COLLECTOR'S
VALUE GUIDE

HALLMARK
Keepsake Ornaments

also featuring
*Merry Miniatures
Kiddie Car Classics*

Foreword by
Clara Johnson Scroggins

**Secondary Market Price Guide
& Collector Handbook**
SECOND EDITION

Happy 25th Anniversary To Hallmark Keepsake Ornaments!

HALLMARK
Keepsake Ornaments

This publication is *not* affiliated with Hallmark Cards, Inc. or any of its affiliates, sub-sidiaries, distributors or representatives. Any opinions expressed are solely those of the authors, and do not necessarily reflect those of Hallmark Cards, Inc. Product names and product designs are the property of Hallmark Cards, Inc., Kansas City, MO.

Front cover (left to right): "The Grinch" (Keepsake, 1998); "Joyful Messenger" (Keepsake, Anniversary Edition, 1998); "Raggedy Ann™" (Keepsake, 1975).

Back cover (top to bottom): "Norman Rockwell" (Keepsake, 1974); "Frosty Friends" (set/2, Crown Reflections, 1998); "1930 Custom Biplane" (Kiddie Car Classics, 1998); "Mickey's Locomotive" (Merry Miniatures, 1998).

Managing Editor:	Jeff Mahony	Art Director:	Joe T. Nguyen
	jeff@collectorspub.com		*joe@collectorspub.com*
Associate Editor:	Jan Cronan	Production Supervisor:	Scott Sierakowski
Editorial Assistants:	Gia C. Manalio	Staff Artists:	David Ten Eyck
	Melissa Bennett		Lance Doyle
	Scarlet H. Riley		Kimberly Eastman
	Nicole W. Blasenak		Ryan Falis
Contributing Editor:	Mike Micciulla		

ISBN 1-888914-21-1

Collectors' Publishing Co., Inc.
598 Pomeroy Avenue
Meriden, CT 06450
www.collectorspub.com

TABLE OF CONTENTS

TABLE OF CONTENTS

FOREWORD BY CLARA JOHNSON SCROGGINS

R *enowned Hallmark expert Clara Johnson Scroggins has been collecting ornaments for over 30 years. She has written several books and numerous articles on ornament collecting and is famous among fellow ornament fans for her ever-growing collection and impressive displays.*

Hello again! For those of you who don't already know, 1998 is the 25th Anniversary of Hallmark Keepsake Ornaments. There are a lot of special events and ornaments planned for this year, so keep your eyes and ears open! I hope to see many of you at the Hallmark convention in Kansas City this August, it will truly be a wonderful – and memorable – event! All the excitement over the anniversary makes me think about how much ornament collecting has changed over the years. When I first started, it seemed like no one else was collecting and now so many people are ornament collectors (even if they don't know they are)!

Clara Johnson Scroggins

One new tradition I am seeing is that people are realizing that ornaments make great gifts, and not just during the Christmas season! If you know a teacher, someone who likes gardening, a sports fan or a movie buff, there are many ornaments you can give them. I give lots of ornaments as gifts; for weddings, birthdays, and anniversaries. I always try to keep in mind the special interests and recent achievements of the person: moving into a new house, a graduation or another special occasion. It's amazing how important the ornament becomes over the years!

With all the fun of Hallmark Ornaments' silver anniversary, this is a great time if you're a longtime collector. It's also a great time to help someone else begin a collection. Giving ornaments lets you introduce Hallmark ornaments to others and share the beauty of ornaments with friends and loved ones.

Happy Collecting!

Clara Johnson Scroggins

INTRODUCING THE COLLECTOR'S VALUE GUIDE™

*W*ith 25 years of ornaments, Hallmark collectors may find it difficult to stay on top of their collection. Therefore, we're happy to bring you the second edition of the Hallmark Keepsake Ornaments Collector's Value Guide™. This easy-to-use guide will help you not only keep track of your ornaments, but will provide insight into one of the country's best-loved collectibles.

Hallmark Ornaments

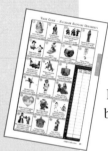

We begin with the history of Hallmark, followed by an overview of the Keepsake Ornaments collection; followed by Spring Ornaments, Merry Miniatures and Kiddie Car Classics. We've also included a section spotlighting the new series, interviews with artists Linda Sickman, Don Palmiter and Tracy Larsen, and biographies on all of the Hallmark artists.

The Value Guide

With Hallmark Ornaments growing by leaps and bounds, there is no better way to record your collection than with our Value Guide. Inside you'll find full-color pictures of every piece released since 1973; as well as important information on each one, including their 1998 secondary market values.

Plus More!

You can take our trivia quiz, read about the hottest ornaments from last year's collection, scan the list of the ten most valuable ornaments or find out how to shop the secondary market. There's information on the gala festivities planned for Hallmark's 25th Anniversary and an interview with noted Hallmark expert Clara Johnson Scroggins. Read on for display tips and a calendar of upcoming events. There's something for everyone in the Collector's Value Guide™!

Two Shoeboxes And A Plan

*J*oyce C. Hall, of Norfolk, Nebraska, arrived in Kansas City, Missouri on January 10, 1910 with the hopes of starting his own business. Although his resources were somewhat limited (he had two shoeboxes full of picture postcards and very little money), he had a great plan. Wishing to capitalize on the then-current trend of sending postcards, Hall began a mail order business by sending packets of the cards to dealers across the Midwest. While some of the store owners returned the cards; soon checks for the merchandise began to arrive. Within just a few months' time Hall had made $200 – a small fortune for an 18 year-old entrepreneur.

Even though his initial endeavor was successful, Hall was certain that the postcard trend wouldn't be more than a passing phase. He predicted that there would soon be a market for higher quality cards with envelopes and, willing to take a gamble on the future, Hall added greeting cards to his product line. The gamble paid off and Hall's brother Rollie joined the company. Within three years the company, then known as the Hall Brothers firm, began producing some of their own greeting cards. Within 10 years of arriving in Missouri, Hall had managed to set the basis for one of the countries most successful businesses.

The Giving Tree

Each year after the holidays, the Christmas tree in Hallmark's Crown Center is taken down and turned to mulch. The core of the tree is preserved and given to the Hallmark artisans to use in the creation of special ornaments known as "Mayor's Ornaments." The ornaments are later sold, with the the proceeds going to help the less-fortunate citizens of Kansas City.

By 1922, a third Hall brother, William, had joined the business which now employed over 120 people. As the company began to grow, they soon found the need for their own building. As a precursor to their reputation as one of the top-rated places to work, they gave the decision to the employees and, in 1926, the new site (chosen by ballot) of 26th and Walnut Street became the new company headquarters. Across the decades, the company continued to grow and expand, outgrowing one location after another before finally settling into their current headquarters in 1956.

As the employee count grew, so did the quantity and variety of products produced. The first addition to greeting cards was decorative gift wrap and by the 1950s, colorful party decorations constructed of paper were added to the line. (The 1950s also brought about the name change of the firm from Hall Brothers to Hallmark Cards, Inc.). Additions such as calendars, candles, photo albums and, amazingly, even made-for-television movies, were soon to follow. Ever the innovator, Hallmark introduced their collection of the first individually-sold ornaments in 1973.

Hallmark has also expanded its enterprises with acquisitions such as the 1967 purchase of Springbok Editions, a maker of jigsaw puzzles, and the 1984 purchase of Binney & Smith, the producer of Crayola Crayons®. Hallmark Entertainment, Inc., founded in their 40 year sponsorship of innovative television programming, was formed in 1994 and has since continued to produce critically acclaimed television for family audiences.

The company has also recently ventured into real estate. Opened in 1968, Crown Center is an 85-acre development built by one of Hallmark's many subsidiaries. Located next to company headquarters in Kansas City, Crown Center contains hotels, a shopping and entertainment center, live theaters, a cinema and over a dozen office buildings. There are plans for further expansion over the next 20 years.

Through the years Hallmark has maintained its strong family leadership. With his two brothers by his side, Joyce Hall headed the company until 1966, when he handed his responsibilities as chief executive officer over to his son, Donald J. Hall. Donald, the current Chairman of the Board, has followed in his father's footsteps, offering liberal employee benefits and profit-sharing. To date, Hallmark employees own more than one quarter of Hallmark's $3 billion operation.

Hallmark Builds On An Age-Old Tradition

Germany is the country most often credited with the development of the tradition of the Christmas tree. Decorations used during the 17th and 18th centuries included paper roses, fruit, wafers, gilded nuts and candies. The practice of using edible decorations continued into the 19th century, when trees were often adorned with candies, cookies or tiny fruits made from marzipan. It was also common to find colored eggshells, strips of bright papers and paper cornucopias containing sweets among the branches of the tree.

Other decorating styles included pine cones, strings of beads, popcorn and bright berries, and the placing of small toys and gifts among the branches. Full color pictures called "scraps" were also popular. These often depicted Victorian-style angels or Santa Claus figures, among other subjects.

The practice of using store-bought ornaments, as opposed to homemade decorations, gained popularity during the 1870s. Ornaments made of tin were the first to be produced, but others made of tinsel, wax and cardboard were soon to follow. With the use of molds, hand-blown glass ornaments were available in a number of intricate designs, including fruits, vegetables, animals, Santas and musical instruments.

Today, trees are decorated with a seemingly endless variety of ornaments, from homemade popcorn strings, to papier-maché animals made in elementary schools, to balls and figures created by skilled artisans. Decorating the tree has become a holiday tradition for families the world over.

*I*nitially known as "Tree Trimmers," "Christmas Tree Trimmers" or "The Tree Trimmer Collection;" the holiday tradition of Hallmark Ornaments started out in 1973 as 12 yarn ornaments and five ball ornaments. It has now been 25 years since the first releases captured the imagination of Christmas enthusiasts and the collection has since grown to over 4,000 pieces. One of the features that makes collecting Hallmark Ornaments so much fun is that the ornaments are very limited. Each year's designs are available from the beginning of the summer until Christmas, so there's only about six months to acquire your favorite ornaments before they're gone forever!

From the classical to the comedic, with Hallmark Ornaments you're sure to find the perfect addition to your Christmas tree or your ornament collection. This is one collection that can truly claim something for everyone and each year the artists at the Hallmark Keepsake Ornament Studio work to ensure that the ornaments are creative, fun and of the finest quality.

KEEPSAKE ORNAMENTS

Ask any ornament collector and they'll be sure to tell you that the foundation of the Hallmark Ornament Collection is the line now known as Keepsake Ornaments. Hallmark broke new ground in 1975 when it departed from the traditional ball-shaped ornament and released the first handcrafted pieces. Collectors where amazed by the choices in materials, including satin, cloth, metal, wood and porcelain and were immediately taken by Hallmark's ability to produce the "realistic" shapes of people and structures.

Through the years, collectors have been astonished at the innovative stylistic changes in the Keepsake line.

Each year, hundreds of new ornament designs surprise and delight collectors. Hallmark continues to produce a good mix of traditional and religious themes, although the most talked-about releases each year are often ornaments depicting popular cultural icons, like this year's Dr. Seuss™ ornament, "The Grinch."

Whether you're a fan of classic cars, BARBIE™ or professional sports, the line of Keepsake Ornaments is sure to touch something dear to your heart. Licensed ornaments, such as those depicting Winnie the Pooh, LOONEY TUNES™ and STAR TREK™, are perfect pieces for collectors who want to relive a bit of their youth. These ornaments lend a whimsical feel to the collection and are so popular, many subjects are repeated year after year and are the basis of collections.

One of the unique aspects of Hallmark Ornament collecting are the collectible series. United by theme or design, the ornaments in a series are often responsible for getting ornament fans "hooked" on Hallmark. Each year new series debut with one ornament, often referred to as the "first edition." In each subsequent year, one new piece will be introduced, adding to the number of editions contained within the series. Part of the popularity of the series can be attributed to the fact that Hallmark has yet to continue a series for less than three years, so that collectors of a particular series are guaranteed future releases to look forward to.

They say that nothing good lasts forever, and in the case of Hallmark Ornament series, this is true as well. A series may be ended for any number of reasons, including production difficulties, conclusion of the theme (for example, after the 8th edition of the *Reindeer Champs* series) or to make room in the line for new series. Unlike other collectibles, however, when

Hallmark decides to retire a series they announce it in the "Dream Book" (the color catalog issued by Hallmark that debuts that years ornament and collectible collections) by designating the last piece as the "final" edition, allowing collectors to be sure that they purchase the ornament before it becomes "the one that got away." For a rundown of the new series for 1998, turn to our *New Series Spotlight* beginning on page 19.

MAGIC ORNAMENTS

Originally known as the "Lighted Ornament Collection" when they debuted in 1984, Magic Ornaments began by featuring ornaments with glowing lights. In 1986, a special motion feature was added to the ornaments, causing quite a stir throughout the industry. An amazing addition to the line, the advent of motion truly brought the ornaments to life. An instant hit with collectors, the line soon grew to encompass a variety of animals, Santas and people.

With movement now incorporated into the collection, the name Lighted Ornaments was no longer appropriate, so in 1987 the line was given the name the "Keepsake Magic Collection." In 1989, Hallmark took the Magic Ornaments collection a step further and added sound, making this line a complete success.

It was not just the sound, movement or lights that drew collectors to these ornaments; the collection features some of the most fun and creative designs ever produced by Hallmark and has touched the "history buff" in all of us by releasing several ornaments that commemorate events, people and milestones in American history.

The Keepsake Magic Collection also offers various collectible series. *Chris Mouse*, the first series to be issued, recently ended with its final edition being offered in 1997. Since the first introductions in 1984, Hallmark has introduced generally about 20 to 25 new Magic ornaments each year.

In 1997, there was a change in the marketing strategy of the Magic ornaments. Hallmark changed the style of the Dream Book and began to mix the Magic ornaments in with the general Keepsake line, using a symbol to denote which ornaments feature light, sound or motion. The displays in Hallmark stores were also modified so that the two lines were interspersed.

CROWN REFLECTIONS

A new introduction for 1998, Crown Reflections is a line of blown glass ornaments styled after the traditional European ornaments of over a century ago. All of the eleven new releases are hand blown and hand painted and this painstaking attention to detail is destined to ensure that these ornaments will be the hit with collectors. To start off the line, one three-piece collection and one collectible series has been introduced. Many collectors will be delighted to find some of their favorite ornaments, such as "Frosty Friends" and "1955 Murray® Fire Truck," recreated in such a beautiful fashion.

SHOWCASE ORNAMENTS

Introduced in 1993, Showcase ornaments first debuted as a separate grouping within the Keepsake line. These ornaments featured materials such as die-cast metal and porcelain and had a much more traditional, "old-world" style that made them stand apart from the rest of the Hallmark collection. Showcase ornaments were available only through Hallmark Gold Crown stores and featured many themes (nature scenes, religious icons and traditional folk art) that were consistent with their styling.

While the umbrella of Showcase ornaments is no longer in existence, their short-lived time in the Hallmark collection indelibly changed the line of general Keepsake ornaments. Several of the new releases share the style of Showcase ornaments, and this reflection can be seen in such pieces as "Cross of Peace" and "Soaring With Angels," which is part of the one-time Showcase collection, *Folk Art Americana*. Currently, only one of the former Showcase series, *The Language Of Flowers*, is still active.

MINIATURE ORNAMENTS

Miniature Ornaments are similar to the general Keepsake line in that they feature many of the same themes, such as family and history; are made of many of the same materials, such as metal, porcelain and glass and offer many series. Hallmark Miniature Ornaments, however, are singularly different, due to their small stature. Ranging from 1/2" to 1-3/4", these tiny ornaments have been a huge hit with collectors since their 1988 arrival in Hallmark Gold Crown stores.

For the most part, Hallmark Miniature Ornaments are generally released in lesser quantities and with a more limited distribution than their Keepsake counterparts so they are, in many instances, harder to find. Notably for 1998, the annual six-piece set of mice that collectors have grown to love since their 1991 debut are missing from the collection. However, many of the 28 new releases and ongoing series are sure to capture collectors' hearts.

OTHER HALLMARK ORNAMENTS

Several types of ornaments have been released throughout the years that have not fallen into the larger lines that make up the Hallmark Ornament collection. The following is a listing of several of the most common additional categories of ornaments.

COLLECTOR'S CLUB ORNAMENTS

Much to the delight of collectors, Hallmark instituted their club in 1987, establishing one of the most popular collector's clubs in the history of collectibles. Benefits of a yearly membership include a subscription to the club newsletter, invitations to special events and exclusive ornaments. Each year there are a number of exclusive pieces offered as gifts with membership, as well as ornaments available for purchase exclusively by club members. In recent years, several of the pieces released have been designed to complement popular series, including this year's "1935 Steelcraft by Murray®" which complements the *Kiddie Car Classics* series.

PREMIERE EXCLUSIVES

Hosted by Gold Crown stores, National Keepsake Ornament Premiere Events mark the arrival of that year's line in retail stores. Adding to the excitement, exclusive ornaments are typically available at the Premiere. This year's exciting Premiere piece is actually a figurine, "Santa's Merry Workshop Musical Figurine," which plays the holiday jingle, "Here Comes Santa Claus." Also available exclusively at the 1998 Premiere events are two sets of Merry Miniatures: "HERSHEY'S™," which is the second in the series and "Bride and Groom–1996 Madame

Alexander®." The sixth annual Premiere will be held this July 18th and 19th.

SPECIAL EVENTS

Since 1993, Hallmark has been the host of various Artists On Tour (10 in 1997 alone) and Expo Events. At these fun-filled events, collectors can meet with the Hallmark artists, win prizes and purchase exclusive ornaments. Many of the ornaments through the years have been a collaboration of several of the artists, including 1997's much sought-after "Trimming Santa's Tree (set/2)." In 1998, to celebrate Hallmark Ornaments' amazing 25 year history, only one event, the 25th Anniversary Celebration, will be held. Taking place from August 20-22 in Kansas City, Missouri, this event is sure to be filled with special announcements, so be on the lookout for things to come.

SPRING ORNAMENTS

Depicting Easter themes and consisting primarily of bunnies, eggs and lambs, this collection was originally called Easter Ornaments when it was introduced by Hallmark in 1991. The name was changed in 1997 to reflect the growing line's broadening themes.

Like the regular Keepsake line, Spring Ornaments reflect many of pop-culture's favorite subjects. Licensed pieces include LOONEY TUNES™, PEANUTS® and BARBIE™. Spring Ornaments also contain several popular series, seven of which are current. Including the 1998 pieces, there have been a total of 144 releases to date.

MERRY MINIATURES

Originating in 1974, Merry Miniatures are a line of whimsical figurines that usually depict a variety of animals such as mice, cats, dogs and even a hedgehog or two. Merry Miniatures generally run with seasonal themes and are often grouped that way. There has been a recent trend toward licensed pieces, including the eight exciting releases for 1998. Merry Miniatures collectors should be sure to attend all the Hallmark special events this year, because several of the pieces are available at either the Spring Preview or Premiere events. A five-piece collection featuring Mickey Mouse and friends will be available only in the weeks following the Open House events in November.

KIDDIE CAR CLASSICS

When Hallmark introduced their die-cast metal recreations of the old pedal cars that were so popular in the 1930s to the 1960s, they had no idea what a hit they had on their hands. Since their 1992 introduction, Kiddie Car Classics have taken off to become one of Hallmark's best-selling, non-ornament creations and have even inspired several series of Keepsake and Miniature ornaments.

The cars and airplanes are awash in bright colors and feature moving pedals and real rubber tires. The Hallmark artists, particularly Don Palmiter who produces the bulk of the line, work hard to ensure that every detail is true to the original car that served to delight thousands of children. Each replica serves as a drive down memory lane.

Kiddie Car Classics are issued in a number of ways; they are either general releases or are limited in either Limited or Luxury Editions, with the piece count 29,500 and 24,500 respectively. This year Hallmark is debuting new, Numbered Editions, where the pieces will be released in sequential production editions, with each edition consisting of 9,999 pieces.

The ever-increasing popularity of Kiddie Car Classics has inspired the release of subsections of the collection. Sidewalk Cruisers, which are recreations of various children's modes of transportation such as bicycles, wagons and milk trucks from the pedal car era were released in 1995 and Kiddie Car Corner is a series of display accessories sculpted by Linda Sickman that debuted in 1997. These replications are sure to capture the imagination and inspire a sense of nostalgia in all, whether young or old.

OTHER HALLMARK COLLECTIBLES

Since the history-making first pieces were released, the Hallmark collection has grown and expanded to include several separate lines of ornaments and collectibles; including such wonders as a separate line of Barbie collectibles called BARBIE™ COLLECTIBLES By Hallmark, a series of die-cast metal Lionel® Trains and even a line of miniature lunch boxes that are sure to recall images of childhood days spent in the schoolyard. Also new for 1998, Spoonful of Stars by Becky Kelly is a collection of figurines modeled after the artist's series of popular drawings. With 25 years of phenomenal history behind us, we can surely expect to be nothing less than amazed at what Hallmark will bring us over the next 25 years!

*I*f you're a veteran Hallmark Ornament collector, you probably already know about the annual introduction of new series. If you're new to this collection, there's a lot to learn! Every year Hallmark announces a number of new series, each of which could continue for any length of time, but never for less than three years. Some of these series prove to be extremely popular. For example, both the *Here Comes Santa* and *Rocking Horse* series have been coveted by collectors and contain ornaments that have shown amazing increases in secondary market value.

The first in any series is usually the most sought-after and tends to become the most valuable. As each edition is only available for one year, it might help to be somewhat clairvoyant (or at least lucky) in this area. One never can tell which new series will continue to gain popularity (and value) and which will be short-lived. Here's a look at the first editions of the new 1998 Hallmark series.

NEW KEEPSAKE SERIES

African-American Holiday BARBIE™ — This year breathes new life into a well-known classic with the first edition of the *African-American Holiday BARBIE*™ series. These figurines will be based upon the Happy Holidays® doll issued each season, and each will surely be dressed in all of her holiday splendor.

Madame Alexander® Holiday Angels — The first in this series of elegantly-styled angels, "Glorious Angel" is a vision of Christmases gone by in her red and gold gown. Each edition of this series will be dressed in a similar, elegant manner and will surely add a sense of old-fashioned style to your tree.

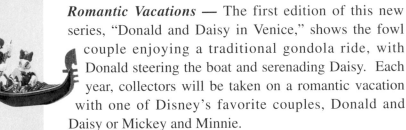

The Old West — Calling all history buffs! This new series pays homage to those brave heroes of the old frontier. The first edition, "Pony Express Rider," is a tribute to the early attempts at long-distance communication. Once the holiday season is over, you might want to keep it near your workstation – it will serve as a nice reminder of how far we've come the next time your computer crashes or that overnight package doesn't arrive!

A Pony for Christmas — If the popularity of artist Linda Sickman's previous series are any indication, this may be the start of something big! Reminiscent of the *Rocking Horse* series which ran for 16 years before ending in 1996, this new series features designs based on old-fashioned toy horses.

Romantic Vacations — The first edition of this new series, "Donald and Daisy in Venice," shows the fowl couple enjoying a traditional gondola ride, with Donald steering the boat and serenading Daisy. Each year, collectors will be taken on a romantic vacation with one of Disney's favorite couples, Donald and Daisy or Mickey and Minnie.

Snow Buddies — The perfect series to add to your holiday decorations this year is the fun new *Snow Buddies* series. Each edition will depict a cheerful snowman frolicking with animal friends. This year's edition features a brightly-dressed snow fellow and a friendly brown and white bunny.

Spotlight on SNOOPY — This new series will spotlight the famous canine companion from the ever-popular PEANUTS® comic strip in a variety of roles. The first edition to this series, "Joe Cool," features the hip beagle as Santa (with his shades, of course).

Unforgettable Villains — Bringing back all those characters we love to hate, this series will pay tribute to the evil ones who bring the drama and suspense to the classic films from Walt Disney. The first is none other than the wicked "Cruella de Vil" of "101 Dalmatians" fame. Will your favorite scoundrel be next?

Winnie the Pooh — The famous pot-bellied bear is back! This honey-lover will be featured in a series of book-style ornaments, each depicting a scene alongside a short narrative. The series debuts with "A Visit From Piglet," in which Pooh and Piglet share a honey feast. Loved by so many, young and old alike, Pooh will make a perfect addition to any ornament collection.

NEW MAGIC SERIES

Candlelight Services — This year brings one new series to the Magic Ornament Collection, *Candlelight Services*. "The Stone Church" is the first edition in this series which will depict a variety of lighted churches that will help spread the warmth of the holiday season.

NEW CROWN REFLECTIONS SERIES

Holiday Traditions — This new series will spotlight blown glass ornaments with a decidedly holiday style. The first edition in this series is "Red Poinsettias," a red, green and gold glass ball which features the traditional holiday flower in the center. Two other blown glass ornaments, "Pink Poinsettias" and "White Poinsettias" complement this series.

NEW MINIATURE SERIES

Miniature Kiddie Car Luxury Edition — Inspired by the Luxury Edition models in Hallmark's Kiddie Car Classics Collection, this new series will feature Miniature die-cast pedal car ornaments designed by artist Don Palmiter. The first edition is the Miniature version of the "1937 Steelcraft Auburn."

The Nativity — This new series will feature pewter ornaments based on the story of the birth of Jesus. This year's ornament is a depiction of Mary, Joseph and the Baby Jesus. Future editions will feature the visitors who played a part in this miraculous story.

Winter Fun With SNOOPY® — This new series will show the famous beagle and his friends enjoying all sorts of winter activities. The first edition features SNOOPY and Woodstock taking a downhill ride in a makeshift sled – an empty water dish.

Last Call!

When Hallmark decides to retire a particular series, it lets collectors know in advance by designating the last piece as the "final" edition. The following eight ornament series will end in 1998:

Keepsake Series
All God's Children®
Cat Naps
A Celebration of Angels
CRAYOLA® Crayon
Yuletide Central

Miniature Series
Alice In Wonderland
Noel R.R.
On The Road

C ollectors' Publishing asked three Hallmark Ornament artists to share a little bit about what it's like to spend a workday designing the famous ornaments that everyone loves! Read on to find out more about some of your favorite artists.

LINDA SICKMAN

Collectors' Publishing: Your *Rocking Horse* series was very successful and in 1998 we see the beginning of a new series, *A Pony for Christmas*. What is it like to return to this style?

Linda Sickman: It feels really good to return to the ponies. It's like returning to some old fantasies of riding in the country with the wind blowing through my hair and the feeling of freedom

CP: A lot of your ornaments have wheels on them – tractors, locomotives, buses, etc. How did you end up sculpting all these vehicles?

LS: I guess it goes back to childhood when I used to ride the train and being on my grandparents' farm, not to mention just loving things with wheels.

CP: You and fellow Hallmark artist Don Palmiter seem to share a fondness for wheels. You have recently started sculpting the Kiddie Car Corner collection to go with Palmiter's new renditions of classic pedal cars. Is this a departure from what you usually do?

LS: It really isn't a departure because I like designing tin products and I have an appreciation for older cars. Don comes up with the car and I try to match it with a situation.

CP: As a sculptor, what is your favorite medium to work with, and why? Once you have an idea, how do you go about translating that into three dimensions?

LS: I would have to say wax, because you can carve it, sand it, mold it, melt it, etc. As far as translating the idea into 3-D, it's another one of those gifts I've been given.

CP: Of all the ornaments that you have sculpted, which is your favorite? Which is your favorite ornament sculpted by another Keepsake artist? What's your favorite ornament idea that never made it into actual production?

LS: These are really hard questions. To the first question, my favorite ornament is the one I'm sculpting at present. To the second, there's just too much talent in the studio to pick and choose. And to the third, the ornament that never made it to production is the one with *all* the bells and whistles.

CP: So many people love collecting Hallmark Keepsake Ornaments. Do you collect anything?

LS: As you may already suspect, I collect tin toys.

CP: Who has been the most influential person(s) in your artistic career?

LS: I would have to say my family, friends and co-workers. I know this is a pretty big group, but without their encouragement and support I wouldn't be where I am today.

CP: Any thoughts on the 25th Anniversary of Hallmark Keepsake Ornaments?

LS: It's been a grand ride.

DON PALMITER

Collectors' Publishing: How did you end up becoming the car king at Hallmark?

Don Palmiter: I've always loved cars and when I came to Keepsakes, I kept turning in ideas for the *Classic American Cars* series. Finally after several years of persistence, they decided to try it. The "1957 Corvette" was the first and it sold great. That was the beginning and it's grown from there.

CP: You have several car series which you've added to this year. Could you take us through the steps, from designing the vehicle, to production, to painting the finishing touches?

DP: I try to research out the more popular cars, trucks, and pedal cars. I plan several years in advance so that contracts can be worked out on each one. I sculpt each vehicle using photo research I have taken after I find the particular car, or truck, or pedal car I want to do. The original sculpture is molded, then I paint that molded piece to look as close to the real car as possible. This original is then used in production to reproduce the ornaments or Kiddie Car Classics.

CP: How did the idea for the Kiddie Car Classics Collection of miniature replicas come about?

DP: A former line designer, Karen Delft Oatman, thought it could be fun to recreate small die-cast replicas of actual pedal cars she had seen in antique and toy shows around the country. Soon after, the line started and because of reproduction problems the decision was made to bring the actual sculpting into the studio. That's when I got involved. In 1992, I started sculpting original Kiddie Car Classics designs.

CP: Of all the cars you've owned, which have been your favorites?

DP: Two cars stand out as my favorites. My 1968 Corvette "T" top and my 1963 Rolls Royce Silver Cloud III.

CP: The *Nostalgic Houses and Shops* series was started by Donna Lee, who retired, and then you took over that series. How did it feel to continue a series that was already started by another artist?

DP: Another of my real interests is architecture. When I first came to Keepsakes, I sculpted a collectible group called Hometown America, which were cold-casted sculptures of houses and buildings. When Donna Lee retired and the line designers decided to keep the house and shop series going, it seemed natural for me to step in. Though my own style of sculpting is a little different than Donna's, I have tried very hard to carry through what she so successfully started. I try to keep it as close as I can, yet bring in some of my own interest in architectural styles.

CP: Who has been the most influential person(s) in your artistic career?

DP: The most influential people in my artistic career have undoubtedly been the many other artists that I have worked with at Hallmark. Seeing the wonderful things they have done only serves to broaden my horizons.

CP: Of all the ornaments that you have sculpted, which is your favorite? Which is your favorite ornament sculpted by another Keepsake artist?

DP: It's hard for me to pick just one ornament. It could be the 1996 "Victorian Painted Lady" from the *Nostalgic Houses and Shops* series. As for other Keepsake artists' works, I have so many favorites, although Linda Sickman's *Here Comes Santa* 20th Anniversary ("Shopping With Santa") is one of my top ones.

CP: So many people love collecting Hallmark Keepsake Ornaments. Do you collect anything?

DP: I collect Keepsake Ornaments along with a number of other things: sculpture, art glass, antique crystal, dolls, toy cars and, of course, I've had a number of collectible cars over the years.

CP: How do you decorate your house for the holidays?

DP: Christmas is the favorite season in our home and we

decorate the entire house with trees, garlands, wreaths, outdoor lights and fill it with the music of the season. We have a two-story Colonial-style home and so we tend to use traditional decorations.

CP: Any thoughts on the 25th Anniversary of Hallmark Keepsake Ornaments?

DP: I hope all of our collectors enjoy looking back on all the fun years and memories that our ornaments have brought to them and their families and friends. I hope I get to visit with many of them in Kansas City this August at the Convention.

TRACY LARSEN

Collectors' Publishing: How did you come up with the idea for the 1998 Three Stooges ornament?

Tracy Larsen: Our Design Manager, David Beal, is a real Stooge fan, so I believe he's the one that planted the seed. The Stooges seem to be going through a revival right now. To create their likenesses, I watched several of their short movies and tried to find recurring expressions and attitudes. I also had a good supply of photographic references. I then took those expressions which I felt represented each character: Moe's scowl, Larry's apprehension and Curly's playfulness.

CP: What was it like to work on "Winter Fun With SNOOPY®," the first piece in the new series?

TL: I started my career at Hallmark over 10 years ago doing greeting cards in an area where licensed characters were our emphasis. My very first assignment was a Snoopy card. Going back and being able to do a 3-D Snoopy was like becoming reacquainted with an old friend. In fact, some of my earliest preserved drawings are of Snoopy and the gang.

CP: Can you tell us about the process of designing and creating the new blown glass ornaments, "Frankincense," "Gold" and "Myrrh?"

TL: Back in 1996, we were asked to submit ideas and designs that could be used with materials that Keepsakes had not been using in their line. I thought the Three Kings could be adapted to several of these materials. It turned out that they fit nicely with blown glass because of the intensity of color and jewel-like quality. I did three drawings (front, back and side) of each character, showing how I wanted them to look. I then did a color study – complete with glitter – over the drawings. These drawings and color studies were then approved and sent over to our blown glass vendor in the Czech Republic, who did a model and mold. After going through various changes, corrections and improvements, we have what is in the stores today.

CP: We love your Howdy Doody and Three Stooges interpretations. Did you watch a lot of television when you were growing up, and if so, do you think it influences your work today?

TL: I was born in 1960 – the year that Howdy Doody went off the air, so I never had a chance to be part of the "Peanut Gallery." I didn't watch a lot of TV, but I did have my favorite shows: The Andy Griffith Show, Beverly Hillbillies, Gilligan's Island, etc. I think my work has been more influenced by some of the animated cartoons I watched – particularly Looney Tunes and Disney.

CP: As one of the newer artists in the Hallmark Ornaments studio, how did it feel to join the team? How is it different from what you were doing as a greeting card artist?

TL: The Keepsake staff is a great group to work with! I enjoy coming to work each day. Everyone has been very helpful to me as I've transitioned from being a 2-D artist to concentrating on mostly 3-D subjects. The other artists have offered tips on how to sculpt and have divulged some of their trade secrets to me. It certainly is different than what I was doing as a greeting card artist in many ways – mainly because as a 2-D artist I was putting characters in environments where in 3-D, the work has to be able to stand on its own.

CP: Can you describe for us the process of getting an ornament idea into production?

TL: We start with what is known as our project time, in which we submit ideas of what we would like to see in the line. Some of these are accepted, most aren't. Those that are accepted eventually return as assigned work. We then either do a more detailed drawing or rough sculpt to show the direction we want to go and then, after approval, do a finished sculpt. This sculpt then needs to be approved and then it goes to molding, where a few resin "white bodies" are made for prototypes. One or two of these come back to the artist so that we can do a color sample. This is then approved and the work is prepared with mold samples, color samples, technical drawings, etc. and sent off to our vendors to be made into product.

CP: What other subjects or characters would you like to work with in the future?

TL: I've worked quite a bit with licensed characters throughout my career at Hallmark. I've enjoyed being on the Disney Team and characters like Howdy Doody and the Three Stooges have been fun. I'm hoping to get more of my own original ideas into the line in the future. I was pleased by the success of my blue plate design from the 1997 line, and I hope to be able to continue to incorporate both 2-D and 3-D elements in my ornaments.

CP: In the 1998 Dream Book, you say you are a music lover. Does music provide you with inspiration?

TL: I enjoy many different kinds of music. I grew up playing the trumpet and I really love Big Band music from the
'30s and '40s. I love classical music. In fact, my wife and I
just attended a concert by the Russian National Orchestra. I
enjoy smooth jazz and I am becoming a real fan of Celtic
music. Whenever I can, I try to incorporate that love for
music into my work. I would love to do an ornament of the
Morman Tabernacle Choir, we'll see . . . .

CP: Of all the ornaments that you have sculpted, which is
your favorite? What's your favorite ornament idea that
never made it into actual production?

TL: I think my favorite ornaments will be coming out in
1999! Of those on the market now, I enjoy the "Larry, Moe,
and Curly The Three Stooges™," "Donald and Daisy in
Venice," and I was pleased by the look of the blown glass
Three Kings. From last year's line, my favorites were
"Howdy Doody™," Mickey and Minnie skating in "New
Pair of Skates" and "The Spirit of Christmas" plate. I'll
keep my favorite idea a secret just in case I can finally
talk Keepsakes into using it!

CP: How do you decorate your house for the holidays?

TL: Pretty traditional. We use a real tree, decorated mostly
with Keepsake ornaments! We have a special place over the
fireplace for a ceramic Nativity scene that my father made.
We're looking for a way to display our growing Department
56 *North Pole* village. Stockings are hung over the fireplace, lights outside, etc.

CP: Any thoughts on the 25th Anniversary of Hallmark
Keepsake Ornaments?

TL: I look back and see all of the wonderful designs that
have been done and I'm grateful to be a part of the growing
tradition.

*B*ehind every great ornament is a great team of artists and the Hallmark Keepsake Ornament artist family is full of both diversity and creativity.

PATRICIA ANDREWS

Patricia Andrews was an engraver at Hallmark for eleven years before becoming a Keepsake Ornament Studio artist in 1987. Married to fellow artist Dill Rhodus, Andrews enjoys gardening on their four acres. She is also an avid collector and is always on the hunt, dreaming of her next find.

As Andrews' most prized possession is her 1961 BARBIE® doll, it comes as no surprise that she would be the sculptor for the *BARBIE*™, *Holiday BARBIE*™ and the new *African-American Holiday BARBIE*™ series. In keeping with her talents for sculpting classic beauties, Andrews has also released two editions in the *Marilyn Monroe* and *Scarlett O'Hara*™ series.

In 1998, Andrews also held the honor of sculpting the limited "Angelic Flight" to commemorate Hallmark Keepsake Ornaments' 25th Anniversary.

NINA AUBÉ

After having been a specialty artist for Hallmark gift products since 1981, Nina Aubé joined the Keepsake Ornament Studio family in 1994. Aubé knew she had made it as an artist when she attended her first Artists On Tour event and collectors recognized her name and her work. The impact that this occurrence had on the artist would not soon fade.

Aubé has transformed a passion for nostalgia into a

love of collecting and she collects everything from Keepsake Ornaments to antique toys and dolls. And while always on a quest for new things, Aubé's most cherished possessions are items such as her great-grandmother's locket and her great-grandfather's writing desk that have been passed down through the generations of her family.

Among Aubé's 1998 contributions are "Writing to Santa" and the innovative "Daughter" and "Son" that open and close like real nutcrackers.

KATRINA BRICKER

Katrina Bricker knew that she wanted to work for Hallmark when she was still in college and was thrilled at the opportunity to work in the specialty department upon graduation. In 1995, after being with the company for a year, she was hired for a spot on the Hallmark Keepsake Ornament team, a position which she refers to as her "dream job."

A self-confessed "horse fanatic," when Bricker is not riding, she's collecting horse figurines. She lives with her husband and cocker spaniel, Molly.

Among Bricker's 1998 releases are the Club Miniature ornament "Kringle Bells," the "Ewoks™" Miniature set and the final edition in the *Cat Naps* series.

ROBERT CHAD

An experienced printmaker and animator, Robert Chad easily extended his talents into the realm of sculpture when he joined the Hallmark Keepsake Ornament Studio in 1987. As a childhood cartoon lover, Chad could never have dreamed that he would someday be recreating the very cartoon characters that filled his world. A lover of travel and all forms of art, Chad takes comfort in the knowledge that his contributions to the artistic world will live on forever through his ornaments.

Among his many contributions to the Hallmark Keepsake Ornament line, Chad sculpted the 11th edition of his popular *Mary's Angels* series, as well as fun characters like "The Grinch" and "Bugs Bunny."

KEN CROW

Ken Crow approaches each day at Hallmark with the awe and excitement of a child – a sentiment that has not faded since the first day he walked through the door.

Crow's other passions include puppetry and his pet crow – a plush companion that has taken on a life of his own as Crow's traveling companion.

Crow's contributions to the 1998 Keepsake Ornament Collection include "Downhill Dash," "Chatty Chipmunk," the tin ornament "Cruising into Christmas" and much more.

JOANNE ESCHRICH

Fresh from Southeastern Massachusetts University with a degree in illustration, Joanne Eschrich looked to Hallmark as a stepping stone in her artistic career. Beginning as a specialty artist, the one year that she allotted for this learning experience soon turned into 15 and in 1996, Eschrich joined the Hallmark Keepsake Ornament Studio family.

While Eschrich enjoys every opportunity to employ her artistic talents, she also loves the contact that she has with collectors. Above all, she cherishes time spent with her family and friends.

In 1998, Eschrich adds pieces such as "Polar Bowler" and "Mistletoe Fairy," as well as the Miniature ornaments "Fishy Surprise" and "Pixie Parachute" to her growing list of accomplishments.

JOHN "COLLIN" FRANCIS

Having joined the Keepsake Ornament Studio in 1986, John "Collin" Francis has been with Hallmark for more than 30 years. Much of his work is inspired by his love of nature and animals, a fondness born from his being a native of Wyoming.

When he's not busy sculpting, Francis' hobbies include exploring his love of nature through his five backyard bird feeders and his love of art through watercolor painting.

In 1998, Francis adds a third edition to his *Madame Alexander®* series and introduces the new Keepsake Ornament *Madame Alexander® Holiday Angels* series and the second edition in the *Lighthouse Greetings* Magic series. In addition to these more classic ornaments, Francis adds a bit of comical sportsmanship with the *NFL Collection.*

TAMMY HADDIX

Since she was five years old, Tammy Haddix knew she wanted to be an artist. Like a dream come true, Haddix was recruited by Hallmark from the Kansas City Art Institute and has been in the Hallmark Keepsake Ornament Studio since 1996.

Haddix lives with her husband and her son Zachary, and enjoys gardening. She attributes her success to her mother, who would never allow her to say, "I can't."

In 1998, Haddix shows her talent with "Good Luck Dice," the cheering snowmen of the *Collegiate Collection*, as well as the designing of several blown glass ornaments such as "Sugarplum Cottage."

KRISTINA KLINE

Kristina Kline probably never realized the career opportunity that would arise from the teddy bear and cat  that she sculpted while at the Kansas City Art Institute. It was here that she met Hallmark's Studio Manager, Jack Benson and artist, Robert Chad.

Kline enjoys extending her creative talents into her free time with sewing (especially stuffed animals) and baking. She also takes gratification in quiet times spent at home.

In 1998, Kline introduces many Keepsake ornaments such as "Sweet Treat" and "Cross of Peace" and expands her expertise into the realm of blown glass with "Sweet Memories."

TRACY LARSEN

Tracy Larsen worked as a greeting card artist at Hallmark for eight years before becoming part of the Hallmark Keepsake Ornament Studio in 1995. An illustrator with a degree from Brigham Young University, Larsen rose to the challenge that sculpting presented.

When he isn't sculpting, Larsen devotes much of his time to church youth activities and choirs. An avid sports participant, Larsen also enjoys coaching Little League. But above all else, he treasures the time he spends with his four children.

In 1998, Larsen lends his talents to "Larry, Moe, and Curly The Three Stooges™," the debut of the first edition in the Miniature ornament *Winter Fun With SNOOPY®* series and the Crown Reflections blown glass ornaments "Frankincense," "Gold" and "Myrrh."

JOYCE LYLE

Originally a physical education major at Oklahoma State University, Joyce Lyle's desire to teach soon overcame her and inspired her to change her focus to art edu-

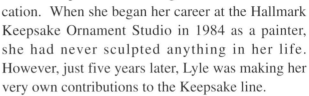

cation. When she began her career at the Hallmark Keepsake Ornament Studio in 1984 as a painter, she had never sculpted anything in her life. However, just five years later, Lyle was making her very own contributions to the Keepsake line.

A lover of the arts, Lyle also takes great pleasure in music. She and her husband Tom are active members of their church vocal and handbell choirs and have traveled extensively with them. Lyle finds it rewarding (and quite fun) to devote her time to directing a choir of five and six year-olds. More than anything, Lyle cherishes the relationships she shares with friends and family. These alliances, as well as her strong faith, are the inspiration behind much of her work.

In 1998, Lyle had the honor of sculpting the Hallmark Keepsake Ornaments 25th Anniversary Commemorative Piece "Joyful Messenger" and "The Holy Family," a three-piece Nativity set.

LYNN NORTON

Before becoming a Keepsake Ornament artist in 1987, Lynn Norton worked for Hallmark as an engraver for 21 years. He attributes his exacting and well-developed technical skills to his lifelong love of building models – a passion first introduced to him by his great-grandfather.

Norton spends much of his time restoring antiques. He finds his inspiration through comedy and enjoys keeping a diary of famous quotations.

Science fiction fans recognize Norton for his designs based on the different generations of ships from STAR TREK™ and STAR WARS™, but in 1998, he also sculpted the "1917 Curtiss JN-4D 'Jenny'" from the *Sky's The Limit* series.

DON PALMITER

A veteran at the Hallmark Keepsake Ornament Studio since 1987, Don Palmiter has been with the company for more than 30 years, having joined the company as an engraver upon graduating from high school.

Palmiter employs his creative impulses on yardwork and interior decorating. He also spends much time traveling, participating in church activities and spending quality time with family and friends.

A car buff himself, Palmiter is the primary designer and research consultant for Kiddie Car Classics and Sidewalk Cruisers and sculpts many of the ornaments based on those collections. Palmiter also lends his talents to the creation of the *Nostalgic Houses and Shops* Keepsake series.

SHARON PIKE

After a four year leave to heal a broken arm, Sharon Pike returned two years ago to what she called "the greatest job there is." Having been with the Hallmark Keepsake Ornament Studio since 1983, Pike was eager to return.

Pike's artistic passion does not end with sculpting. She also enjoys making jewelry and spending time painting. A true lover of all forms of art, Pike spends much of her time attending art shows and the theater.

Much of Pike's work reflects her love of animals. This endearment is evident in such 1998 pieces as "Purr-fect Little Deer" and the 9th edition in the *Fabulous Decade* series.

DILL RHODUS

Before becoming a Keepsake Ornament artist in 1986, Dill Rhodus was an engraver at Hallmark for 20 years.

Rhodus spends his free time cultivating his zeal for sports by coaching his daughter's soccer team and through his true passion – golf. Married to fellow artist Patricia Andrews, Rhodus values his family above all else.

While he enjoys the wide range of subject matters, as an avid sports fan, Rhodus is especially excited about his *At The Ballpark* and *Football Legends* series, which boast new introductions in 1998. And space fans are sure to love his renditions of the STAR WARS™ characters "Princess Leia™" and "Boba Fett™."

ANITA MARRA ROGERS

Anita Marra Rogers says that it was like falling in love the first time she entered the Keepsake Ornament Studio. After three years of working as a part-time artist, Rogers became a full-time member of the Keepsake Ornament family in 1987. It was with the 1994 "The Beatles Gift Set" that Rogers proved to the world (and herself) that she had a knack for sculpting realistic representations of people.

In her free time, Rogers enjoys collecting Hallmark Ornaments and Longaberger baskets and pottery. She also has a passion for intricate puzzles, baking and enjoys traveling and spending time with her family.

While Rogers is perhaps best known for her renditions of STAR TREK™ characters, she is a versatile artist and lends her talents to a variety of ornaments in 1998, including "Madonna and Child."

ED SEALE

Since 1980, Ed Seale has been bringing his design magic to the Hallmark Keepsake Ornament studio. Many of his unique creations are based on elements of surprise and whimsy as he places animals in scenes where one would most likely expect to find a person. Seale believes that sometimes animals represent humans better than humans can themselves.

When he's not sculpting, Seale likes to sail his catamaran, travel and take photographs. He also boasts himself to be a die-hard home improver and takes great pride in having recently become a grandfather.

Among Seale's 1998 contributions to the Keepsake Ornament line is the Premiere Exclusive "Santa's Merry Workshop Musical Figurine" and ornaments such as "Santa's Flying Machine" and the 19th edition of the *Frosty Friends* series.

LINDA SICKMAN

Linda Sickman has been with Hallmark for over 35 years, and has been a Keepsake Ornament Studio artist since 1976. A seasoned and prolific sculptor, Sickman has created more than 300 ornaments.

When she is not sculpting ornaments, Sickman is collecting them. She also takes great pleasure in her tin toys and nutcracker collection. An afficionado of the symphony and theater, Sickman spends much of her time in the world of the arts.

Sickman is known for her popular and long-running series, including the Keepsake Ornament *Rocking Horse* and *Tin Locomotive* series. She has also created many Miniature ornament series, including *Antique Tractors*, *Miniature Clothespin Soldier*, *Noel R.R.*, *Nutcracker Guild* and *On the Road*.

BOB SIEDLER

Bob Siedler probably had no idea of the impact of his lunch breaks while working as a graphic artist in

Hallmark's sales promotion department. During those breaks, Siedler would create clay figurines that he refers to as "noon doodles." Once he had a bit of a collection of them, Siedler took them to the Hallmark Keepsake Ornament art director and in 1982, Siedler was transformed from a "noon

doodler" to a Keepsake Ornament Studio artist.

When he's not sculpting, Siedler likes to spend his free time actively. He prefers sports such as golf and snow skiing. His most prized possession is a microscope, the first Christmas present he recalls receiving that was neither socks nor underwear.

Siedler gets his inspiration from watching people and enjoys the challenge of creating a wide variety of Hallmark ornaments. His 1998 contributions include the *NBA Collection*, the second edition of *The Clauses on Vacation* series and the introduction of "Joe Cool," the first edition of the *Spotlight On SNOOPY* series.

SUE TAGUE

Sue Tague has been with Hallmark for 32 years. While she didn't actually become a Keepsake Ornament artist until 1994, she played a key part in the production of many ornaments before taking her position as a Keepsake artist.

Always in the creative mode, Tague enjoys making dolls and puppets. She jokes that she enjoys spending her free time doing the same kinds of things that she does while at work.

Tague is perhaps best known for her *Language Of Flowers* series and in 1998, offers the third edition, "Iris Angel."

DUANE UNRUH

After a winning career as a high school coach, Duane Unruh realized that the artistic talent that he had discovered as a child could no longer be ignored. In

1984, his lifelong love of wax-sculpting and wood-carving evolved into a position as a Hallmark Keepsake Ornament Studio artist.

In his free time, Unruh enjoys working on his seventy-six acres of land. He also cherishes time spent with his wife of over 40 years and their dog.

As a sports afficionado, Unruh was honored to create the Commemorative Olympic Piece "Lighting The Flame" in 1996. A recent accomplishment; his "Journey To Bethlehem" ornament was named as the 1998 Collector's Choice by Hallmark ornament expert Clara Johnson Scroggins.

LaDene Votruba

LaDene Votruba became a Hallmark Keepsake Ornament Studio artist in 1983 after ten years of working for Hallmark in other creative capacities. She finds inspiration in all aspects of her life and believes that the best work is a reflection of those cherished moments in life.

A woman of many interests, Votruba enjoys spending time in all realms of the artistic world including film, music and literature. She also takes great pleasure in hiking, antiquing and shopping.

Votruba's accomplishments include the Miniature Ornament *Nutcracker Ballet* series. She has also made numerous contributions to the Keepsake Ornament line throughout the years.

NELLO WILLIAMS

As a free-time ornament artist, Nello Williams never thought that his hobby would lead him to an actual career. An illustrator by profession, Williams at first interviewed with Hallmark's card division. When the ornament that the artist just happened to have with him impressed the interviewer; one thing led to another and Williams was given an internship in the Keepsake Studio. In 1995, he became a member of the Keepsake Ornament Studio family.

The multi-talented Williams is also an accomplished musician who enjoys playing guitar and keyboard. He also takes great pride in his Buck Rogers and Flash Gordon memorabilia collection. He has even combined the two, as he boasts that his electric guitar is covered with Buck Rogers-type images.

Williams is known for his whimsical creations. His 1998 contributions include "Holiday Decorator," which features a mouse drawing a picture of a Christmas tree on a frost-covered window. This piece is unique as it can be hung on a tree like an ornament or put somewhere special with lights behind it so as to take advantage of its lighting effect.

How To Use Your Value Guide

1. Locate your piece in the value guide. The value guide section begins with Hallmark Keepsake Ornaments, which is split into two sections: collectible series (listed in alphabetical order by series name) followed by general ornaments (listed in reverse

1956 Ford Truck
(1st, 1995)
Handcrafted • PALM
1395QX5527 • **Value $34**

chronological order, from 1998 to 1973). Within each year, the general ornaments are grouped according to Keepsake, Magic, Crown Reflections, Showcase and Miniature (if applicable) and then miscellaneous collections. Separate sections are devoted to Spring Ornaments, Merry Miniatures and Kiddie Car Classics. To help locate an ornament, refer to the complete alphabetical index that begins on page 320.

2. Fill in the price you originally paid for each ornament in the "Price Paid" column. To figure out the original retail price, look at the first 3 or 4 digits of each piece's Hallmark stock number. (For example, the ornament with stock number "1395QX5527" originally retailed for $13.95.)

3. Record the current market value of each ornament in the "Value of My Collection" column. The current value of each piece is located next to its item number. If the market value of a piece is not established, it is listed as "N/E."

4. Calculate the value for each page by adding all of the boxes in each column. Next, transfer the totals from each page to the "Total Value Of My Collection" worksheets on pages 288-302. Now add all of the totals together to determine the overall value of your collection. (Remember: Use a pencil so you can change the totals as your collection grows!)

Hallmark Artist Key

ANDR	Patricia Andrews
AUBE	Nina Aubé
BAUR	Tim Bauer
BISH	Ron Bishop
BLAC	Thomas Blackshear
BRIC	Katrina Bricker
BRWN	Andrew Brownsword
CHAD	Robert Chad
CROW	Ken Crow
DLEE	Donna Lee
DUTK	Peter Dutkin
ESCH	Joanne Eschrich
FRAL	Tobin Fraley
FRAN	John "Collin" Francis
HADD	Tammy Haddix
HAMI	Mary Hamilton
JLEE	Julia Lee
JOHN	Cathy Johnson
KLIN	Kristina Kline
LARS	Tracy Larsen
LYLE	Joyce Lyle
MAHO	Jim Mahon
MCGE	Diana McGehee
N/A	not available
NORT	Lynn Norton
PALM	Don Palmiter
PATT	Joyce Pattee
PIKE	Sharon Pike
PYDA	Michele Pyda-Sevcik
RGRS	Anita Marra Rogers
RHOD	Dill Rhodus
SCHU	Lee Schuler
SEAL	Ed Seale
SICK	Linda Sickman
SIED	Bob Siedler
TAGU	Sue Tague
UNRU	Duane Unruh
VARI	various artists
VOTR	LaDene Votruba
WILL	Nello Williams

Keepsake Series

Since Hallmark Ornaments were introduced in 1973, there have been 85 Keepsake collectible series, including 47 that are ongoing. An impressive 10 Keepsake series, including "A Pony for Christmas" and "Winnie the Pooh" are making their debut in 1998; while 5 series, including the popular "CRAYOLA® Crayon," are concluding.

(1) NEW!

African-American Holiday BARBIE™ (1st, 1998)
Handcrafted • ANDR
1595QX6936 • Value $15.95

(2) 1956 Ford Truck (1st, 1995)
Handcrafted • PALM
1395QX5527 • Value $34

(3) 1955 Chevrolet Cameo (2nd, 1996)
Handcrafted • PALM
1395QX5241 • Value $31

(4) 1953 GMC (3rd, 1997)
Handcrafted • PALM
1395QX6105 • Value $26

(5) NEW!
1937 Ford V-8 (4th, 1998)
Handcrafted • PALM
1395QX6263 • Value $13.95

(6) Christy (1st, 1996)
Handcrafted • N/A
1295QX5564 • Value $26

(7) Nikki (2nd, set/2, 1997)
Handcrafted • N/A
1295QX6142 • Value $23

(8) NEW!
Ricky (3rd & final, 1998)
Handcrafted • N/A
1295QX6363 • Value $12.95

(9) Madonna and Child and St. John (1st, 1984)
Bezeled Satin • MCGE
650QX3494 • Value $20

(10) Madonna of the Pomegranate (2nd, 1985)
Bezeled Satin • MCGE
675QX3772 • Value $19

(11) Madonna and Child with the Infant St. John (3rd & final, 1986)
Bezeled Satin • MCGE
675QX3506 • Value $30

(12) Nolan Ryan (1st, 1996)
Handcrafted • RHOD
1495QXI5711 • Value $35

(13) Hank Aaron (2nd, 1997)
Handcrafted • RHOD
1495QX6152 • Value $27

(14) NEW!
Cal Ripken Jr. (3rd, 1998)
Handcrafted • RHOD
1495QXI4033 • Value $14.95

(15) BARBIE™ (1st, 1994)
Handcrafted • ANDR
1495QX5006 • Value $48

(16) Solo in the Spotlight (2nd, 1995)
Handcrafted • ANDR
1495QXI5049 • Value $33

(17) Brunette Debut – 1959 (club edition, 1995)
Handcrafted • ANDR
1495QXC5397 • Value $73

AFRICAN-AMERICAN HOLIDAY BARBIE	
	Price Paid	Value of My Collection
1.		
ALL-AMERICAN TRUCKS		
2.		
3.		
4.		
5.		
ALL GOD'S CHILDREN®		
6.		
7.		
8.		
ART MASTERPIECE		
9.		
10.		
11.		
AT THE BALLPARK		
12.		
13.		
14.		
BARBIE™		
15.		
16.		
17.		
PENCIL TOTALS		

KEEPSAKE SERIES

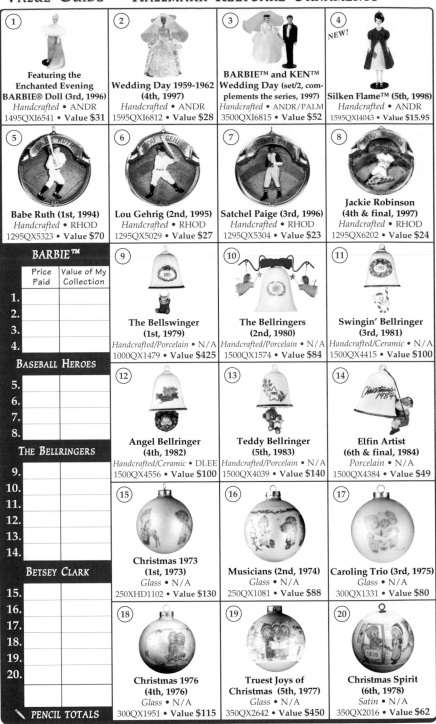

(1) Featuring the
Enchanted Evening
BARBIE® Doll (3rd, 1996)
Handcrafted • ANDR
1495QXI6541 • **Value $31**

(2) Wedding Day 1959-1962
(4th, 1997)
Handcrafted • ANDR
1595QXI6812 • **Value $28**

(3) BARBIE™ and KEN™
Wedding Day (set/2, complements the series, 1997)
Handcrafted • ANDR/PALM
3500QXI6815 • **Value $52**

(4) NEW!
Silken Flame™ (5th, 1998)
Handcrafted • ANDR
1595QXI4043 • **Value $15.95**

(5) Babe Ruth (1st, 1994)
Handcrafted • RHOD
1295QX5323 • **Value $70**

(6) Lou Gehrig (2nd, 1995)
Handcrafted • RHOD
1295QX5029 • **Value $27**

(7) Satchel Paige (3rd, 1996)
Handcrafted • RHOD
1295QX5304 • **Value $23**

(8) Jackie Robinson
(4th & final, 1997)
Handcrafted • RHOD
1295QX6202 • **Value $24**

BARBIE™

	Price Paid	Value of My Collection
1.		
2.		
3.		
4.		

BASEBALL HEROES

5.		
6.		
7.		
8.		

THE BELLRINGERS

9.		
10.		
11.		
12.		
13.		
14.		

BETSEY CLARK

15.		
16.		
17.		
18.		
19.		
20.		

PENCIL TOTALS

(9) The Bellswinger
(1st, 1979)
Handcrafted/Porcelain • N/A
1000QX1479 • **Value $425**

(10) The Bellringers
(2nd, 1980)
Handcrafted/Porcelain • N/A
1500QX1574 • **Value $84**

(11) Swingin' Bellringer
(3rd, 1981)
Handcrafted/Ceramic • N/A
1500QX4415 • **Value $100**

(12) Angel Bellringer
(4th, 1982)
Handcrafted/Ceramic • DLEE
1500QX4556 • **Value $100**

(13) Teddy Bellringer
(5th, 1983)
Handcrafted/Porcelain • N/A
1500QX4039 • **Value $140**

(14) Elfin Artist
(6th & final, 1984)
Porcelain • N/A
1500QX4384 • **Value $49**

(15) Christmas 1973
(1st, 1973)
Glass • N/A
250XHD1102 • **Value $130**

(16) Musicians (2nd, 1974)
Glass • N/A
250QX1081 • **Value $88**

(17) Caroling Trio (3rd, 1975)
Glass • N/A
300QX1331 • **Value $80**

(18) Christmas 1976
(4th, 1976)
Glass • N/A
300QX1951 • **Value $115**

(19) Truest Joys of
Christmas (5th, 1977)
Glass • N/A
350QX2642 • **Value $450**

(20) Christmas Spirit
(6th, 1978)
Satin • N/A
350QX2016 • **Value $62**

VALUE GUIDE — HALLMARK KEEPSAKE ORNAMENTS

(1)
Holiday Fun (7th, 1979)
Satin • N/A
350QX2019 • **Value $40**

(2)
Joy-in-the-Air (8th, 1980)
Glass • N/A
400QX2154 • **Value $32**

(3)
Christmas 1981 (9th, 1981)
Glass • N/A
450QX8022 • **Value $34**

(4)
Joys of Christmas (10th, 1982)
Satin • N/A
450QX2156 • **Value $36**

(5)
Christmas Happiness (11th, 1983)
Glass • N/A
450QX2119 • **Value $31**

(6)
Days are Merry (12th, 1984)
Glass • N/A
500QX2494 • **Value $35**

(7)
Special Kind of Feeling (13th & final, 1985)
Glass • PIKE
500QX2632 • **Value $37**

(8)
Betsey Clark: Home For Christmas (1st, 1986)
Glass • PIKE
500QX2776 • **Value $37**

(9)
Betsey Clark: Home For Christmas (2nd, 1987)
Glass • PIKE
500QX2727 • **Value $26**

(10)
Betsey Clark: Home For Christmas (3rd, 1988)
Glass • PIKE
500QX2714 • **Value $25**

(11)
Betsey Clark: Home For Christmas (4th, 1989)
Glass • N/A
500QX2302 • **Value $38**

(12)
Betsey Clark: Home For Christmas (5th, 1990)
Glass • N/A
500QX2033 • **Value $25**

(13)
Betsey Clark: Home For Christmas (6th & final, 1991)
Glass • N/A
500QX2109 • **Value $32**

(14)
Betsey 's Country Christmas (1st, 1992)
Glass • N/A
500QX2104 • **Value $30**

(15)
Betsey 's Country Christmas (2nd, 1993)
Glass • N/A
500QX2062 • **Value $21**

(16)
Betsey 's Country Christmas (3rd & final, 1994)
Glass • N/A
500QX2403 • **Value $18**

(17)
Antique Toys (1st, 1978)
Handcrafted • N/A
600QX1463 • **Value $400**

(18)
Christmas Carrousel (2nd, 1979)
Handcrafted • N/A
650QX1467 • **Value $190**

(19)
Merry Carrousel (3rd, 1980)
Handcrafted • N/A
750QX1414 • **Value $168**

(20)
Skaters' Carrousel (4th, 1981)
Handcrafted • N/A
900QX4275 • **Value $92**

	Price Paid	Value of My Collection
BETSEY CLARK		
1.		
2.		
3.		
4.		
5.		
6.		
7.		
BETSEY CLARK: HOME FOR CHRISTMAS		
8.		
9.		
10.		
11.		
12.		
13.		
BETSEY'S COUNTRY CHRISTMAS		
14.		
15.		
16.		
CARROUSEL SERIES		
17.		
18.		
19.		
20.		
PENCIL TOTALS		

Value Guide — Hallmark Keepsake Ornaments

1 — Snowman Carrousel (5th, 1982)
Handcrafted • SEAL
1000QX4783 • **Value $104**

2 — Santa and Friends (6th & final, 1983)
Handcrafted • SICK
1100QX4019 • **Value $52**

3 — Cat Naps (1st, 1994)
Handcrafted • RHOD
795QX5313 • **Value $45**

4 — Cat Naps (2nd, 1995)
Handcrafted • RHOD
795QX5097 • **Value $28**

5 — Cat Naps (3rd, 1996)
Handcrafted • RHOD
795QX5641 • **Value $22**

6 — Cat Naps (4th, 1997)
Handcrafted • BRIC
895QX6205 • **Value $16**

7 — NEW! Cat Naps (5th & final, 1998)
Handcrafted • BRIC
895QX6383 • **Value $8.95**

8 — A Celebration Of Angels (1st, 1995)
Handcrafted • ANDR
1295QX5077 • **Value $23**

9 — A Celebration Of Angels (2nd, 1996)
Handcrafted • ANDR
1295QX5634 • **Value $30**

10 — A Celebration of Angels (3rd, 1997)
Handcrafted • ANDR
1395QX6175 • **Value $26**

11 — NEW! A Celebration of Angels (4th & final, 1998)
Handcrafted • ANDR
1395QX6366 • **Value $13.95**

12 — Christmas Kitty (1st, 1989)
Porcelain • RGRS
1475QX5445 • **Value $31**

13 — Christmas Kitty (2nd, 1990)
Porcelain • RGRS
1475QX4506 • **Value $33**

14 — Christmas Kitty (3rd & final, 1991)
Porcelain • RGRS
1475QX4377 • **Value $32**

15 — St. Nicholas (1st, 1995)
Handcrafted • RGRS
1495QX5087 • **Value $30**

16 — Christkindl (2nd, 1996)
Handcrafted • VOTR
1495QX5631 • **Value $28**

17 — Kolyada (3rd & final, 1997)
Handcrafted • VOTR
1495QX6172 • **Value $24**

	Price Paid	Value of My Collection
CARROUSEL SERIES		
1.		
2.		
CAT NAPS		
3.		
4.		
5.		
6.		
7.		
A CELEBRATION OF ANGELS		
8.		
9.		
10.		
11.		
CHRISTMAS KITTY		
12.		
13.		
14.		
CHRISTMAS VISITORS		
15.		
16.		
17.		
PENCIL TOTALS		

(1)

1957 Corvette (1st, 1991)
Handcrafted • PALM
1275QX4319 • **Value $205**

(2)
1966 Mustang (2nd, 1992)
Handcrafted • PALM
1275QX4284 • **Value $50**

(3)
1956 Ford Thunderbird (3rd, 1993)
Handcrafted • PALM
1275QX5275 • **Value $37**

(4)
1957 Chevrolet Bel Air (4th, 1994)
Handcrafted • PALM
1295QX5422 • **Value $36**

(5)
1969 Chevrolet Camaro (5th, 1995)
Handcrafted • PALM
1295QX5239 • **Value $22**

(6)
1958 Ford Edsel Citation Convertible (club edition, 1995)
Handcrafted • PALM
1295QXC4167 • **Value $77**

(7)
1959 Cadillac De Ville (6th, 1996)
Handcrafted • PALM
1295QX5384 • **Value $30**

(8)
1969 Hurst Oldsmobile 442 (7th, 1997)
Handcrafted • PALM
1395QX6102 • **Value $26**

(9) NEW!
1970 Plymouth® Hemi 'Cuda (8th, 1998)
Handcrafted • PALM
1395QX6256 • **Value $13.95**

(10)

The Clauses on Vacation (1st, 1997)
Handcrafted • SIED
1495QX6112 • **Value $28**

(11) NEW!
The Clauses on Vacation (2nd, 1998)
Handcrafted • SIED
1495QX6276 • **Value $14.95**

(12)
British (1st, 1982)
Handcrafted • SICK
500QX4583 • **Value $130**

(13)
Early American (2nd, 1983)
Handcrafted • SICK
500QX4029 • **Value $47**

(14)
Canadian Mountie (3rd, 1984)
Handcrafted • SICK
500QX4471 • **Value $31**

(15)
Scottish Highlander (4th, 1985)
Handcrafted • SICK
550QX4715 • **Value $30**

(16)
French Officer (5th, 1986)
Handcrafted • SICK
550QX4063 • **Value $30**

(17)
Sailor (6th & final, 1987)
Handcrafted • SICK
550QX4807 • **Value $29**

(18)

Light Shines at Christmas (1st, 1987)
Porcelain • VOTR
800QX4817 • **Value $78**

(19)
Waiting for Santa (2nd, 1988)
Porcelain • VOTR
800QX4061 • **Value $50**

(20)
Morning of Wonder (3rd, 1989)
Porcelain • VOTR
825QX4612 • **Value $33**

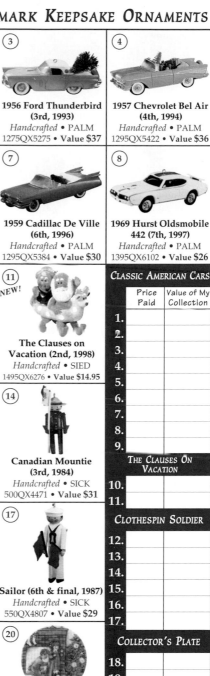

CLASSIC AMERICAN CARS		
	Price Paid	Value of My Collection
1.		
2.		
3.		
4.		
5.		
6.		
7.		
8.		
9.		
THE CLAUSES ON VACATION		
10.		
11.		
CLOTHESPIN SOLDIER		
12.		
13.		
14.		
15.		
16.		
17.		
COLLECTOR'S PLATE		
18.		
19.		
20.		
PENCIL TOTALS		

1 Cookies for Santa
(4th, 1990)
Porcelain • VOTR
875QX4436 • **Value $36**

2 Let It Snow! (5th, 1991)
Porcelain • VOTR
875QX4369 • **Value $30**

3 Sweet Holiday Harmony
(6th & final, 1992)
Porcelain • VOTR
875QX4461 • **Value $32**

4 Bright Journey
(1st, 1989)
Handcrafted • SICK
875QX4352 • **Value $50**

5 Bright Moving Colors
(2nd, 1990)
Handcrafted • CROW
875QX4586 • **Value $47**

6 Bright Vibrant Carols
(3rd, 1991)
Handcrafted • CROW
975QX4219 • **Value $41**

7 Bright Blazing Colors
(4th, 1992)
Handcrafted • CROW
975QX4264 • **Value $42**

8 Bright Shining Castle
(5th, 1993)
Handcrafted • CROW
1075QX4422 • **Value $33**

9 Bright Playful Colors
(6th, 1994)
Handcrafted • CROW
1095QX5273 • **Value $31**

10 Bright 'n' Sunny Tepee
(7th, 1995)
Handcrafted • ANDR
1095QX5247 • **Value $22**

11 Bright Flying Colors
(8th, 1996)
Handcrafted • CROW
1095QX5391 • **Value $27**

12 Bright Rocking Colors
(9th, 1997)
Handcrafted • TAGU
1295QX6235 • **Value $26**

13 NEW! Bright Sledding Colors
(10th & final, 1998)
Handcrafted • TAGU
1295QX6166 • **Value $12.95**

14 Native American
BARBIE™ (1st, 1996)
Handcrafted • ANDR
1495QX5561 • **Value $32**

15 Chinese BARBIE™
(2nd, 1997)
Handcrafted • RGRS
1495QX6162 • **Value $32**

16 NEW! Mexican BARBIE™
(3rd, 1998)
Handcrafted • RGRS
1495QX6356 • **Value $14.95**

17 Cinderella (1st, 1997)
Handcrafted • CROW
1495QXD4045 • **Value $31**

18 NEW! Walt Disney's *Snow White* (2nd, 1998)
Handcrafted • N/A
1495QXD4056 • **Value $14.95**

COLLECTOR'S PLATE

	Price Paid	Value of My Collection
1.		
2.		
3.		

CRAYOLA® Crayon

4.		
5.		
6.		
7.		
8.		
9.		
10.		
11.		
12.		
13.		

DOLLS OF THE WORLD

14.		
15.		
16.		

THE ENCHANTED MEMORIES COLLECTION

17.		
18.		

PENCIL TOTALS

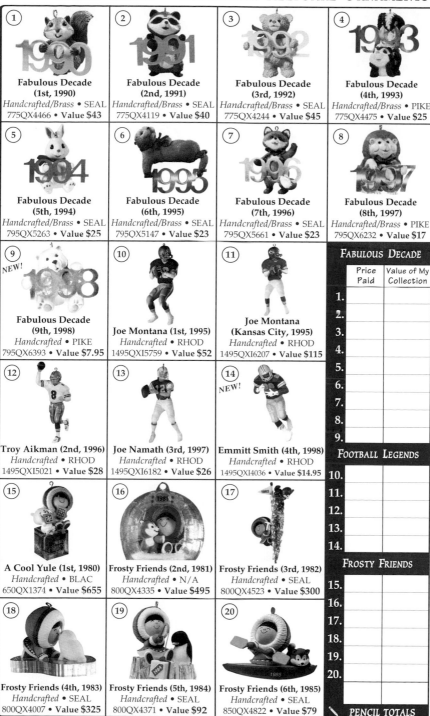

① Fabulous Decade (1st, 1990)
Handcrafted/Brass • SEAL
775QX4466 • **Value $43**

② Fabulous Decade (2nd, 1991)
Handcrafted/Brass • SEAL
775QX4119 • **Value $40**

③ Fabulous Decade (3rd, 1992)
Handcrafted/Brass • SEAL
775QX4244 • **Value $45**

④ Fabulous Decade (4th, 1993)
Handcrafted/Brass • PIKE
775QX4475 • **Value $25**

⑤ Fabulous Decade (5th, 1994)
Handcrafted/Brass • SEAL
795QX5263 • **Value $25**

⑥ Fabulous Decade (6th, 1995)
Handcrafted/Brass • SEAL
795QX5147 • **Value $23**

⑦ Fabulous Decade (7th, 1996)
Handcrafted/Brass • SEAL
795QX5661 • **Value $23**

⑧ Fabulous Decade (8th, 1997)
Handcrafted/Brass • PIKE
795QX6232 • **Value $17**

⑨ NEW! Fabulous Decade (9th, 1998)
Handcrafted • PIKE
795QX6393 • **Value $7.95**

⑩ Joe Montana (1st, 1995)
Handcrafted • RHOD
1495QXI5759 • **Value $52**

⑪ Joe Montana (Kansas City, 1995)
Handcrafted • RHOD
1495QXI6207 • **Value $115**

⑫ Troy Aikman (2nd, 1996)
Handcrafted • RHOD
1495QXI5021 • **Value $28**

⑬ Joe Namath (3rd, 1997)
Handcrafted • RHOD
1495QXI6182 • **Value $26**

⑭ NEW! Emmitt Smith (4th, 1998)
Handcrafted • RHOD
1495QXI4036 • **Value $14.95**

⑮ A Cool Yule (1st, 1980)
Handcrafted • BLAC
650QX1374 • **Value $655**

⑯ Frosty Friends (2nd, 1981)
Handcrafted • N/A
800QX4335 • **Value $495**

⑰ Frosty Friends (3rd, 1982)
Handcrafted • SEAL
800QX4523 • **Value $300**

⑱ Frosty Friends (4th, 1983)
Handcrafted • SEAL
800QX4007 • **Value $325**

⑲ Frosty Friends (5th, 1984)
Handcrafted • SEAL
800QX4371 • **Value $92**

⑳ Frosty Friends (6th, 1985)
Handcrafted • SEAL
850QX4822 • **Value $79**

FABULOUS DECADE	Price Paid	Value of My Collection
1.		
2.		
3.		
4.		
5.		
6.		
7.		
8.		
9.		
FOOTBALL LEGENDS		
10.		
11.		
12.		
13.		
14.		
FROSTY FRIENDS		
15.		
16.		
17.		
18.		
19.		
20.		
PENCIL TOTALS		

(1) Frosty Friends (7th, 1986)
Handcrafted • SIED
850QX4053 • **Value $76**

(2) Frosty Friends (8th, 1987)
Handcrafted • SEAL
850QX4409 • **Value $61**

(3) Frosty Friends (9th, 1988)
Handcrafted • SEAL
875QX4031 • **Value $67**

(4) Frosty Friends
(10th, 1989)
Handcrafted • SEAL
925QX4572 • **Value $68**

(5) Frosty Friends
(11th, 1990)
Handcrafted • SEAL
975QX4396 • **Value $40**

(6) Frosty Friends
(12th, 1991)
Handcrafted • PIKE
975QX4327 • **Value $44**

(7) Frosty Friends
(13th, 1992)
Handcrafted • JLEE
975QX4291 • **Value $35**

(8) Frosty Friends
(14th, 1993)
Handcrafted • JLEE
975QX4142 • **Value $38**

FROSTY FRIENDS		
	Price Paid	Value of My Collection
1.		
2.		
3.		
4.		
5.		
6.		
7.		
8.		
9.		
10.		
11.		
12.		
13.		

(9) Frosty Friends (complements the series, 1993)
Handcrafted • SEAL
2000QX5682 • **Value $50**

(10) Frosty Friends
(15th, 1994)
Handcrafted • SEAL
995QX5293 • **Value $35**

(11) Frosty Friends
(16th, 1995)
Handcrafted • SEAL
1095QX5169 • **Value $33**

(12) Frosty Friends
(17th, 1996)
Handcrafted • SEAL
1095QX5681 • **Value $26**

(13) Frosty Friends
(18th, 1997)
Handcrafted • SEAL
1095QX6255 • **Value $25**

(14) NEW! Frosty Friends
(19th, 1998)
Handcrafted • SEAL
1095QX6226 • **Value $10.95**

THE GIFT BRINGERS		
15.		
16.		
17.		
18.		
19.		

(15) St. Nicholas (1st, 1989)
Glass • VOTR
500QX2795 • **Value $26**

(16) St. Lucia (2nd, 1990)
Glass • VOTR
500QX2803 • **Value $25**

(17) Christkindl (3rd, 1991)
Glass • VOTR
500QX2117 • **Value $25**

GREATEST STORY		
20.		
PENCIL TOTALS		

(18) Kolyada (4th, 1992)
Glass • VOTR
500QX2124 • **Value $22**

(19) The Magi
(5th & final, 1993)
Glass • VOTR
500QX2065 • **Value $21**

(20) Greatest Story (1st, 1990)
Porcelain/Brass • VOTR
1275QX4656 • **Value $32**

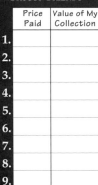

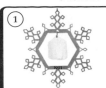

(1)
Greatest Story (2nd, 1991)
Porcelain/Brass • VOTR
1275QX4129 • **Value $29**

(2)
Greatest Story
(3rd & final, 1992)
Porcelain/Brass • VOTR
1275QX4251 • **Value $27**

(3)
Donald's Surprising
Gift (1st, 1997)
Handcrafted • BRIC
1295QXD4025 • **Value $25**

(4) NEW!
Ready for Christmas
(2nd, 1998)
Handcrafted • N/A
1295QXD4006 • **Value $12.95**

(5)
Hark! It's Herald
(1st, 1989)
Handcrafted • CROW
675QX4555 • **Value $30**

(6)
Hark! It's Herald
(2nd, 1990)
Handcrafted • CROW
675QX4463 • **Value $25**

(7)
Hark! It's Herald
(3rd, 1991)
Handcrafted • RGRS
675QX4379 • **Value $28**

(8)
Hark! It's Herald
(4th & final, 1992)
Handcrafted • JLEE
775QX4464 • **Value $25**

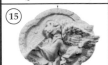

(9)
Heart of Christmas
(1st, 1990)
Handcrafted • SEAL
1375QX4726 • **Value $80**

(10)
Heart of Christmas
(2nd, 1991)
Handcrafted • SEAL
1375QX4357 • **Value $37**

(11)
Heart of Christmas
(3rd, 1992)
Handcrafted • SEAL
1375QX4411 • **Value $30**

(12)
Heart of Christmas
(4th, 1993)
Handcrafted • SEAL
1475QX4482 • **Value $30**

(13)
Heart of Christmas
(5th & final, 1994)
Handcrafted • SEAL
1495QX5266 • **Value $28**

(14)
Heavenly Angels
(1st, 1991)
Handcrafted • LYLE
775QX4367 • **Value $32**

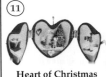

(15)
Heavenly Angels
(2nd, 1992)
Handcrafted • LYLE
775QX4454 • **Value $27**

(16)
Heavenly Angels
(3rd & final, 1993)
Handcrafted • LYLE
775QX4945 • **Value $21**

(17)
Santa's Motorcar
(1st, 1979)
Handcrafted • MAHO
900QX1559 • **Value $710**

(18)
Santa's Express
(2nd, 1980)
Handcrafted • MAHO
1200QX1434 • **Value $260**

GREATEST STORY		
	Price Paid	Value of My Collection
1.		
2.		
HALLMARK ARCHIVES		
3.		
4.		
HARK! IT'S HERALD		
5.		
6.		
7.		
8.		
HEART OF CHRISTMAS		
9.		
10.		
11.		
12.		
13.		
HEAVENLY ANGELS		
14.		
15.		
16.		
HERE COMES SANTA		
17.		
18.		
PENCIL TOTALS		

Value Guide – Hallmark Keepsake Ornaments

1 Rooftop Deliveries (3rd, 1981) *Handcrafted* • MAHO 1300QX4382 • **Value $350**	2 Jolly Trolley (4th, 1982) *Handcrafted* • SICK 1500QX4643 • **Value $145**	3 Santa Express (5th, 1983) *Handcrafted* • DLEE 1300QX4037 • **Value $285**	4 Santa's Deliveries (6th, 1984) *Handcrafted* • SICK 1300QX4324 • **Value $93**
5 Santa's Fire Engine (7th, 1985) *Handcrafted* • SICK 1400QX4965 • **Value $67**	6 Kringle's Kool Treats (8th, 1986) *Handcrafted* • SIED 1400QX4043 • **Value $80**	7 Santa's Woody (9th, 1987) *Handcrafted* • CROW 1400QX4847 • **Value $103**	8 Kringle Koach (10th, 1988) *Handcrafted* • CROW 1400QX4001 • **Value $50**
9 Christmas Caboose (11th, 1989) *Handcrafted* • CROW 1475QX4585 • **Value $52**	10 Festive Surrey (12th, 1990) *Handcrafted* • SICK 1475QX4923 • **Value $44**	11 Santa's Antique Car (13th, 1991) *Handcrafted* • SICK 1475QX4349 • **Value $62**	
12 Kringle Tours (14th, 1992) *Handcrafted* • SICK 1475QX4341 • **Value $44**	13 Happy Haul-idays (15th, 1993) *Handcrafted* • SICK 1475QX4102 • **Value $40**	14 Shopping With Santa (complements the series, 1993) *Handcrafted* • SICK 2400QX5675 • **Value $50**	
15 Makin' Tractor Tracks (16th, 1994) *Handcrafted* • SICK 1495QX5296 • **Value $63**	16 Santa's Roadster (17th, 1995) *Handcrafted* • SICK 1495QX5179 • **Value $32**	17 Santa's 4 x 4 (18th, 1996) *Handcrafted* • SEAL 1495QX5684 • **Value $32**	
18 The Claus-Mobile (19th, 1997) *Handcrafted* • TAGU 1495QX6262 • **Value $26**	19 NEW! Santa's Bumper Car (20th, 1998) *Handcrafted* • TAGU 1495QX6283 • **Value $14.95**	20 Wayne Gretzky (1st, 1997) *Handcrafted* • UNRU 1595QXI6275 • **Value $29**	

Here Comes Santa

	Price Paid	Value of My Collection
1.		
2.		
3.		
4.		
5.		
6.		
7.		
8.		
9.		
10.		
11.		
12.		
13.		
14.		
15.		
16.		
17.		
18.		
19.		

Hockey Greats

20.		

PENCIL TOTALS

1
NEW!

Mario Lemieux
(2nd, 1998)
Handcrafted • FRAN
1595QXI6476 • **Value $15.95**

2

Holiday BARBIE™
(1st, 1993)
Handcrafted • ANDR
1475QX5725 • **Value $180**

3

Holiday BARBIE™
(2nd, 1994)
Handcrafted • ANDR
1495QX5216 • **Value $58**

4

Holiday BARBIE™
(3rd, 1995)
Handcrafted • ANDR
1495QXI5057 • **Value $40**

5

Holiday BARBIE™
(4th, 1996)
Handcrafted • ANDR
1495QXI5371 • **Value $38**

6

Holiday BARBIE™
(5th, 1997)
Handcrafted • ANDR
1595QXI6212 • **Value $28**

7
NEW!

Holiday BARBIE™
(6th, 1998)
Handcrafted • ANDR
1595QXI4023 • **Value $15.95**

8

Based on the 1988 Happy Holidays® BARBIE® Doll
(1st, club edition, 1996)
Handcrafted • ANDR
1495QXC4181 • **Value $60**

9

Based on the 1989 Happy Holidays® BARBIE® Doll
(2nd, club edition, 1997)
Handcrafted • ANDR
1595QXC5162 • **Value $28**

10
NEW!

Based on the 1990 Happy Holidays® BARBIE® Doll
(3rd, club edition, 1998)
Handcrafted • ANDR
1595QXC4493 • **Value $15.95**

11

Holiday Heirloom
(1st, LE-34,600, 1987)
Crystal/Silver-Plated • UNRU
2500QX4857 • **Value $30**

12

Holiday Heirloom
(2nd, club edition, LE-34,600, 1988)
Crystal/Silver-Plated • N/A
2500QX4064 • **Value $32**

13

Holiday Heirloom
(3rd & final, club edition, LE-34,600, 1989)
Crystal/Silver-Plated • N/A
2500QXC4605 • **Value $40**

14

Cardinalis (1st, 1982)
Wood • N/A
700QX3133 • **Value $395**

15

Black-Capped Chickadees (2nd, 1983)
Wood • N/A
700QX3099 • **Value $72**

16

Ring-Necked Pheasant
(3rd, 1984)
Wood • N/A
725QX3474 • **Value $30**

17
California Partridge
(4th, 1985)
Wood • N/A
750QX3765 • **Value $30**

18

Cedar Waxwing
(5th, 1986)
Wood • N/A
750QX3216 • **Value $30**

19
Snow Goose (6th, 1987)
Wood • VOTR
750QX3717 • **Value $26**

HOCKEY GREATS	Price Paid	Value of My Collection
1.		
HOLIDAY BARBIE™		
2.		
3.		
4.		
5.		
6.		
7.		
HOLIDAY BARBIE™ – COLLECTOR'S CLUB		
8.		
9.		
10.		
HOLIDAY HEIRLOOM		
11.		
12.		
13.		
HOLIDAY WILDLIFE		
14.		
15.		
16.		
17.		
18.		
19.		
PENCIL TOTALS		

VALUE GUIDE – HALLMARK KEEPSAKE ORNAMENTS

(1) Purple Finch
(7th & final, 1988)
Wood • N/A
775QX3711 • **Value $29**

(2) Shaquille O'Neal
(1st, 1995)
Handcrafted • N/A
1495QXI5517 • **Value $55**

(3) Larry Bird (2nd, 1996)
Handcrafted • N/A
1495QXI5014 • **Value $38**

(4) Magic Johnson
(3rd, 1997)
Handcrafted • N/A
1495QXI6832 • **Value $28**

(5) NEW!
Grant Hill (4th, 1998)
Handcrafted • UNRU
1495QXI6846 • **Value $14.95**

(6) Murray® "Champion"
(1st, 1994)
Die-Cast Metal • PALM
1395QX5426 • **Value $72**

(7) Murray® Fire Truck
(2nd, 1995)
Die-Cast Metal • PALM
1395QX5027 • **Value $32**

(8) Murray® Airplane
(3rd, 1996)
Die-Cast Metal • PALM
1395QX5364 • **Value $30**

(9) 1937 Steelcraft Auburn
by Murray®
(club edition, 1996)
Die-Cast Metal • PALM
1595QXC4174 • **Value $57**

(10) Murray® Dump Truck
(4th, 1997)
Die-Cast Metal • PALM
1395QX6195 • **Value $27**

(11) 1937 Steelcraft Airflow
by Murray®
(club edition, 1997)
Die-Cast Metal • PALM
1595QXC5185 • **Value $58**

(12) NEW!
1955 Murray® Tractor
and Trailer (5th, 1998)
Die-Cast Metal • PALM
1695QX6376 • **Value $16.95**

(13) NEW!
1935 Steelcraft
by Murray®
(club edition, 1998)
Die-Cast Metal • PALM
1595QXC4496 • **Value $15.95**

(14) Pansy (1st, 1996)
Handcrafted • TAGU
1595QK1171 • **Value $75**

(15) Snowdrop Angel
(2nd, 1997)
Handcrafted • TAGU
1595QX1095 • **Value $28**

(16) NEW!
Iris Angel (3rd, 1998)
Handcrafted • TAGU
1595QX6156 • **Value $15.95**

(17) 700E Hudson Steam
Locomotive (1st, 1996)
Die-Cast Metal • N/A
1895QX5531 • **Value $60**

(18) 1950 Santa Fe F3 Diesel
Locomotive (2nd, 1997)
Die-Cast Metal • N/A
1895QX6145 • **Value $40**

(19) NEW!
Pennsylvania GG-1
Locomotive (3rd, 1998)
Die-Cast Metal • N/A
1895QX6346 • **Value $18.95**

HOLIDAY WILDLIFE

	Price Paid	Value of My Collection
1.		

HOOP STARS

2.		
3.		
4.		
5.		

KIDDIE CAR CLASSICS

6.		
7.		
8.		
9.		
10.		
11.		
12.		
13.		

THE LANGUAGE OF FLOWERS

14.		
15.		
16.		

LIONEL® TRAIN

17.		
18.		
19.		

PENCIL TOTALS

1
Cinderella – 1995 (1st, 1996)
Handcrafted • FRAN
1495QX6311 • **Value $46**

2
Little Red Riding Hood – 1991 (2nd, 1997)
Handcrafted • FRAN
1495QX6155 • **Value $30**

3 NEW!
Mop Top Wendy (3rd, 1998)
Handcrafted • FRAN
1495QX6353 • **Value $14.95**

4 NEW!
Glorious Angel (1st, 1998)
Handcrafted • FRAN
1495QX6493 • **Value $14.95**

5
Snowshoe Rabbits in Winter Mark Newman (1st, 1997)
Handcrafted • N/A
1295QX5694 • **Value $28**

6 NEW!
Timber Wolves at Play Mark Newman (2nd, 1998)
Handcrafted • N/A
1295QX6273 • **Value $12.95**

7
Marilyn Monroe (1st, 1997)
Handcrafted • ANDR
1495QX5704 • **Value $26**

8 NEW!
Marilyn Monroe (2nd, 1998)
Handcrafted • ANDR
1495QX6333 • **Value $14.95**

9
Buttercup (1st, 1988)
Handcrafted • CHAD
500QX4074 • **Value $46**

10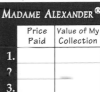
Bluebell (2nd, 1989)
Handcrafted • CHAD
575QX4545 • **Value $100**

11
Rosebud (3rd, 1990)
Handcrafted • CHAD
575QX4423 • **Value $40**

12
Iris (4th, 1991)
Handcrafted • CHAD
675QX4279 • **Value $42**

13
Lily (5th, 1992)
Handcrafted • CHAD
675QX4274 • **Value $50**

14
Ivy (6th, 1993)
Handcrafted • CHAD
675QX4282 • **Value $28**

15
Jasmine (7th, 1994)
Handcrafted • CHAD
695QX5276 • **Value $23**

16
Camellia (8th, 1995)
Handcrafted • CHAD
695QX5149 • **Value $18**

17
Violet (9th, 1996)
Handcrafted • CHAD
695QX5664 • **Value $19**

18
Daisy (10th, 1997)
Handcrafted • CHAD
795QX6242 • **Value $16**

19 NEW!
Daphne (11th, 1998)
Handcrafted • CHAD
795QX6153 • **Value $7.95**

MADAME ALEXANDER®	Price Paid	Value of My Collection
1.		
2.		
3.		
MADAME ALEXANDER® HOLIDAY ANGELS		
4.		
MAJESTIC WILDERNESS		
5.		
6.		
MARILYN MONROE		
7.		
8.		
MARY'S ANGELS		
9.		
10.		
11.		
12.		
13.		
14.		
15.		
16.		
17.		
18.		
19.		
PENCIL TOTALS		

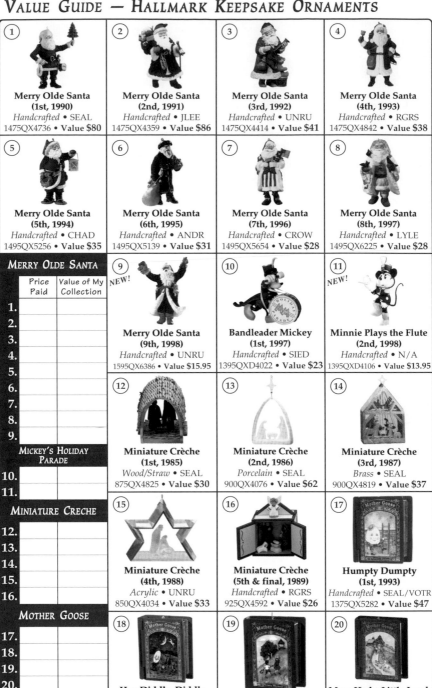

1
Merry Olde Santa
(1st, 1990)
Handcrafted • SEAL
1475QX4736 • **Value $80**

2
Merry Olde Santa
(2nd, 1991)
Handcrafted • JLEE
1475QX4359 • **Value $86**

3
Merry Olde Santa
(3rd, 1992)
Handcrafted • UNRU
1475QX4414 • **Value $41**

4
Merry Olde Santa
(4th, 1993)
Handcrafted • RGRS
1475QX4842 • **Value $38**

5
Merry Olde Santa
(5th, 1994)
Handcrafted • CHAD
1495QX5256 • **Value $35**

6
Merry Olde Santa
(6th, 1995)
Handcrafted • ANDR
1495QX5139 • **Value $31**

7
Merry Olde Santa
(7th, 1996)
Handcrafted • CROW
1495QX5654 • **Value $28**

8
Merry Olde Santa
(8th, 1997)
Handcrafted • LYLE
1495QX6225 • **Value $28**

9 NEW!
Merry Olde Santa
(9th, 1998)
Handcrafted • UNRU
1595QX6386 • **Value $15.95**

10
Bandleader Mickey
(1st, 1997)
Handcrafted • SIED
1395QXD4022 • **Value $23**

11 NEW!
Minnie Plays the Flute
(2nd, 1998)
Handcrafted • N/A
1395QXD4106 • **Value $13.95**

12
Miniature Crèche
(1st, 1985)
Wood/Straw • SEAL
875QX4825 • **Value $30**

13
Miniature Crèche
(2nd, 1986)
Porcelain • SEAL
900QX4076 • **Value $62**

14
Miniature Crèche
(3rd, 1987)
Brass • SEAL
900QX4819 • **Value $37**

15
Miniature Crèche
(4th, 1988)
Acrylic • UNRU
850QX4034 • **Value $33**

16
Miniature Crèche
(5th & final, 1989)
Handcrafted • RGRS
925QX4592 • **Value $26**

17
Humpty Dumpty
(1st, 1993)
Handcrafted • SEAL/VOTR
1375QX5282 • **Value $47**

18
Hey Diddle, Diddle
(2nd, 1994)
Handcrafted • SEAL
1395QX5213 • **Value $43**

19
Jack and Jill (3rd, 1995)
Handcrafted • SEAL/VOTR
1395QX5099 • **Value $28**

20
Mary Had a Little Lamb
(4th, 1996)
Handcrafted • SEAL/VOTR
1395QX5644 • **Value $31**

MERRY OLDE SANTA	Price Paid	Value of My Collection
1.		
2.		
3.		
4.		
5.		
6.		
7.		
8.		
9.		
MICKEY'S HOLIDAY PARADE		
10.		
11.		
MINIATURE CRECHE		
12.		
13.		
14.		
15.		
16.		
MOTHER GOOSE		
17.		
18.		
19.		
20.		
PENCIL TOTALS		

(1) 	(2) 	(3)	(4)
Little Boy Blue (5th & final, 1997) *Handcrafted* • SEAL/VOTR 1395QX6215 • **Value $25**	**Merry Mistletoe Time** (1st, 1986) *Handcrafted* • UNRU 1300QX4026 • **Value $105**	**Home Cooking** (2nd, 1987) *Handcrafted* • UNRU 1325QX4837 • **Value $70**	**Shall We Dance** (3rd, 1988) *Handcrafted* • UNRU 1300QX4011 • **Value $60**
(5)	(6)	(7)	(8)
Holiday Duet (4th, 1989) *Handcrafted* • UNRU 1325QX4575 • **Value $51**	**Popcorn Party (5th, 1990)** *Handcrafted* • UNRU 1375QX4393 • **Value $80**	**Checking His List** (6th, 1991) *Handcrafted* • UNRU 1375QX4339 • **Value $52**	**Gift Exchange** (7th, 1992) *Handcrafted* • UNRU 1475QX4294 • **Value $46**

(9)	(10)	(11)
A Fitting Moment (8th, 1993) *Handcrafted* • FRAN 1475QX4202 • **Value $45**	**A Handwarming Present (9th, 1994)** *Handcrafted* • UNRU 1495QX5283 • **Value $39**	**Christmas Eve Kiss** (10th & final, 1995) *Handcrafted* • UNRU 1495QX5157 • **Value $33**
(12)	(13)	(14)
Santa's Visitors (1st, 1980) *Cameo* • N/A 650QX3061 • **Value $235**	**The Carolers (2nd, 1981)** *Cameo* • N/A 850QX5115 • **Value $50**	**Filling the Stockings** (3rd, 1982) *Cameo* • N/A 850QX3053 • **Value $32**
(15)	(16)	(17)
Dress Rehearsal (4th, 1983) *Cameo* • N/A 750QX3007 • **Value $36**	**Caught Napping** (5th, 1984) *Cameo* • MCGE 750QX3411 • **Value $35**	**Jolly Postman (6th, 1985)** *Cameo* • MCGE 750QX3745 • **Value $35**
(18)	(19)	(20) 
Checking Up (7th, 1986) *Cameo* • PIKE 775QX3213 • **Value $28**	**The Christmas Dance** (8th, 1987) *Cameo* • PALM 775QX3707 • **Value $25**	**And to All a Good Night (9th & final, 1988)** *Cameo* • N/A 775QX3704 • **Value $24**

	Price Paid	Value of My Collection
MOTHER GOOSE		
1.		
MR. AND MRS. CLAUS		
2.		
3.		
4.		
5.		
6.		
7.		
8.		
9.		
10.		
11.		
NORMAN ROCKWELL		
12.		
13.		
14.		
15.		
16.		
17.		
18.		
19.		
20.		
PENCIL TOTALS		

(1) Victorian Dollhouse (1st, 1984) *Handcrafted* • DLEE 1300QX4481 • **Value $210**	**(2)** Old-Fashioned Toy Shop (2nd, 1985) *Handcrafted* • DLEE 1375QX4975 • **Value $162**	**(3)** Christmas Candy Shoppe (3rd, 1986) *Handcrafted* • DLEE 1375QX4033 • **Value $310**	**(4)** House on Main St. (4th, 1987) *Handcrafted* • DLEE 1400QX4839 • **Value $82**
(5) Hall Bro's Card Shop (5th, 1988) *Handcrafted* • DLEE 1450QX4014 • **Value $66**	**(6)** U.S. Post Office (6th, 1989) *Handcrafted* • DLEE 1425QX4582 • **Value $70**	**(7)** Holiday Home (7th, 1990) *Handcrafted* • DLEE 1475QX4696 • **Value $82**	**(8)** Fire Station (8th, 1991) *Handcrafted* • DLEE 1475QX4139 • **Value $70**

Nostalgic Houses and Shops

	Price Paid	Value of My Collection
1.		
2.		
3.		
4.		
5.		
6.		
7.		
8.		
9.		
10.		
11.		
12.		
13.		
14.		
15.		
16.		
17.		
18.		

(9) Five and Ten Cent Store (9th, 1992) *Handcrafted* • DLEE 1475QX4254 • **Value $47**	**(10)** Cozy Home (10th, 1993) *Handcrafted* • DLEE 1475QX4175 • **Value $52**	**(11)** Tannenbaum's Dept. Store (complements the series, 1993) *Handcrafted* • DLEE 2600QX5612 • **Value $55**
(12) Neighborhood Drugstore (11th, 1994) *Handcrafted* • DLEE 1495QX5286 • **Value $37**	**(13)** Town Church (12th, 1995) *Handcrafted* • PALM 1495QX5159 • **Value $32**	**(14)** Accessories for Nostalgic Houses and Shops (set/3, 1995) *Handcrafted* • JLEE 895QX5089 • **Value $10**
(15) Victorian Painted Lady (13th, 1996) *Handcrafted* • PALM 1495QX5671 • **Value $28**	**(16)** Cafe (14th, 1997) *Handcrafted* • PALM 1695QX6245 • **Value $32**	**(17)** NEW! Grocery Store (15th, 1998) *Handcrafted* • PALM 1695QX6266 • **Value $16.95**

The Old West

19.

(18) NEW! Halls Station (complements the series, 1998) *Handcrafted* • PALM 2500QX6833 • **Value $25**	**(19)** NEW! Pony Express Rider (1st, 1998) *Handcrafted* • UNRU 1395QX6323 • **Value $13.95**

PENCIL TOTALS

KEEPSAKE SERIES

(1)
Owliver (1st, 1992)
Handcrafted • SIED
775QX4544 • **Value $22**

(2)
Owliver (2nd, 1993)
Handcrafted • SIED
775QX5425 • **Value $20**

(3)
**Owliver
(3rd & final, 1994)**
Handcrafted • SIED
795QX5226 • **Value $20**

(4)
Italy (1st, 1991)
Handcrafted • SICK
1175QX5129 • **Value $30**

(5)
Spain (2nd, 1992)
Handcrafted • SICK
1175QX5174 • **Value $28**

(6)
Poland (3rd & final, 1993)
Handcrafted • SICK
1175QX5242 • **Value $25**

(7)
**The PEANUTS® Gang
(1st, 1993)**
Handcrafted • RHOD
975QX5315 • **Value $68**

(8)
**The PEANUTS® Gang
(2nd, 1994)**
Handcrafted • BISH
995QX5203 • **Value $26**

(9)
**The PEANUTS® Gang
(3rd, 1995)**
Handcrafted • SIED
995QX5059 • **Value $26**

(10)
**The PEANUTS® Gang
(4th & final, 1996)**
Handcrafted • FRAN
995QX5381 • **Value $20**

(11) NEW!
**A Pony for Christmas
(1st, 1998)**
Handcrafted • SICK
1095QX6316 • **Value $10.95**

(12)
**Cinnamon Teddy
(1st, 1983)**
Porcelain • DUTK
700QX4289 • **Value $78**

(13)
**Cinnamon Bear
(2nd, 1984)**
Porcelain • N/A
700QX4541 • **Value $52**

(14)
**Porcelain Bear
(3rd, 1985)**
Porcelain • DUTK
750QX4792 • **Value $60**

(15)
**Porcelain Bear
(4th, 1986)**
Porcelain • N/A
775QX4056 • **Value $46**

(16)
**Porcelain Bear
(5th, 1987)**
Porcelain • N/A
775QX4427 • **Value $40**

(17)
**Porcelain Bear
(6th, 1988)**
Porcelain • PIKE
800QX4044 • **Value $42**

(18)
**Porcelain Bear
(7th, 1989)**
Porcelain • PIKE
875QX4615 • **Value $38**

(19)
**Porcelain Bear
(8th & final, 1990)**
Porcelain • N/A
875QX4426 • **Value $36**

OWLIVER		
	Price Paid	Value of My Collection
1.		
2.		
3.		
PEACE ON EARTH		
4.		
5.		
6.		
THE PEANUTS® GANG		
7.		
8.		
9.		
10.		
A PONY FOR CHRISTMAS		
11.		
PORCELAIN BEAR		
12.		
13.		
14.		
15.		
16.		
17.		
18.		
19.		
PENCIL TOTALS		

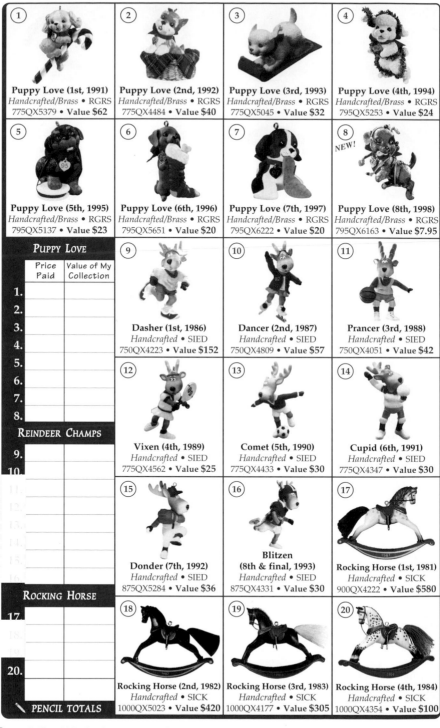

(1) Puppy Love (1st, 1991)
Handcrafted/Brass • RGRS
775QX5379 • **Value $62**

(2) Puppy Love (2nd, 1992)
Handcrafted/Brass • RGRS
775QX4484 • **Value $40**

(3) Puppy Love (3rd, 1993)
Handcrafted/Brass • RGRS
775QX5045 • **Value $32**

(4) Puppy Love (4th, 1994)
Handcrafted/Brass • RGRS
795QX5253 • **Value $24**

(5) Puppy Love (5th, 1995)
Handcrafted/Brass • RGRS
795QX5137 • **Value $23**

(6) Puppy Love (6th, 1996)
Handcrafted/Brass • RGRS
795QX5651 • **Value $20**

(7) Puppy Love (7th, 1997)
Handcrafted/Brass • RGRS
795QX6222 • **Value $20**

NEW!
(8) Puppy Love (8th, 1998)
Handcrafted/Brass • RGRS
795QX6163 • **Value $7.95**

(9)
(10)
(11)

Dasher (1st, 1986)
Handcrafted • SIED
750QX4223 • **Value $152**

Dancer (2nd, 1987)
Handcrafted • SIED
750QX4809 • **Value $57**

Prancer (3rd, 1988)
Handcrafted • SIED
750QX4051 • **Value $42**

(12)
(13)
(14)

Vixen (4th, 1989)
Handcrafted • SIED
775QX4562 • **Value $25**

Comet (5th, 1990)
Handcrafted • SIED
775QX4433 • **Value $30**

Cupid (6th, 1991)
Handcrafted • SIED
775QX4347 • **Value $30**

(15)
(16)
(17)

Donder (7th, 1992)
Handcrafted • SIED
875QX5284 • **Value $36**

Blitzen (8th & final, 1993)
Handcrafted • SIED
875QX4331 • **Value $30**

Rocking Horse (1st, 1981)
Handcrafted • SICK
900QX4222 • **Value $580**

(18)
(19)
(20)

Rocking Horse (2nd, 1982)
Handcrafted • SICK
1000QX5023 • **Value $420**

Rocking Horse (3rd, 1983)
Handcrafted • SICK
1000QX4177 • **Value $305**

Rocking Horse (4th, 1984)
Handcrafted • SICK
1000QX4354 • **Value $100**

PUPPY LOVE

	Price Paid	Value of My Collection
1.		
2.		
3.		
4.		
5.		
6.		
7.		
8.		

REINDEER CHAMPS

9.		
10.		
11.		
12.		
13.		
14.		
15.		
16.		

ROCKING HORSE

17.		
18.		
19.		
20.		

PENCIL TOTALS

KEEPSAKE SERIES

(1)
Rocking Horse (5th, 1985)
Handcrafted • SICK
1075QX4932 • **Value $95**

(2)
Rocking Horse (6th, 1986)
Handcrafted • SICK
1075QX4016 • **Value $86**

(3)
Rocking Horse (7th, 1987)
Handcrafted • SICK
1075QX4829 • **Value $78**

(4)
Rocking Horse (8th, 1988)
Handcrafted • SICK
1075QX4024 • **Value $70**

(5)
Rocking Horse (9th, 1989)
Handcrafted • SICK
1075QX4622 • **Value $72**

(6)
Rocking Horse (10th, 1990)
Handcrafted • SICK
1075QX4646 • **Value $105**

(7)
Rocking Horse (11th, 1991)
Handcrafted • SICK
1075QX4147 • **Value $55**

(8)
Rocking Horse (12th, 1992)
Handcrafted • SICK
1075QX4261 • **Value $45**

(9)
Rocking Horse (13th, 1993)
Handcrafted • SICK
1075QX4162 • **Value $47**

(10)
Rocking Horse (14th, 1994)
Handcrafted • SICK
1095QX5016 • **Value $30**

(11)
Rocking Horse (15th, 1995)
Handcrafted • SICK
1095QX5167 • **Value $32**

(12)
Pewter Rocking Horse (15th Anniversary Edition, 1995)
Pewter • SICK
2000QX6167 • **Value $45**

(13)
Rocking Horse (16th & final, 1996)
Handcrafted • SICK
1095QX5674 • **Value $30**

(14) NEW!
Donald and Daisy in Venice (1st, 1998)
Handcrafted • LARS
1495QXD4103 • **Value $14.95**

(15)
Scarlett O'Hara™ (1st, 1997)
Handcrafted • ANDR
1495QX6125 • **Value $26**

(16) NEW!
Scarlett O'Hara™ (2nd, 1998)
Handcrafted • ANDR
1495QX6336 • **Value $14.95**

(17)
The Flight at Kitty Hawk (1st, 1997)
Handcrafted • NORT
1495QX5574 • **Value $30**

(18) NEW!
1917 Curtiss JN-4D "Jenny" (2nd, 1998)
Handcrafted • NORT
1495QX6286 • **Value $14.95**

ROCKING HORSE		
	Price Paid	Value of My Collection
1.		
2.		
3.		
4.		
5.		
6.		
7.		
8.		
9.		
10.		
11.		
12.		
13.		
ROMANTIC VACATIONS		
14.		
SCARLETT O'HARA™		
15.		
16.		
SKY'S THE LIMIT		
17.		
18.		
PENCIL TOTALS		

VALUE GUIDE — HALLMARK KEEPSAKE ORNAMENTS

① Ice Hockey Holiday
(1st, 1979)
Handcrafted • N/A
800QX1419 • **Value $140**

② Ski Holiday (2nd, 1980)
Handcrafted • FRAN
900QX1541 • **Value $125**

③ SNOOPY® and Friends
(3rd, 1981)
Handcrafted • FRAN
1200QX4362 • **Value $130**

④ SNOOPY® and Friends
(4th, 1982)
Handcrafted • SEAL
1300QX4803 • **Value $105**

⑤ Santa SNOOPY®
(5th & final, 1983)
Handcrafted • SICK
1300QX4169 • **Value $100**

⑥ NEW! Snow Buddies (1st, 1998)
Handcrafted • HADD
795QX6853 • **Value $7.95**

⑦ NEW! Joe Cool (1st, 1998)
Handcrafted • SIED
995QX6453 • **Value $9.95**

⑧ Luke Skywalker™
(1st, 1997)
Handcrafted • RHOD
1395QXI5484 • **Value $28**

⑨ NEW! Princess Leia™
(2nd, 1998)
Handcrafted • RHOD
1395QXI4026 • **Value $13.95**

⑩ Jeff Gordon (1st, 1997)
Handcrafted • SEAL
1595QXI6165 • **Value $30**

⑪ NEW! Richard Petty (2nd, 1998)
Handcrafted • SEAL
1595QXI4143 • **Value $15.95**

⑫ Mouse in a Thimble (1st, 1978, re-issued in 1979)
Handcrafted • N/A
250QX1336 • **Value $300**

⑬ A Christmas Salute (2nd, 1979, re-issued in 1980)
Handcrafted • N/A
300QX1319 • **Value $175**

⑭ Mouse in a Thimble (1979, re-issued from 1978)
Handcrafted • N/A
300QX1336 • **Value $300**

⑮ Thimble Elf (3rd, 1980)
Handcrafted • N/A
400QX1321 • **Value $173**

⑯ A Christmas Salute (1980, re-issued from 1979)
Handcrafted • N/A
400QX1319 • **Value $175**

⑰ Thimble Angel (4th, 1981)
Handcrafted • N/A
450QX4135 • **Value $152**

⑱ Thimble Mouse
(5th, 1982)
Handcrafted • N/A
500QX4513 • **Value $75**

SNOOPY® And Friends

	Price Paid	Value of My Collection
1.		
2.		
3.		
4.		
5.		

Snow Buddies

6.		

Spotlight On Snoopy

7.		

Star Wars™

8.		
9.		

Stock Car Champions

10.		
11.		

Thimble Series

12.		
13.		
14.		
15.		
16.		
17.		
18.		

PENCIL TOTALS

VALUE GUIDE — HALLMARK KEEPSAKE ORNAMENTS

(1)

Thimble Elf (6th, 1983)
Handcrafted • N/A
500QX4017 • **Value $38**

(2)

Thimble Angel (7th, 1984)
Handcrafted • N/A
500QX4304 • **Value $60**

(3)

Thimble Santa (8th, 1985)
Handcrafted • SIED
550QX4725 • **Value $35**

(4)

**Thimble Partridge
(9th, 1986)**
Handcrafted • N/A
575QX4066 • **Value $27**

(5)

**Thimble Drummer
(10th, 1987)**
Handcrafted • SIED
575QX4419 • **Value $28**

(6)

**Thimble Snowman
(11th, 1988)**
Handcrafted • SIED
575QX4054 • **Value $24**

(7)

**Thimble Puppy
(12th & final, 1989)**
Handcrafted • RGRS
575QX4552 • **Value $28**

(8)

**Victorian Christmas
Thomas Kinkade, Painter
of Light™ (1st, 1997)**
Porcelain • SEAL
1095QXI6135 • **Value $20**

(9) NEW!

**Victorian Christmas II
Thomas Kinkade, Painter
of Light™ (2nd, 1998)**
Ceramic • N/A
1095QX6343 • **Value $10.95**

(10)

Tin Locomotive (1st, 1982)
Pressed Tin • SICK
1300QX4603 • **Value $695**

(11)

Tin Locomotive (2nd, 1983)
Pressed Tin • SICK
1300QX4049 • **Value $305**

(12)

Tin Locomotive (3rd, 1984)
Pressed Tin • SICK
1400QX4404 • **Value $87**

(13)

Tin Locomotive (4th, 1985)
Pressed Tin • SICK
1475QX4972 • **Value $85**

(14)

Tin Locomotive (5th, 1986)
Pressed Tin • SICK
1475QX4036 • **Value $80**

(15)

Tin Locomotive (6th, 1987)
Pressed Tin • SICK
1475QX4849 • **Value $68**

(16)

Tin Locomotive (7th, 1988)
Pressed Tin • SICK
1475QX4004 • **Value $62**

(17)

**Tin Locomotive
(8th & final, 1989)**
Pressed Tin • SICK
1475QX4602 • **Value $60**

(18)
**Tobin Fraley Carousel
(1st, 1992)**
Porcelain/Brass • FRAL
2800QX4891 • **Value $65**

(19)
**Tobin Fraley Carousel
(2nd, 1993)**
Porcelain/Brass • FRAL
2800QX5502 • **Value $50**

(20)
**Tobin Fraley Carousel
(3rd, 1994)**
Porcelain/Brass • FRAL
2800QX5223 • **Value $60**

THIMBLE SERIES	Price Paid	Value of My Collection
1.		
2.		
3.		
4.		
5.		
6.		
7.		
THOMAS KINKADE		
8.		
9.		
TIN LOCOMOTIVE		
10.		
11.		
12.		
13.		
14.		
15.		
16.		
17.		
TOBIN FRALEY CAROUSEL		
18.		
19.		
20.		
PENCIL TOTALS		

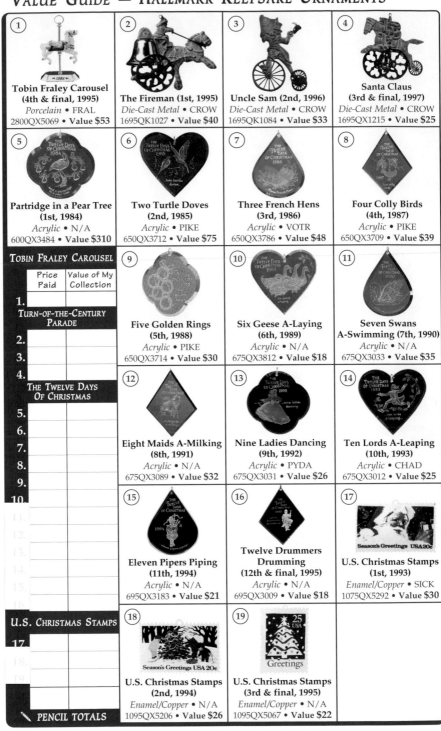

1

Tobin Fraley Carousel
(4th & final, 1995)
Porcelain • FRAL
2800QX5069 • **Value $53**

2

The Fireman (1st, 1995)
Die-Cast Metal • CROW
1695QK1027 • **Value $40**

3

Uncle Sam (2nd, 1996)
Die-Cast Metal • CROW
1695QK1084 • **Value $33**

4

Santa Claus
(3rd & final, 1997)
Die-Cast Metal • CROW
1695QX1215 • **Value $25**

5

Partridge in a Pear Tree
(1st, 1984)
Acrylic • N/A
600QX3484 • **Value $310**

6

Two Turtle Doves
(2nd, 1985)
Acrylic • PIKE
650QX3712 • **Value $75**

7

Three French Hens
(3rd, 1986)
Acrylic • VOTR
650QX3786 • **Value $48**

8

Four Colly Birds
(4th, 1987)
Acrylic • PIKE
650QX3709 • **Value $39**

9

Five Golden Rings
(5th, 1988)
Acrylic • PIKE
650QX3714 • **Value $30**

10

Six Geese A-Laying
(6th, 1989)
Acrylic • N/A
675QX3812 • **Value $18**

11

Seven Swans
A-Swimming (7th, 1990)
Acrylic • N/A
675QX3033 • **Value $35**

12

Eight Maids A-Milking
(8th, 1991)
Acrylic • N/A
675QX3089 • **Value $32**

13

Nine Ladies Dancing
(9th, 1992)
Acrylic • PYDA
675QX3031 • **Value $26**

14

Ten Lords A-Leaping
(10th, 1993)
Acrylic • CHAD
675QX3012 • **Value $25**

15

Eleven Pipers Piping
(11th, 1994)
Acrylic • N/A
695QX3183 • **Value $21**

16

Twelve Drummers
Drumming
(12th & final, 1995)
Acrylic • N/A
695QX3009 • **Value $18**

17

U.S. Christmas Stamps
(1st, 1993)
Enamel/Copper • SICK
1075QX5292 • **Value $30**

18

U.S. Christmas Stamps
(2nd, 1994)
Enamel/Copper • N/A
1095QX5206 • **Value $26**

19

U.S. Christmas Stamps
(3rd & final, 1995)
Enamel/Copper • N/A
1095QX5067 • **Value $22**

Tobin Fraley Carousel

	Price Paid	Value of My Collection
1.		

Turn-of-the-Century Parade

2.		
3.		
4.		

The Twelve Days of Christmas

5.		
6.		
7.		
8.		
9.		
10.		
11.		
12.		
13.		
14.		
15.		
16.		

U.S. Christmas Stamps

17.		
18.		
19.		

✎ Pencil Totals

(1) NEW!

Cruella de Vil
Walt Disney's *101*
***Dalmatians* (1st, 1998)**
Handcrafted • ESCH
1495QXD4063 • **Value $14.95**

(2)

Feliz Navidad (1st, 1985)
Handcrafted • DLEE
975QX4902 • **Value $98**

(3)
Vrolyk Kerstfeest
(2nd, 1986)
Handcrafted • SIED
1000QX4083 • **Value $66**

(4)

Mele Kalikimaka
(3rd, 1987)
Handcrafted • DLEE
1000QX4827 • **Value $30**

(5)

Joyeux Noël (4th, 1988)
1000QX4021 • **Value $34**

(6) 11

Fröhliche Weihnachten
(5th, 1989)
Handcrafted • DLEE
1075QX4625 • **Value $33**

(7)

Nollaig Shona
(6th & final, 1990)
Handcrafted • DLEE
1075QX4636 • **Value $30**

(8) NEW!

A Visit From Piglet
(1st, 1998)
Handcrafted • N/A
1395QXD4086 • **Value $13.95**

(9)

Winter Surprise
(1st, 1989)
Handcrafted • FRAN
1075QX4272 • **Value $28**

(10)
Winter Surprise
(2nd, 1990)
Handcrafted • FRAN
1075QX4443 • **Value $27**

(11)

Winter Surprise
(3rd, 1991)
Handcrafted • LYLE
1075QX4277 • **Value $33**

(12)

Winter Surprise
(4th & final, 1992)
Handcrafted • FRAN
1175QX4271 • **Value $32**

(13)

Wooden Lamb (1st, 1984)
Wood • N/A
650QX4394 • **Value $48**

(14)

Wooden Train (2nd, 1985)
Wood • DUTK
700QX4722 • **Value $50**

(15)
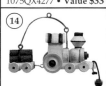
Wooden Reindeer
(3rd, 1986)
Wood • CROW
750QX4073 • **Value $29**

(16)

Wooden Horse (4th, 1987)
Wood • SIED
750QX4417 • **Value $26**

(17)

Wooden Airplane
(5th, 1988)
Wood • DUTK
750QX4041 • **Value $27**

(18)

Wooden Truck
(6th & final, 1989)
Wood • N/A
775QX4595 • **Value $25**

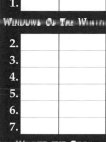

	Price Paid	Value of My Collection
UNFORGETTABLE VILLAINS		
1.		
WINDOWS OF THE WORLD		
2.		
3.		
4.		
5.		
6.		
7.		
WINNIE THE POOH		
8.		
WINTER SURPRISE		
9.		
10.		
11.		
12.		
WOOD CHILDHOOD ORNAMENTS		
13.		
14.		
15.		
16.		
17.		
18.		
PENCIL TOTALS		

 ①	 ②	 ③	 ④
Yuletide Central (1st, 1994) *Pressed Tin* • SICK 1895QX5316 • **Value $55**	**Yuletide Central** (2nd, 1995) *Pressed Tin* • SICK 1895QX5079 • **Value $33**	**Yuletide Central** (3rd, 1996) *Pressed Tin* • SICK 1895QX5011 • **Value $38**	**Yuletide Central** (4th, 1997) *Pressed Tin* • SICK 1895QX5812 • **Value $30**

⑤ NEW!

Yuletide Central (5th & final, 1998)
Pressed Tin • SICK
1895QX6373 • **Value $18.95**

Magic Series

There have been 9 Magic collectible series since the ornaments featuring light, sound and motion debuted in 1984. Three series are ongoing. "Candlelight Services" is a brand new series for 1998, while the popular series "Journeys Into Space" and "Lighthouse Greetings" welcome new editions.

Yuletide Central

	Price Paid	Value of My Collection
1.		
2.		
3.		
4.		
5.		

Candlelight Services

6.		

Chris Mouse

7.		
8.		
9.		
10.		

PENCIL TOTALS

⑥ NEW!	⑦	⑧

The Stone Church (1st, 1998) *Handcrafted* • SEAL 1895QLX7636 • **Value $18.95**	**Chris Mouse** (1st, 1985) *Handcrafted* • SIED 1250QLX7032 • **Value $92**	**Chris Mouse Dreams** (2nd, 1986) *Handcrafted* • DUTK 1300QLX7056 • **Value $80**
⑨	⑩	⑪
Chris Mouse Glow (3rd, 1987) *Handcrafted* • SIED 1100QLX7057 • **Value $62**	**Chris Mouse Star** (4th, 1988) *Handcrafted* • SIED 875QLX7154 • **Value $62**	**Chris Mouse Cookout** (5th, 1989) *Handcrafted* • RGRS 950QLX7225 • **Value $63**
⑫	⑬	⑭
Chris Mouse Wreath (6th, 1990) *Handcrafted* • RGRS 1000QLX7296 • **Value $48**	**Chris Mouse Mail** (7th, 1991) *Handcrafted* • SIED 1000QLX7207 • **Value $40**	**Chris Mouse Tales** (8th, 1992) *Handcrafted* • RGRS 1200QLX7074 • **Value $30**
⑮	⑯	⑰
Chris Mouse Flight (9th, 1993) *Handcrafted* • RGRS 1200QLX7152 • **Value $34**	**Chris Mouse Jelly** (10th, 1994) *Handcrafted* • RGRS 1200QLX7393 • **Value $29**	**Chris Mouse Tree** (11th, 1995) *Handcrafted* • RGRS 1250QLX7307 • **Value $29**

①
Chris Mouse Inn
(12th, 1996)
Handcrafted • SIED
1450QLX7371 • **Value $32**

②
Chris Mouse Luminaria
(13th & final, 1997)
Handcrafted • SIED
1495QLX7525 • **Value $30**

③
The Nutcracker Ballet
– Sugarplum Fairy
(1st, 1986)
Handcrafted • N/A
1750QLX7043 • **Value $90**

④
A Christmas Carol
(2nd, 1987)
Handcrafted • N/A
1600QLX7029 • **Value $73**

⑤
Night Before Christmas
(3rd, 1988)
Handcrafted • DLEE
1500QLX7161 • **Value $43**

⑥
Little Drummer Boy
(4th, 1989)
Handcrafted • DLEE
1350QLX7242 • **Value $42**

⑦
The Littlest Angel
(5th & final, 1990)
Handcrafted • FRAN
1400QLX7303 • **Value $53**

⑧
Forest Frolics (1st, 1989)
Handcrafted • PIKE
2450QLX7282 • **Value $100**

⑨
Forest Frolics (2nd, 1990)
Handcrafted • PIKE
2500QLX7236 • **Value $74**

⑩
Forest Frolics (3rd, 1991)
Handcrafted • PIKE
2500QLX7219 • **Value $70**

⑪
Forest Frolics (4th, 1992)
Handcrafted • PIKE
2800QLX7254 • **Value $66**

⑫
Forest Frolics (5th, 1993)
Handcrafted • PIKE
2500QLX7165 • **Value $52**

⑬
Forest Frolics (6th, 1994)
Handcrafted • PIKE
2800QLX7436 • **Value $57**

⑭
Forest Frolics
(7th & final, 1995)
Handcrafted • PIKE
2800QLX7299 • **Value $55**

⑮
Freedom 7 (1st, 1996)
Handcrafted • SEAL
2400QLX7524 • **Value $48**

⑯
Friendship 7 (2nd, 1997)
Handcrafted • SEAL
2400QLX7532 • **Value $40**

⑰ **NEW!**
Apollo Lunar Module
(3rd, 1998)
Handcrafted • N/A
2400QLX7543 • **Value $24**

⑱
Lighthouse Greetings
(1st, 1997)
Handcrafted • FRAN
2400QLX7442 • **Value $70**

⑲ **NEW!**
Lighthouse Greetings
(2nd, 1998)
Handcrafted • FRAN
2400QLX7536 • **Value $24**

CHRIS MOUSE	Price Paid	Value of My Collection
1.		
2.		
CHRISTMAS CLASSICS		
3.		
4.		
5.		
6.		
7.		
FOREST FROLICS		
8.		
9.		
10.		
11.		
12.		
13.		
14.		
JOURNEYS INTO SPACE		
15.		
16.		
17.		
LIGHTHOUSE GREETINGS		
18.		
19.		
PENCIL TOTALS		

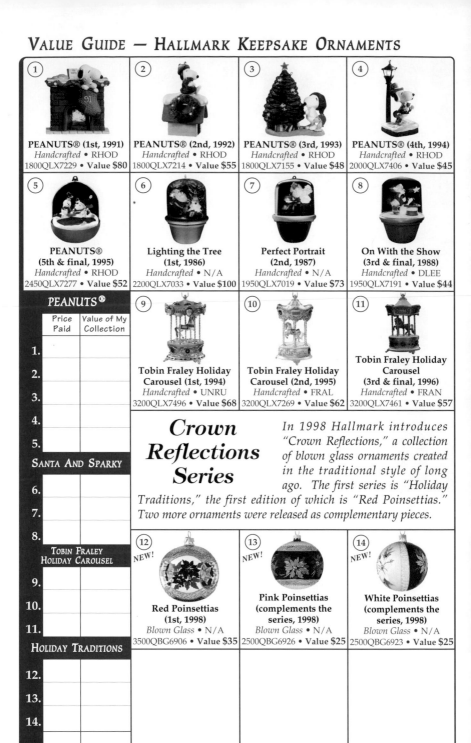

PEANUTS® (1st, 1991)
Handcrafted • RHOD
1800QLX7229 • **Value $80**

PEANUTS® (2nd, 1992)
Handcrafted • RHOD
1800QLX7214 • **Value $55**

PEANUTS® (3rd, 1993)
Handcrafted • RHOD
1800QLX7155 • **Value $48**

PEANUTS® (4th, 1994)
Handcrafted • RHOD
2000QLX7406 • **Value $45**

**PEANUTS®
(5th & final, 1995)**
Handcrafted • RHOD
2450QLX7277 • **Value $52**

**Lighting the Tree
(1st, 1986)**
Handcrafted • N/A
2200QLX7033 • **Value $100**

**Perfect Portrait
(2nd, 1987)**
Handcrafted • N/A
1950QLX7019 • **Value $73**

**On With the Show
(3rd & final, 1988)**
Handcrafted • DLEE
1950QLX7191 • **Value $44**

**Tobin Fraley Holiday
Carousel (1st, 1994)**
Handcrafted • UNRU
3200QLX7496 • **Value $68**

**Tobin Fraley Holiday
Carousel (2nd, 1995)**
Handcrafted • FRAL
3200QLX7269 • **Value $62**

**Tobin Fraley Holiday
Carousel
(3rd & final, 1996)**
Handcrafted • FRAN
3200QLX7461 • **Value $57**

Crown Reflections Series

In 1998 Hallmark introduces "Crown Reflections," a collection of blown glass ornaments created in the traditional style of long ago. The first series is "Holiday Traditions," the first edition of which is "Red Poinsettias." Two more ornaments were released as complementary pieces.

**Red Poinsettias
(1st, 1998)**
Blown Glass • N/A
3500QBG6906 • **Value $35**

**Pink Poinsettias
(complements the
series, 1998)**
Blown Glass • N/A
2500QBG6926 • **Value $25**

**White Poinsettias
(complements the
series, 1998)**
Blown Glass • N/A
2500QBG6923 • **Value $25**

PEANUTS®	Price Paid	Value of My Collection
1.		
2.		
3.		
4.		
5.		
SANTA AND SPARKY		
6.		
7.		
8.		
TOBIN FRALEY HOLIDAY CAROUSEL		
9.		
10.		
11.		
HOLIDAY TRADITIONS		
12.		
13.		
14.		
PENCIL TOTALS		

Miniature Series

Hallmark adds three new Miniature collectible series this year, ("Miniature Kiddie Car Luxury Edition," "The Nativity" and "Winter Fun With SNOOPY®") bringing the total number of series since 1988 to 28. While 16 of these series are ongoing, three will close this year including the popular "On the Road."

Alice in Wonderland
(1st, 1995)
Handcrafted • ANDR
675QXM4777 • **Value $18**

Mad Hatter (2nd, 1996)
Handcrafted • ANDR
675QXM4074 • **Value $16**

White Rabbit (3rd, 1997)
Handcrafted • ANDR
695QXM4142 • **Value $14**

NEW!
Cheshire Cat
(4th & final, 1998)
Handcrafted • ANDR
695QXM4186 • **Value $6.95**

Antique Tractors
(1st, 1997)
Die-Cast Metal • SICK
695QXM4185 • **Value $17**

NEW!
Antique Tractors
(2nd, 1998)
Die-Cast Metal • SICK
695QXM4166 • **Value $6.95**

The Bearymores
(1st, 1992)
Handcrafted • RGRS
575QXM5544 • **Value $24**

The Bearymores
(2nd, 1993)
Handcrafted • RGRS
575QXM5125 • **Value $20**

The Bearymores
(3rd & final, 1994)
Handcrafted • RGRS
575QXM5133 • **Value $17**

Centuries of Santa
(1st, 1994)
Handcrafted • SICK
600QXM5153 • **Value $27**

Centuries of Santa
(2nd, 1995)
Handcrafted • SICK
575QXM4789 • **Value $22**

Centuries of Santa
(3rd, 1996)
Handcrafted • SICK
575QXM4091 • **Value $16**

Centuries of Santa
(4th, 1997)
Handcrafted • SICK
595QXM4295 • **Value $12**

NEW!
Centuries of Santa
(5th, 1998)
Handcrafted • SICK
595QXM4206 • **Value $5.95**

Christmas Bells
(1st, 1995)
Handcrafted/Metal • SEAL
475QXM4007 • **Value $20**

Christmas Bells
(2nd, 1996)
Handcrafted/Metal • SEAL
475QXM4071 • **Value $16**

Christmas Bells
(3rd, 1997)
Handcrafted/Metal • SEAL
495QXM4162 • **Value $12**

	Price Paid	Value of My Collection
ALICE IN WONDERLAND		
1.		
2.		
3.		
4.		
ANTIQUE TRACTORS		
5.		
6.		
THE BEARYMORES		
7.		
8.		
9.		
CENTURIES OF SANTA		
10.		
11.		
12.		
13.		
14.		
CHRISTMAS BELLS		
15.		
16.		
17.		
	PENCIL TOTALS	

VALUE GUIDE — HALLMARK KEEPSAKE ORNAMENTS

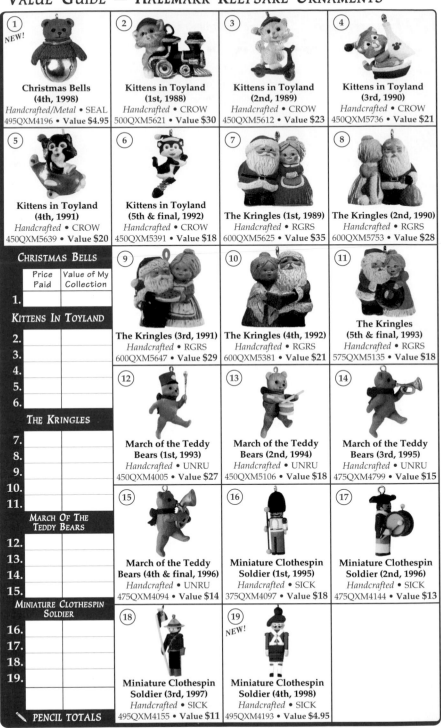

(1) NEW!
Christmas Bells
(4th, 1998)
Handcrafted/Metal • SEAL
495QXM4196 • **Value $4.95**

(2)
Kittens in Toyland
(1st, 1988)
Handcrafted • CROW
500QXM5621 • **Value $30**

(3)
Kittens in Toyland
(2nd, 1989)
Handcrafted • CROW
450QXM5612 • **Value $23**

(4)
Kittens in Toyland
(3rd, 1990)
Handcrafted • CROW
450QXM5736 • **Value $21**

(5)
Kittens in Toyland
(4th, 1991)
Handcrafted • CROW
450QXM5639 • **Value $20**

(6)
Kittens in Toyland
(5th & final, 1992)
Handcrafted • CROW
450QXM5391 • **Value $18**

(7)
The Kringles (1st, 1989)
Handcrafted • RGRS
600QXM5625 • **Value $35**

(8)
The Kringles (2nd, 1990)
Handcrafted • RGRS
600QXM5753 • **Value $28**

(9)
The Kringles (3rd, 1991)
Handcrafted • RGRS
600QXM5647 • **Value $29**

(10)
The Kringles (4th, 1992)
Handcrafted • RGRS
600QXM5381 • **Value $21**

(11)
The Kringles
(5th & final, 1993)
Handcrafted • RGRS
575QXM5135 • **Value $18**

(12)
March of the Teddy Bears (1st, 1993)
Handcrafted • UNRU
450QXM4005 • **Value $27**

(13)
March of the Teddy Bears (2nd, 1994)
Handcrafted • UNRU
450QXM5106 • **Value $18**

(14)
March of the Teddy Bears (3rd, 1995)
Handcrafted • UNRU
475QXM4799 • **Value $15**

(15)
March of the Teddy Bears (4th & final, 1996)
Handcrafted • UNRU
475QXM4094 • **Value $14**

(16)
Miniature Clothespin Soldier (1st, 1995)
Handcrafted • SICK
375QXM4097 • **Value $18**

(17)
Miniature Clothespin Soldier (2nd, 1996)
Handcrafted • SICK
475QXM4144 • **Value $13**

(18)
Miniature Clothespin Soldier (3rd, 1997)
Handcrafted • SICK
495QXM4155 • **Value $11**

(19) NEW!
Miniature Clothespin Soldier (4th, 1998)
Handcrafted • SICK
495QXM4193 • **Value $4.95**

CHRISTMAS BELLS

	Price Paid	Value of My Collection
1.		

KITTENS IN TOYLAND

2.		
3.		
4.		
5.		
6.		

THE KRINGLES

7.		
8.		
9.		
10.		
11.		

MARCH OF THE TEDDY BEARS

12.		
13.		
14.		
15.		

MINIATURE CLOTHESPIN SOLDIER

16.		
17.		
18.		
19.		

PENCIL TOTALS

1

Murray® "Champion" (1st, 1995)
Die-Cast Metal • PALM
575QXM4079 • **Value $21**

2

Murray® "Fire Truck" (2nd, 1996)
Die-Cast Metal • PALM
675QXM4031 • **Value $18**

3

Murray Inc.® "Pursuit" Airplane (3rd, 1997)
Die-Cast Metal • PALM
695QXM4132 • **Value $15**

4 NEW!

Murray Inc.® Dump Truck (4th, 1998)
Die-Cast Metal • PALM
695QXM4183 • **Value $6.95**

5 NEW!

1937 Steelcraft Auburn (1st, 1998)
Die-Cast Metal • PALM
695QXM4143 • **Value $6.95**

6 NEW!

The Nativity (1st, 1998)
Pewter • UNRU
995QXM4156 • **Value $9.95**

7

Nature's Angels (1st, 1990)
Handcrafted/Brass • SEAL
450QXM5733 • **Value $26**

8

Nature's Angels (2nd, 1991)
Handcrafted/Brass • PIKE
450QXM5657 • **Value $22**

9

Nature's Angels (3rd, 1992)
Handcrafted/Brass • PIKE
450QXM5451 • **Value $20**

10

Nature's Angels (4th, 1993)
Handcrafted/Brass • ANDR
450QXM5122 • **Value $22**

11

Nature's Angels (5th, 1994)
Handcrafted/Brass • VOTR
450QXM5126 • **Value $13**

12

Nature's Angels (6th, 1995)
Handcrafted/Brass • ANDR
475QXM4809 • **Value $20**

13

Nature's Angels (7th & final, 1996)
Handcrafted/Brass • PIKE
475QXM4111 • **Value $13**

14

The Night Before Christmas (1st, 1992, w/display house)
Handcrafted • UNRU
1375QXM5541 • **Value $37**

15

The Night Before Christmas (2nd, 1993)
Handcrafted • UNRU
450QXM5115 • **Value $24**

16

The Night Before Christmas (3rd, 1994)
Handcrafted • UNRU
450QXM5123 • **Value $14**

17

The Night Before Christmas (4th, 1995)
Handcrafted • UNRU
475QXM4807 • **Value $20**

18

The Night Before Christmas (5th & final, 1996)
Handcrafted • UNRU
575QXM4104 • **Value $14**

	Price Paid	Value of My Collection
MINIATURE KIDDIE CAR CLASSICS		
1.		
2.		
3.		
4.		
MINIATURE KIDDIE CAR LUXURY EDITION		
5.		
THE NATIVITY		
6.		
NATURE'S ANGELS		
7.		
8.		
9.		
10.		
11.		
12.		
13.		
THE NIGHT BEFORE CHRISTMAS		
14.		
15.		
16.		
17.		
18.		
PENCIL TOTALS		

VALUE GUIDE — HALLMARK KEEPSAKE ORNAMENTS

(1)
Locomotive (1st, 1989)
Handcrafted • SICK
850QXM5762 • **Value $47**

(2)
Coal Car (2nd, 1990)
Handcrafted • SICK
850QXM5756 • **Value $35**

(3)
Passenger Car (3rd, 1991)
Handcrafted • SICK
850QXM5649 • **Value $50**

(4)
Box Car (4th, 1992)
Handcrafted • SICK
700QXM5441 • **Value $23**

(5)
Flatbed Car (5th, 1993)
Handcrafted • SICK
700QXM5105 • **Value $24**

(6)
Stock Car (6th, 1994)
Handcrafted • SICK
700QXM5113 • **Value $23**

(7)
Milk Tank Car (7th, 1995)
Handcrafted • SICK
675QXM4817 • **Value $19**

(8)
Cookie Car (8th, 1996)
Handcrafted • SICK
675QXM4114 • **Value $18**

NOEL R.R.

	Price Paid	Value of My Collection
1.		
2.		
3.		
4.		
5.		
6.		
7.		
8.		
9.		
10.		
11.		

THE NUTCRACKER BALLET

12.		
13.		
14.		

NUTCRACKER GUILD

15.		
16.		
17.		
18.		
19.		

OLD ENGLISH VILLAGE

20.		

PENCIL TOTALS

(9)
Candy Car (9th, 1997)
Handcrafted • SICK
695QXM4175 • **Value $14**

(10) NEW!
Caboose (10th & final, 1998)
Handcrafted • SICK
695QXM4216 • **Value $6.95**

(11) NEW!
Noel R.R. Locomotive 1989-1998 (Anniversary Edition, 1998)
Pewter • SICK
1095QXM4286 • **Value $10.95**

(12)
The Nutcracker Ballet (1st, 1996, w/display stage)
Handcrafted • VOTR
1475QXM4064 • **Value $30**

(13)
Herr Drosselmeyer (2nd, 1997)
Handcrafted • VOTR
595QXM4135 • **Value $11**

(14) NEW!
Nutcracker (3rd, 1998)
Handcrafted • VOTR
595QXM4146 • **Value $5.95**

(15)
Nutcracker Guild (1st, 1994)
Handcrafted • SICK
575QXM5146 • **Value $20**

(16)
Nutcracker Guild (2nd, 1995)
Handcrafted • SICK
575QXM4787 • **Value $18**

(17)
Nutcracker Guild (3rd, 1996)
Handcrafted • SICK
575QXM4084 • **Value $16**

(18)
Nutcracker Guild (4th, 1997)
Handcrafted • SICK
695QXM4165 • **Value $13**

(19) NEW!
Nutcracker Guild (5th, 1998)
Handcrafted • SICK
695QXM4203 • **Value $6.95**

(20)
Family Home (1st, 1988)
Handcrafted • DLEE
850QXM5634 • **Value $46**

1
Sweet Shop (2nd, 1989)
Handcrafted • JLEE
850QXM5615 • **Value $37**

2
School (3rd, 1990)
Handcrafted • JLEE
850QXM5763 • **Value $26**

3
Inn (4th, 1991)
Handcrafted • JLEE
850QXM5627 • **Value $30**

4
Church (5th, 1992)
Handcrafted • JLEE
700QXM5384 • **Value $33**

5
Toy Shop (6th, 1993)
Handcrafted • JLEE
700QXM5132 • **Value $23**

6
Hat Shop (7th, 1994)
Handcrafted • ANDR
700QXM5143 • **Value $21**

7
Tudor House (8th, 1995)
Handcrafted • JLEE
675QXM4819 • **Value $20**

8
Village Mill (9th, 1996)
Handcrafted • RHOD
675QXM4124 • **Value $17**

9
**Village Depot
(10th & final, 1997)**
Handcrafted • LARS
695QXM4182 • **Value $14**

10
On the Road (1st, 1993)
Pressed Tin • SICK
575QXM4002 • **Value $22**

11
On the Road (2nd, 1994)
Pressed Tin • SICK
575QXM5103 • **Value $19**

12
On the Road (3rd, 1995)
Pressed Tin • SICK
575QXM4797 • **Value $16**

13
On the Road (4th, 1996)
Pressed Tin • SICK
575QXM4101 • **Value $14**

14
On the Road (5th, 1997)
Pressed Tin • SICK
595QXM4172 • **Value $13**

15 NEW!
**On the Road
(6th & final, 1998)**
Pressed Tin • SICK
595QXM4213 • **Value $5.95**

16
Penguin Pal (1st, 1988)
Handcrafted • SIED
375QXM5631 • **Value $30**

17
Penguin Pal (2nd, 1989)
Handcrafted • N/A
450QXM5602 • **Value $21**

18
Penguin Pal (3rd, 1990)
Handcrafted • N/A
450QXM5746 • **Value $20**

19
**Penguin Pal
(4th & final, 1991)**
Handcrafted • SIED
450QXM5629 • **Value $18**

Old English Village

	Price Paid	Value of My Collection
1.		
2.		
3.		
4.		
5.		
6.		
7.		
8.		
9.		

On the Road

10.		
11.		
12.		
13.		
14.		
15.		

Penguin Pal

16.		
17.		
18.		
19.		

PENCIL TOTALS

1. Rocking Horse (1st, 1988)
Handcrafted • SICK
450QXM5624 • **Value $46**

2. Rocking Horse (2nd, 1989)
Handcrafted • SICK
450QXM5605 • **Value $32**

3. Rocking Horse (3rd, 1990)
Handcrafted • SICK
450QXM5743 • **Value $26**

4. Rocking Horse (4th, 1991)
Handcrafted • SICK
450QXM5637 • **Value $31**

5. Rocking Horse (5th, 1992)
Handcrafted • SICK
450QXM5454 • **Value $22**

6. Rocking Horse (6th, 1993)
Handcrafted • SICK
450QXM5112 • **Value $17**

7. Rocking Horse (7th, 1994)
Handcrafted • SICK
450QXM5116 • **Value $18**

8. Rocking Horse (8th, 1995)
Handcrafted • SICK
450QXM4827 • **Value $17**

9. Rocking Horse (9th, 1996)
Handcrafted • SICK
475QXM4121 • **Value $16**

10. Rocking Horse (10th & final, 1997)
Handcrafted • SICK
495QXM4302 • **Value $13**

11. Santa's Little Big Top (1st, 1995)
Handcrafted • CROW
675QXM4779 • **Value $21**

12. Santa's Little Big Top (2nd, 1996)
Handcrafted • CROW
675QXM4081 • **Value $16**

13. Santa's Little Big Top (3rd & final, 1997)
Handcrafted • CROW
695QXM4152 • **Value $13**

14. Snowflake Ballet (1st, 1997)
Handcrafted • ANDR
595QXM4192 • **Value $12**

15. NEW! Snowflake Ballet (2nd, 1998)
Handcrafted • ANDR
595QXM4173 • **Value $5.95**

16. Teddy-Bear Style (1st, 1997)
Handcrafted • UNRU
595QXM4215 • **Value $13**

17. NEW! Teddy-Bear Style (2nd, 1998)
Handcrafted • UNRU
595QXM4176 • **Value $5.95**

Rocking Horse

	Price Paid	Value of My Collection
1.		
2.		
3.		
4.		
5.		
6.		
7.		
8.		
9.		
10.		

Santa's Little Big Top

11.		
12.		
13.		

Snowflake Ballet

14.		
15.		

Teddy-Bear Style

16.		
17.		

PENCIL TOTALS

MINIATURE SERIES

1 Thimble Bells
(1st, 1990)
Porcelain • PYDA
600QXM5543 • **Value $28**

2 Thimble Bells
(2nd, 1991)
Porcelain • PYDA
600QXM5659 • **Value $26**

3 Thimble Bells
(3rd, 1992)
Porcelain • LYLE
600QXM5461 • **Value $24**

4 Thimble Bells
(4th & final, 1993)
Porcelain • VOTR
575QXM5142 • **Value $17**

5 Welcome Friends
(1st, 1997)
Handcrafted • PIKE
695QXM4205 • **Value $13**

6 NEW!
Welcome Friends
(2nd, 1998)
Handcrafted • PIKE
695QXM4153 • **Value $6.95**

7 NEW!
Winter Fun With
SNOOPY® (1st, 1998)
Handcrafted • LARS
695QXM4243 • **Value $6.95**

8 Woodland Babies
(1st, 1991)
Handcrafted • CROW
600QXM5667 • **Value $25**

9 Woodland Babies
(2nd, 1992)
Handcrafted • PALM
600QXM5444 • **Value $16**

10 Woodland Babies
(3rd & final, 1993)
Handcrafted • FRAN
575QXM5102 • **Value $17**

THIMBLE BELLS		
	Price Paid	Value of My Collection
1.		
2.		
3.		
4.		
WELCOME FRIENDS		
5.		
6.		
WINTER FUN WITH SNOOPY®		
7.		
WOODLAND BABIES		
8.		
9.		
10.		
PENCIL TOTALS		

1998

Among the highlights for 1998 are a number of special Anniversary Edition pieces commemorating the 25th year of Hallmark Keepsake Ornaments. In addition to the 165 new ornaments in the Keepsake line, there are 12 new Magic and 25 new Miniature ornaments. See the collectible series section for more 1998 ornaments.

(1)

#1 Student
Handcrafted • N/A
795QX6646 • **Value $7.95**

(2)

**1998 Corvette®
Convertible**
Handcrafted • PALM
1395QX6416 • **Value $13.95**

(3)

Angelic Flight (LE-25,000)
Crystal/Silver-Plated • ANDR
8500QXI4146 • **Value $85**

(4)

Baby's First Christmas
Handcrafted • FRAN
795QX6603 • **Value $7.95**

(5)

Baby's First Christmas
Handcrafted • KLIN
895QX6596 • **Value $8.95**

GENERAL KEEPSAKE

	Price Paid	Value of My Collection
1.		
2.		
3.		
4.		
5.		
6.		
7.		
8.		
9.		
10.		

(6)

Baby's First Christmas
Handcrafted • TAGU
995QX6233 • **Value $9.95**

(7)

Baby's First Christmas
Handcrafted • ESCH
995QX6586 • **Value $9.95**

(8)

**Baby's Second
Christmas**
Handcrafted • CROW
795QX6606 • **Value $7.95**

(9)

Boba Fett™
Handcrafted • RHOD
1495QXI4053 • **Value $14.95**

(10)

Bouncy Baby-sitter
Handcrafted • SIED
1295QXD4096 • **Value $12.95**

(11)

Bugs Bunny
Handcrafted • CHAD
1395QX6443 • **Value $13.95**

(12)

Building a Snowman
Handcrafted • SIED
1495QXD4133 • **Value $14.95**

(13)

Buzz Lightyear
Handcrafted • CROW
1495QXD4066 • **Value $14.95**

(14)

**Captain Kathryn
Janeway™**
Handcrafted • RGRS
1495QXI4046 • **Value $14.95**

(15)

Catch of the Season
Handcrafted • SEAL
1495QX6786 • **Value $14.95**

(16)

Chatty Chipmunk
Handcrafted • CROW
995QX6716 • **Value $9.95**

(17)

Checking Santa's Files
Handcrafted • TAGU
895QX6806 • **Value $8.95**

PENCIL TOTALS

1

A Child Is Born
Handcrafted • VOTR
1295QX6176 • **Value $12.95**

2

Child's Fifth Christmas
Handcrafted • CROW
795QX6623 • **Value $7.95**

3

Child's Fourth Christmas
Handcrafted • CROW
795QX6616 • **Value $7.95**

4

Child's Third Christmas
Handcrafted • CROW
795QX6613 • **Value $7.95**

5

A Christmas Eve Story Becky Kelly
Handcrafted • TAGU
1395QXD6873 • **Value $13.95**

6

Christmas Request
Handcrafted • FRAN
1495QX6193 • **Value $14.95**

7

Christmas Sleigh Ride
Die-Cast Metal • CROW
1295QX6556 • **Value $12.95**

8

Cinderella's Coach
Handcrafted • WILL
1495QXD4083 • **Value $14.95**

9

Compact Skater
Handcrafted • TAGU
995QX6766 • **Value $9.95**

10

Country Home Marjolein Bastin
Handcrafted • FRAN
1095QX5172 • **Value $10.95**

11

Cross of Peace
Metal • KLIN
995QX6856 • **Value $9.95**

12

Cruising into Christmas
Handcrafted/Tin • CROW
1695QX6196 • **Value $16.95**

13

Dad
Handcrafted • KLIN
895QX6663 • **Value $8.95**

14

Daughter
Handcrafted • AUBE
895QX6673 • **Value $8.95**

15

Daydreams
Handcrafted • BRIC
1395QXD4136 • **Value $13.95**

16

Decorating Maxine-Style
Handcrafted • N/A
1095QXE6883 • **Value $10.95**

17

Downhill Dash
Handcrafted • CROW
1395QX6776 • **Value $13.95**

18

Fancy Footwork
Handcrafted • VOTR
895QX6536 • **Value $8.95**

19

Feliz Navidad
Handcrafted • CHAD
895QX6173 • **Value $8.95**

20

Flik
Handcrafted • N/A
1295QXD4153 • **Value $12.95**

1998

General Keepsake

	Price Paid	Value of My Collection
1.		
2.		
3.		
4.		
5.		
6.		
7.		
8.		
9.		
10.		
11.		
12.		
13.		
14.		
15.		
16.		
17.		
18.		
19.		
20.		
PENCIL TOTALS		

(1) Forever Friends Bear
Handcrafted • PIKE
895QX6303 • **Value $8.95**

(2) Friend of My Heart (set/2)
Handcrafted • SEAL
1495QX6723 • **Value $14.95**

(3) Future Ballerina
Handcrafted • TAGU
795QX6756 • **Value $7.95**

(4) Gifted Gardener
Handcrafted • CHAD
795QX6736 • **Value $7.95**

(5) Godchild
Handcrafted • CHAD
795QX6703 • **Value $7.95**

(6) Good Luck Dice
Handcrafted • HADD
995QX6813 • **Value $9.95**

(7) Goofy Soccer Star
Handcrafted • CHAD
1095QXD4123 • **Value $10.95**

(8) Granddaughter
Handcrafted • FRAN
795QX6683 • **Value $7.95**

(9) Grandma's Memories
Handcrafted • KLIN
895QX6686 • **Value $8.95**

(10) Grandson
Handcrafted • FRAN
795QX6676 • **Value $7.95**

(11) The Grinch
Handcrafted • CHAD
1395QXI6466 • **Value $13.95**

(12) Guardian Friend
Handcrafted • LYLE
895QX6543 • **Value $8.95**

(13) Heavenly Melody
Handcrafted • VOTR
1895QX6576 • **Value $18.95**

(14) Holiday Camper
Handcrafted • SEAL
1295QX6783 • **Value $12.95**

(15) Holiday Decorator
Handcrafted • WILL
1395QX6566 • **Value $13.95**

(16) The Holy Family (set/3)
Porcelain • LYLE
2500QX6523 • **Value $25**

(17) Hot Wheels™
Handcrafted • CROW
1395QX6436 • **Value $13.95**

(18) Iago, Abu and the Genie
Handcrafted • WILL
1295QXD4076 • **Value $12.95**

(19) Joe Montana Notre Dame
Handcrafted • UNRU
1495QXI6843 • **Value $14.95**

(20) Journey To Bethlehem
Handcrafted • UNRU
1695QX6223 • **Value $16.95**

GENERAL KEEPSAKE	Price Paid	Value of My Collection
1.		
2.		
3.		
4.		
5.		
6.		
7.		
8.		
9.		
10.		
11.		
12.		
13.		
14.		
15.		
16.		
17.		
18.		
19.		
20.		

PENCIL TOTALS

1
Joyful Messenger
Handcrafted/Silver-Plated • LYLE
1895QXI6733 • **Value $18.95**

2
**King Kharoof–
Second King**
Handcrafted • ANDR
1295QX6186 • **Value $12.95**

3
**Larry, Moe, and Curly
The Three Stooges™
(set/3)**
Handcrafted • LARS
2700QX6503 • **Value $27**

4
Madonna and Child
Handcrafted • RGRS
1295QX6516 • **Value $12.95**

5
Make-Believe Boat
Handcrafted • ESCH
1295QXD4113 • **Value $12.95**

6
Maxine
Handcrafted • PIKE
995QX6446 • **Value $9.95**

7
Memories of Christmas
Glass • LARS
595QX2406 • **Value $5.95**

8
Merry Chime
Handcrafted/Brass • CROW
995QX6692 • **Value $9.95**

1998

9
**The Mickey and
Minnie Handcar**
Handcrafted • WILL
1495QXD4116 • **Value $14.95**

10
**Mickey's Favorite
Reindeer**
Handcrafted • LARS
1395QXD4013 • **Value $13.95**

11
Miracle in Bethlehem
Handcrafted • SEAL
1295QX6513 • **Value $12.95**

12
Mistletoe Fairy
Handcrafted • ESCH
1295QX6216 • **Value $12.95**

13
Mom
Handcrafted • KLIN
895QX6656 • **Value $8.95**

14
Mom and Dad
Handcrafted • KLIN
995QX6653 • **Value $9.95**

15
Mother and Daughter
Porcelain • VOTR
895QX6696 • **Value $8.95**

16
Mrs. Potato Head®
Handcrafted • N/A
1095QX6886 • **Value $10.95**

17
**Mulan, Mushu
and Cri-Kee (set/2)**
Handcrafted • N/A
1495QXD4156 • **Value $14.95**

18
**Munchkinland™ Mayor
and Coroner (set/2)**
Handcrafted • LYLE
1395QX6463 • **Value $13.95**

19
National Salute
Handcrafted • RHOD
895QX6293 • **Value $8.95**

20
New Arrival
Porcelain • VOTR
1895QX6306 • **Value $18.95**

GENERAL KEEPSAKE		
	Price Paid	Value of My Collection
1.		
2.		
3.		
4.		
5.		
6.		
7.		
8.		
9.		
10.		
11.		
12.		
13.		
14.		
15.		
16.		
17.		
18.		
19.		
20.		
PENCIL TOTALS		

(1) New Home
Handcrafted • SEAL
995QX6713 • **Value $9.95**

(2) Nick's Wish List
Handcrafted • ANDR
895QX6863 • **Value $8.95**

(3) Night Watch
Handcrafted • SIED
995QX6725 • **Value $9.95**

(4) North Pole Reserve
Handcrafted • SEAL
1095QX6803 • **Value $10.95**

(5) Our First Christmas Together
Acrylic • VOTR
795QX3193 • **Value $7.95**

(6) Our First Christmas Together
Brass/Porcelain • VOTR
1895QX6643 • **Value $18.95**

(7) Our First Christmas Together
Handcrafted • TAGU
895QX6636 • **Value $8.95**

(8) OUR SONG
Ceramic • N/A
995QX6183 • **Value $9.95**

GENERAL KEEPSAKE

	Price Paid	Value of My Collection
1.		
2.		
3.		
4.		
5.		
6.		
7.		
8.		
9.		
10.		
11.		
12.		
13.		
14.		
15.		
16.		
17.		
18.		
19.		
20.		

(9) Peekaboo Bears
Handcrafted • CROW
1295QX6563 • **Value $12.95**

(10) A Perfect Match
Handcrafted • RHOD
1095QX6633 • **Value $10.95**

(11) Polar Bowler
Handcrafted • ESCH
795QX6746 • **Value $7.95**

(12) Princess Aurora (set/2)
Handcrafted • BRIC
1295QXD4126 • **Value $12.95**

(13) Purr-fect Little Deer
Handcrafted • PIKE
795QX6526 • **Value $7.95**

(14) Puttin' Around
Handcrafted • RHOD
895QX6763 • **Value $8.95**

(15) Rocket to Success
Handcrafted • PIKE
895QX6793 • **Value $8.95**

(16) Runaway Toboggan (set/2)
Handcrafted • N/A
1695QXD4003 • **Value $16.95**

(17) Santa's Deer Friend
Handcrafted • CHAD
2400QX6583 • **Value $24**

(18) Santa's Flying Machine
Handcrafted/Tin • SEAL
1695QX6573 • **Value $16.95**

(19) Santa's Hidden Surprise
Ceramic • N/A
1495QX6913 • **Value $14.95**

(20) "Sew" Gifted
Handcrafted • TAGU
795QX6743 • **Value $7.95**

PENCIL TOTALS

VALUE GUIDE — HALLMARK KEEPSAKE ORNAMENTS

(1)  **Simba & Nala** *Handcrafted* • N/A 1395QXD4073 • **Value $13.95**	**(2)**  **Sister to Sister** *Handcrafted* • PIKE 895QX6693 • **Value $8.95**

(3)
Soaring With Angels
Handcrafted • SICK
1695QX6213 • **Value $16.95**

(4)
Son
Handcrafted • AUBE
895QX6666 • **Value $8.95**

(5)
Special Dog
Handcrafted • N/A
795QX6706 • **Value $7.95**

(6)
Spoonful of Love
Handcrafted • TAGU
895QX6796 • **Value $8.95**

(7)
Superman™
Pressed Tin • N/A
1295QX6423 • **Value $12.95**

(8)
Surprise Catch
Handcrafted • FRAN
795QX6753 • **Value $7.95**

(9)
Sweet Rememberings
Handcrafted • TAGU
895QX6876 • **Value $8.95**

(10)
Sweet Treat
Handcrafted • KLIN
1095QX6433 • **Value $10.95**

(11)
Tin Locomotive
Pressed Tin • SICK
2500QX6826 • **Value $25**

(12)
Tonka® Road Grader
Die-Cast Metal • N/A
1395QX6483 • **Value $13.95**

(13)
Treetop Choir
Handcrafted • FRAN
995QX6506 • **Value $9.95**

(14)
Warm and Cozy
Handcrafted • SICK
895QX6866 • **Value $8.95**

(15)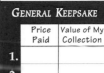
Watchful Shepherd
Handcrafted • KLIN
895QX6496 • **Value $8.95**

(16)
Woody the Sheriff
Handcrafted • N/A
1495QXD4163 • **Value $14.95**

(17)
Writing to Santa
Handcrafted • AUBE
795QX6533 • **Value $7.95**

(18)
1998 Corvette®
Handcrafted • PALM
2400QLX7605 • **Value $24**

(19)
Cinderella at the Ball
Handcrafted • N/A
2400QXD7576 • **Value $24**

(20)
Mickey's Comet
Handcrafted • WILL
2400QXD7586 • **Value $24**

GENERAL KEEPSAKE

	Price Paid	Value of My Collection
1.		
2.		
3.		
4.		
5.		
6.		
7.		
8.		
9.		
10.		
11.		
12.		
13.		
14.		
15.		
16.		
17.		

GENERAL MAGIC

18.		
19.		
20.		
PENCIL TOTALS		

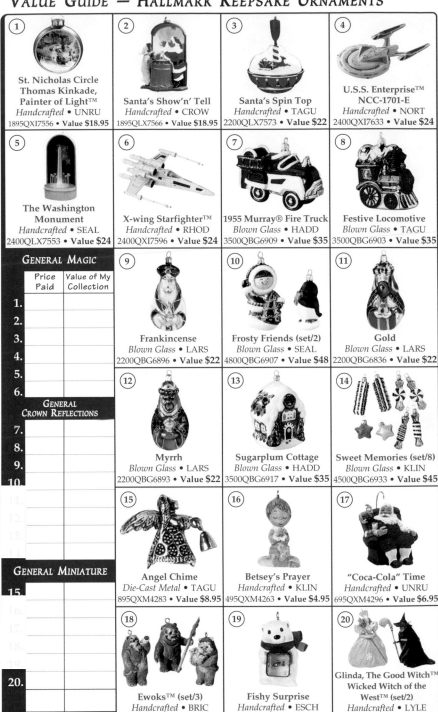

1 St. Nicholas Circle Thomas Kinkade, Painter of Light™
Handcrafted • UNRU
1895QXI7556 • **Value $18.95**

2 Santa's Show'n' Tell
Handcrafted • CROW
1895QLX7566 • **Value $18.95**

3 Santa's Spin Top
Handcrafted • TAGU
2200QLX7573 • **Value $22**

4 U.S.S. Enterprise™ NCC-1701-E
Handcrafted • NORT
2400QXI7633 • **Value $24**

5 The Washington Monument
Handcrafted • SEAL
2400QLX7553 • **Value $24**

6 X-wing Starfighter™
Handcrafted • RHOD
2400QXI7596 • **Value $24**

7 1955 Murray® Fire Truck
Blown Glass • HADD
3500QBG6909 • **Value $35**

8 Festive Locomotive
Blown Glass • TAGU
3500QBG6903 • **Value $35**

9 Frankincense
Blown Glass • LARS
2200QBG6896 • **Value $22**

10 Frosty Friends (set/2)
Blown Glass • SEAL
4800QBG6907 • **Value $48**

11 Gold
Blown Glass • LARS
2200QBG6836 • **Value $22**

12 Myrrh
Blown Glass • LARS
2200QBG6893 • **Value $22**

13 Sugarplum Cottage
Blown Glass • HADD
3500QBG6917 • **Value $35**

14 Sweet Memories (set/8)
Blown Glass • KLIN
4500QBG6933 • **Value $45**

15 Angel Chime
Die-Cast Metal • TAGU
895QXM4283 • **Value $8.95**

16 Betsey's Prayer
Handcrafted • KLIN
495QXM4263 • **Value $4.95**

17 "Coca-Cola" Time
Handcrafted • UNRU
695QXM4296 • **Value $6.95**

18 Ewoks™ (set/3)
Handcrafted • BRIC
1695QXI4223 • **Value $16.95**

19 Fishy Surprise
Handcrafted • ESCH
695QXM4276 • **Value $6.95**

20 Glinda, The Good Witch™ Wicked Witch of the West™ (set/2)
Handcrafted • LYLE
1495QXM4233 • **Value $14.95**

GENERAL MAGIC

GENERAL CROWN REFLECTIONS

GENERAL MINIATURE

	Price Paid	Value of My Collection
1.		
2.		
3.		
4.		
5.		
6.		
7.		
8.		
9.		
10.		
11.		
12.		
13.		
14.		
15.		
16.		
17.		
18.		
19.		
20.		

✎ **PENCIL TOTALS**

1 **Holly-Jolly Jig** *Handcrafted* • TAGU 695QXM4266 • **Value $6.95**	**2**  **Peaceful Pandas** *Handcrafted* • SICK 595QXM4253 • **Value $5.95**	**3** **Pixie Parachute** *Handcrafted* • ESCH 495QXM4256 • **Value $4.95**	**4** **Sharing Joy** *Handcrafted* • N/A 495QXM4273 • **Value $4.95**

5 **Singin' in the Rain™ (set/2)** *Handcrafted* • ANDR 1095QXM4303 • **Value $10.95**	**6**  **Superman™ (set/2)** *Handcrafted* • CHAD 1095QXM4313 • **Value $10.95**	**7** **Tree Trimmin' Time (set/3)** *Handcrafted* • N/A 1995QXD4236 • **Value $19.95**	**8**  **Follow the Leader (club edition, set/2)** *Handcrafted* • SIED 1695QXC4503 • **Value $16.95**

1998

9 **Kringle Bells (keepsake of membership, miniature)** *Handcrafted* • BRIC QXC4486 • **Value N/E**	**10** **Making His Way (keepsake of membership)** *Handcrafted* • SICK QXC4523 • **Value N/E**	**11** **New Christmas Friend (keepsake of membership)** *Handcrafted* • ESCH QXC4516 • **Value N/E**

12 _____ **Surprise 25th Anniversary Gift** *To Be Announced*	**13** **Santa's Merry Workshop Musical Figurine** *Handcrafted* • SEAL 3200QX6816 • **Value $32**	**14** **Holiday Memories™ BARBIE™ Ornament** *Handcrafted* • N/A 1495QHB6020 • **Value $14.95**

General Miniature

	Price Paid	Value of My Collection
1.		
2.		
3.		
4.		
5.		
6.		
7.		

Collector's Club

8.		
9.		
10.		
11.		
12.		

15 **Holiday Memories™ BARBIE™ Porcelain Plate (LE-24,500)** *Porcelain* • N/A 3000QHB6021 • **Value $30**	**16** **Holiday Voyage™ BARBIE™ Card-Display Figurine** *Handcrafted* • N/A 4000QHB6019 • **Value $40**	**17**  **Holiday Voyage™ BARBIE® Doll (2nd in *Holiday Homecoming Collector Series™*)** *Vinyl* • N/A 5000QHB6022 • **Value $50**

Premiere Figurines

13.		

Barbie™ Collectibles

14.		
15.		
16.		
17.		
18.		
19.		
20.		

18 **Holiday Voyage™ BARBIE™ Ornament** *Handcrafted* • N/A 1495QHB6016 • **Value $14.95**	**19** **Holiday Voyage™ BARBIE™ Porcelain Figurine (LE-24,500)** *Porcelain* • N/A 4500QHB6017 • **Value $45**	**20** **Holiday Voyage™ BARBIE™ Porcelain Plate (LE-24,500)** *Porcelain* • N/A 3000QHB6018 • **Value $30**

Pencil Totals

(1) **Collegiate Collection** **(5 assorted)** *Handcrafted* • HADD	1. Florida State Seminoles™ 995QSR2316 • **Value $9.95** 2. Michigan Wolverines™ 995QSR2323 • **Value $9.95** 3. North Carolina Tar Heels™ 995QSR2333 • **Value $9.95** 4. Notre Dame Fighting Irish™ 995QSR2313 • **Value $9.95** 5. Penn State Nittany Lions™ 995QSR2326 • **Value $9.95**	**1998 Hallmark Keepsake Ornaments'** **25th Anniversary Celebration** **August 20 - 22, 1998 in Kansas City, Missouri** *If you're a Hallmark collector attending the silver anniversary convention for Hallmark Keepsake Ornaments, you're sure to be privy to many suprises; including some exclusive pieces to add to your collection. Use the boxes below to record any special treats you receive at the convention. Have fun!!*

(2) **(3)** **(4)** **(5)**

COLLEGIATE COLLECTION

	Price Paid	Value of My Collection
1.		

(6) **(7)** **(8)**

CONVENTION PIECES

2.		
3.		
4.		
5.		
6.		
7.		
8.		

(9)
 1926 Lionel® Catalog Cover Tin Sign
 Pressed Tin • N/A
 1800QHT3701 • **Value $18**

(10)
 1929 Lionel® Catalog Cover Tin Sign
 Pressed Tin • N/A
 1800QHT3703 • **Value $18**

(11)
 1952 Lionel® Catalog Cover Tin Sign
 Pressed Tin • N/A
 1800QHT3702 • **Value $18**

LIONEL® LIMITED

9.		
10.		
11.		
12.		
13.		
14.		

(12)
 Lionel® 726 Berkshire Steam Locomotive (1st in *20th Century Series***)**
 Die-Cast Metal • N/A
 ($120)1QHT7801 • **Value $120**

(13)
 Lionel® 746 Norfolk and Western Steam Locomotive (1st in *Norfolk and Western Train Series***)**
 Die-Cast Metal • N/A
 9000QHT7803 • **Value $90**

(14)
 Lionel® 2332 Pennsylvania GG1 Electric Locomotive (2nd in *20th Century Series***)**
 Die-Cast Metal • N/A
 9500QHT7804 • **Value $95**

NBA COLLECTION

15.		

(15)
 NBA Collection
 (10 assorted)
 Handcrafted • SIED

1. **Charlotte Hornets**
 995QSR1033 • **Value $9.95**
2. **Chicago Bulls**
 995QSR1036 • **Value $9.95**
3. **Detroit Pistons**
 995QSR1043 • **Value $9.95**
4. **Houston Rockets**
 995QSR1046 • **Value $9.95**
5. **Indiana Pacers**
 995QSR1053 • **Value $9.95**

6. **Los Angeles Lakers**
 995QSR1056 • **Value $9.95**
7. **New York Knickerbockers**
 995QSR1063 • **Value $9.95**
8. **Orlando Magic**
 995QSR1066 • **Value $9.95**
9. **Seattle Supersonics**
 995QSR1076 • **Value $9.95**
10. **Utah Jazz**
 995QSR1083 • **Value $9.95**

PENCIL TOTALS

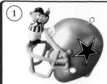

NFL Collection
(15 assorted)
Handcrafted • FRAN

1. Carolina Panthers™
995QSR5026 • **Value $9.95**
2. Chicago Bears™
995QSR5033 • **Value $9.95**
3. Dallas Cowboys™
995QSR5046 • **Value $9.95**
4. Denver Broncos™
995QSR5053 • **Value $9.95**
5. Green Bay Packers™
995QSR5063 • **Value $9.95**

6. Kansas City Chiefs™
995QSR5013 • **Value $9.95**
7. Miami Dolphins™
995QSR5096 • **Value $9.95**
8. Minnesota Vikings™
995QSR5126 • **Value $9.95**
9. New York Giants™
995QSR5143 • **Value $9.95**
10. Oakland Raiders™
995QSR5086 • **Value $9.95**

11. Philadelphia Eagles™
995QSR5153 • **Value $9.95**
12. Pittsburgh Steelers™
995QSR5163 • **Value $9.95**
13. St. Louis Rams™
995QSR5093 • **Value $9.95**
14. San Francisco 49ers™
995QSR5173 • **Value $9.95**
15. Washington Redskins™
995QSR5186 • **Value $9.95**

1997

1950s HOWDY DOODY™
Pressed Tin • N/A
1950QHM8801 • **Value $19.50**

1950s Lone Ranger™
Pressed Tin • N/A
1950QHM8802 • **Value $19.50**

1950s SUPERMAN™
Pressed Tin • N/A
1950QHM8803 • **Value $19.50**

1970s Hot Wheels™
Pressed Tin • N/A
1950QHM8813 • **Value $19.50**

Christmas Caring
Resin • BRIC
1800QHC8251 • **Value $18**

Dreams and Wishes
Resin • VOTR
2500QHC8250 • **Value $25**

Splendid Days
Resin • TAGU
1800QHC8216 • **Value $18**

Thoughtful Ways
Resin • HADD/TAGU
1800QHC8215 • **Value $18**

Together Days
Resin • BRIC
1800QHC8217 • **Value $18**

1997

Highlights for 1997 included a new collection of Disney ornaments, as well as several ornaments based on the STAR WARS movies. The 1997 collection featured 144 Keepsake ornaments, 17 Magic ornaments and 36 Miniature ornaments. See the collectible series section for more 1997 ornaments.

1997 Corvette
Handcrafted • PALM
1395QXI6455 • **Value $28**

All-Round Sports Fan
Handcrafted • WILL
895QX6392 • **Value $30**

All-Weather Walker
Handcrafted • WILL
895QX6415 • **Value $18**

NFL Collection

	Price Paid	Value of My Collection
1.		

School Days Lunch Boxes

2.		
3.		
4.		
5.		

Spoonful of Star

6.		
7.		
8.		
9.		
10.		

General Keepsake

11.		
12.		
13.		

Pencil Totals

1997

Value Guide — Hallmark Keepsake Ornaments

1. **Angel Friend**
Handcrafted • FRAN
1495QX6762 • **Value $25**

2. **Ariel, The Little Mermaid**
Handcrafted • BRIC
1295QXI4072 • **Value $23**

3. **Baby's First Christmas**
Handcrafted • N/A
795QX6482 • **Value $20**

4. **Baby's First Christmas**
Handcrafted • CROW
795QX6495 • **Value $19**

5. **Baby's First Christmas**
Handcrafted • VOTR
995QX6485 • **Value $24**

6. **Baby's First Christmas**
Handcrafted • ANDR
995QX6492 • **Value $20**

7. **Baby's First Christmas**
Porcelain • VOTR
1495QX6535 • **Value $21**

8. **Baby's Second Christmas**
Handcrafted • CROW
795QX6502 • **Value $17**

9. **Biking Buddies**
Handcrafted • PALM
1295QX6682 • **Value $24**

10. **Book of the Year**
Handcrafted • BRIC
795QX6645 • **Value $18**

11. **Breezin' Along**
Handcrafted • SEAL
895QX6722 • **Value $20**

12. **Bucket Brigade**
Handcrafted • FRAN
895QX6382 • **Value $17**

13. **Catch of the Day**
Handcrafted • TAGU
995QX6712 • **Value $20**

14. **Child's Fifth Christmas**
Handcrafted • CROW
795QX6515 • **Value $16**

15. **Child's Fourth Christmas**
Handcrafted • CROW
795QX6512 • **Value $16**

16. **Child's Third Christmas**
Handcrafted • CROW
795QX6505 • **Value $15**

17. **Christmas Checkup**
Handcrafted • SIED
795QX6385 • **Value $17**

18. **Classic Cross**
Precious Metal • VOTR
1395QX6805 • **Value $20**

19. **Clever Camper**
Handcrafted • CHAD
795QX6445 • **Value $17**

20. **Commander Data™**
Handcrafted • RGRS
1495QXI6345 • **Value $30**

GENERAL KEEPSAKE

	Price Paid	Value of My Collection
1.		
2.		
3.		
4.		
5.		
6.		
7.		
8.		
9.		
10.		
11.		
12.		
13.		
14.		
15.		
16.		
17.		
18.		
19.		
20.		
PENCIL TOTALS		

1 — **Cycling Santa**
Handcrafted • WILL
1495QX6425 • **Value $28**

2 — **Dad**
Handcrafted • SIED
895QX6532 • **Value $22**

3 — **Daughter**
Pressed Tin • BRIC
795QX6612 • **Value $19**

4 — **Downhill Run**
Handcrafted • CROW
995QX6705 • **Value $23**

5 — **Dr. Leonard H. McCoy™**
Handcrafted • RGRS
1495QXI6352 • **Value $30**

6 — **Elegance on Ice**
Handcrafted • LYLE
995QX6432 • **Value $20**

7 — **Expressly for Teacher**
Handcrafted • TAGU
795QX6375 • **Value $15**

8 — **Feliz Navidad**
Handcrafted • SEAL
895QX6665 • **Value $33**

9 — **Friendship Blend**
Handcrafted • SEAL
995QX6655 • **Value $19**

10 — **Garden Bouquet**
Handcrafted • LYLE
1495QX6752 • **Value $30**

11 — **Gift of Friendship**
Porcelain • N/A
1295QXE6835 • **Value N/E**

12 — **Godchild**
Handcrafted • BRIC
795QX6662 • **Value $15**

13 — **God's Gift of Love**
Porcelain • LYLE
1695QX6792 • **Value $33**

14 — **Goofy's Ski Adventure**
Handcrafted • CHAD
1295QXD4042 • **Value $25**

15 — **Granddaughter**
Handcrafted • TAGU
795QX6622 • **Value $18**

16 — **Grandma**
Handcrafted • PIKE
895QX6625 • **Value $16**

17 — **Grandson**
Handcrafted • TAGU
795QX6615 • **Value $18**

18 — **Gus & Jaq, Cinderella**
Handcrafted • CROW
1295QXD4052 • **Value $28**

19 — **Heavenly Song**
Acrylic • VOTR
1295QX6795 • **Value $22**

20 — **Hercules**
Handcrafted • WILL
1295QXI4005 • **Value $25**

General Keepsake

	Price Paid	Value of My Collection
1.		
2.		
3.		
4.		
5.		
6.		
7.		
8.		
9.		
10.		
11.		
12.		
13.		
14.		
15.		
16.		
17.		
18.		
19.		
20.		
PENCIL TOTALS		

1997

① Honored Guests
Handcrafted • FRAN
1495QX6745 • **Value $32**

② Howdy Doody™
Handcrafted • LARS
1295QX6272 • **Value $25**

③ The Incredible Hulk®
Handcrafted • N/A
1295QX5471 • **Value $21**

④ Jasmine & Aladdin, Aladdin & the King of Thieves
Handcrafted • RGRS
1495QXD4062 • **Value $26**

⑤ Jingle Bell Jester
Handcrafted • PIKE
995QX6695 • **Value $18**

⑥ Juggling Stars
Handcrafted • TAGU
995QX6595 • **Value $19**

⑦ King Noor–First King
Handcrafted • ANDR
1295QX6552 • **Value $27**

⑧ Leading The Way
Handcrafted • SICK
1695QX6782 • **Value $32**

⑨ Lion and Lamb
Handcrafted • WILL
795QX6602 • **Value $18**

⑩ The Lone Ranger™
Pressed Tin • N/A
1295QX6265 • **Value $34**

⑪ Love to Sew
Handcrafted • TAGU
795QX6435 • **Value $18**

⑫ Madonna del Rosario
Handcrafted • SICK
1295QX6545 • **Value $24**

⑬ Marbles Champion
Handcrafted • UNRU
1095QX6342 • **Value $20**

⑭ Meadow Snowman
Pressed Tin • SICK
1295QX6715 • **Value $30**

⑮ Megara and Pegasus
Handcrafted • CROW
1695QXI4012 • **Value $32**

⑯ Michigan J. Frog
Handcrafted • CHAD
995QX6332 • **Value $22**

⑰ Mickey's Long Shot
Handcrafted • SIED
1095QXD6412 • **Value $22**

⑱ Mickey's Snow Angel
Handcrafted • SIED
995QXD4035 • **Value $20**

⑲ Miss Gulch
Handcrafted • LYLE
1395QX6372 • **Value $27**

⑳ Mom
Handcrafted • SIED
895QX6525 • **Value $18**

GENERAL KEEPSAKE

	Price Paid	Value of My Collection
1.		
2.		
3.		
4.		
5.		
6.		
7.		
8.		
9.		
10.		
11.		
12.		
13.		
14.		
15.		
16.		
17.		
18.		
19.		
20.		

PENCIL TOTALS

1
Mom and Dad
Handcrafted • SIED
995QX6522 • **Value $20**

2
Mr. Potato Head®
Handcrafted • SIED
1095QX6335 • **Value $25**

3
Nativity Tree
Handcrafted • UNRU
1495QX6575 • **Value $35**

4
New Home
Handcrafted • PIKE
895QX6652 • **Value $18**

5
New Pair of Skates
Handcrafted • LARS
1395QXD4032 • **Value $28**

6
The Night Before Christmas
Handcrafted • CROW
2400QX5721 • **Value $45**

7
Our Christmas Together
Pewter • N/A
1695QX6475 • **Value $30**

8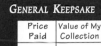
Our First Christmas Together
Acrylic • N/A
795QX3182 • **Value $16**

9
Our First Christmas Together
Handcrafted • PIKE
895QX6472 • **Value $20**

10
Our First Christmas Together
Handcrafted • SEAL
1095QX6465 • **Value $23**

11
Phoebus & Esmeralda, The Hunchback of Notre Dame
Handcrafted • CROW
1495QXD6344 • **Value $26**

12
Playful Shepherd
Handcrafted • TAGU
995QX6592 • **Value $21**

13
Porcelain Hinged Box
Porcelain • VOTR
1495QX6772 • **Value $30**

14
Praise Him
Handcrafted • SICK
895QX6542 • **Value $19**

15
Prize Topiary
Handcrafted • SEAL
1495QXD6675 • **Value $28**

16
Sailor Bear
Handcrafted • UNRU
1495QX6765 • **Value $27**

17
Santa Mail
Handcrafted • WILL
1095QX6702 • **Value $22**

18
Santa's Friend
Handcrafted • UNRU
1295QX6685 • **Value $25**

19
Santa's Magical Sleigh
Handcrafted • UNRU
2400QX6672 • **Value $42**

20
Santa's Merry Path
Handcrafted • SICK
1695QX6785 • **Value $35**

1997

GENERAL KEEPSAKE

	Price Paid	Value of My Collection
1.		
2.		
3.		
4.		
5.		
6.		
7.		
8.		
9.		
10.		
11.		
12.		
13.		
14.		
15.		
16.		
17.		
18.		
19.		
20.		

PENCIL TOTALS

(1) 	(2)	(3)	(4)
Santa's Polar Friend *Handcrafted* • CHAD 1695QX6755 • **Value $32**	**Santa's Ski Adventure** *Handcrafted* • CHAD 1295QX6422 • **Value $25**	**Sister to Sister** *Handcrafted* • PIKE 995QX6635 • **Value $20**	**Snow Bowling** *Handcrafted* • WILL 695QX6395 • **Value $16**

(5) 	(6)	(7)	(8)
Snow White, Anniversary Edition (set/2) *Handcrafted* • ESCH 1695QXD4055 • **Value $35**	**Snowgirl** *Handcrafted* • TAGU 795QX6562 • **Value $17**	**Son** *Pressed Tin* • BRIC 795QX6605 • **Value $16**	**Special Dog** *Handcrafted* • BRIC 795QX6632 • **Value $16**

(9)	(10)	(11)
The Spirit of Christmas *Handcrafted* • LARS 995QX6585 • **Value $20**	**Stealing a Kiss** *Handcrafted* • TAGU 1495QX6555 • **Value $28**	**Sweet Discovery** *Handcrafted* • SICK 1195QX6325 • **Value $23**

(12) 	(13)	(14)
Sweet Dreamer *Handcrafted* • BRIC 695QX6732 • **Value $15**	**Swinging in the Snow** *Handcrafted/Glass* • TAGU 1295QX6775 • **Value $25**	**Taking A Break** *Handcrafted* • UNRU 1495QX6305 • **Value $28**

(15)	(16)	(17) 
Timon & Pumbaa, The Lion King *Handcrafted* • WILL 1295QXD4065 • **Value $20**	**Tomorrow's Leader** *Ceramic* • N/A 995QX6452 • **Value $18**	**Tonka® Mighty Front Loader** *Die-Cast Metal* • N/A 1395QX6362 • **Value $27**

(18)	(19)	(20)
Two-Tone, 101 Dalmatians *Handcrafted* • CHAD 995QXD4015 • **Value $20**	**Waitin' on Santa– Winnie the Pooh** *Handcrafted* • SIED 1295QXD6365 • **Value $27**	**What a Deal!** *Handcrafted* • PIKE 895QX6442 • **Value $16**

(1) **Yoda™** *Handcrafted* • BRIC 995QXI6355 • **Value $35**	**(2)** **Darth Vader™** *Handcrafted* • RHOD 2400QXI7531 • **Value $47**	**(3)** **Decorator Taz** *Handcrafted* • CHAD 3000QLX7502 • **Value $55**	**(4)** **Glowing Angel** *Handcrafted* • VOTR 1895QLX7435 • **Value $27**
(5)  **Holiday Serenade** *Handcrafted* • FRAN 2400QLX7485 • **Value $47**	**(6)** **Joy to the World** *Handcrafted* • TAGU 1495QLX7512 • **Value $30**	**(7)** **The Lincoln Memorial** *Handcrafted* • SEAL 2400QLX7522 • **Value $44**	**(8)** **Madonna and Child** *Handcrafted* • LYLE 1995QLX7425 • **Value $38**
(9)  **Motorcycle Chums** *Handcrafted* • SEAL 2400QLX7495 • **Value $45**	**(10)** **Santa's Secret Gift** *Handcrafted* • CHAD 2400QLX7455 • **Value $43**	**(11)** 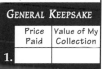 **Santa's Showboat** *Handcrafted* • CROW 4200QLX7465 • **Value $76**	

GENERAL KEEPSAKE		
	Price Paid	Value of My Collection
1.		

GENERAL MAGIC

2.	
3.	
4.	
5.	
6.	
7.	
8.	
9.	
10.	
11.	
12.	
13.	
14.	
15.	

(12) **SNOOPY Plays Santa** *Handcrafted* • RGRS 2200QLX7475 • **Value $40**	**(13)** **Teapot Party** *Handcrafted* • TAGU 1895QLX7482 • **Value $36**	**(14)** **U.S.S. Defiant™** *Handcrafted* • NORT 2400QXI7481 • **Value $40**
(15)  **The Warmth of Home** *Handcrafted* • LARS 1895QXI7545 • **Value $30**	**(16)**  **C-3PO™ and R2-D2™ (set/2)** *Handcrafted* • RHOD 1295QXI4265 • **Value $25**	**(17)**  **Casablanca™ (set/3)** *Handcrafted* • ANDR 1995QXM4272 • **Value $34**

GENERAL MINIATURE

16.	
17.	
18.	
19.	
20.	

(18) **Future Star** *Handcrafted* • PIKE 595QXM4232 • **Value $12**	**(19)** **Gentle Giraffes** *Handcrafted* • SICK 595QXM4221 • **Value $11**	**(20)** **He Is Born** *Handcrafted* • VOTR 795QXM4235 • **Value $18**

PENCIL TOTALS

(1) Heavenly Music
Handcrafted • TAGU
595QXM4292 • **Value $11**

(2) Home Sweet Home
Handcrafted • SEAL
595QXM4222 • **Value $13**

**(3) Honey of a Gift–
Winnie the Pooh**
Handcrafted • LARS
695QXD4255 • **Value $16**

(4) Ice Cold Coca-Cola®
Handcrafted • CHAD
695QXM4252 • **Value $15**

(5) King of the Forest (set/4)
Handcrafted • RGRS
2400QXM4262 • **Value $42**

(6) Miniature 1997 Corvette
Handcrafted • PALM
695QXI4322 • **Value $14**

(7) Our Lady of Guadalupe
Pewter • CHAD
895QXM4275 • **Value $17**

(8) Peppermint Painter
Handcrafted • TAGU
495QXM4312 • **Value $11**

(9) Polar Buddies
Handcrafted • FRAN
495QXM4332 • **Value $12**

(10) Seeds of Joy
Handcrafted • TAGU
695QXM4242 • **Value $13**

(11) Sew Talented
Handcrafted • SEAL
595QXM4195 • **Value $13**

(12) Shutterbug
Handcrafted • TAGU
595QXM4212 • **Value $14**

(13) Snowboard Bunny
Handcrafted • TAGU
495QXM4315 • **Value $12**

**(14) Tiny Home Improvers
(set/6)**
Handcrafted • SEAL
2900QXM4282 • **Value $46**

(15) Victorian Skater
Handcrafted • UNRU
595QXM4305 • **Value $12**

(16) Away to the Window
(keepsake of membership)
Handcrafted • WILL
QXC5135 • **Value $20**

**(17) Farmer's Market,
Tender Touches**
(club edition)
Handcrafted • SEAL
1500QXC5182 • **Value $27**

(18) Happy Christmas to All!
(keepsake of membership)
Handcrafted • WILL
QXC5132 • **Value $20**

(19) Jolly Old Santa
(keepsake of membership,
miniature)
Handcrafted • WILL
QXC5145 • **Value $18**

(20) Ready for Santa
(keepsake of membership,
miniature)
Handcrafted • WILL
QXC5142 • **Value $11**

General Miniature

	Price Paid	Value of My Collection
1.		
2.		
3.		
4.		
5.		
6.		
7.		
8.		
9.		
10.		
11.		
12.		
13.		
14.		
15.		

Collector's Club

	Price Paid	Value of My Collection
16.		
17.		
18.		
19.		
20.		

Pencil Totals

The Perfect Tree, Tender Touches
Handcrafted • SEAL
1500QX6572 • **Value $28**

1953 GMC (green)
Handcrafted • PALM
(N/C) No stock # • **Value N/E**

First Class Thank You
Handcrafted • RGRS
(N/C) No stock # • **Value N/E**

Mrs. Claus's Story
Handcrafted • ESCH/KLIN
($14.95) No stock # • **Value $25**

Murray® Dump Truck (orange)
Die-Cast Metal • PALM
(N/C) No stock # • **Value N/E**

Murray Inc.® "Pursuit" Airplane (miniature, tan)
Die-Cast Metal • PALM
(N/C) No stock # • **Value N/E**

Santa's Magical Sleigh (silver runners)
Handcrafted • UNRU
(N/C) No stock # • **Value N/E**

Trimming Santa's Tree (set/2)
Handcrafted • VARI
6000QXC5175 • **Value N/E**

BARBIE™ Lapel Pin (re-issued from 1996)
Handcrafted • N/A
495XLP3544 • **Value $4.95**

Holiday BARBIE™ Stocking Hanger (re-issued from 1996)
Handcrafted • N/A
1995XSH3101 • **Value $35**

Holiday Traditions™ BARBIE® Doll (1st in *Holiday Homecoming Collector Series™*)
Vinyl • N/A
5000QHB3402 • **Value N/E**

Holiday Traditions™ BARBIE™ Ornament
Handcrafted • N/A
1495QHB6002 • **Value $21**

Holiday Traditions™ BARBIE™ Porcelain Figurine
Porcelain • N/A
4500QHB6001 • **Value N/E**

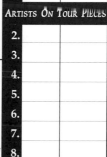

Holiday Traditions™ BARBIE™ Porcelain Plate
Porcelain • N/A
3000QHB6003 • **Value N/E**

Victorian Elegance™ BARBIE™ Ornament
Handcrafted • N/A
1495QHB6004 • **Value $22**

Victorian Elegance™ BARBIE™ Porcelain Plate
Porcelain • N/A
3000QHB6005 • **Value N/E**

NBA COLLECTION (10 assorted)
Ceramic • N/A

1. **Charlotte Hornets™**
995QSR1222 • **Value N/E**
2. **Chicago Bulls™**
995QSR1232 • **Value N/E**
3. **Detroit Pistons™**
995QSR1242 • **Value N/E**
4. **Houston Rockets™**
995QSR1245 • **Value N/E**
5. **Indiana Pacers™**
995QSR1252 • **Value N/E**
6. **Los Angeles Lakers™**
995QSR1262 • **Value N/E**
7. **New York Knickerbockers™**
995QSR1272 • **Value N/E**
8. **Orlando Magic™**
995QSR1282 • **Value N/E**
9. **Phoenix Suns™**
995QSR1292 • **Value N/E**
10. **Seattle Supersonics™**
995QSR1295 • **Value N/E**

1997

PREMIERE ORNAMENTS	Price Paid	Value of My Collection
1.		
ARTISTS ON TOUR PIECES		
2.		
3.		
4.		
5.		
6.		
7.		
8.		
BARBIE™ COLLECTIBLES		
9.		
10.		
11.		
12.		
13.		
14.		
15.		
16.		
NBA COLLECTION		
17.		
PENCIL TOTALS		

NFL COLLECTION
(30 assorted)
Handcrafted • SIED

1. **Arizona Cardinals™**
995QSR5505 • Value N/E
2. **Atlanta Falcons™**
995QSR5305 • Value N/E
3. **Baltimore Ravens™**
995QSR5352 • Value N/E
4. **Buffalo Bills™**
995QSR5312 • Value N/E
5. **Carolina Panthers™**
995QSR5315 • Value N/E
6. **Chicago Bears™**
995QSR5322 • Value N/E
7. **Cincinnati Bengals™**
995QSR5325 • Value N/E
8. **Dallas Cowboys™**
995QSR5355 • Value N/E
9. **Denver Broncos™**
995QSR5362 • Value N/E
10. **Detroit Lions™**
995QSR5365 • Value N/E

11. **Green Bay Packers™**
995QSR5372 • Value N/E
12. **Houston Oilers™**
995QSR5375 • Value N/E
13. **Indianapolis Colts™**
995QSR5411 • Value N/E
14. **Jacksonville Jaguars™**
995QSR5415 • Value N/E
15. **Kansas City Chiefs™**
995QSR5302 • Value N/E
16. **Miami Dolphins™**
995QSR5472 • Value N/E
17. **Minnesota Vikings™**
995QSR5475 • Value N/E
18. **New England Patriots™**
995QSR5482 • Value N/E
19. **New Orleans Saints™**
995QSR5485 • Value N/E
20. **New York Giants™**
995QSR5492 • Value N/E

21. **New York Jets™**
995QSR5495 • Value N/E
22. **Oakland Raiders™**
995QSR5422 • Value N/E
23. **Philadelphia Eagles™**
995QSR5502 • Value N/E
24. **Pittsburgh Steelers™**
995QSR5512 • Value N/E
25. **St. Louis Rams™**
995QSR5425 • Value N/E
26. **San Diego Chargers™**
995QSR5515 • Value N/E
27. **San Francisco 49ers™**
995QSR5522 • Value N/E
28. **Seattle Seahawks™**
995QSR5525 • Value N/E
29. **Tampa Bay Buccaneers™**
995QSR5532 • Value N/E
30. **Washington Redskins™**
995QSR5535 • Value N/E

	NFL Collection	
	Price Paid	Value of My Collection
1.		

General Keepsake

2.		
3.		
4.		
5.		
6.		
7.		
8.		
9.		
10.		

PENCIL TOTALS

1996

Hallmark introduced several ornaments and collectibles commemorating the Centennial Olympic Games in Atlanta, Georgia in 1996. Overall, there were 135 Keepsake ornaments in the collection, as well as 23 Magic, 13 Showcase and 34 Miniature ornaments. See the collectible series section for more 1996 ornaments.

101 Dalmatians
Handcrafted • N/A
1295QXI6544 • **Value $24**

Antlers Aweigh!
Handcrafted • CHAD
995QX5901 • **Value $22**

Apple for Teacher
Handcrafted • AUBE
795QX6121 • **Value $15**

Baby's First Christmas
Handcrafted • SEAL
795QX5761 • **Value $20**

Baby's First Christmas
Handcrafted • CROW
795QX5764 • **Value $20**

Baby's First Christmas
Handcrafted • ANDR
995QX5754 • **Value $22**

Baby's First Christmas
Porcelain • N/A
1095QX5751 • **Value $22**

Baby's First Christmas
Porcelain • VOTR
1895QX5744 • **Value $30**

Baby's Second Christmas
Handcrafted • CROW
795QX5771 • **Value $18**

1 Bounce Pass
Handcrafted • SIED
795QX6031 • **Value $16**

2 Bowl 'em Over
Handcrafted • SIED
795QX6014 • **Value $15**

3 Child Care Giver
Handcrafted • SIED
895QX6071 • **Value $15**

4 Child's Fifth Christmas
Handcrafted • RHOD
695QX5784 • **Value $16**

5 Child's Fourth Christmas
Handcrafted • CROW
795QX5781 • **Value $16**

6 Child's Third Christmas
Handcrafted • CROW
795QX5774 • **Value $16**

7 Christmas Joy
Handcrafted • UNRU
1495QX6241 • **Value $29**

8 Christmas Snowman
Handcrafted • UNRU
995QX6214 • **Value $20**

9 Close-Knit Friends
Handcrafted • BRIC
995QX5874 • **Value $17**

10 Come All Ye Faithful
Handcrafted • CROW
1295QX6244 • **Value $25**

11 Commander William T. Riker™
Handcrafted • RGRS
1495QXI5551 • **Value $25**

12 Dad
Handcrafted • SIED
795QX5831 • **Value $16**

13 Daughter
Handcrafted • PALM
895QX6077 • **Value $18**

14 Esmeralda and Djali
Handcrafted • CROW
1495QXI6351 • **Value $20**

15 Evergreen Santa
Handcrafted • LYLE
2200QX5714 • **Value $40**

16 Fan-tastic Season
Handcrafted • CHAD
995QX5924 • **Value $22**

17 Feliz Navidad
Handcrafted • SICK
995QX6304 • **Value $22**

18 Foghorn Leghorn and Henery Hawk (set/2)
Handcrafted • CHAD
1395QX5444 • **Value $25**

19 Glad Tidings
Handcrafted • LYLE
1495QX6231 • **Value $33**

20 Goal Line Glory (set/2)
Handcrafted • SEAL
1295QX6001 • **Value $25**

1996

GENERAL KEEPSAKE	Price Paid	Value of My Collection
1.		
2.		
3.		
4.		
5.		
6.		
7.		
8.		
9.		
10.		
11.		
12.		
13.		
14.		
15.		
16.		
17.		
18.		
19.		
20.		
PENCIL TOTALS		

(1)

Godchild
Handcrafted • RGRS
895QX5841 • **Value $18**

(2)

Granddaughter
Handcrafted • RGRS
795QX5697 • **Value $17**

(3)

Grandma
Handcrafted • VOTR
895QX5844 • **Value $20**

(4)

Grandpa
Handcrafted • VOTR
895QX5851 • **Value $20**

(5)

Grandson
Handcrafted • RGRS
795QX5699 • **Value $16**

(6)

Growth of a Leader
Ceramic • N/A
995QX5541 • **Value $17**

(7)

Happy Holi-doze
Handcrafted • RHOD
995QX5904 • **Value $23**

(8)

Hearts Full of Love
Handcrafted • RHOD
995QX5814 • **Value $20**

General Keepsake

	Price Paid	Value of My Collection
1.		
2.		
3.		
4.		
5.		
6.		
7.		
8.		
9.		
10.		
11.		
12.		
13.		
14.		
15.		
16.		
17.		
18.		
19.		
20.		

PENCIL TOTALS

(9)

High Style
Handcrafted • CHAD
895QX6064 • **Value $20**

(10)

Hillside Express
Handcrafted • AUBE
1295QX6134 • **Value $27**

(11)

Holiday Haul
Handcrafted • SICK
1495QX6201 • **Value $35**

(12)

Hurrying Downstairs
Handcrafted • FRAN
895QX6074 • **Value $17**

(13)

I Dig Golf
Handcrafted • RHOD
1095QX5891 • **Value $21**

(14)

Invitation to the Games (set/2)
Ceramic • MCGE
1495QXE5511 • **Value $27**

(15)

It's A Wonderful Life™
Handcrafted • CROW
1495QXI6531 • **Value $34**

(16)

IZZY™ – The Mascot
Handcrafted • PALM
995QXE5724 • **Value $18**

(17)

Jackpot Jingle
Handcrafted • SIED
995QX5911 • **Value $19**

(18)

Jolly Wolly Ark
Handcrafted • CROW
1295QX6221 • **Value $26**

(19)

Kindly Shepherd
Handcrafted • ANDR
1295QX6274 • **Value $28**

(20)

Laverne, Victor and Hugo
Handcrafted • CROW
1295QXI6354 • **Value $19**

(1)  **Lighting the Way** *Handcrafted* • CHAD 1295QX6124 • **Value $25**	(2)  **A Little Song and Dance** *Handcrafted* • CROW 995QX6211 • **Value $17**	(3) **Little Spooners** *Handcrafted* • UNRU 1295QX5504 • **Value $23**	(4) **Madonna and Child** *Tin* • SICK 1295QX6324 • **Value $21**

(5) **Making His Rounds** *Handcrafted* • FRAN 1495QX6271 • **Value $28**	(6) **Marvin the Martian** *Handcrafted* • CHAD 1095QX5451 • **Value $23**	(7) **Matchless Memories** *Handcrafted* • CROW 995QX6061 • **Value $18**	(8) **Maxine** *Handcrafted* • PIKE 995QX6224 • **Value $28**

(9) **Merry Carpoolers** *Handcrafted* • CROW 1495QX5884 • **Value $30**	(10) **Mom** *Handcrafted* • LYLE 795QX5824 • **Value $17**	(11) **Mom and Dad** *Handcrafted* • RHOD 995QX5821 • **Value $18**

	Price Paid	Value of My Collection
1.		
2.		
3.		
4.		
5.		
6.		
7.		
8.		
9.		
10.		
11.		
12.		
13.		
14.		
15.		
16.		
17.		
18.		
19.		
20.		
PENCIL TOTALS		

(12) 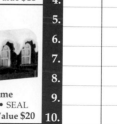 **Mom-to-Be** *Handcrafted* • UNRU 795QX5791 • **Value $16**	(13) **Mr. Spock** *Handcrafted* • RGRS 1495QXI5544 • **Value $30**	(14) **New Home** *Handcrafted* • SEAL 895QX5881 • **Value $20**

(15) **Olive Oyl and Swee' Pea** *Handcrafted* • CHAD 1095QX5481 • **Value $25**	(16) 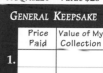 **Olympic Triumph** *Handcrafted* • SEAL 1095QXE5731 • **Value $21**	(17) **On My Way** *Handcrafted* • TAGU 795QX5861 • **Value $13**

(18) **Our Christmas Together** *Handcrafted* • PALM 1895QX5794 • **Value $35**	(19) **Our Christmas Together Photo Holder** *Handcrafted* • CROW 895QX5804 • **Value $17**	(20)  **Our First Christmas Together** *Acrylic* • VOTR 695QX3051 • **Value $16**

1996

①
Our First Christmas
Together
Handcrafted • PALM
995QX5811 • **Value $20**

②
Our First Christmas
Together Collector's
Plate
Porcelain • N/A
1095QX5801 • **Value $22**

③
Parade of Nations
Porcelain • N/A
1095QXE5741 • **Value $22**

④
Peppermint Surprise
Handcrafted • PIKE
795QX6234 • **Value $17**

⑤
Percy the Small Engine
– No. 6
Handcrafted • RHOD
995QX6314 • **Value $20**

⑥
PEZ® Snowman
Handcrafted • N/A
795QX6534 • **Value $16**

⑦
Polar Cycle
Handcrafted • UNRU
1295QX6034 • **Value $24**

⑧
Prayer for Peace
Handcrafted • LYLE
795QX6261 • **Value $16**

GENERAL KEEPSAKE

	Price Paid	Value of My Collection
1.		
2.		
3.		
4.		
5.		
6.		
7.		
8.		
9.		
10.		
11.		
12.		
13.		
14.		
15.		
16.		
17.		
18.		
19.		

⑨
Precious Child
Handcrafted • VOTR
895QX6251 • **Value $16**

⑩
Pup-Tenting
Handcrafted • PALM
795QX6011 • **Value $17**

⑪
Quasimodo
Handcrafted • CROW
995QXI6341 • **Value $15**

⑫
Regal Cardinal
Handcrafted • FRAN
995QX6204 • **Value $22**

⑬
Sew Sweet
Handcrafted • AUBE
895QX5921 • **Value $19**

⑭
Sister to Sister
Handcrafted • LYLE
995QX5834 • **Value $20**

⑮
Son
Handcrafted • PALM
895QX6079 • **Value $17**

⑯
Special Dog
Handcrafted • TAGU
795QX5864 • **Value $23**

⑰
SPIDER-MAN™
Handcrafted • CHAD
1295QX5757 • **Value $26**

⑱
Star of the Show
Handcrafted • AUBE
895QX6004 • **Value $18**

⑲
Tamika
Handcrafted • BRIC
795QX6301 • **Value $15**

PENCIL TOTALS

1

Tender Lovin' Care
Handcrafted • SEAL
795QX6114 • **Value $16**

2

Thank You, Santa
Handcrafted • BRIC
795QX5854 • **Value $15**

3

This Big!
Handcrafted • SEAL
995QX5914 • **Value $18**

4

Time for a Treat
Handcrafted • SICK
1195QX5464 • **Value $24**

5

**Tonka® Mighty
Dump Truck**
Die-Cast Metal • N/A
1395QX6321 • **Value $32**

6

A Tree for SNOOPY
Handcrafted • SIED
895QX5507 • **Value $17**

7

Welcome Guest
Handcrafted • UNRU
1495QX5394 • **Value $28**

8

Welcome Him
Handcrafted • TAGU
895QX6264 • **Value $17**

1996

9

**Winnie the Pooh
and Piglet**
Handcrafted • SIED
1295QX5454 • **Value $34**

10

Witch of the West
Handcrafted • LYLE
1395QX5554 • **Value $30**

11

WONDER WOMAN™
Handcrafted • RGRS
1295QX5941 • **Value $27**

GENERAL KEEPSAKE

	Price Paid	Value of My Collection
1.		
2.		
3.		
4.		
5.		
6.		
7.		
8.		
9.		
10.		
11.		
12.		
13.		
14.		
15.		

12

Woodland Santa
Pressed Tin • SICK
1295QX6131 • **Value $25**

13

**Yogi Bear™ and
Boo Boo™**
Handcrafted • RGRS
1295QX5521 • **Value $27**

14

Yuletide Cheer
Handcrafted • VOTR
795QX6054 • **Value $16**

15

Ziggy®
Handcrafted • CHAD
995QX6524 • **Value $25**

16

Baby's First Christmas
Handcrafted • FRAN
2200QLX7404 • **Value $45**

17

Chicken Coop Chorus
Handcrafted • CROW
2450QLX7491 • **Value $50**

GENERAL MAGIC

16.		
17.		
18.		
19.		
20.		

18

Emerald City
Handcrafted • CROW
3200QLX7454 • **Value $66**

19

Father Time
Handcrafted • CHAD
2450QLX7391 • **Value $53**

20

THE JETSONS™
Handcrafted • CROW
2800QLX7411 • **Value $57**

PENCIL TOTALS

(1) Jukebox Party
Handcrafted • PALM
2450QLX7339 • **Value $59**

(2) Let Us Adore Him
Handcrafted • LYLE
1650QLX7381 • **Value $35**

(3) Lighting the Flame
Handcrafted • UNRU
2800QXE7444 • **Value $51**

(4) Millennium Falcon™
Handcrafted • N/A
2400QLX7474 • **Value $48**

(5) North Pole Volunteers
Handcrafted • SEAL
4200QLX7471 • **Value $82**

(6) Over the Rooftops
Handcrafted • SEAL
1450QLX7374 • **Value $29**

(7) PEANUTS®
Handcrafted • CHAD
1850QLX7394 • **Value $43**

(8) Pinball Wonder
Handcrafted • CROW
2800QLX7451 • **Value $56**

(9) Sharing a Soda
Handcrafted • CROW
2450QLX7424 • **Value $48**

(10) Slippery Day
Handcrafted • SIED
2450QLX7414 • **Value $52**

(11) STAR TREK®, 30 Years
(set/2, w/display base)
Handcrafted • NORT/RHOD
4500QXI7534 • **Value $83**

(12) The Statue of Liberty
Handcrafted • SEAL
2450QLX7421 • **Value $47**

(13) Treasured Memories
Handcrafted • SICK
1850QLX7384 • **Value $39**

(14) U.S.S. Voyager™
Handcrafted • NORT
2400QXI7544 • **Value $50**

(15) Video Party
Handcrafted • SIED
2800QLX7431 • **Value $54**

(16) Carmen
Cookie Jar Friends
Porcelain • RGRS
1595QK1164 • **Value $27**

(17) Clyde
Cookie Jar Friends
Porcelain • AUBE
1595QK1161 • **Value $20**

(18) Caroling Angel
Folk Art Americana
Handcrafted/Copper • SICK
1695QK1134 • **Value $30**

(19) Mrs. Claus
Folk Art Americana
Handcrafted/Copper • SICK
1895QK1204 • **Value $32**

(20) Santa's Gifts
Folk Art Americana
Handcrafted/Copper • SICK
1895QK1124 • **Value $42**

GENERAL MAGIC

	Price Paid	Value of My Collection
1.		
2.		
3.		
4.		
5.		
6.		
7.		
8.		
9.		
10.		
11.		
12.		
13.		
14.		
15.		

GENERAL SHOWCASE

16.		
17.		
18.		
19.		
20.		

PENCIL TOTALS

VALUE GUIDE — HALLMARK KEEPSAKE ORNAMENTS

Balthasar (Frankincense) *Magi Bells* *Porcelain* • VOTR 1395QK1174 • **Value $24**	**Caspar (Myrrh)** *Magi Bells* *Porcelain* • VOTR 1395QK1184 • **Value $24**	**Melchoir (Gold)** *Magi Bells* *Porcelain* • VOTR 1395QK1181 • **Value $24**	**The Birds' Christmas Tree** *Nature's Sketchbook* *Handcrafted* • UNRU 1895QK1114 • **Value $30**
Christmas Bunny *Nature's Sketchbook* *Handcrafted* • FRAN 1895QK1104 • **Value $34**	**The Holly Basket** *Nature's Sketchbook* *Handcrafted* • LYLE 1895QK1094 • **Value $28**	**Madonna and Child** *Sacred Masterworks* *Handcrafted* • SICK 1595QK1144 • **Value $27**	**Praying Madonna** *Sacred Masterworks* *Handcrafted* • SICK 1595QK1154 • **Value $27**

1996

 **African Elephants** *Handcrafted* • SICK 575QXM4224 • **Value $16**	**Baby Sylvester** *Handcrafted* • PALM 575QXM4154 • **Value $17**	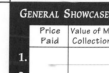 **Baby Tweety** *Handcrafted* • PALM 575QXM4014 • **Value $26**	**GENERAL SHOWCASE**

GENERAL SHOWCASE

	Price Paid	Value of My Collection
1.		
2.		
3.		
4.		
5.		
6.		
7.		
8.		

A Child's Gifts *Handcrafted* • ANDR 675QXM4234 • **Value $13**	**Christmas Bear** *Handcrafted* • SEAL 475QXM4241 • **Value $13**	 **Cloisonné Medallion** *Cloisonné* • MCGE 975QXE4041 • **Value $19**

GENERAL MINIATURE

9.		
10.		

Cool Delivery Coca-Cola® *Handcrafted* • PIKE 575QXM4021 • **Value $14**	**GONE WITH THE WIND™ (set/3)** *Handcrafted* • ANDR 1995QXM4211 • **Value $36**	**Hattie Chapeau** *Handcrafted* • RHOD 475QXM4251 • **Value $10**

11.	
12.	
13.	
14.	
15.	
16.	

Joyous Angel *Handcrafted* • ANDR 475QXM4231 • **Value $10**	**Long Winter's Nap** *Handcrafted* • ANDR 575QXM4244 • **Value $12**	 **Message for Santa** *Handcrafted* • SEAL 675QXM4254 • **Value $13**

17.	
18.	
19.	
20.	

PENCIL TOTAL

Value Guide — Hallmark Keepsake Ornaments

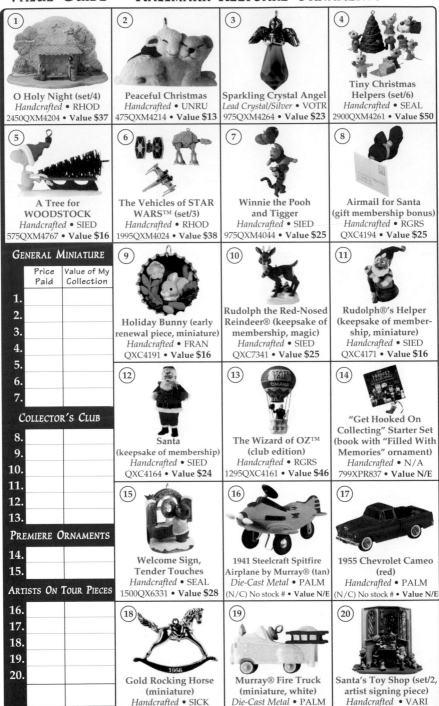

1
O Holy Night (set/4)
Handcrafted • RHOD
2450QXM4204 • **Value $37**

2
Peaceful Christmas
Handcrafted • UNRU
475QXM4214 • **Value $13**

3
Sparkling Crystal Angel
Lead Crystal/Silver • VOTR
975QXM4264 • **Value $23**

4
Tiny Christmas Helpers (set/6)
Handcrafted • SEAL
2900QXM4261 • **Value $50**

5
A Tree for WOODSTOCK
Handcrafted • SIED
575QXM4767 • **Value $16**

6
The Vehicles of STAR WARS™ (set/3)
Handcrafted • RHOD
1995QXM4024 • **Value $38**

7
Winnie the Pooh and Tigger
Handcrafted • SIED
975QXM4044 • **Value $25**

8
Airmail for Santa (gift membership bonus)
Handcrafted • RGRS
QXC4194 • **Value $25**

9
Holiday Bunny (early renewal piece, miniature)
Handcrafted • FRAN
QXC4191 • **Value $16**

10
Rudolph the Red-Nosed Reindeer® (keepsake of membership, magic)
Handcrafted • SIED
QXC7341 • **Value $25**

11
Rudolph®'s Helper (keepsake of membership, miniature)
Handcrafted • SIED
QXC4171 • **Value $16**

12
Santa (keepsake of membership)
Handcrafted • SIED
QXC4164 • **Value $24**

13
The Wizard of OZ™ (club edition)
Handcrafted • RGRS
1295QXC4161 • **Value $46**

14
"Get Hooked On Collecting" Starter Set (book with "Filled With Memories" ornament)
Handcrafted • N/A
799XPR837 • **Value N/E**

15
Welcome Sign, Tender Touches
Handcrafted • SEAL
1500QX6331 • **Value $28**

16
1941 Steelcraft Spitfire Airplane by Murray® (tan)
Die-Cast Metal • PALM
(N/C) No stock # • **Value N/E**

17
1955 Chevrolet Cameo (red)
Handcrafted • PALM
(N/C) No stock # • **Value N/E**

18
Gold Rocking Horse (miniature)
Handcrafted • SICK
($12.95) No stock # • **Value $43**

19
Murray® Fire Truck (miniature, white)
Die-Cast Metal • PALM
(N/C) No stock # • **Value N/E**

20
Santa's Toy Shop (set/2, artist signing piece)
Handcrafted • VARI
6000QXC4201 • **Value $120**

General Miniature

	Price Paid	Value of My Collection
1.		
2.		
3.		
4.		
5.		
6.		
7.		

Collector's Club

8.		
9.		
10.		
11.		
12.		
13.		

Premiere Ornaments

14.		
15.		

Artists On Tour Pieces

16.		
17.		
18.		
19.		
20.		

PENCIL TOTALS

1
Toy Shop Santa
Handcrafted • UNRU
($14.95) No stock # • **Value $34**

2
BARBIE™ Lapel Pin
(re-issued in 1997)
Handcrafted • N/A
495XLP3544 • **Value $4.95**

3
Holiday BARBIE™
Stocking Hanger
(re-issued in 1997)
Handcrafted • N/A
1995XSH3101 • **Value $35**

4
Yuletide Romance ™
BARBIE® Doll (3rd &
final in series)
Vinyl • N/A
5000QHX3401 • **Value $100**

5
Reindeer Rooters
Handcrafted • CROW
(N/C) No stock # • **Value N/E**

6
Golden Age
Batman and Robin™
"The Dynamic Duo™"
Handcrafted • UNRU
7000QHF3103 • **Value N/E**

7
Golden Age
Superman™ "Man of
Steel™" (LE-14,500)
Handcrafted • N/A
8000QHF3101 • **Value N/E**

8
Golden Age Wonder
Woman™ "Champion
of Freedom"
Handcrafted • RGRS
3500QHF3107 • **Value N/E**

9
Modern Era Batman™
"Guardian of Gotham
City™"
Handcrafted • CHAD
5500QHF3104 • **Value N/E**

10
Modern Era Robin™
"World's Bravest
Teenager"
Handcrafted • CHAD
4000QHF3105 • **Value N/E**

11
Modern Era
Superman™ "In A
Single Bound"
Handcrafted • N/A
6000QHF3102 • **Value N/E**

12
Modern Era Wonder
Woman™ "Warrior of
Strength and Wisdom"
Handcrafted • RGRS
3500QHF3106 • **Value N/E**

13
NFL COLLECTION
(14 assorted)
Glass • N/A

1. **Buffalo Bills™**
   595BIL2035 • **Value $10**
2. **Carolina Panthers™**
   (re-issued from 1995)
   595PNA2035 • **Value $10**
3. **Chicago Bears™**
   (re-issued from 1995)
   595BRS2035 • **Value $10**
4. **Dallas Cowboys™**
   (re-issued from 1995)
   595COW2035 • **Value $10**
5. **Green Bay Packers™**
   595PKR2035 • **Value $10**
6. **Kansas City Chiefs™**
   (re-issued from 1995)
   595CHF2035 • **Value $10**
7. **Los Angeles Raiders™**
   (re-issued from 1995)
   595RDR2035 • **Value $10**
8. **Minnesota Vikings™**
   (re-issued from 1995)
   595VIK2035 • **Value $10**
9. **New England Patriots™**
   (re-issued from 1995)
   595NEP2035 • **Value $10**
10. **Philadelphia Eagles™**
    (re-issued from 1995)
    595EAG2035 • **Value $10**
11. **Pittsburgh Steelers™**
    595PIT2035 • **Value $10**
12. **St. Louis Rams™**
    595RAM2035 • **Value $10**
13. **San Francisco 49ers™**
    (re-issued from 1995)
    595FOR2035 • **Value $10**
14. **Washington Redskins™**
    (re-issued from 1995)
    595RSK2035 • **Value $10**

14
NFL COLLECTION
(30 assorted)
Handcrafted • UNRU

1. **Arizona Cardinals™**
   995QSR6484 • **Value $15**
2. **Atlanta Falcons™**
   995QSR6364 • **Value $15**
3. **Browns™**
   995QSR6391 • **Value $15**
4. **Buffalo Bills™**
   995QSR6371 • **Value $15**
5. **Carolina Panthers™**
   995QSR6374 • **Value $15**
6. **Chicago Bears™**
   995QSR6381 • **Value $15**
7. **Cincinnati Bengals™**
   995QSR6384 • **Value $15**
8. **Dallas Cowboys™**
   995QSR6394 • **Value $15**
9. **Denver Broncos™**
   995QSR6411 • **Value $15**
10. **Detroit Lions™**
    995QSR6414 • **Value $15**
11. **Green Bay Packers™**
    995QSR6421 • **Value $15**
12. **Indianapolis Colts™**
    995QSR6431 • **Value $15**

1996

ARTISTS ON TOUR PIECES

	Price Paid	Value of My Collection
1.		

BARBIE™ COLLECTIBLES

2.		
3.		
4.		

CLUB TOUR ORNAMENT

5.		

D.C. SUPER HEROES FIGURINES

6.		
7.		
8.		
9.		
10.		
11.		
12.		

NFL COLLECTION

13.		
14.		

PENCIL TOTALS

13. Jacksonville Jaguars™
995QSR6434 • Value **$15**
14. Kansas City Chiefs™
995QSR6361 • Value **$15**
15. Miami Dolphins™
995QSR6451 • Value **$15**
16. Minnesota Vikings™
995QSR6454 • Value **$15**
17. New England Patriots™
995QSR6461 • Value **$15**
18. New Orleans Saints™
995QSR6464 • Value **$15**

19. New York Giants™
995QSR6471 • Value **$15**
20. New York Jets™
995QSR6474 • Value **$15**
21. Oakland Raiders™
995QSR6441 • Value **$15**
22. Oilers™
995QSR6424 • Value **$15**
23. Philadelphia Eagles™
995QSR6481 • Value **$15**
24. Pittsburgh Steelers™
995QSR6491 • Value **$15**

25. St. Louis Rams™
995QSR6444 • Value **$15**
26. San Diego Chargers™
995QSR6494 • Value **$15**
27. San Francisco 49ers™
995QSR6501 • Value **$15**
28. Seattle Seahawks™
995QSR6504 • Value **$15**
29. Tampa Bay Buccaneers™
995QSR6511 • Value **$15**
30. Washington Redskins™
995QSR6514 • Value **$15**

(1)

Gymnastics Figurine
Handcrafted • LYLE
1750QHC8204 • **Value N/E**

(2)

**Olympic Triumph
Figurine (LE-24,500)**
Handcrafted • UNRU
5000QHC8191 • **Value N/E**

(3)

Parade of Nations Plate
Porcelain • N/A
3000QHC8194 • **Value N/E**

(4)

Swimming Figurine
Handcrafted • CHAD
1750QHC8211 • **Value N/E**

(5)

**Track and Field
Figurine**
Handcrafted • N/A
1750QHC8201 • **Value N/E**

OLYMPIC COLLECTIBLES

	Price Paid	Value of My Collection
1.		
2.		
3.		
4.		
5.		

GENERAL KEEPSAKE

6.		
7.		
8.		
9.		
10.		
11.		
12.		
13.		
14.		

PENCIL TOTALS

1995

More great BARBIE™, STAR TREK™ and sports ornaments were released in 1995, as well as a record number of Showcase ornaments. In the 1995 line, there were 146 Keepsake, 20 Magic, 20 Showcase and 36 Miniature ornaments. See the collectible series section for more 1995 ornaments.

(6)

Acorn 500
Handcrafted • SIED
1095QX5929 • **Value $23**

(7)

Across the Miles
Handcrafted • FRAN
895QX5847 • **Value $20**

(8)

Air Express
Handcrafted • SEAL
795QX5977 • **Value $19**

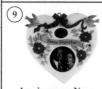
(9)

Anniversary Year
Handcrafted • UNRU
895QX5819 • **Value $17**

(10)

Baby's First Christmas
Handcrafted • VOTR
795QX5549 • **Value $18**

(11)

Baby's First Christmas
Handcrafted • CROW
795QX5559 • **Value $21**

(12)

Baby's First Christmas
Handcrafted • ANDR
995QX5557 • **Value $20**

(13)

Baby's First Christmas
Handcrafted • ANDR
1895QX5547 • **Value $50**

(14)

**Baby's First Christmas
– Baby Boy**
Glass • N/A
500QX2319 • **Value $16**

(1) 	(2)	(3)	(4)
Baby's First Christmas – Baby Girl *Glass* • N/A 500QX2317 • **Value $16**	**Baby's Second Christmas** *Handcrafted* • CROW 795QX5567 • **Value $22**	**Barrel-Back Rider** *Handcrafted* • FRAN 995QX5189 • **Value $27**	**Batmobile** *Handcrafted* • PALM 1495QX5739 • **Value $32**
(5)	(6)	(7) 	(8)
Betty and Wilma *Handcrafted* • RHOD 1495QX5417 • **Value $27**	**Beverly and Teddy** *Handcrafted* • UNRU 2175QX5259 • **Value $38**	**Bingo Bear** *Handcrafted* • VOTR 795QX5919 • **Value $19**	**Bobbin' Along** *Handcrafted* • CROW 895QX5879 • **Value $38**
(9) 	(10)	(11)	
Brother *Handcrafted* • LYLE 695QX5679 • **Value $14**	**Bugs Bunny** *Handcrafted* • CHAD 895QX5019 • **Value $22**	**Captain James T. Kirk** *Handcrafted* • RGRS 1395QXI5539 • **Value $25**	

1995

GENERAL KEEPSAKE

	Price Paid	Value of My Collection
1.		
2.		
3.		
4.		
5.		
6.		
7.		
8.		
9.		
10.		
11.		
12.		
13.		
14.		
15.		
16.		
17.		
18.		
19.		
20.		

(12)	(13)	(14) 
Captain Jean-Luc Picard *Handcrafted* • RGRS 1395QXI5737 • **Value $25**	**Captain John Smith and Meeko** *Handcrafted* • CROW 1295QXI6169 • **Value $22**	**Catch the Spirit** *Handcrafted* • SIED 795QX5899 • **Value $20**
(15)	(16) 	(17) 
Child's Fifth Christmas *Handcrafted* • RHOD 695QX5637 • **Value $17**	**Child's Fourth Christmas** *Handcrafted* • FRAN 695QX5629 • **Value $19**	**Child's Third Christmas** *Handcrafted* • CROW 795QX5627 • **Value $20**
(18)	(19)	(20)
Christmas Fever *Handcrafted* • AUBE 795QX5967 • **Value $19**	**Christmas Morning** *Handcrafted* • FRAN 1095QX5997 • **Value $17**	**Christmas Patrol** *Handcrafted* • ANDR 795QX5959 • **Value $18**

PENCIL TOTALS

(1) Colorful World	(2) Cows of Bali	(3) Dad	(4) Dad-to-Be
Handcrafted • CROW	Handcrafted • ANDR	Handcrafted • SIED	Handcrafted • RHOD
1095QX5519 • Value $26	895QX5999 • Value $19	795QX5649 • Value $17	795QX5667 • Value $14

(5) Daughter	(6) Delivering Kisses	(7) Dream On	(8) Dudley the Dragon
Handcrafted • PALM	Handcrafted • SICK	Handcrafted • FRAN	Handcrafted • PIKE
695QX5677 • Value $20	1095QX4107 • Value $26	1095QX6007 • Value $22	1095QX6209 • Value $23

General Keepsake

	Price Paid	Value of My Collection
1.		
2.		
3.		
4.		
5.		
6.		
7.		
8.		
9.		
10.		
11.		
12.		
13.		
14.		
15.		
16.		
17.		
18.		
19.		
20.		

(9) Faithful Fan	(10) Feliz Navidad	(11) For My Grandma
Handcrafted • SIED	Handcrafted • RHOD	Handcrafted • PALM
895QX5897 • Value $18	795QX5869 • Value $20	695QX5729 • Value $14

(12) Forever Friends Bear	(13) Friendly Boost	(14) GARFIELD®
Handcrafted • BRWN	Handcrafted • PALM	Handcrafted • N/A
895QX5258 • Value $23	895QX5827 • Value $23	1095QX5007 • Value $26

(15) Glinda, Witch of the North	(16) Godchild	(17) Godparent
Handcrafted • LYLE	Handcrafted/Brass • PALM	Glass • VOTR
1395QX5749 • Value $34	795QX5707 • Value $22	500QX2417 • Value $11

(18) Gopher Fun	(19) Grandchild's First Christmas	(20) Granddaughter
Handcrafted • SIED	Handcrafted • FRAN	Handcrafted • RGRS
995QX5887 • Value $23	795QX5777 • Value $15	695QX5779 • Value $16

PENCIL TOTALS

1. Grandmother
Handcrafted • ANDR
795QX5767 • **Value $23**

2. Grandpa
Handcrafted • CROW
895QX5769 • **Value $17**

3. Grandparents
Glass • LYLE
500QX2419 • **Value $12**

4. Grandson
Handcrafted • RGRS
695QX5787 • **Value $16**

5. Happy Wrappers (set/2)
Handcrafted • CROW
1095QX6037 • **Value $22**

6. Heaven's Gift (set/2)
Handcrafted • ANDR
2000QX6057 • **Value $41**

7. Hockey Pup
Handcrafted • CROW
995QX5917 • **Value $27**

8. Important Memo
Handcrafted • SICK
895QX5947 • **Value $19**

9. In a Heartbeat
Handcrafted • ANDR
895QX5817 • **Value $21**

10. In Time With Christmas
Handcrafted • CROW
1295QX6049 • **Value $28**

11. Joy to the World
Handcrafted • ANDR
895QX5867 • **Value $21**

12. LEGO® Fireplace With Santa
Handcrafted • CROW
1095QX4769 • **Value $25**

13. Lou Rankin Bear
Handcrafted • SIED
995QX4069 • **Value $23**

14. The Magic School Bus™
Handcrafted • RHOD
1095QX5849 • **Value $22**

15. Mary Engelbreit
Glass • N/A
500QX2409 • **Value $16**

16. Merry RV
Handcrafted • PALM
1295QX6027 • **Value $28**

17. Mom
Handcrafted • SIED
795QX5647 • **Value $17**

18. Mom and Dad
Handcrafted • RGRS
995QX5657 • **Value $25**

19. Mom-to-Be
Handcrafted • RHOD
795QX5659 • **Value $15**

20. Muletide Greetings
Handcrafted • CHAD
795QX6009 • **Value $17**

1995

General Keepsake

	Price Paid	Value of My Collection
1.		
2.		
3.		
4.		
5.		
6.		
7.		
8.		
9.		
10.		
11.		
12.		
13.		
14.		
15.		
16.		
17.		
18.		
19.		
20.		
PENCIL TOTALS		

1 New Home
Handcrafted • ANDR
895QX5839 • **Value $17**

2 North Pole 911
Handcrafted • SEAL
1095QX5957 • **Value $24**

3 Number One Teacher
Handcrafted • SEAL
795QX5949 • **Value $17**

4 The Olympic Spirit
Centennial Games
Atlanta 1996
Acrylic • N/A
795QX3169 • **Value $19**

5 On the Ice
Handcrafted • CROW
795QX6047 • **Value $23**

6 Our Christmas Together
Handcrafted • LYLE
995QX5809 • **Value $19**

7 Our Family
Handcrafted • CHAD
795QX5709 • **Value $17**

8 Our First Christmas
Together
Acrylic • LYLE
695QX3177 • **Value $19**

9 Our First Christmas
Together
Handcrafted • SIED
895QX5799 • **Value $21**

10 Our First Christmas
Together
Handcrafted • SEAL
895QX5807 • **Value $19**

11 Our First Christmas
Handcrafted • LYLE
1695QX5797 • **Value $32**

12 Our Little Blessings
Handcrafted • CROW
1295QX5209 • **Value $26**

13 Packed With Memories
Handcrafted • SEAL
795QX5639 • **Value $18**

14 Percy, Flit and Meeko
Handcrafted • CROW
995QXI6179 • **Value $20**

15 Perfect Balance
Handcrafted • SIED
795QX5927 • **Value $17**

16 PEZ® Santa
Handcrafted • FRAN
795QX5267 • **Value $20**

17 Pocahontas
Handcrafted • CROW
1295QXI6177 • **Value $21**

18 Pocahontas and Captain
John Smith
Handcrafted • CROW
1495QXI6197 • **Value $25**

19 Polar Coaster
Handcrafted • CROW
895QX6117 • **Value $28**

20 Popeye®
Handcrafted • CHAD
1095QX5257 • **Value $30**

General Keepsake

	Price Paid	Value of My Collection
1.		
2.		
3.		
4.		
5.		
6.		
7.		
8.		
9.		
10.		
11.		
12.		
13.		
14.		
15.		
16.		
17.		
18.		
19.		
20.		

PENCIL TOTALS

1
Refreshing Gift
Handcrafted • UNRU
1495QX4067 • **Value $31**

2
Rejoice!
Handcrafted • LYLE
1095QX5987 • **Value $24**

3
Roller Whiz
Handcrafted • SEAL
795QX5937 • **Value $19**

4
Santa In Paris
Handcrafted • SICK
895QX5877 • **Value $28**

5
Santa's Serenade
Handcrafted • CROW
895QX6017 • **Value $19**

6
Santa's Visitors
Glass • N/A
500QX2407 • **Value $18**

7
Simba, Pumbaa and Timon
Handcrafted • CROW
1295QX6159 • **Value $16**

8
Sister
Handcrafted • LYLE
695QX5687 • **Value $13**

9
Sister to Sister
Handcrafted • VOTR
895QX5689 • **Value $17**

10
Ski Hound
Handcrafted • RHOD
895QX5909 • **Value $18**

11
Son
Handcrafted • PALM
695QX5669 • **Value $18**

12
Special Cat
Handcrafted • CHAD
795QX5717 • **Value $16**

13
Special Dog
Handcrafted • CHAD
795QX5719 • **Value $16**

14
Surfin' Santa
Handcrafted • CROW
995QX6019 • **Value $23**

15
Sylvester and Tweety (set/2)
Handcrafted • CHAD
1395QX5017 • **Value $27**

16
Takin' a Hike
Handcrafted • FRAN
795QX6029 • **Value $19**

17
Tennis, Anyone?
Handcrafted • AUBE
795QX5907 • **Value $19**

18
Thomas the Tank Engine – No. 1
Handcrafted • RHOD
995QX5857 • **Value $32**

19
Three Wishes
Handcrafted • ANDR
795QX5979 • **Value $20**

20
Two for Tea
Handcrafted • JLEE
995QX5829 • **Value $34**

1995

GENERAL KEEPSAKE

	Price Paid	Value of My Collection
1.		
2.		
3.		
4.		
5.		
6.		
7.		
8.		
9.		
10.		
11.		
12.		
13.		
14.		
15.		
16.		
17.		
18.		
19.		
20.		
PENCIL TOTALS		

1995 Collection   111

VALUE GUIDE — HALLMARK KEEPSAKE ORNAMENTS

(1)

Vera the Mouse
Porcelain • N/A
895QX5537 • **Value $18**

(2)

Waiting Up for Santa
Handcrafted • PALM
895QX6106 • **Value $19**

(3)

Water Sports (set/2)
Handcrafted • SIED
1495QX6039 • **Value $33**

(4)

Wheel of Fortune®
Handcrafted • SICK
1295QX6187 • **Value $28**

(5)

Winnie the Pooh and Tigger
Handcrafted • SIED
1295QX5009 • **Value $32**

(6)

The Winning Play
Handcrafted • SIED
795QX5889 • **Value $24**

(7)

Baby's First Christmas
Handcrafted • CROW
2200QLX7317 • **Value $45**

(8)

Coming to See Santa
Handcrafted • PALM
3200QLX7369 • **Value $63**

	Price Paid	Value of My Collection
GENERAL KEEPSAKE		
1.		
2.		
3.		
4.		
5.		
6.		
GENERAL MAGIC		
7.		
8.		
9.		
10.		
11.		
12.		
13.		
14.		
15.		
16.		
17.		
18.		
19.		
20.		
PENCIL TOTALS		

(9)

Fred and Dino
Handcrafted • RHOD
2800QLX7289 • **Value $60**

(10)

Friends Share Fun
Handcrafted • RGRS
1650QLX7349 • **Value $36**

(11)

Goody Gumballs!
Handcrafted • SIED
1250QLX7367 • **Value $34**

(12)

Headin' Home
Handcrafted • JLEE
2200QLX7327 • **Value $50**

(13)

Holiday Swim
Handcrafted • RGRS
1850QLX7319 • **Value $39**

(14)

Jumping for Joy
Handcrafted • FRAN
2800QLX7347 • **Value $58**

(15)

My First HOT WHEELS™
Handcrafted • CROW
2800QLX7279 • **Value $48**

(16)

Romulan Warbird™
Handcrafted • NORT
2400QXI7267 • **Value $40**

(17)

Santa's Diner
Handcrafted • VOTR
2450QLX7337 • **Value $34**

(18)

Space Shuttle
Handcrafted • CROW
2450QLX7396 • **Value $40**

(19)

Superman™
Handcrafted • CHAD
2800QLX7309 • **Value $53**

(20)

Victorian Toy Box
Handcrafted • LYLE
4200QLX7357 • **Value $61**

(1)

Wee Little Christmas
Handcrafted • CROW
2200QLX7329 • **Value $43**

(2)

Winnie the Pooh Too Much Hunny
Handcrafted • SIED
2450QLX7297 • **Value $50**

(3)

Angel of Light
All Is Bright
Handcrafted • ANDR
1195QK1159 • **Value $24**

(4)

Gentle Lullaby
All Is Bright
Handcrafted • ANDR
1195QK1157 • **Value $24**

(5)

Carole
Angel Bells
Porcelain • VOTR
1295QK1147 • **Value $25**

(6)

Joy
Angel Bells
Porcelain • VOTR
1295QK1137 • **Value $28**

(7)

Noelle
Angel Bells
Porcelain • VOTR
1295QK1139 • **Value $25**

(8)

Fetching the Firewood
Folk Art Americana
Handcrafted • SICK
1595QK1057 • **Value $36**

(9)

Fishing Party
Folk Art Americana
Handcrafted • SICK
1595QK1039 • **Value $37**

(10)

Guiding Santa
Folk Art Americana
Handcrafted • SICK
1895QK1037 • **Value $53**

(11)

Learning to Skate
Folk Art Americana
Handcrafted • SICK
1495QK1047 • **Value $40**

(12)

Away in a Manger
Holiday Enchantment
Porcelain • N/A
1395QK1097 • **Value $27**

(13)

Following the Star
Holiday Enchantment
Porcelain • VOTR
1395QK1099 • **Value $27**

(14)

Cozy Cottage Teapot
Invitation To Tea
Handcrafted • ANDR
1595QK1127 • **Value $30**

(15)

European Castle Teapot
Invitation To Tea
Handcrafted • ANDR
1595QK1129 • **Value $30**

(16)

Victorian Home Teapot
Invitation To Tea
Handcrafted • ANDR
1595QK1119 • **Value $37**

(17)

Backyard Orchard
Nature's Sketchbook
Handcrafted • FRAN
1895QK1069 • **Value $33**

(18)

Christmas Cardinal
Nature's Sketchbook
Handcrafted • LYLE
1895QK1077 • **Value $42**

(19)

Raising a Family
Nature's Sketchbook
Handcrafted • LYLE
1895QK1067 • **Value $30**

(20)

Violets and Butterflies
Nature's Sketchbook
Handcrafted • LYLE
1695QK1079 • **Value $32**

1995

GENERAL MAGIC

	Price Paid	Value of My Collection
1.		
2.		

GENERAL SHOWCASE

3.		
4.		
5.		
6.		
7.		
8.		
9.		
10.		
11.		
12.		
13.		
14.		
15.		
16.		
17.		
18.		
19.		
20.		
PENCIL TOTALS		

1
Jolly Santa
Symbols Of Christmas
Handcrafted • ANDR
1595QK1087 • **Value $32**

2
Sweet Song
Symbols Of Christmas
Handcrafted • ANDR
1595QK1089 • **Value $29**

3
Baby's First Christmas
Handcrafted • SEAL
475QXM4027 • **Value $13**

4
Calamity Coyote
Handcrafted • RGRS
675QXM4467 • **Value $16**

5
Christmas Wishes
Handcrafted • SEAL
375QXM4087 • **Value $15**

6
Cloisonné Partridge
Cloisonné • VOTR
975QXM4017 • **Value $19**

7
Downhill Double
Handcrafted • PALM
475QXM4837 • **Value $12**

8
Friendship Duet
Handcrafted • UNRU
475QXM4019 • **Value $13**

GENERAL SHOWCASE

	Price Paid	Value of My Collection
1.		
2.		
GENERAL MINIATURE		
3.		
4.		
5.		
6.		
7.		
8.		
9.		
10.		
11.		
12.		
13.		
14.		
15.		
16.		
17.		
18.		
19.		
20.		
PENCIL TOTALS		

9
Furrball
Handcrafted • RGRS
575QXM4459 • **Value $16**

10
Grandpa's Gift
Handcrafted • RGRS
575QXM4829 • **Value $12**

11
Heavenly Praises
Handcrafted • ANDR
575QXM4037 • **Value $12**

12
Joyful Santa
Handcrafted • UNRU
475QXM4089 • **Value $12**

13
Little Beeper
Handcrafted • RGRS
575QXM4469 • **Value $15**

14
Merry Walruses
Handcrafted • SICK
575QXM4057 • **Value $19**

15
A Moustershire Christmas (set/4)
Handcrafted • RHOD
2450QXM4839 • **Value $46**

16
Pebbles and Bamm-Bamm
Handcrafted • RHOD
975QXM4757 • **Value $17**

17
Playful Penguins
Handcrafted • SICK
575QXM4059 • **Value $21**

18
Precious Creations
Handcrafted • SICK
975QXM4077 • **Value $19**

19
Santa's Visit
Handcrafted • CROW
775QXM4047 • **Value $21**

20
The Ships of STAR TREK® (set/3)
Handcrafted • N/A
1995QXI4109 • **Value $26**

(1)

Starlit Nativity
Handcrafted • UNRU
775QXM4039 • **Value $18**

(2)

Sugarplum Dreams
Handcrafted • CROW
475QXM4099 • **Value $14**

(3)

Tiny Treasures (set/6)
Handcrafted • SEAL
2900QXM4009 • **Value $51**

(4)

Tunnel of Love
Handcrafted • CROW
475QXM4029 • **Value $13**

(5)

Cinderella's Stepsisters (gift membership bonus, Merry Miniature)
Handcrafted • PIKE
375QXC4159 • **Value $80**

(6)

Collecting Memories (keepsake of membership)
Handcrafted • SIED
QXC4117 • **Value $20**

(7)

Cool Santa (keepsake of membership, miniature)
Handcrafted • FRAN
QXC4457 • **Value $16**

(8)

Cozy Christmas (early renewal gift, miniature)
Handcrafted • FRAN
QXC4119 • **Value $20**

(9)

Fishing For Fun (keepsake of membership)
Handcrafted • SEAL
QXC5207 • **Value $22**

(10)

A Gift From Rodney (keepsake of membership, miniature)
Handcrafted • SICK
QXC4129 • **Value $18**

(11)

Home From The Woods (club edition)
Handcrafted • SICK
1595QXC1059 • **Value $58**

(12)

May Flower (club edition, Easter sidekick)
Handcrafted • SIED
495QXC8246 • **Value $50**

(13)

Happy Holidays
Handcrafted • VOTR
295QX6307 • **Value $14**

(14)

Hooked On Collecting – 1995 – Ornament Premiere
Handcrafted • PALM
(N/C) No stock # • **Value $10**

(15)

Wish List
Handcrafted • SEAL
1500QX5859 • **Value $30**

(16)

Charlie Brown
A Charlie Brown Christmas
Handcrafted • SIED
395QRP4207 • **Value $24**

(17)

Linus
A Charlie Brown Christmas
Handcrafted • RGRS
395QRP4217 • **Value $20**

(18)

Lucy
A Charlie Brown Christmas
Handcrafted • SIED
395QRP4209 • **Value $18**

(19)

SNOOPY
A Charlie Brown Christmas
Handcrafted • RGRS
395QRP4219 • **Value $23**

(20)

WOODSTOCK w/tree and snowbase
A Charlie Brown Christmas
Handcrafted • RGRS
395QRP4227 • **Value $17**

	Price Paid	Value of My Collection
GENERAL MINIATURE		
1.		
2.		
3.		
4.		
COLLECTOR'S CLUB		
5.		
6.		
7.		
8.		
9.		
10.		
11.		
12.		
PREMIERE ORNAMENTS		
13.		
14.		
15.		
REACH ORNAMENTS		
16.		
17.		
18.		
19.		
20.		
PENCIL TOTALS		

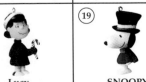

VALUE GUIDE — HALLMARK KEEPSAKE ORNAMENTS

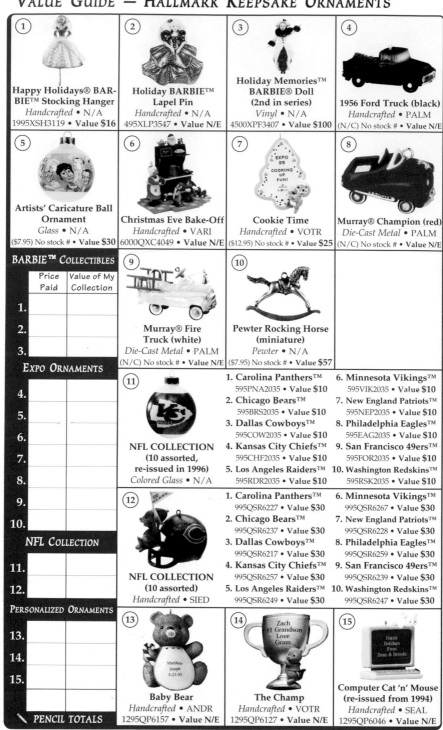

(1) Happy Holidays® BAR-BIE™ Stocking Hanger
Handcrafted • N/A
1995XSH3119 • **Value $16**

(2) Holiday BARBIE™ Lapel Pin
Handcrafted • N/A
495XLP3547 • **Value N/E**

(3) Holiday Memories™ BARBIE® Doll (2nd in series)
Vinyl • N/A
4500XPF3407 • **Value $100**

(4) 1956 Ford Truck (black)
Handcrafted • PALM
(N/C) No stock # • **Value N/E**

(5) Artists' Caricature Ball Ornament
Glass • N/A
($7.95) No stock # • **Value $30**

(6) Christmas Eve Bake-Off
Handcrafted • VARI
6000QXC4049 • **Value N/E**

(7) Cookie Time
Handcrafted • VOTR
($12.95) No stock # • **Value $25**

(8) Murray® Champion (red)
Die-Cast Metal • PALM
(N/C) No stock # • **Value N/E**

(9) Murray® Fire Truck (white)
Die-Cast Metal • PALM
(N/C) No stock # • **Value N/E**

(10) Pewter Rocking Horse (miniature)
Pewter • N/A
($7.95) No stock # • **Value $57**

BARBIE™ COLLECTIBLES

	Price Paid	Value of My Collection
1.		
2.		
3.		

EXPO ORNAMENTS

4.		
5.		
6.		
7.		
8.		
9.		
10.		

NFL COLLECTION

11.		
12.		

PERSONALIZED ORNAMENTS

13.		
14.		
15.		

PENCIL TOTALS

(11) NFL COLLECTION (10 assorted, re-issued in 1996)
Colored Glass • N/A

1. Carolina Panthers™ 595PNA2035 • **Value $10**
2. Chicago Bears™ 595BRS2035 • **Value $10**
3. Dallas Cowboys™ 595COW2035 • **Value $10**
4. Kansas City Chiefs™ 595CHF2035 • **Value $10**
5. Los Angeles Raiders™ 595RDR2035 • **Value $10**
6. Minnesota Vikings™ 595VIK2035 • **Value $10**
7. New England Patriots™ 595NEP2035 • **Value $10**
8. Philadelphia Eagles™ 595EAG2035 • **Value $10**
9. San Francisco 49ers™ 595FOR2035 • **Value $10**
10. Washington Redskins™ 595RSK2035 • **Value $10**

(12) NFL COLLECTION (10 assorted)
Handcrafted • SIED

1. Carolina Panthers™ 995QSR6227 • **Value $30**
2. Chicago Bears™ 995QSR6237 • **Value $30**
3. Dallas Cowboys™ 995QSR6217 • **Value $30**
4. Kansas City Chiefs™ 995QSR6257 • **Value $30**
5. Los Angeles Raiders™ 995QSR6249 • **Value $30**
6. Minnesota Vikings™ 995QSR6267 • **Value $30**
7. New England Patriots™ 995QSR6228 • **Value $30**
8. Philadelphia Eagles™ 995QSR6259 • **Value $30**
9. San Francisco 49ers™ 995QSR6239 • **Value $30**
10. Washington Redskins™ 995QSR6247 • **Value $30**

(13) Baby Bear
Handcrafted • ANDR
1295QP6157 • **Value N/E**

(14) The Champ
Handcrafted • VOTR
1295QP6127 • **Value N/E**

(15) Computer Cat 'n' Mouse (re-issued from 1994)
Handcrafted • SEAL
1295QP6046 • **Value N/E**

(1)  **Cookie Time** (re-issued from 1994) *Handcrafted* • VOTR 1295QP6073 • **Value N/E**	(2) **Etch-A-Sketch®** (re-issued from 1994) *Handcrafted* • CROW 1295QP6015 • **Value N/E**	(3)  **From The Heart** (re-issued from 1994) *Handcrafted* • RHOD 1495QP6036 • **Value N/E**	(4) **Key Note** *Handcrafted* • SEAL 1295QP6149 • **Value N/E**

(5)  **Mailbox Delivery** (re-issued from 1993) *Handcrafted* • CROW 1495QP6015 • **Value N/E**	(6)  **Novel Idea** (re-issued from 1994) *Handcrafted* • VOTR 1295QP6066 • **Value N/E**	(7)  **On the Billboard** (re-issued from 1993) *Handcrafted* • CROW 1295QP6022 • **Value N/E**	(8) **Playing Ball** (re-issued from 1993) *Handcrafted* • FRAN 1295QP6032 • **Value N/E**

(9)
Reindeer Rooters
(re-issued from 1994)
Handcrafted • CROW
1295QP6056 • **Value N/E**

1994

Hallmark created a sensation in 1994 with the release of "The Beatles Gift Set," as well as several new ornaments featuring LOONEY TUNES™ and Wizard of OZ™ characters. The 1994 collection featured 149 Keepsake, 24 Magic, 18 Showcase and 38 Miniature ornaments. See the collectible series section for more 1994 ornaments.

PERSONALIZED ORNAMENTS

	Price Paid	Value of My Collection
1.		
2.		
3.		
4.		
5.		
6.		
7.		
8.		
9.		

GENERAL KEEPSAKE

(10) **Across the Miles** *Handcrafted* • ANDR 895QX5656 • **Value $19**	(11) **All Pumped Up** *Handcrafted* • RHOD 895QX5923 • **Value $19**	(12) **Angel Hare** *Handcrafted/Brass* • SICK 895QX5896 • **Value $25**

10.		
11.		
12.		
13.		
14.		
15.		

(13)  **Anniversary Year** *Brass/Chrome* • BISH 1095QX5683 • **Value $21**	(14) **Baby's First Christmas** *Handcrafted* • VOTR 795QX5636 • **Value $22**	(15) 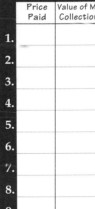 **Baby's First Christmas** *Handcrafted* • N/A 795QX5713 • **Value $30**

PENCIL TOTALS

(1) Baby's First Christmas
Handcrafted • SEAL
1295QX5743 • **Value $28**

(2) Baby's First Christmas
Porcelain/Brass • UNRU
1895QX5633 • **Value $37**

(3) Baby's First Christmas
– Baby Boy
Glass • N/A
500QX2436 • **Value $16**

(4) Baby's First Christmas
– Baby Girl
Glass • N/A
500QX2433 • **Value $18**

(5) Baby's Second
Christmas
Handcrafted • CROW
795QX5716 • **Value $22**

(6) Barney™
Handcrafted • RHOD
995QX5966 • **Value $26**

(7) Batman
Handcrafted • CHAD
1295QX5853 • **Value $27**

(8) The Beatles Gift Set
Handcrafted • RGRS
4800QX5373 • **Value $110**

GENERAL KEEPSAKE

	Price Paid	Value of My Collection
1.		
2.		
3.		
4.		
5.		
6.		
7.		
8.		
9.		
10.		
11.		
12.		
13.		
14.		
15.		
16.		
17.		
18.		
19.		
20.		

PENCIL TOTALS

(9) Big Shot
Handcrafted • SIED
795QX5873 • **Value $18**

(10) Brother
Handcrafted • PIKE
695QX5516 • **Value $16**

(11) Busy Batter
Handcrafted • SIED
795QX5876 • **Value $18**

(12) Candy Caper
Handcrafted • ANDR
895QX5776 • **Value $20**

(13) Caring Doctor
Handcrafted • RGRS
895QX5823 • **Value $19**

(14) Champion Teacher
Handcrafted • SIED
695QX5836 • **Value $16**

(15) Cheers To You!
Handcrafted/Brass • CROW
1095QX5796 • **Value $28**

(16) Cheery Cyclists
Handcrafted • CROW
1295QX5786 • **Value $30**

(17) Child Care Giver
Handcrafted • VOTR
795QX5906 • **Value $17**

(18) Child's Fifth Christmas
Handcrafted • RHOD
695QX5733 • **Value $20**

(19) Child's Fourth
Christmas
Handcrafted • FRAN
695QX5726 • **Value $20**

(20) Child's Third Christmas
Handcrafted • FRAN
695QX5723 • **Value $20**

VALUE GUIDE — HALLMARK KEEPSAKE ORNAMENTS

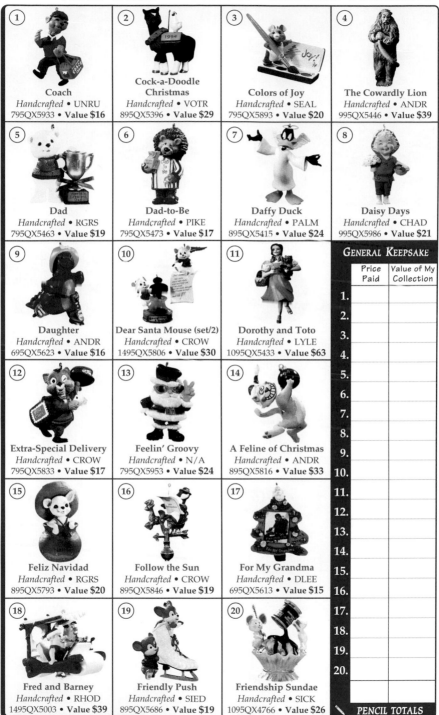

(1) Coach
Handcrafted • UNRU
795QX5933 • **Value $16**

(2) Cock-a-Doodle Christmas
Handcrafted • VOTR
895QX5396 • **Value $29**

(3) Colors of Joy
Handcrafted • SEAL
795QX5893 • **Value $20**

(4) The Cowardly Lion
Handcrafted • ANDR
995QX5446 • **Value $39**

(5) Dad
Handcrafted • RGRS
795QX5463 • **Value $19**

(6) Dad-to-Be
Handcrafted • PIKE
795QX5473 • **Value $17**

(7) Daffy Duck
Handcrafted • PALM
895QX5415 • **Value $24**

(8) Daisy Days
Handcrafted • CHAD
995QX5986 • **Value $21**

(9) Daughter
Handcrafted • ANDR
695QX5623 • **Value $16**

(10) Dear Santa Mouse (set/2)
Handcrafted • CROW
1495QX5806 • **Value $30**

(11) Dorothy and Toto
Handcrafted • LYLE
1095QX5433 • **Value $63**

(12) Extra-Special Delivery
Handcrafted • CROW
795QX5833 • **Value $17**

(13) Feelin' Groovy
Handcrafted • N/A
795QX5953 • **Value $24**

(14) A Feline of Christmas
Handcrafted • ANDR
895QX5816 • **Value $33**

(15) Feliz Navidad
Handcrafted • RGRS
895QX5793 • **Value $20**

(16) Follow the Sun
Handcrafted • CROW
895QX5846 • **Value $19**

(17) For My Grandma
Handcrafted • DLEE
695QX5613 • **Value $15**

(18) Fred and Barney
Handcrafted • RHOD
1495QX5003 • **Value $39**

(19) Friendly Push
Handcrafted • SIED
895QX5686 • **Value $19**

(20) Friendship Sundae
Handcrafted • SICK
1095QX4766 • **Value $26**

1994

	General Keepsake	
	Price Paid	Value of My Collection
1.		
2.		
3.		
4.		
5.		
6.		
7.		
8.		
9.		
10.		
11.		
12.		
13.		
14.		
15.		
16.		
17.		
18.		
19.		
20.		
PENCIL TOTALS		

Value Guide — Hallmark Keepsake Ornaments

1. GARFIELD
Handcrafted • N/A
1295QX5753 • **Value $28**

2. Gentle Nurse
Handcrafted • LYLE
695QX5973 • **Value $20**

3. Godchild
Handcrafted • RGRS
895QX4453 • **Value $24**

4. Godparent
Glass • N/A
500QX2423 • **Value $20**

5. Grandchild's First Christmas
Handcrafted • UNRU
795QX5676 • **Value $18**

6. Granddaughter
Handcrafted • PIKE
695QX5523 • **Value $20**

7. Grandmother
Handcrafted • ANDR
795QX5673 • **Value $19**

8. Grandpa
Handcrafted • UNRU
795QX5616 • **Value $20**

9. Grandparents
Glass • N/A
500QX2426 • **Value $14**

10. Grandson
Handcrafted • PIKE
695QX5526 • **Value $20**

11. Happy Birthday, Jesus
Handcrafted • LYLE
1295QX5423 • **Value $30**

12. Harvest Joy
Handcrafted • CHAD
995QX5993 • **Value $20**

13. Hearts in Harmony
Porcelain • ANDR
1095QX4406 • **Value $22**

14. Helpful Shepherd
Handcrafted • CHAD
895QX5536 • **Value $21**

15. Holiday Patrol
Handcrafted • RHOD
895QX5826 • **Value $20**

16. Ice Show
Handcrafted • ANDR
795QX5946 • **Value $20**

17. In the Pink
Handcrafted • ANDR
995QX5763 • **Value $23**

18. It's a Strike
Handcrafted • SIED
895QX5856 • **Value $19**

19. Jingle Bell Band
Handcrafted • CROW
1095QX5783 • **Value $31**

20. Joyous Song
Handcrafted • ANDR
895QX4473 • **Value $20**

General Keepsake

	Price Paid	Value of My Collection
1.		
2.		
3.		
4.		
5.		
6.		
7.		
8.		
9.		
10.		
11.		
12.		
13.		
14.		
15.		
16.		
17.		
18.		
19.		
20.		
PENCIL TOTALS		

(1)  **Jump-along Jackalope** *Handcrafted* • FRAN 895QX5756 • **Value $20**	**(2)**  **Keep on Mowin'** *Handcrafted* • SIED 895QX5413 • **Value $20**	**(3)** **Kickin' Roo** *Handcrafted* • SIED 795QX5916 • **Value $18**	**(4)** **Kitty's Catamaran** *Handcrafted* • SEAL 1095QX5416 • **Value $21**
(5)  **Kringle's Kayak** *Handcrafted* • SEAL 795QX5886 • **Value $24**	**(6)**  **Lou Rankin Seal** *Handcrafted* • BISH 995QX5456 • **Value $22**	**(7)** **Lucinda and Teddy** *Handcrafted/Fabric* • UNRU 2175QX4813 • **Value $46**	**(8)** **Magic Carpet Ride** *Handcrafted* • SEAL 795QX5883 • **Value $25**

(9)  **Making It Bright** *Handcrafted* • RHOD 895QX5403 • **Value $20**	**(10)** **Mary Engelbreit** *Glass* • N/A 500QX2416 • **Value $20**	**(11)** **Merry Fishmas** *Handcrafted* • PALM 895QX5913 • **Value $22**	

General Keepsake

	Price Paid	Value of My Collection
1.		
2.		
3.		
4.		
5.		
6.		
7.		
8.		
9.		
10.		
11.		
12.		
13.		
14.		
15.		
16.		
17.		
18.		
19.		
20.		

(12)  **Mistletoe Surprise (set/2)** *Handcrafted* • SEAL 1295QX5996 • **Value $31**	**(13)** **Mom** *Handcrafted* • RGRS 795QX5466 • **Value $18**	**(14)** **Mom and Dad** *Handcrafted* • SIED 995QX5666 • **Value $21**
(15) **Mom-to-Be** *Handcrafted* • PIKE 795QX5506 • **Value $17**	**(16)**  **Mufasa and Simba** *Handcrafted* • CROW 1495QX5406 • **Value $32**	**(17)** **Nephew** *Handcrafted* • FRAN 795QX5546 • **Value $16**
(18) **New Home** *Handcrafted* • ANDR 895QX5663 • **Value $22**	**(19)**  **Niece** *Handcrafted* • FRAN 795QX5543 • **Value $16**	**(20)** **Norman Rockwell Art** *Glass* • LYLE 500QX2413 • **Value $20**

PENCIL TOTALS

(1) Open-and-Shut Holiday
Handcrafted • SIED
995QX5696 • **Value $22**

(2) Our Christmas Together
Handcrafted • RGRS
995QX4816 • **Value $22**

(3) Our Family
Handcrafted • ANDR
795QX5576 • **Value $19**

(4) Our First Christmas Together
Acrylic • VOTR
695QX3186 • **Value $16**

(5) Our First Christmas Together
Brass/Fabric • ANDR
1895QX5706 • **Value $41**

(6) Our First Christmas Together
Handcrafted • PALM
895QX5653 • **Value $20**

(7) Our First Christmas Together
Handcrafted • BISH
995QX5643 • **Value $25**

(8) Out of This World Teacher
Handcrafted • UNRU
795QX5766 • **Value $20**

GENERAL KEEPSAKE

	Price Paid	Value of My Collection
1.		
2.		
3.		
4.		
5.		
6.		
7.		
8.		
9.		
10.		
11.		
12.		
13.		
14.		
15.		
16.		
17.		
18.		
19.		
20.		

PENCIL TOTALS

(9) Practice Makes Perfect
Handcrafted • PALM
895QX5863 • **Value $18**

(10) Red Hot Holiday
Handcrafted • RGRS
795QX5843 • **Value $20**

(11) Reindeer Pro
Handcrafted • RHOD
795QX5926 • **Value $19**

(12) Relaxing Moment
Handcrafted • FRAN
1495QX5356 • **Value $34**

(13) Road Runner and Wile E. Coyote
Handcrafted • CHAD
1295QX5602 • **Value $29**

(14) Santa's LEGO® Sleigh
Handcrafted • CROW
1095QX5453 • **Value $32**

(15) The Scarecrow
Handcrafted • UNRU
995QX5436 • **Value $44**

(16) Secret Santa
Handcrafted • UNRU
795QX5736 • **Value $17**

(17) A Sharp Flat
Handcrafted • CROW
1095QX5773 • **Value $27**

(18) Simba and Nala (set/2)
Handcrafted • CROW
1295QX5303 • **Value $28**

(19) Sister
Handcrafted • PIKE
695QX5513 • **Value $19**

(20) Sister to Sister
Handcrafted • RHOD
995QX5533 • **Value $25**

1. Son
Handcrafted • ANDR
695QX5626 • **Value $16**

2. Special Cat
Acrylic • RHOD
795QX5606 • **Value $17**

3. Special Dog
Handcrafted • RHOD
795QX5603 • **Value $17**

4. Speedy Gonzales
Handcrafted • PALM
895QX5343 • **Value $23**

5. Stamp of Approval
Handcrafted • SICK
795QX5703 • **Value $18**

6. Sweet Greeting (set/2)
Handcrafted • PALM
1095QX5803 • **Value $23**

7. The Tale of Peter Rabbit
BEATRIX POTTER
Glass • N/A
500QX2443 • **Value $20**

8. Tasmanian Devil
Handcrafted • PALM
895QX5605 • **Value $64**

1994

9. Thick 'n' Thin
Handcrafted • RGRS
1095QX5693 • **Value $22**

10. Thrill a Minute
Handcrafted • SIED
895QX5866 • **Value $19**

11. Time of Peace
Handcrafted • ANDR
795QX5813 • **Value $18**

12. Timon and Pumbaa
Handcrafted • CROW
895QX5366 • **Value $24**

13. The Tin Man
Handcrafted • UNRU
995QX5443 • **Value $42**

14. Tou Can Love
Handcrafted • RGRS
895QX5646 • **Value $19**

15. Tulip Time
Handcrafted • CHAD
995QX5983 • **Value $21**

16. Winnie the Pooh
and Tigger
Handcrafted • SIED
1295QX5746 • **Value $35**

17. Yosemite Sam
Handcrafted • PALM
895QX5346 • **Value $20**

18. Yuletide Cheer
Handcrafted • CHAD
995QX5976 • **Value $23**

19. Away in a Manger
Handcrafted • LYLE
1600QLX7383 • **Value $43**

20. Baby's First Christmas
Handcrafted • FRAN
2000QLX7466 • **Value $43**

	Price Paid	Value of My Collection
General Keepsake		
1.		
2.		
3.		
4.		
5.		
6.		
7.		
8.		
9.		
10.		
11.		
12.		
13.		
14.		
15.		
16.		
17.		
18.		
General Magic		
19.		
20.		
Pencil Totals		

① Barney™
Handcrafted • N/A
2400QLX7506 • **Value $48**

② Candy Cane Lookout
Handcrafted • FRAN
1800QLX7376 • **Value $77**

③ Conversations With Santa
Handcrafted • SEAL
2800QLX7426 • **Value $56**

④ Country Showtime
Handcrafted • SICK
2200QLX7416 • **Value $45**

⑤ The Eagle Has Landed
Handcrafted • SEAL
2400QLX7486 • **Value $50**

⑥ Feliz Navidad
Handcrafted • CROW
2800QLX7433 • **Value $69**

⑦ Gingerbread Fantasy
Handcrafted • PALM
4400QLX7382 • **Value $93**

⑧ Klingon Bird of Prey™
Handcrafted • NORT
2400QLX7386 • **Value $50**

⑨ Kringle Trolley
Handcrafted • CROW
2000QLX7413 • **Value $48**

⑩ Maxine
Handcrafted • SICK
2000QLX7503 • **Value $47**

⑪ Peekaboo Pup
Handcrafted • RGRS
2000QLX7423 • **Value $42**

⑫ Rock Candy Miner
Handcrafted • SIED
2000QLX7403 • **Value $41**

⑬ Santa's Sing-Along
Handcrafted • CROW
2400QLX7473 • **Value $57**

⑭ Simba, Sarabi and Mufasa
Handcrafted • CROW
2000QLX7516 • **Value $40**

⑮ Simba, Sarabi and Mufasa (recalled due to defective sound)
Handcrafted • CROW
3200QLX7513 • **Value $73**

⑯ Very Merry Minutes
Handcrafted • VOTR
2400QLX7443 • **Value $47**

⑰ White Christmas
Handcrafted • DLEE
2800QLX7463 • **Value $65**

⑱ Winnie the Pooh Parade
Handcrafted • CROW
3200QLX7493 • **Value $69**

⑲ Home for the Holidays
Christmas Lights
Porcelain • PALM
1575QK1123 • **Value $20**

⑳ Moonbeams
Christmas Lights
Porcelain • ANDR
1575QK1116 • **Value $20**

GENERAL MAGIC	Price Paid	Value of My Collection
1.		
2.		
3.		
4.		
5.		
6.		
7.		
8.		
9.		
10.		
11.		
12.		
13.		
14.		
15.		
16.		
17.		
18.		
GENERAL SHOWCASE		
19.		
20.		
PENCIL TOTALS		

1  **Mother and Child** *Christmas Lights* *Porcelain* • RGRS 1575QK1126 • **Value $20**	**2** **Peaceful Village** *Christmas Lights* *Porcelain* • CHAD 1575QK1106 • **Value $20**	**3**  **Catching 40 Winks** *Folk Art Americana* *Handcrafted* • SICK 1675QK1183 • **Value $37**	**4** **Going to Town** *Folk Art Americana* *Handcrafted* • SICK 1575QK1166 • **Value $37**

5 **Racing Through the Snow** *Folk Art Americana* *Handcrafted* • SICK 1575QK1173 • **Value $51**	**6** **Rarin' to Go** *Folk Art Americana* *Handcrafted* • SICK 1575QK1193 • **Value $38**	**7** **Roundup Time** *Folk Art Americana* *Handcrafted* • SICK 1675QK1176 • **Value $36**	**8** **Dapper Snowman** *Holiday Favorites* *Porcelain* • VOTR 1375QK1053 • **Value $20**

9 **Graceful Fawn** *Holiday Favorites* *Porcelain* • VOTR 1175QK1033 • **Value $20**	**10**  **Jolly Santa** *Holiday Favorites* *Porcelain* • VOTR 1375QK1046 • **Value $26**	**11**  **Joyful Lamb** *Holiday Favorites* *Porcelain* • VOTR 1175QK1036 • **Value $20**

12 **Peaceful Dove** *Holiday Favorites* *Porcelain* • VOTR 1175QK1043 • **Value $19**	**13** 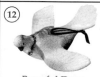 **Silver Bells** *Old-World Silver* *Silver-Plated* • UNRU 2475QK1026 • **Value $30**	**14** **Silver Bows** *Old-World Silver* *Silver-Plated* • PALM 2475QK1023 • **Value $31**

15 **Silver Poinsettia** *Old-World Silver* *Silver-Plated* • UNRU 2475QK1006 • **Value $36**	**16**  **Silver Snowflakes** *Old-World Silver* *Silver-Plated* • UNRU 2475QK1016 • **Value $31**	**17** **Babs Bunny** *Handcrafted* • PALM 575QXM4116 • **Value $15**

18  **Baby's First Christmas** *Handcrafted* • LYLE 575QXM4003 • **Value $15**	**19** **Baking Tiny Treats (set/6)** *Handcrafted* • SEAL 2900QXM4033 • **Value $60**	**20** 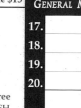 **Beary Perfect Tree** *Handcrafted* • BISH 475QXM4076 • **Value $12**

GENERAL SHOWCASE

	Price Paid	Value of My Collection
1.		
2.		
3.		
4.		
5.		
6.		
7.		
8.		
9.		
10.		
11.		
12.		
13.		
14.		
15.		
16.		

GENERAL MINIATURE

17.		
18.		
19.		
20.		

PENCIL TOTALS

(1) **Buster Bunny**
Handcrafted • PALM
575QXM5163 • **Value $13**

(2) **Corny Elf**
Handcrafted • RHOD
450QXM4063 • **Value $11**

(3) **Cute as a Button**
Handcrafted • CROW
375QXM4103 • **Value $15**

(4) **Dazzling Reindeer**
Handcrafted • VOTR
975QXM4026 • **Value $22**

(5) **Dizzy Devil**
Handcrafted • PALM
575QXM4133 • **Value $15**

(6) **Friends Need Hugs**
Handcrafted • LYLE
450QXM4016 • **Value $14**

(7) **Graceful Carousel Horse**
Pewter • BISH
775QXM4056 • **Value $19**

(8) **Hamton**
Handcrafted • PALM
575QXM4126 • **Value $14**

(9) **Have a Cookie**
Handcrafted • DLEE
575QXM5166 • **Value $14**

(10) **Hearts A-Sail**
Handcrafted • BISH
575QXM4006 • **Value $12**

(11) **Jolly Visitor**
Handcrafted • SICK
575QXM4053 • **Value $15**

(12) **Jolly Wolly Snowman**
Handcrafted • VOTR
375QXM4093 • **Value $14**

(13) **Journey to Bethlehem**
Handcrafted • LYLE
575QXM4036 • **Value $17**

(14) **Just My Size**
Handcrafted • BISH
375QXM4086 • **Value $11**

(15) **Love Was Born**
Handcrafted • SICK
450QXM4043 • **Value $15**

(16) **Melodic Cherub**
Handcrafted • RGRS
375QXM4066 • **Value $10**

(17) **A Merry Flight**
Handcrafted • CROW
575QXM4073 • **Value $12**

(18) **Mom**
Handcrafted • RGRS
450QXM4013 • **Value $14**

(19) **Noah's Ark (set/3)**
Handcrafted • SICK
2450QXM4106 • **Value $60**

(20) **Plucky Duck**
Handcrafted • PALM
575QXM4123 • **Value $12**

GENERAL MINIATURE

	Price Paid	Value of My Collection
1.		
2.		
3.		
4.		
5.		
6.		
7.		
8.		
9.		
10.		
11.		
12.		
13.		
14.		
15.		
16.		
17.		
18.		
19.		
20.		

PENCIL TOTALS

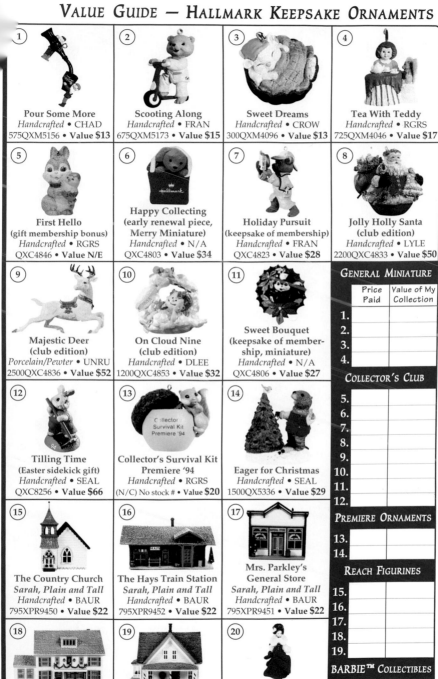

1
Pour Some More
Handcrafted • CHAD
575QXM5156 • **Value $13**

2
Scooting Along
Handcrafted • FRAN
675QXM5173 • **Value $15**

3
Sweet Dreams
Handcrafted • CROW
300QXM4096 • **Value $13**

4
Tea With Teddy
Handcrafted • RGRS
725QXM4046 • **Value $17**

5
First Hello
(gift membership bonus)
Handcrafted • RGRS
QXC4846 • **Value N/E**

6
Happy Collecting
(early renewal piece,
Merry Miniature)
Handcrafted • N/A
QXC4803 • **Value $34**

7
Holiday Pursuit
(keepsake of membership)
Handcrafted • FRAN
QXC4823 • **Value $28**

8
Jolly Holly Santa
(club edition)
Handcrafted • LYLE
2200QXC4833 • **Value $50**

9
Majestic Deer
(club edition)
Porcelain/Pewter • UNRU
2500QXC4836 • **Value $52**

10
On Cloud Nine
(club edition)
Handcrafted • DLEE
1200QXC4853 • **Value $32**

11
Sweet Bouquet
(keepsake of member-
ship, miniature)
Handcrafted • N/A
QXC4806 • **Value $27**

12
Tilling Time
(Easter sidekick gift)
Handcrafted • SEAL
QXC8256 • **Value $66**

13
**Collector's Survival Kit
Premiere '94**
Handcrafted • RGRS
(N/C) No stock # • **Value $20**

14
Eager for Christmas
Handcrafted • SEAL
1500QX5336 • **Value $29**

15
The Country Church
Sarah, Plain and Tall
Handcrafted • BAUR
795XPR9450 • **Value $22**

16
The Hays Train Station
Sarah, Plain and Tall
Handcrafted • BAUR
795XPR9452 • **Value $22**

17
**Mrs. Parkley's
General Store**
Sarah, Plain and Tall
Handcrafted • BAUR
795XPR9451 • **Value $22**

18
Sarah's Maine Home
Sarah, Plain and Tall
Handcrafted • BAUR
795XPR9454 • **Value $23**

19
Sarah's Prairie Home
Sarah, Plain and Tall
Handcrafted • BAUR
795XPR9453 • **Value $22**

20
**Victorian Elegance™
BARBIE® Doll**
(1st in series)
Vinyl • N/A
4000XPF3546 • **Value $95**

1994

	Price Paid	Value of My Collection
General Miniature		
1.		
2.		
3.		
4.		
Collector's Club		
5.		
6.		
7.		
8.		
9.		
10.		
11.		
12.		
Premiere Ornaments		
13.		
14.		
Reach Figurines		
15.		
16.		
17.		
18.		
19.		
Barbie™ Collectibles		
20.		
Pencil Totals		

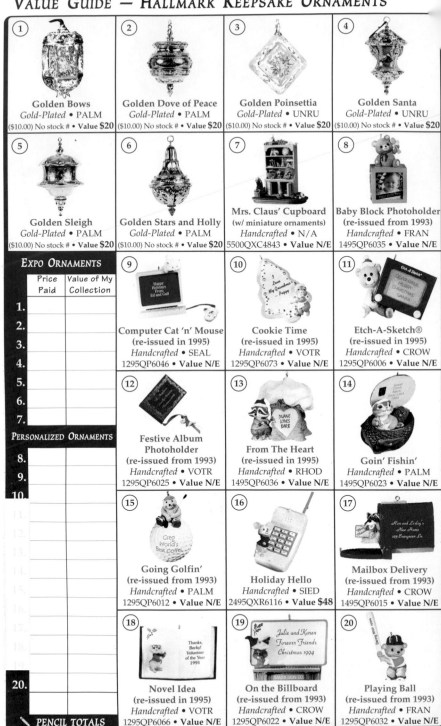

1. Golden Bows
Gold-Plated • PALM
($10.00) No stock # • **Value $20**

2. Golden Dove of Peace
Gold-Plated • PALM
($10.00) No stock # • **Value $20**

3. Golden Poinsettia
Gold-Plated • UNRU
($10.00) No stock # • **Value $20**

4. Golden Santa
Gold-Plated • UNRU
($10.00) No stock # • **Value $20**

5. Golden Sleigh
Gold-Plated • PALM
($10.00) No stock # • **Value $20**

6. Golden Stars and Holly
Gold-Plated • PALM
($10.00) No stock # • **Value $20**

7. Mrs. Claus' Cupboard
(w/ miniature ornaments)
Handcrafted • N/A
5500QXC4843 • **Value N/E**

8. Baby Block Photoholder
(re-issued from 1993)
Handcrafted • FRAN
1495QP6035 • **Value N/E**

9. Computer Cat 'n' Mouse
(re-issued in 1995)
Handcrafted • SEAL
1295QP6046 • **Value N/E**

10. Cookie Time
(re-issued in 1995)
Handcrafted • VOTR
1295QP6073 • **Value N/E**

11. Etch-A-Sketch®
(re-issued in 1995)
Handcrafted • CROW
1295QP6006 • **Value N/E**

12. Festive Album Photoholder
(re-issued from 1993)
Handcrafted • VOTR
1295QP6025 • **Value N/E**

13. From The Heart
(re-issued in 1995)
Handcrafted • RHOD
1495QP6036 • **Value N/E**

14. Goin' Fishin'
Handcrafted • PALM
1495QP6023 • **Value N/E**

15. Going Golfin'
(re-issued from 1993)
Handcrafted • PALM
1295QP6012 • **Value N/E**

16. Holiday Hello
Handcrafted • SIED
2495QXR6116 • **Value $48**

17. Mailbox Delivery
(re-issued from 1993)
Handcrafted • CROW
1495QP6015 • **Value N/E**

18. Novel Idea
(re-issued in 1995)
Handcrafted • VOTR
1295QP6066 • **Value N/E**

19. On the Billboard
(re-issued from 1993)
Handcrafted • CROW
1295QP6022 • **Value N/E**

20. Playing Ball
(re-issued from 1993)
Handcrafted • FRAN
1295QP6032 • **Value N/E**

EXPO ORNAMENTS

	Price Paid	Value of My Collection
1.		
2.		
3.		
4.		
5.		
6.		
7.		

PERSONALIZED ORNAMENTS

8.		
9.		
10.		
11.		
12.		
13.		
14.		
15.		
16.		
17.		
18.		
19.		
20.		

PENCIL TOTALS

(1)

Reindeer Rooters
(re-issued in 1995)
Handcrafted • CROW
1295QP6056 • **Value N/E**

(2)

Santa Says
(re-issued from 1993)
Handcrafted • SEAL
1495QP6005 • **Value N/E**

1993

The 20th anniversary of Keepsake Ornaments was celebrated in 1993 with four special ornaments, including "Glowing Pewter Wreath" and pieces to complement three popular collectible series. Overall, there were 141 Keepsake, 21 Magic, 19 Showcase and 36 Miniature ornaments. See the collectible series section for more 1993 ornaments.

(3)

Across the Miles
Handcrafted • FRAN
875QX5912 • **Value $20**

1993

(4)

Anniversary Year Photoholder
Brass/Chrome • LYLE
975QX5972 • **Value $20**

(5)

Apple for Teacher
Handcrafted • SEAL
775QX5902 • **Value $16**

(6)

Baby's First Christmas
Handcrafted • CROW
775QX5525 • **Value $29**

(7)

Baby's First Christmas
Handcrafted • ANDR
1075QX5515 • **Value $25**

(8)

Baby's First Christmas
Silver-Plated • PALM
1875QX5512 • **Value $38**

(9)

Baby's First Christmas
– Baby Boy
Glass • VOTR
475QX2105 • **Value $17**

(10)

Baby's First Christmas
– Baby Girl
Glass • VOTR
475QX2092 • **Value $17**

(11)

Baby's First Christmas Photoholder
Handcrafted/Lace • RGRS
775QX5522 • **Value $26**

(12)

Baby's Second Christmas
Handcrafted • FRAN
675QX5992 • **Value $21**

(13)

Beary Gifted
Handcrafted • CROW
775QX5762 • **Value $19**

(14)

Big on Gardening
Handcrafted • VOTR
975QX5842 • **Value $18**

(15)

Big Roller
Handcrafted • SIED
875QX5352 • **Value $19**

	Price Paid	Value of My Collection
PERSONALIZED ORNAMENTS		
1.		
2.		
GENERAL KEEPSAKE		
3.		
4.		
5.		
6.		
7.		
8.		
9.		
10.		
11.		
12.		
13.		
14.		
15.		
PENCIL TOTA		

(1) Bird-Watcher
Handcrafted • JLEE
975QX5252 • **Value $20**

(2) Bowling for ZZZs
Handcrafted • FRAN
775QX5565 • **Value $19**

(3) Brother
Handcrafted • RGRS
675QX5542 • **Value $14**

(4) Bugs Bunny
Handcrafted • SICK
875QX5412 • **Value $27**

(5) Caring Nurse
Handcrafted • FRAN
675QX5785 • **Value $19**

(6) A Child's Christmas
Handcrafted • FRAN
975QX5882 • **Value $22**

(7) Child's Fifth Christmas
Handcrafted • RHOD
675QX5222 • **Value $18**

(8) Child's Fourth Christmas
Handcrafted • FRAN
675QX5215 • **Value $16**

(9) Child's Third Christmas
Handcrafted • FRAN
675QX5995 • **Value $17**

(10) Christmas Break
Handcrafted • SEAL
775QX5825 • **Value $25**

(11) Clever Cookie
Handcrafted/Tin • SICK
775QX5662 • **Value $23**

(12) Coach
Handcrafted • PALM
675QX5935 • **Value $15**

(13) Curly 'n' Kingly
Handcrafted/Brass • CROW
1075QX5285 • **Value $24**

(14) Dad
Handcrafted • JLEE
775QX5855 • **Value $19**

(15) Dad-to-Be
Handcrafted • JLEE
675QX5532 • **Value $15**

(16) Daughter
Handcrafted • VOTR
675QX5872 • **Value $25**

(17) Dickens Caroler Bell – Lady Daphne
Porcelain • CHAD
2175QX5505 • **Value $50**

(18) Dunkin' Roo
Handcrafted • SIED
775QX5575 • **Value $17**

(19) Eeyore
Handcrafted • SIED
975QX5712 • **Value $21**

(20) Elmer Fudd
Handcrafted • LYLE
875QX5495 • **Value $20**

GENERAL KEEPSAKE

	Price Paid	Value of My Collection
1.		
2.		
3.		
4.		
5.		
6.		
7.		
8.		
9.		
10.		
11.		
12.		
13.		
14.		
15.		
16.		
17.		
18.		
19.		
20.		
PENCIL TOTALS		

①	**②**	**③**	**④** 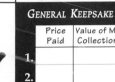
Faithful Fire Fighter *Handcrafted* • VOTR 775QX5782 • **Value $19**	**Feliz Navidad** *Handcrafted/Brass* • DLEE 875QX5365 • **Value $21**	**Fills the Bill** *Handcrafted* • SIED 875QX5572 • **Value $18**	**Glowing Pewter Wreath** *Pewter* • UNRU 1875QX5302 • **Value $37**

⑤	**⑥**	**⑦**	**⑧**
Godchild *Handcrafted* • CHAD 875QX5875 • **Value $20**	**Grandchild's First Christmas** *Handcrafted* • FRAN 675QX5552 • **Value $15**	**Granddaughter** *Handcrafted* • CHAD 675QX5635 • **Value $18**	**Grandmother** *Handcrafted* • ANDR 675QX5665 • **Value $16**

1993

⑨	**⑩**	**⑪**	
Grandparents *Glass* • VOTR 475QX2085 • **Value $15**	**Grandson** *Handcrafted* • CHAD 675QX5632 • **Value $18**	**Great Connections (set/2)** *Handcrafted* • RGRS 1075QX5402 • **Value $28**	

	Price Paid	Value of My Collection
1.		
2.		
3.		
4.		
5.		
6.		
7.		
8.		
9.		
10.		
11.		
12.		
13.		
14.		
15.		
16.		
17.		
18.		
19.		
20.		
PENCIL TOTALS		

⑫	**⑬**	**⑭**
He Is Born *Handcrafted* • LYLE 975QX5362 • **Value $43**	**High Top-Purr** *Handcrafted* • SEAL 875QX5332 • **Value $26**	**Home for Christmas** *Handcrafted* • SIED 775QX5562 • **Value $18**

⑮ 	**⑯**	**⑰**
Howling Good Time *Handcrafted* • RGRS 975QX5255 • **Value $22**	**Icicle Bicycle** *Handcrafted* • JLEE 975QX5835 • **Value $21**	**Julianne and Teddy** *Handcrafted* • UNRU 2175QX5295 • **Value $49**

⑱	**⑲**	**⑳**
Kanga and Roo *Handcrafted* • SIED 975QX5672 • **Value $23**	**Little Drummer Boy** *Handcrafted* • PALM 875QX5372 • **Value $24**	**Look for the Wonder** *Handcrafted* • DLEE 1275QX5685 • **Value $30**

(1) Lou Rankin Polar Bear
Handcrafted • RHOD
975QX5745 • **Value $29**

(2) Makin' Music
Handcrafted/Brass • SEAL
975QX5325 • **Value $21**

(3) Making Waves
Handcrafted • PALM
975QX5775 • **Value $28**

(4) Mary Engelbreit
Glass • N/A
500QX2075 • **Value $17**

(5) Maxine
Handcrafted • SICK
875QX5385 • **Value $33**

(6) Mom
Handcrafted • JLEE
775QX5852 • **Value $19**

(7) Mom and Dad
Handcrafted • PALM
975QX5845 • **Value $19**

(8) Mom-to-Be
Handcrafted • JLEE
675QX5535 • **Value $16**

(9) Nephew
Handcrafted • RGRS
675QX5735 • **Value $14**

(10) New Home
Enamel/Metal • PALM
775QX5905 • **Value $48**

(11) Niece
Handcrafted • RGRS
675QX5732 • **Value $14**

(12) On Her Toes
Handcrafted • ANDR
875QX5265 • **Value $26**

(13) One-Elf Marching Band
Handcrafted/Brass • CHAD
1275QX5342 • **Value $28**

(14) Our Christmas Together
Handcrafted • DLEE
1075QX5942 • **Value $25**

(15) Our Family Photoholder
Handcrafted • UNRU
775QX5892 • **Value $19**

(16) Our First Christmas Together
Acrylic • ANDR
675QX3015 • **Value $18**

(17) Our First Christmas Together
Brass/Silver-Plated • RGRS
1875QX5955 • **Value $39**

(18) Our First Christmas Together
Handcrafted • LYLE
975QX5642 • **Value $17**

(19) Our First Christmas Together Photoholder
Handcrafted • UNRU
875QX5952 • **Value $17**

(20) Owl
Handcrafted • SIED
975QX5695 • **Value $21**

General Keepsake

	Price Paid	Value of My Collection
1.		
2.		
3.		
4.		
5.		
6.		
7.		
8.		
9.		
10.		
11.		
12.		
13.		
14.		
15.		
16.		
17.		
18.		
19.		
20.		
PENCIL TOTALS		

1

PEANUTS®
Glass • N/A
500QX2072 • **Value $28**

2

Peek-a-Boo Tree
Handcrafted • CROW
1075QX5245 • **Value $25**

3

Peep Inside
Handcrafted • DLEE
1375QX5322 • **Value $27**

4

People Friendly
Handcrafted • SEAL
875QX5932 • **Value $18**

5

Perfect Match
Handcrafted • SIED
875QX5772 • **Value $19**

6

The Pink Panther
Handcrafted • PALM
1275QX5755 • **Value $26**

7

Playful Pals
Handcrafted • RGRS
1475QX5742 • **Value $31**

8

Popping Good Times
(set/2)
Handcrafted • CHAD
1475QX5392 • **Value $30**

1993

9

Porky Pig
Handcrafted • ANDR
875QX5652 • **Value $20**

10

Putt-Putt Penguin
Handcrafted • JLEE
975QX5795 • **Value $22**

11

Quick as a Fox
Handcrafted • CROW
875QX5792 • **Value $19**

12

Rabbit
Handcrafted • SIED
975QX5702 • **Value $22**

13

Ready for Fun
Handcrafted/Tin • LYLE
775QX5124 • **Value $17**

14

Room for One More
Handcrafted • CROW
875QX5382 • **Value $52**

15

Silvery Noel
Silver-Plated • LYLE
1275QX5305 • **Value $36**

16

Sister
Handcrafted • RGRS
675QX5545 • **Value $23**

17

Sister to Sister
Handcrafted • SEAL
975QX5885 • **Value $54**

18

Smile! It's Christmas
Photoholder
Handcrafted • SEAL
975QX5335 • **Value $21**

19

Snow Bear Angel
Handcrafted • JLEE
775QX5355 • **Value $19**

20

Snowbird
Handcrafted • JLEE
775QX5765 • **Value $19**

GENERAL KEEPSAKE		
	Price Paid	Value of My Collection
1.		
2.		
3.		
4.		
5.		
6.		
7.		
8.		
9.		
10.		
11.		
12.		
13.		
14.		
15.		
16.		
17.		
18.		
19.		
20.		
PENCIL TOTALS		

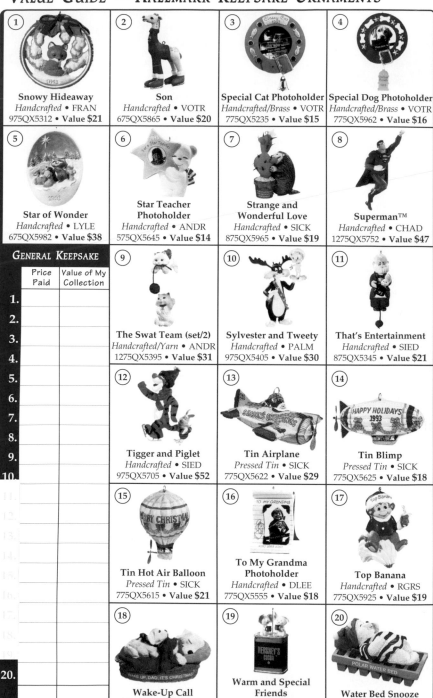

(1) Snowy Hideaway
Handcrafted • FRAN
975QX5312 • **Value $21**

(2) Son
Handcrafted • VOTR
675QX5865 • **Value $20**

(3) Special Cat Photoholder
Handcrafted/Brass • VOTR
775QX5235 • **Value $15**

(4) Special Dog Photoholder
Handcrafted/Brass • VOTR
775QX5962 • **Value $16**

(5) Star of Wonder
Handcrafted • LYLE
675QX5982 • **Value $38**

(6) Star Teacher Photoholder
Handcrafted • ANDR
575QX5645 • **Value $14**

(7) Strange and Wonderful Love
Handcrafted • SICK
875QX5965 • **Value $19**

(8) Superman™
Handcrafted • CHAD
1275QX5752 • **Value $47**

(9) The Swat Team (set/2)
Handcrafted/Yarn • ANDR
1275QX5395 • **Value $31**

(10) Sylvester and Tweety
Handcrafted • PALM
975QX5405 • **Value $30**

(11) That's Entertainment
Handcrafted • SIED
875QX5345 • **Value $21**

(12) Tigger and Piglet
Handcrafted • SIED
975QX5705 • **Value $52**

(13) Tin Airplane
Pressed Tin • SICK
775QX5622 • **Value $29**

(14) Tin Blimp
Pressed Tin • SICK
775QX5625 • **Value $18**

(15) Tin Hot Air Balloon
Pressed Tin • SICK
775QX5615 • **Value $21**

(16) To My Grandma Photoholder
Handcrafted • DLEE
775QX5555 • **Value $18**

(17) Top Banana
Handcrafted • RGRS
775QX5925 • **Value $19**

(18) Wake-Up Call
Handcrafted • UNRU
875QX5262 • **Value $22**

(19) Warm and Special Friends
Handcrafted/Metal • VOTR
1075QX5895 • **Value $26**

(20) Water Bed Snooze
Handcrafted • JLEE
975QX5375 • **Value $23**

GENERAL KEEPSAKE

	Price Paid	Value of My Collection
1.		
2.		
3.		
4.		
5.		
6.		
7.		
8.		
9.		
10.		
11.		
12.		
13.		
14.		
15.		
16.		
17.		
18.		
19.		
20.		
PENCIL TOTALS		

1

Winnie the Pooh
Handcrafted • SIED
975QX5715 • **Value $33**

2

Baby's First Christmas
Handcrafted • FRAN
2200QLX7365 • **Value $47**

3

Bells Are Ringing
Handcrafted • CROW
2800QLX7402 • **Value $66**

4

Dog's Best Friend
Handcrafted • JLEE
1200QLX7172 • **Value $24**

5

Dollhouse Dreams
Handcrafted • CROW
2200QLX7372 • **Value $50**

6

Home on the Range
Handcrafted • SICK
3200QLX7395 • **Value $72**

7

The Lamplighter
Handcrafted • PALM
1800QLX7192 • **Value $41**

8

Last Minute Shopping
Handcrafted • VOTR
2800QLX7385 • **Value $62**

1993

9

Messages of Christmas
Handcrafted • SIED
3500QLX7476 • **Value $58**

10

North Pole Merrython
Handcrafted • SEAL
2500QLX7392 • **Value $53**

11

Our First Christmas Together
Handcrafted • CHAD
2000QLX7355 • **Value $42**

	Price Paid	Value of My Collection
1.		

GENERAL MAGIC

2.		
3.		

12

Radio News Flash
Handcrafted • DLEE
2200QLX7362 • **Value $50**

13

Raiding the Fridge
Handcrafted • RGRS
1600QLX7185 • **Value $37**

14

Road Runner and Wile E. Coyote™
Handcrafted • CHAD
3000QLX7415 • **Value $74**

4.		
5.		
6.		
7.		
8.		
9.		

15

Santa's Snow-Getter
Handcrafted • CROW
1800QLX7352 • **Value $39**

16

Santa's Workshop
Handcrafted • SIED
2800QLX7375 • **Value $58**

17

Song of the Chimes
Handcrafted/Brass • ANDR
2500QLX7405 • **Value $53**

10.		
11.		
12.		
13.		
14.		
15.		

18

U.S.S. Enterprise™ THE NEXT GENERATION™
Handcrafted • NORT
2400QLX7412 • **Value $52**

19

Winnie the Pooh
Handcrafted • SIED
2400QLX7422 • **Value $54**

16.		
17.		
18.		
19.		

PENCIL TOTALS

(1) Angel in Flight
Folk Art Americana
Handcrafted • SICK
1575QK1052 • **Value $52**

(2) Polar Bear Adventure
Folk Art Americana
Handcrafted • SICK
1500QK1055 • **Value $68**

(3) Riding in the Woods
Folk Art Americana
Handcrafted • SICK
1575QK1065 • **Value $72**

(4) Riding the Wind
Folk Art Americana
Handcrafted • SICK
1575QK1045 • **Value $63**

(5) Santa Claus
Folk Art Americana
Handcrafted • SICK
1675QK1072 • **Value $215**

(6) Angelic Messengers
Holiday Enchantment
Porcelain • VOTR
1375QK1032 • **Value $40**

(7) Bringing Home the Tree
Holiday Enchantment
Porcelain • CHAD
1375QK1042 • **Value $35**

(8) Journey to the Forest
Holiday Enchantment
Porcelain • N/A
1375QK1012 • **Value $32**

(9) The Magi
Holiday Enchantment
Porcelain • N/A
1375QK1025 • **Value $38**

(10) Visions of Sugarplums
Holiday Enchantment
Porcelain • N/A
1375QK1005 • **Value $36**

(11) Silver Dove of Peace
Old-World Silver
Silver-Plated • PALM
2475QK1075 • **Value $36**

(12) Silver Santa
Old-World Silver
Silver-Plated • UNRU
2475QK1092 • **Value $60**

(13) Silver Sleigh
Old-World Silver
Silver-Plated • PALM
2475QK1082 • **Value $37**

(14) Silver Stars and Holly
Old-World Silver
Silver-Plated • PALM
2475QK1085 • **Value $36**

(15) Christmas Feast
Portraits in Bisque
Porcelain • PIKE
1575QK1152 • **Value $35**

(16) Joy of Sharing
Portraits in Bisque
Porcelain • LYLE
1575QK1142 • **Value $35**

(17) Mistletoe Kiss
Portraits in Bisque
Porcelain • PIKE
1575QK1145 • **Value $32**

(18) Norman Rockwell – Filling the Stockings
Portraits in Bisque
Porcelain • DUTK
1575QK1155 • **Value $36**

(19) Norman Rockwell – Jolly Postman
Portraits in Bisque
Porcelain • DUTK
1575QK1162 • **Value $36**

General Showcase

	Price Paid	Value of My Collection
1.		
2.		
3.		
4.		
5.		
6.		
7.		
8.		
9.		
10.		
11.		
12.		
13.		
14.		
15.		
16.		
17.		
18.		
19.		

PENCIL TOTALS

1
Baby's First Christmas
Handcrafted • VOTR
575QXM5145 • **Value $12**

2
Cheese Please
Handcrafted • SIED
375QXM4072 • **Value $9**

3
Christmas Castle
Handcrafted • SEAL
575QXM4085 • **Value $12**

4
Cloisonné Snowflake
Cloisonné/Brass • VOTR
975QXM4012 • **Value $20**

5
Country Fiddling
Handcrafted • FRAN
375QXM4062 • **Value $12**

6
Crystal Angel
Crystal/Gold-Plated • PALM
975QXM4015 • **Value $51**

7
Ears to Pals
Handcrafted • ANDR
375QXM4075 • **Value $9**

8
Grandma
Handcrafted • SEAL
450QXM5162 • **Value $13**

9
I Dream of Santa
Handcrafted • SICK
375QXM4055 • **Value $14**

10
Into the Woods
Handcrafted • SEAL
375QXM4045 • **Value $9**

11
Learning to Skate
Handcrafted • CHAD
300QXM4122 • **Value $10**

12
Lighting a Path
Handcrafted • CHAD
300QXM4115 • **Value $9**

13
Merry Mascot
Handcrafted • SIED
375QXM4042 • **Value $10**

14
Mom
Handcrafted • ANDR
450QXM5155 • **Value $14**

15
Monkey Melody
Handcrafted • SICK
575QXM4092 • **Value $16**

16
North Pole Fire Truck
Handcrafted • PALM
475QXM4105 • **Value $14**

17
Pear-Shaped Tones
Handcrafted • LYLE
375QXM4052 • **Value $10**

18
Pull Out a Plum
Handcrafted • FRAN
575QXM4095 • **Value $14**

19
Refreshing Flight
Handcrafted • CHAD
575QXM4112 • **Value $15**

20
'Round the Mountain
Handcrafted • CROW
725QXM4025 • **Value $20**

1993

General Miniature

	Price Paid	Value of My Collection
1.		
2.		
3.		
4.		
5.		
6.		
7.		
8.		
9.		
10.		
11.		
12.		
13.		
14.		
15.		
16.		
17.		
18.		
19.		
20.		

PENCIL TOTALS

VALUE GUIDE – HALLMARK KEEPSAKE ORNAMENTS

① Secret Pal
Handcrafted • RGRS
375QXM5172 • **Value $11**

② Snuggle Birds
Handcrafted • ANDR
575QXM5182 • **Value $15**

③ Special Friends
Handcrafted • FRAN
450QXM5165 • **Value $12**

④ Tiny Green Thumbs (set/6)
Handcrafted • SEAL
2900QXM4032 • **Value $52**

⑤ Visions of Sugarplums
Pewter • PALM
725QXM4022 • **Value $18**

⑥ Circle of Friendship (gift membership bonus)
Glass • N/A
QXC2112 • **Value N/E**

⑦ Forty Winks (keepsake of membership, miniature)
Handcrafted • FRAN
QXC5294 • **Value $25**

⑧ Gentle Tidings (club edition, LE-17,500)
Porcelain • ANDR
2500QXC5442 • **Value $55**

GENERAL MINIATURE

	Price Paid	Value of My Collection
1.		
2.		
3.		
4.		
5.		

COLLECTOR'S CLUB

6.		
7.		
8.		
9.		
10.		
11.		

PREMIERE ORNAMENTS

12.		

REACH ORNAMENTS

13.		
14.		
15.		
16.		
17.		

ANNIVERSARY BELLS

18.		
19.		

PENCIL TOTALS

⑨ It's in the Mail (keepsake of membership)
Handcrafted • SEAL
QXC5272 • **Value $27**

⑩ Sharing Christmas (club edition, LE-16,500)
Handcrafted • LYLE
2000QXC5435 • **Value $49**

⑪ Trimmed With Memories (club edition)
Handcrafted • SICK
1200QXC5432 • **Value $43**

⑫ You're Always Welcome
Handcrafted • SEAL
975QX5692 • **Value $62**

⑬ Abearnathy
The Bearingers of Victoria Circle
Handcrafted • N/A
495XPR9747 • **Value $12**

⑭ Bearnadette
The Bearingers of Victoria Circle
Handcrafted • N/A
495XPR9748 • **Value $12**

⑮ Fireplace Base
The Bearingers of Victoria Circle
Handcrafted • N/A
495XPR9749 • **Value $14**

⑯ Mama Bearinger
The Bearingers of Victoria Circle
Handcrafted • N/A
495XPR9745 • **Value $14**

⑰ Papa Bearinger
The Bearingers of Victoria Circle
Handcrafted • N/A
495XPR9746 • **Value $12**

⑱ 25 Years Together
Porcelain • N/A
800AGA7687 • **Value $20**

⑲ 50 Years Together
Porcelain • N/A
800AGA7788 • **Value $20**

1 Our First Anniversary
Porcelain • N/A
1000AGA7865 • **Value $20**

2 Our Fifth Anniversary
Porcelain • N/A
1000AGA7866 • **Value $20**

3 Our Tenth Anniversary
Porcelain • N/A
1000AGA7867 • **Value $20**

4 25 Years Together
Porcelain • N/A
1000AGA7686 • **Value $20**

5 40 Years Together
Porcelain • N/A
1000AGA7868 • **Value $20**

6 50 Years Together
Porcelain • N/A
1000AGA7787 • **Value $20**

7 Santa's Favorite Stop
Handcrafted • VARI
5500QXC4125 • **Value N/E**

8 Baby's Christening
Handcrafted • N/A
1200BBY2917 • **Value $20**

9 Baby's Christening Photoholder
Silver-Plated • N/A
1000BBY1335 • **Value $15**

10 Baby's First Christmas
Handcrafted • N/A
1200BBY2918 • **Value $18**

11 Baby's First Christmas
Handcrafted • N/A
1400BBY2919 • **Value $20**

12 Baby's First Christmas Photoholder
Silver-Plated • N/A
1000BBY1470 • **Value $15**

13 Granddaughter's First Christmas
Handcrafted • N/A
1400BBY2802 • **Value $20**

14 Grandson's First Christmas
Handcrafted • N/A
1400BBY2801 • **Value $20**

15 K.C. Angel
Silver-Plated • N/A
(N/C) No stock # • **Value $500**

16 Baby Block Photoholder (re-issued in 1994)
Handcrafted • FRAN
1475QP6035 • **Value N/E**

17 Cool Snowman
Glass • N/A
875QP6052 • **Value N/E**

18 Festive Album Photoholder (re-issued in 1994)
Handcrafted • VOTR
1275QP6025 • **Value N/E**

19 Filled With Cookies
Handcrafted • RGRS
1275QP6042 • **Value N/E**

20 Going Golfin' (re-issued in 1994)
Handcrafted • PALM
1275QP6012 • **Value N/E**

1993

	Price Paid	Value of My Collection
ANNIVERSARY ORNAMENTS		
1.		
2.		
3.		
4.		
5.		
6.		
ARTISTS ON TOUR PIECES		
7.		
BABY ORNAMENTS		
8.		
9.		
10.		
11.		
12.		
13.		
14.		
CONVENTION ORNAMENTS		
15.		
PERSONALIZED ORNAMENTS		
16.		
17.		
18.		
19.		
20.		
PENCIL TOTALS		

①	②	③	④
Here's Your Fortune	**Mailbox Delivery** (re-issued in 1994 and 1995)	**On the Billboard** (re-issued in 1994 and 1995)	**PEANUTS®**
Handcrafted • SEAL	*Handcrafted* • CROW	*Handcrafted* • CROW	*Glass* • N/A
1075QP6002 • **Value N/E**	1475QP6015 • **Value N/E**	1275QP6022 • **Value N/E**	900QP6045 • **Value N/E**

⑤ 	⑥	⑦
Playing Ball (re-issued in 1994 and 1995)	**Reindeer in the Sky**	**Santa Says** (re-issued in 1994)
Handcrafted • FRAN	*Glass* • N/A	*Handcrafted* • SEAL
1275QP6032 • **Value N/E**	875QP6055 • **Value N/E**	1475QP6005 • **Value N/E**

PERSONALIZED ORNAMENTS

	Price Paid	Value of My Collection
1.		
2.		
3.		
4.		
5.		
6.		
7.		

1992

Of note in the 1992 collection was the debut of the "unofficial series" of handcrafted Coca-Cola® Santa ornaments in the Keepsake and Miniature lines. For 1992, there were 126 Keepsake ornaments, 21 Magic ornaments and 48 Miniature ornaments. See the collectible series section for more 1992 ornaments.

⑧ 	⑨	⑩
Across The Miles	**Anniversary Year Photoholder**	**Baby's First Christmas**
Acrylic • RHOD	*Chrome/Brass* • UNRU	*Handcrafted* • FRAN
675QX3044 • **Value $14**	975QX4851 • **Value $28**	775QX4644 • **Value $32**

GENERAL KEEPSAKE

⑪	⑫ 	⑬
Baby's First Christmas	**Baby's First Christmas – Baby Boy**	**Baby's First Christmas – Baby Girl**
Porcelain • ANDR	*Satin* • VOTR	*Satin* • VOTR
1875QX4581 • **Value $40**	475QX2191 • **Value $19**	475QX2204 • **Value $19**

8.		
9.		
10.		
11.		
12.		
13.		
14.		
15.		
16.		

⑭ 	⑮	⑯ 
Baby's First Christmas Photoholder	**Baby's Second Christmas**	**Bear Bell Champ**
Fabric • VOTR	*Handcrafted* • FRAN	*Handcrafted/Brass* • SEAL
775QX4641 • **Value $26**	675QX4651 • **Value $23**	775QX5071 • **Value $31**

PENCIL TOTALS

1. **Brother**
Handcrafted • CROW
675QX4684 • **Value $16**

2. **Cheerful Santa**
Handcrafted • UNRU
975QX5154 • **Value $37**

3. **A Child's Christmas**
Handcrafted • FRAN
975QX4574 • **Value $19**

4. **Child's Fifth Christmas**
Handcrafted • RHOD
675QX4664 • **Value $22**

5. **Child's Fourth Christmas**
Handcrafted • FRAN
675QX4661 • **Value $26**

6. **Child's Third Christmas**
Handcrafted • FRAN
675QX4654 • **Value $23**

7. **Cool Fliers (set/2)**
Handcrafted • JLEE
1075QX5474 • **Value $26**

8. **Dad**
Handcrafted • SIED
775QX4674 • **Value $24**

9. **Dad-to-Be**
Handcrafted • JLEE
675QX4611 • **Value $17**

10. **Daughter**
Handcrafted • FRAN
675QX5031 • **Value $27**

11. **Deck the Hogs**
Handcrafted • FRAN
875QX5204 • **Value $24**

12. **Dickens Caroler Bell – Lord Chadwick**
Porcelain • CHAD
2175QX4554 • **Value $48**

13. **Down-Under Holiday**
Handcrafted • CROW
775QX5144 • **Value $20**

14. **Egg Nog Nest**
Handcrafted • N/A
775QX5121 • **Value $18**

15. **Elfin Marionette**
Handcrafted • CHAD
1175QX5931 • **Value $23**

16. **Elvis**
Brass-Plated • RHOD/LYLE
1475QX5624 • **Value $28**

17. **Eric the Baker**
Handcrafted • SICK
875QX5244 • **Value $21**

18. **Feliz Navidad**
Handcrafted • ANDR
675QX5181 • **Value $23**

19. **For My Grandma Photoholder**
Fabric • N/A
775QX5184 • **Value $15**

20. **For The One I Love**
Porcelain • LYLE
975QX4844 • **Value $23**

GENERAL KEEPSAKE

	Price Paid	Value of My Collection
1.		
2.		
3.		
4.		
5.		
6.		
7.		
8.		
9.		
10.		
11.		
12.		
13.		
14.		
15.		
16.		
17.		
18.		
19.		
20.		
PENCIL TOTALS		

1992

(1) Franz the Artist
Handcrafted • SICK
875QX5261 • **Value $27**

(2) Frieda the Animals' Friend
Handcrafted • SICK
875QX5264 • **Value $25**

(3) Friendly Greetings
Handcrafted • CHAD
775QX5041 • **Value $15**

(4) Friendship Line
Handcrafted • SEAL
975QX5034 • **Value $30**

(5) From Our Home to Yours
Glass • VOTR
475QX2131 • **Value $13**

(6) Fun on a Big Scale
Handcrafted • CROW
1075QX5134 • **Value $23**

(7) GARFIELD
Handcrafted • PALM
775QX5374 • **Value $18**

(8) Genius at Work
Handcrafted • CROW
1075QX5371 • **Value $22**

General Keepsake

	Price Paid	Value of My Collection
1.		
2.		
3.		
4.		
5.		
6.		
7.		
8.		
9.		
10.		
11.		
12.		
13.		
14.		
15.		
16.		
17.		
18.		
19.		
20.		

Pencil Totals

(9) Godchild
Handcrafted • UNRU
675QX5941 • **Value $20**

(10) Golf's a Ball
Handcrafted • SCHU
675QX5984 • **Value $29**

(11) Gone Wishin'
Handcrafted • DLEE
875QX5171 • **Value $19**

(12) Granddaughter
Handcrafted • SEAL
675QX5604 • **Value $23**

(13) Granddaughter's First Christmas
Handcrafted • SIED
675QX4634 • **Value $19**

(14) Grandmother
Glass • N/A
475QX2011 • **Value $18**

(15) Grandparents
Glass • N/A
475QX2004 • **Value $17**

(16) Grandson
Handcrafted • SEAL
675QX5611 • **Value $21**

(17) Grandson's First Christmas
Handcrafted • SIED
675QX4621 • **Value $18**

(18) Green Thumb Santa
Handcrafted • PALM
775QX5101 • **Value $17**

(19) Hello-Ho-Ho
Handcrafted • CROW
975QX5141 • **Value $24**

(20) Holiday Memo
Handcrafted • RGRS
775QX5044 • **Value $17**

VALUE GUIDE — HALLMARK KEEPSAKE ORNAMENTS

(1) Holiday Teatime (set/2)
Handcrafted • RGRS
1475QX5431 • **Value $32**

(2) Holiday Wishes
Handcrafted • PIKE
775QX5131 • **Value $17**

(3) Honest George
Handcrafted • JLEE
775QX5064 • **Value $20**

(4) Jesus Loves Me
Cameo • ANDR
775QX3024 • **Value $17**

(5) Love to Skate
Handcrafted • RGRS
875QX4841 • **Value $22**

(6) Loving Shepherd
Handcrafted/Brass • ANDR
775QX5151 • **Value $18**

(7) Ludwig the Musician
Handcrafted • SICK
875QX5281 • **Value $22**

(8) Max the Tailor
Handcrafted • SICK
875QX5251 • **Value $22**

(9) Memories to Cherish Photoholder
Porcelain • ANDR
1075QX5161 • **Value $23**

(10) Merry "Swiss" Mouse
Handcrafted • SEAL
775QX5114 • **Value $16**

(11) Mom
Handcrafted • RGRS
775QX5164 • **Value $21**

(12) Mom and Dad
Handcrafted • SIED
975QX4671 • **Value $39**

(13) Mom-to-Be
Handcrafted • JLEE
675QX4614 • **Value $18**

(14) Mother Goose
Handcrafted • CROW
1375QX4984 • **Value $30**

(15) New Home
Handcrafted • PIKE
875QX5191 • **Value $18**

(16) Norman Rockwell Art
Glass • LYLE
500QX2224 • **Value $25**

(17) North Pole Fire Fighter
Handcrafted/Brass • SEAL
975QX5104 • **Value $24**

(18) Otto the Carpenter
Handcrafted • SICK
875QX5254 • **Value $22**

(19) Our First Christmas Together
Acrylic • VOTR
675QX3011 • **Value $19**

(20) Our First Christmas Together
Handcrafted • JLEE
975QX5061 • **Value $21**

1992

GENERAL KEEPSAKE

	Price Paid	Value of My Collection
1.		
2.		
3.		
4.		
5.		
6.		
7.		
8.		
9.		
10.		
11.		
12.		
13.		
14.		
15.		
16.		
17.		
18.		
19.		
20.		
PENCIL TOTALS		

Value Guide – Hallmark Keepsake Ornaments

1

Our First Christmas Together Photoholder
Handcrafted • SEAL
875QX4694 • **Value $24**

2

Owl
Handcrafted • SIED
975QX5614 • **Value $28**

3

Partridge IN a Pear Tree
Handcrafted • SIED
875QX5234 • **Value $19**

4

PEANUTS®
Glass • N/A
500QX2244 • **Value $30**

5

Please Pause Here
Handcrafted • DLEE
1475QX5291 • **Value $35**

6

Polar Post
Handcrafted • SEAL
875QX4914 • **Value $22**

7

Rapid Delivery
Handcrafted • PALM
875QX5094 • **Value $23**

8

A Santa-Full!
Handcrafted • FRAN
975QX5991 • **Value $42**

General Keepsake

	Price Paid	Value of My Collection
1.		
2.		
3.		
4.		
5.		
6.		
7.		
8.		
9.		
10.		
11.		
12.		
13.		
14.		
15.		
16.		
17.		
18.		
19.		
20.		

PENCIL TOTALS

9

Santa Maria
Handcrafted • CROW
1275QX5074 • **Value $26**

10

Santa's Hook Shot (set/2)
Handcrafted • SEAL
1275QX5434 • **Value $30**

11

Santa's Roundup
Handcrafted • JLEE
875QX5084 • **Value $26**

12

Secret Pal
Handcrafted • RGRS
775QX5424 • **Value $14**

13

Silver Star Train Set (set/3)
Die-Cast Metal • SICK
2800QX5324 • **Value $58**

14

Sister
Handcrafted • CROW
675QX4681 • **Value $15**

15

Skiing 'Round
Handcrafted • JLEE
875QX5214 • **Value $21**

16

Sky Line Caboose
Die-Cast Metal • SICK
975QX5321 • **Value $27**

17

Sky Line Coal Car
Die-Cast Metal • SICK
975QX5401 • **Value $22**

18

Sky Line Locomotive
Die-Cast Metal • SICK
975QX5311 • **Value $45**

19

Sky Line Stock Car
Die-Cast Metal • SICK
975QX5314 • **Value $22**

20

SNOOPY® and WOODSTOCK
Handcrafted • RGRS
875QX5954 • **Value $42**

(1)  **Son** *Handcrafted* • FRAN 675QX5024 • **Value $27**	**(2)** **Special Cat Photoholder** *Handcrafted* • CHAD 775QX5414 • **Value $19**	**(3)** **Special Dog Photoholder** *Handcrafted* • CHAD 775QX5421 • **Value $30**	**(4)** **Spirit of Christmas Stress** *Handcrafted* • CHAD 875QX5231 • **Value $26**
(5)  **Stocked With Joy** *Pressed Tin* • SICK 775QX5934 • **Value $23**	**(6)** **Tasty Christmas** *Handcrafted* • FRAN 975QX5994 • **Value $26**	**(7)** **Teacher** *Glass* • N/A 475QX2264 • **Value $16**	**(8)** **Toboggan Tail** *Handcrafted* • ANDR 775QX5459 • **Value $19**

			GENERAL KEEPSAKE
(9) **Tread Bear** *Handcrafted* • SEAL 875QX5091 • **Value $25**	**(10)** **Turtle Dreams** *Handcrafted* • JLEE 875QX4991 • **Value $27**	**(11)** **Uncle Art's Ice Cream** *Handcrafted* • SIED 875QX5001 • **Value $28**	

	Price Paid	Value of My Collection
1.		
2.		
3.		
4.		
5.		
6.		
7.		
8.		
9.		
10.		
11.		
12.		
13.		

(12) **V.P. of Important Stuff** *Handcrafted* • SIED 675QX5051 • **Value $16**	**(13)**  **World-Class Teacher** *Handcrafted* • SIED 775QX5054 • **Value $19**	**(14)** **Baby's First Christmas** *Handcrafted* • CROW 2200QLX7281 • **Value $90**
(15) **Christmas Parade** *Handcrafted* • SICK 3000QLX7271 • **Value $62**	**(16)**  **Continental Express** *Handcrafted* • SICK 3200QLX7264 • **Value $73**	**(17)** **The Dancing Nutcracker** *Handcrafted* • VOTR 3000QLX7261 • **Value $56**

GENERAL MAGIC

14.		
15.		
16.		
17.		
18.		
19.		
20.		

(18) **Enchanted Clock** *Handcrafted* • CROW 3000QLX7274 • **Value $60**	**(19)** **Feathered Friends** *Handcrafted* • SICK 1400QLX7091 • **Value $30**	**(20)**  **Good Sledding Ahead** *Handcrafted* • PALM 2800QLX7244 • **Value $59**

PENCIL TOTALS

1992

(1) 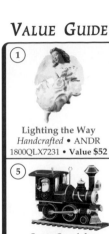 **Lighting the Way** *Handcrafted* • ANDR 1800QLX7231 • **Value $52**	(2) **Look! It's Santa** *Handcrafted* • DLEE 1400QLX7094 • **Value $48**	(3) **Nut Sweet Nut** *Handcrafted* • CROW 1000QLX7081 • **Value $24**	(4) **Our First Christmas Together** *Panorama Ball* • CHAD 2000QLX7221 • **Value $44**

(5) **Santa Special** (re-issued from 1991) *Handcrafted* • SEAL 4000QLX7167 • **Value $78**	(6) **Santa Sub** *Handcrafted* • CROW 1800QLX7321 • **Value $40**	(7)  **Santa's Answering Machine** *Handcrafted* • JLEE 2200QLX7241 • **Value $45**	(8) **Shuttlecraft Galileo™ From the Starship Enterprise™** *Handcrafted* • RHOD 2400QLX7331 • **Value $52**

	Price Paid	Value of My Collection
1.		
2.		
3.		
4.		
5.		
6.		
7.		
8.		
9.		
10.		

11.		
12.		
13.		
14.		
15.		
16.		
17.		
18.		
19.		
20.		

PENCIL TOTALS

(9) **Under Construction** *Handcrafted* • PALM 1800QLX7324 • **Value $42**	(10) **Watch Owls** *Porcelain* • FRAN 1200QLX7084 • **Value $28**	(11) **Yuletide Rider** *Handcrafted* • SEAL 2800QLX7314 • **Value $56**

(12) **A+ Teacher** *Handcrafted* • UNRU 375QXM5511 • **Value $8**	(13) **Angelic Harpist** *Handcrafted* • LYLE 450QXM5524 • **Value $15**	(14) **Baby's First Christmas** *Handcrafted/Brass* • LYLE 450QXM5494 • **Value $21**

(15) **Black-Capped Chickadee** *Handcrafted* • FRAN 300QXM5484 • **Value $15**	(16) 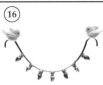 **Bright Stringers** *Handcrafted* • SEAL 375QXM5841 • **Value $15**	(17) **Buck-A-Roo** *Handcrafted* • CROW 450QXM5814 • **Value $15**

(18)  **Christmas Bonus** *Handcrafted* • PALM 300QXM5811 • **Value $9**	(19) **Christmas Copter** *Handcrafted* • FRAN 575QXM5844 • **Value $15**	(20) **Coca-Cola® Santa** *Handcrafted* • UNRU 575QXM5884 • **Value $18**

Value Guide — Hallmark Keepsake Ornaments

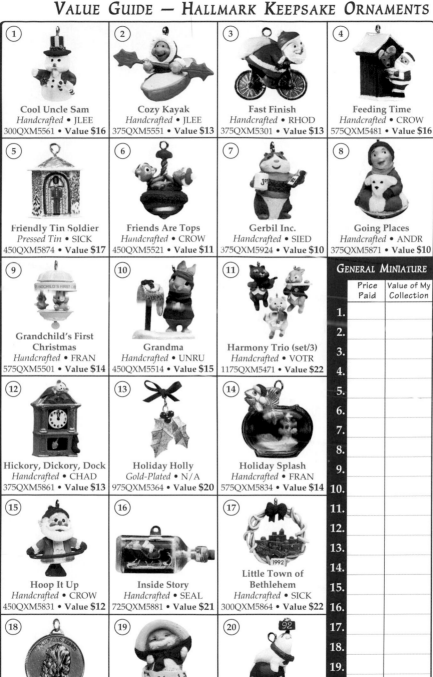

(1) Cool Uncle Sam
Handcrafted • JLEE
300QXM5561 • **Value $16**

(2) Cozy Kayak
Handcrafted • JLEE
375QXM5551 • **Value $13**

(3) Fast Finish
Handcrafted • RHOD
375QXM5301 • **Value $13**

(4) Feeding Time
Handcrafted • CROW
575QXM5481 • **Value $16**

(5) Friendly Tin Soldier
Pressed Tin • SICK
450QXM5874 • **Value $17**

(6) Friends Are Tops
Handcrafted • CROW
450QXM5521 • **Value $11**

(7) Gerbil Inc.
Handcrafted • SIED
375QXM5924 • **Value $10**

(8) Going Places
Handcrafted • ANDR
375QXM5871 • **Value $10**

(9) Grandchild's First Christmas
Handcrafted • FRAN
575QXM5501 • **Value $14**

(10) Grandma
Handcrafted • UNRU
450QXM5514 • **Value $15**

(11) Harmony Trio (set/3)
Handcrafted • VOTR
1175QXM5471 • **Value $22**

(12) Hickory, Dickory, Dock
Handcrafted • CHAD
375QXM5861 • **Value $13**

(13) Holiday Holly
Gold-Plated • N/A
975QXM5364 • **Value $20**

(14) Holiday Splash
Handcrafted • FRAN
575QXM5834 • **Value $14**

(15) Hoop It Up
Handcrafted • CROW
450QXM5831 • **Value $12**

(16) Inside Story
Handcrafted • SEAL
725QXM5881 • **Value $21**

(17) Little Town of Bethlehem
Handcrafted • SICK
300QXM5864 • **Value $22**

(18) Minted for Santa
Copper • UNRU
375QXM5854 • **Value $14**

(19) Mom
Handcrafted • ANDR
450QXM5504 • **Value $17**

(20) Perfect Balance
Handcrafted • RGRS
300QXM5571 • **Value $12**

1992

General Miniature

	Price Paid	Value of My Collection
1.		
2.		
3.		
4.		
5.		
6.		
7.		
8.		
9.		
10.		
11.		
12.		
13.		
14.		
15.		
16.		
17.		
18.		
19.		
20.		
PENCIL TOTALS		

(1) Polar Polka
Handcrafted • SEAL
450QXM5534 • **Value $15**

(2) Puppet Show
Handcrafted • SIED
300QXM5574 • **Value $13**

(3) Sew, Sew Tiny (set/6)
Handcrafted • SEAL
2900QXM5794 • **Value $55**

(4) Ski for Two
Handcrafted • ANDR
450QXM5821 • **Value $14**

(5) Snowshoe Bunny
Handcrafted • VOTR
375QXM5564 • **Value $12**

(6) Snug Kitty
Handcrafted • PIKE
375QXM5554 • **Value $13**

(7) Spunky Monkey
Handcrafted • CHAD
300QXM5921 • **Value $16**

(8) Visions of Acorns
Handcrafted • ANDR
450QXM5851 • **Value $16**

(9) Wee Three Kings
Handcrafted • PALM
575QXM5531 • **Value $20**

(10) Chipmunk Parcel Service (early renewal piece, miniature)
Handcrafted • SEAL
QXC5194 • **Value $26**

(11) Christmas Treasures (set/4, club edition, LE-15,500, miniature)
Handcrafted • CHAD
2200QXC5464 • **Value $160**

(12) Rodney Takes Flight (keepsake of membership)
Handcrafted • DLEE
QXC5081 • **Value $28**

(13) Santa's Club List (club edition, magic)
Handcrafted • SEAL
1500QXC7291 • **Value $42**

(14) Victorian Skater (club edition, LE-14,700)
Porcelain • UNRU
2500QXC4067 • **Value $71**

(15) O Christmas Tree
Porcelain • VOTR
1075QX5411 • **Value $38**

(16) Comet and Cupid
Santa and His Reindeer
Handcrafted/Brass • CROW
495XPR9737 • **Value $22**

(17) Dasher and Dancer
Santa and His Reindeer
Handcrafted/Brass • CROW
495XPR9735 • **Value $53**

(18) Donder and Blitzen
Santa and His Reindeer
Handcrafted/Brass • CROW
495XPR9738 • **Value $40**

(19) Prancer and Vixen
Santa and His Reindeer
Handcrafted/Brass • CROW
495XPR9736 • **Value $22**

(20) Santa Claus
Santa and His Reindeer
Handcrafted/Brass • CROW
495XPR9739 • **Value $31**

General Miniature

	Price Paid	Value of My Collection
1.		
2.		
3.		
4.		
5.		
6.		
7.		
8.		
9.		

Collector's Club

10.		
11.		
12.		
13.		
14.		

Premiere Ornaments

15.		

Reach Ornaments

16.		
17.		
18.		
19.		
20.		

Pencil Totals

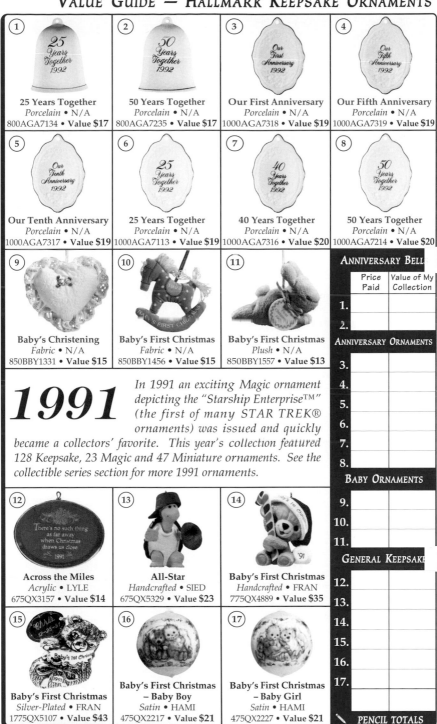

① 25 Years Together
Porcelain • N/A
800AGA7134 • **Value $17**

② 50 Years Together
Porcelain • N/A
800AGA7235 • **Value $17**

③ Our First Anniversary
Porcelain • N/A
1000AGA7318 • **Value $19**

④ Our Fifth Anniversary
Porcelain • N/A
1000AGA7319 • **Value $19**

⑤ Our Tenth Anniversary
Porcelain • N/A
1000AGA7317 • **Value $19**

⑥ 25 Years Together
Porcelain • N/A
1000AGA7113 • **Value $19**

⑦ 40 Years Together
Porcelain • N/A
1000AGA7316 • **Value $20**

⑧ 50 Years Together
Porcelain • N/A
1000AGA7214 • **Value $20**

⑨ Baby's Christening
Fabric • N/A
850BBY1331 • **Value $15**

⑩ Baby's First Christmas
Fabric • N/A
850BBY1456 • **Value $15**

⑪ Baby's First Christmas
Plush • N/A
850BBY1557 • **Value $13**

1991

In 1991 an exciting Magic ornament depicting the "Starship Enterprise™" (the first of many STAR TREK® ornaments) was issued and quickly became a collectors' favorite. This year's collection featured 128 Keepsake, 23 Magic and 47 Miniature ornaments. See the collectible series section for more 1991 ornaments.

⑫ Across the Miles
Acrylic • LYLE
675QX3157 • **Value $14**

⑬ All-Star
Handcrafted • SIED
675QX5329 • **Value $23**

⑭ Baby's First Christmas
Handcrafted • FRAN
775QX4889 • **Value $35**

⑮ Baby's First Christmas
Silver-Plated • FRAN
1775QX5107 • **Value $43**

⑯ Baby's First Christmas – Baby Boy
Satin • HAMI
475QX2217 • **Value $21**

⑰ Baby's First Christmas – Baby Girl
Satin • HAMI
475QX2227 • **Value $21**

	Price Paid	Value of My Collection
ANNIVERSARY BELL		
1.		
2.		
ANNIVERSARY ORNAMENTS		
3.		
4.		
5.		
6.		
7.		
8.		
BABY ORNAMENTS		
9.		
10.		
11.		
GENERAL KEEPSAKE		
12.		
13.		
14.		
15.		
16.		
17.		
PENCIL TOTALS		

1991

(1)  **Baby's First Christmas Photoholder** *Fabric* • VOTR 775QX4869 • **Value $30**	**(2)** **Baby's Second Christmas** *Handcrafted* • FRAN 675QX4897 • **Value $34**	**(3)** **Basket Bell Players** *Handcrafted/Wicker* • SEAL 775QX5377 • **Value $26**	**(4)** **The Big Cheese** *Handcrafted* • SIED 675QX5327 • **Value $20**

(5) **Bob Cratchit** *Porcelain* • UNRU 1375QX4997 • **Value $37**

(6) **Brother** *Handcrafted* • SIED 675QX5479 • **Value $22**

(7) **A Child's Christmas** *Handcrafted* • FRAN 975QX4887 • **Value $17**

(8) **Child's Fifth Christmas** *Handcrafted* • RHOD 675QX4909 • **Value $19**

GENERAL KEEPSAKE

	Price Paid	Value of My Collection
1.		
2.		
3.		
4.		
5.		
6.		
7.		
8.		
9.		
10.		
11.		
12.		
13.		
14.		
15.		
16.		
17.		
18.		
19.		
20.		

PENCIL TOTALS

(9) **Child's Fourth Christmas** *Handcrafted* • FRAN 675QX4907 • **Value $20**

(10) **Child's Third Christmas** *Handcrafted* • FRAN 675QX4899 • **Value $30**

(11) **Chilly Chap** *Handcrafted* • DLEE 675QX5339 • **Value $18**

(12) **Christmas Welcome** *Handcrafted* • SICK 975QX5299 • **Value $25**

(13) **Christopher Robin** *Handcrafted* • SIED 975QX5579 • **Value $38**

(14) **Cuddly Lamb** *Handcrafted* • RGRS 675QX5199 • **Value $20**

(15) **Dad** *Handcrafted* • JLEE 775QX5127 • **Value $19**

(16) **Dad-to-Be** *Handcrafted* • JLEE 575QX4879 • **Value $18**

(17) **Daughter** *Handcrafted* • SIED 575QX5477 • **Value $52**

(18) **Dickens Caroler Bell – Mrs. Beaumont** *Porcelain* • CHAD 2175QX5039 • **Value $48**

(19) **Dinoclaus** *Handcrafted* • CHAD 775QX5277 • **Value $23**

(20) **Ebenezer Scrooge** *Porcelain* • UNRU 1375QX4989 • **Value $46**

1 Evergreen Inn
Handcrafted • SEAL
875QX5389 • **Value $18**

2 Extra-Special Friends
Glass • N/A
475QX2279 • **Value $17**

3 Fanfare Bear
Handcrafted • SEAL
875QX5337 • **Value $20**

4 Feliz Navidad
Handcrafted • JLEE
675QX5279 • **Value $26**

5 Fiddlin' Around
Handcrafted • VOTR
775QX4387 • **Value $20**

6 Fifty Years Together
Photoholder
Handcrafted/Brass • VOTR
875QX4947 • **Value $19**

7 First Christmas
Together
Acrylic • PIKE
675QX3139 • **Value $24**

8 First Christmas
Together
Glass • N/A
475QX2229 • **Value $20**

9 First Christmas
Together
Handcrafted • SICK
875QX4919 • **Value $28**

10 First Christmas
Together Photoholder
Handcrafted/Brass • VOTR
875QX4917 • **Value $32**

11 Five Years Together
Faceted Glass • N/A
775QX4927 • **Value $21**

12 Flag of Liberty
Handcrafted • DLEE
675QX5249 • **Value $18**

13 Folk Art Reindeer
Wood/Brass • VOTR
875QX5359 • **Value $20**

14 Forty Years Together
Faceted Glass • N/A
775QX4939 • **Value $20**

15 Friends Are Fun
Handcrafted • CROW
975QX5289 • **Value $24**

16 From Our Home
to Yours
Glass • VOTR
475QX2287 • **Value $23**

17 GARFIELD®
Handcrafted • RHOD
775QX5177 • **Value $31**

18 Gift of Joy
Brass/Chrome/Copper • MCGE
875QX5319 • **Value $25**

19 Glee Club Bears
Handcrafted • SEAL
875QX4969 • **Value $22**

20 Godchild
Handcrafted • BISH
675QX5489 • **Value $22**

GENERAL KEEPSAKE

	Price Paid	Value of My Collection
1.		
2.		
3.		
4.		
5.		
6.		
7.		
8.		
9.		
10.		
11.		
12.		
13.		
14.		
15.		
16.		
17.		
18.		
19.		
20.		
PENCIL TOTALS		

1991

Value Guide — Hallmark Keepsake Ornaments

(1) **Granddaughter** *Glass* • PYDA 475QX2299 • **Value $28**	**(2)** **Granddaughter's First Christmas** *Handcrafted* • CHAD 675QX5119 • **Value $24**

(1) **Granddaughter**
Glass • PYDA
475QX2299 • **Value $28**

(2) **Granddaughter's First Christmas**
Handcrafted • CHAD
675QX5119 • **Value $24**

(3) **Grandmother**
Glass • N/A
475QX2307 • **Value $19**

(4) **Grandparents**
Glass • PYDA
475QX2309 • **Value $16**

(5) **Grandson**
Glass • PYDA
475QX2297 • **Value $25**

(6) **Grandson's First Christmas**
Handcrafted • CHAD
675QX5117 • **Value $27**

(7) **Holiday Cafe**
Handcrafted • SEAL
875QX5399 • **Value $16**

(8) **Hooked on Santa**
Handcrafted • JLEE
775QX4109 • **Value $28**

(9) **Jesus Loves Me**
Cameo • RHOD
775QX3147 • **Value $18**

(10) **Jolly Wolly Santa**
Pressed Tin • SICK
775QX5419 • **Value $32**

(11) **Jolly Wolly Snowman**
Pressed Tin • SICK
775QX5427 • **Value $24**

(12) **Jolly Wolly Soldier**
Pressed Tin • SICK
775QX5429 • **Value $21**

(13) **Joyous Memories Photoholder**
Handcrafted • VOTR
675QX5369 • **Value $28**

(14) **Kanga and Roo**
Handcrafted • SIED
975QX5617 • **Value $49**

(15) **Look Out Below**
Handcrafted • SEAL
875QX4959 • **Value $21**

(16) **Loving Stitches**
Handcrafted • SEAL
875QX4987 • **Value $34**

(17) **Mary Engelbreit**
Glass • N/A
475QX2237 • **Value $32**

(18) **Merry Carolers**
Porcelain • UNRU
2975QX4799 • **Value $94**

(19) **Mom and Dad**
Handcrafted • N/A
975QX5467 • **Value $25**

(20) **Mom-to-Be**
Handcrafted • JLEE
575QX4877 • **Value $25**

General Keepsake

	Price Paid	Value of My Collection
1.		
2.		
3.		
4.		
5.		
6.		
7.		
8.		
9.		
10.		
11.		
12.		
13.		
14.		
15.		
16.		
17.		
18.		
19.		
20.		

PENCIL TOTALS

1

Mother
Porcelain/Tin • N/A
975QX5457 • **Value $37**

2

Mrs. Cratchit
Porcelain • UNRU
1375QX4999 • **Value $32**

3

New Home
Handcrafted • BISH
675QX5449 • **Value $33**

4

Night Before Christmas
Handcrafted • SICK
975QX5307 • **Value $25**

5

Noah's Ark
Handcrafted • CROW
1375QX4867 • **Value $50**

6

Norman Rockwell Art
Glass • LYLE
500QX2259 • **Value $32**

7

Notes of Cheer
Handcrafted • SIED
575QX5357 • **Value $14**

8

Nutshell Nativity
Handcrafted • RGRS
675QX5176 • **Value $26**

9

Nutty Squirrel
Handcrafted • PIKE
575QX4833 • **Value $14**

10

Old-Fashioned Sled
Handcrafted • SICK
875QX4317 • **Value $20**

11

On a Roll
Handcrafted • CROW
675QX5347 • **Value $21**

12

Partridge in a Pear Tree
Handcrafted • SICK
975QX5297 • **Value $20**

13

PEANUTS®
Glass • N/A
500QX2257 • **Value $31**

14

Piglet and Eeyore
Handcrafted • SIED
975QX5577 • **Value $56**

15

Plum Delightful
Handcrafted • SEAL
875QX4977 • **Value $20**

16

Polar Circus Wagon
Handcrafted • SICK
1375QX4399 • **Value $30**

17

Polar Classic
Handcrafted • SIED
675QX5287 • **Value $22**

18

Rabbit
Handcrafted • SIED
975QX5607 • **Value $33**

19

Santa Sailor
Handcrafted/Metal • SEAL
975QX4389 • **Value $27**

20

Santa's Studio
Handcrafted • SEAL
875QX5397 • **Value $19**

	Price Paid	Value of My Collection
General Keepsake		
1.		
2.		
3.		
4.		
5.		
6.		
7.		
8		
9.		
10.		
11.		
12.		
13.		
14.		
15.		
16.		
17.		
18.		
19.		
20.		
PENCIL TOTALS		

1991

1
Sister
Handcrafted • LYLE
675QX5487 • **Value $20**

2
Ski Lift Bunny
Handcrafted • JLEE
675QX5447 • **Value $22**

3
SNOOPY® and WOODSTOCK
Handcrafted • RHOD
675QX5197 • **Value $40**

4
Snow Twins
Handcrafted • SEAL
875QX4979 • **Value $22**

5
Snowy Owl
Handcrafted • SICK
775QX5269 • **Value $20**

6
Son
Handcrafted • SIED
575QX5469 • **Value $20**

7
Sweet Talk
Handcrafted • UNRU
875QX5367 • **Value $23**

8
Sweetheart
Porcelain • N/A
975QX4957 • **Value $27**

9
Teacher
Glass • RGRS
475QX2289 • **Value $12**

10
Ten Years Together
Faceted Glass • N/A
775QX4929 • **Value $21**

11
Terrific Teacher
Handcrafted • SICK
675QX5309 • **Value $17**

12
Tigger
Handcrafted • SIED
975QX5609 • **Value $125**

13
Tiny Tim
Porcelain • UNRU
1075QX5037 • **Value $40**

14
Tramp and Laddie
Handcrafted • FRAN
775QX4397 • **Value $42**

15
Twenty-Five Years Together Photoholder
Handcrafted/Chrome • VOTR
875QX4937 • **Value $19**

16
Under the Mistletoe
Handcrafted • PIKE
875QX4949 • **Value $20**

17
Up 'N' Down Journey
Handcrafted • CROW
975QX5047 • **Value $28**

18
Winnie-the-Pooh
Handcrafted • SIED
975QX5569 • **Value $59**

19
Yule Logger
Handcrafted • SEAL
875QX4967 • **Value $29**

20
Arctic Dome
Handcrafted • CROW
2500QLX7117 • **Value $56**

GENERAL KEEPSAKE

	Price Paid	Value of My Collection
1.		
2.		
3.		
4.		
5.		
6.		
7.		
8.		
9.		
10.		
11.		
12.		
13.		
14.		
15.		
16.		
17.		
18.		
19.		

GENERAL MAGIC

20.		

PENCIL TOTALS

①
Baby's First Christmas
Handcrafted • SEAL
3000QLX7247 • **Value $97**

②
Bringing Home the Tree
Handcrafted • UNRU
2800QLX7249 • **Value $65**

③
Elfin Engineer
Handcrafted • CHAD
1000QLX7209 • **Value $25**

④
Father Christmas
Handcrafted • UNRU
1400QLX7147 • **Value $40**

⑤
Festive Brass Church
Brass • MCGE
1400QLX7179 • **Value $32**

⑥
First Christmas Together
Handcrafted • SICK
2500QLX7137 • **Value $58**

⑦
Friendship Tree
Handcrafted • DUTK
1000QLX7169 • **Value $25**

⑧
Holiday Glow
Panorama Ball • PIKE
1400QLX7177 • **Value $30**

⑨
It's a Wonderful Life
Handcrafted • DLEE
2000QLX7237 • **Value $78**

⑩
Jingle Bears
Handcrafted • JLEE
2500QLX7323 • **Value $55**

⑪
Kringle's Bumper Cars
Handcrafted • SICK
2500QLX7119 • **Value $57**

⑫
Mole Family Home
Handcrafted • JLEE
2000QLX7149 • **Value $45**

⑬
Salvation Army Band
Handcrafted • UNRU
3000QLX7273 • **Value $72**

⑭
Santa Special
(re-issued in 1992)
Handcrafted • SEAL
4000QLX7167 • **Value $78**

⑮
Santa's Hot Line
Handcrafted • CROW
1800QLX7159 • **Value $44**

⑯
Ski Trip
Handcrafted • SEAL
2800QLX7266 • **Value $57**

⑰
Sparkling Angel
Handcrafted • CHAD
1800QLX7157 • **Value $38**

⑱
Starship Enterprise™
Handcrafted • NORT
2000QLX7199 • **Value $390**

⑲
Toyland Tower
Handcrafted • CROW
2000QLX7129 • **Value $42**

⑳
All Aboard
Handcrafted • CHAD
450QXM5869 • **Value $18**

1991

GENERAL MAGIC

	Price Paid	Value of My Collection
1.		
2.		
3.		
4.		
5.		
6.		
7.		
8.		
9.		
10.		
11.		
12.		
13.		
14.		
15.		
16.		
17.		
18.		
19.		

GENERAL MINIATURE

20.		

PENCIL TOTALS

(1) Baby's First Christmas
Handcrafted • FRAN
600QXM5799 • **Value $22**

(2) Brass Bells
Brass • ANDR
300QXM5977 • **Value $10**

(3) Brass Church
Brass • N/A
300QXM5979 • **Value $10**

(4) Brass Soldier
Brass • N/A
300QXM5987 • **Value $10**

(5) Bright Boxers
Handcrafted • RHOD
450QXM5877 • **Value $17**

(6) Busy Bear
Wood • RHOD
450QXM5939 • **Value $13**

(7) Cardinal Cameo
Handcrafted • LYLE
600QXM5957 • **Value $17**

(8) Caring Shepherd
Porcelain • FRAN
600QXM5949 • **Value $18**

(9) Cool 'n Sweet
Porcelain • PIKE
450QXM5867 • **Value $21**

(10) Country Sleigh
Enamel • VOTR
450QXM5999 • **Value $15**

(11) Courier Turtle
Handcrafted • PIKE
450QXM5857 • **Value $15**

(12) Fancy Wreath
Handcrafted • LYLE
450QXM5917 • **Value $14**

(13) Feliz Navidad
Handcrafted/Straw • RGRS
600QXM5887 • **Value $18**

(14) First Christmas Together
Handcrafted/Brass • UNRU
600QXM5819 • **Value $16**

(15) Fly By
Handcrafted • CROW
450QXM5859 • **Value $17**

(16) Friendly Fawn
Handcrafted • JLEE
600QXM5947 • **Value $16**

(17) Grandchild's First Christmas
Porcelain • RGRS
450QXM5697 • **Value $15**

(18) Heavenly Minstrel
Handcrafted • DLEE
975QXM5687 • **Value $32**

(19) Holiday Snowflake
Acrylic • RHOD
300QXM5997 • **Value $14**

(20) Key to Love
Handcrafted • CROW
450QXM5689 • **Value $17**

GENERAL MINIATURE

	Price Paid	Value of My Collection
1.		
2.		
3.		
4.		
5.		
6.		
7.		
8.		
9.		
10.		
11.		
12.		
13.		
14.		
15.		
16.		
17.		
18.		
19.		
20.		
PENCIL TOTALS		

1 Kitty in a Mitty
Handcrafted • ANDR
450QXM5879 • **Value $12**

2 Li'l Popper
Handcrafted • SICK
450QXM5897 • **Value $20**

3 Love Is Born
Porcelain • VOTR
600QXM5959 • **Value $20**

4 Lulu & Family
Handcrafted • RGRS
600QXM5677 • **Value $21**

5 Mom
Handcrafted • SIED
600QXM5699 • **Value $17**

6 N. Pole Buddy
Handcrafted • PALM
450QXM5927 • **Value $19**

7 Noel
Acrylic • N/A
300QXM5989 • **Value $12**

8 Ring-A-Ding Elf
Handcrafted/Brass • CHAD
850QXM5669 • **Value $20**

9 Seaside Otter
Handcrafted • SIED
450QXM5909 • **Value $13**

10 Silvery Santa
Silver-Plated • JLEE
975QXM5679 • **Value $25**

11 Special Friends
Handcrafted/Wicker • JLEE
850QXM5797 • **Value $21**

12 Tiny Tea Party Set (set/6)
Handcrafted/Porcelain • SEAL
2900QXM5827 • **Value $168**

13 Top Hatter
Handcrafted • SEAL
600QXM5889 • **Value $18**

14 Treeland Trio
Handcrafted • CHAD
850QXM5899 • **Value $17**

15 Upbeat Bear
Handcrafted/Metal • FRAN
600QXM5907 • **Value $17**

16 Vision of Santa
Handcrafted • CHAD
450QXM5937 • **Value $14**

17 Wee Toymaker
Handcrafted • BISH
850QXM5967 • **Value $17**

18 Beary Artistic (club edition, magic)
Handcrafted/Acrylic • SIED
1000QXC7259 • **Value $40**

19 Five Years Together (charter member gift)
Acrylic • N/A
QXC3159 • **Value $50**

20 Galloping Into Christmas (club edition, LE-28,400)
Pressed Tin • SICK
1975QXC4779 • **Value $122**

GENERAL MINIATURE

	Price Paid	Value of My Collection
1.		
2.		
3.		
4.		
5.		
6.		
7.		
8.		
9.		
10.		
11.		
12.		
13.		
14.		
15.		
16.		
17.		

COLLECTOR'S CLUB

18.		
19.		
20.		

PENCIL TOTALS

1991

VALUE GUIDE — HALLMARK KEEPSAKE ORNAMENTS

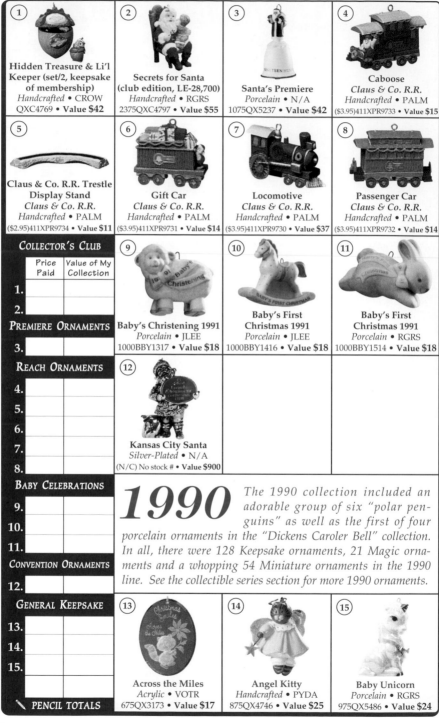

(1)
Hidden Treasure & Li'l Keeper (set/2, keepsake of membership)
Handcrafted • CROW
QXC4769 • **Value $42**

(2)
Secrets for Santa (club edition, LE-28,700)
Handcrafted • RGRS
2375QXC4797 • **Value $55**

(3)
Santa's Premiere
Porcelain • N/A
1075QX5237 • **Value $42**

(4)
Caboose
Claus & Co. R.R.
Handcrafted • PALM
($3.95)411XPR9733 • **Value $15**

(5)
Claus & Co. R.R. Trestle Display Stand
Claus & Co. R.R.
Handcrafted • PALM
($2.95)411XPR9734 • **Value $11**

(6)
Gift Car
Claus & Co. R.R.
Handcrafted • PALM
($3.95)411XPR9731 • **Value $14**

(7)
Locomotive
Claus & Co. R.R.
Handcrafted • PALM
($3.95)411XPR9730 • **Value $37**

(8)
Passenger Car
Claus & Co. R.R.
Handcrafted • PALM
($3.95)411XPR9732 • **Value $14**

COLLECTOR'S CLUB

	Price Paid	Value of My Collection
1.		
2.		

PREMIERE ORNAMENTS

| 3. | | |

REACH ORNAMENTS

4.		
5.		
6.		
7.		
8.		

BABY CELEBRATIONS

9.		
10.		
11.		

CONVENTION ORNAMENTS

| 12. | | |

GENERAL KEEPSAKE

13.		
14.		
15.		

PENCIL TOTALS

(9)
Baby's Christening 1991
Porcelain • JLEE
1000BBY1317 • **Value $18**

(10)
Baby's First Christmas 1991
Porcelain • JLEE
1000BBY1416 • **Value $18**

(11)
Baby's First Christmas 1991
Porcelain • RGRS
1000BBY1514 • **Value $18**

(12)
Kansas City Santa
Silver-Plated • N/A
(N/C) No stock # • **Value $900**

1990

The 1990 collection included an adorable group of six "polar penguins" as well as the first of four porcelain ornaments in the "Dickens Caroler Bell" collection. In all, there were 128 Keepsake ornaments, 21 Magic ornaments and a whopping 54 Miniature ornaments in the 1990 line. See the collectible series section for more 1990 ornaments.

(13)
Across the Miles
Acrylic • VOTR
675QX3173 • **Value $17**

(14)
Angel Kitty
Handcrafted • PYDA
875QX4746 • **Value $25**

(15)
Baby Unicorn
Porcelain • RGRS
975QX5486 • **Value $24**

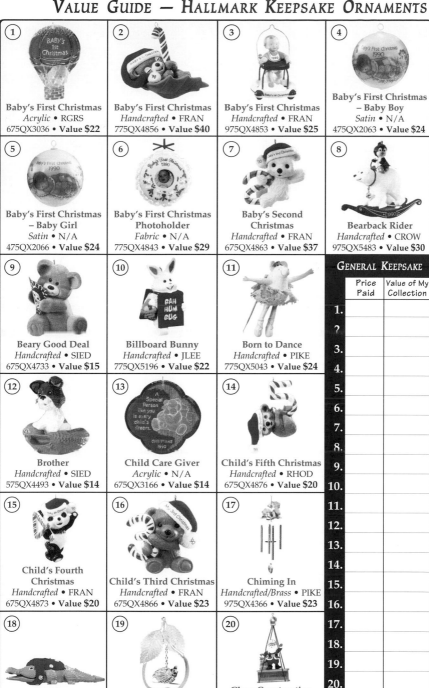

(1) Baby's First Christmas
Acrylic • RGRS
675QX3036 • **Value $22**

(2) Baby's First Christmas
Handcrafted • FRAN
775QX4856 • **Value $40**

(3) Baby's First Christmas
Handcrafted • FRAN
975QX4853 • **Value $25**

(4) Baby's First Christmas
– Baby Boy
Satin • N/A
475QX2063 • **Value $24**

(5) Baby's First Christmas
– Baby Girl
Satin • N/A
475QX2066 • **Value $24**

(6) Baby's First Christmas
Photoholder
Fabric • N/A
775QX4843 • **Value $29**

(7) Baby's Second
Christmas
Handcrafted • FRAN
675QX4863 • **Value $37**

(8) Bearback Rider
Handcrafted • CROW
975QX5483 • **Value $30**

(9) Beary Good Deal
Handcrafted • SIED
675QX4733 • **Value $15**

(10) Billboard Bunny
Handcrafted • JLEE
775QX5196 • **Value $22**

(11) Born to Dance
Handcrafted • PIKE
775QX5043 • **Value $24**

(12) Brother
Handcrafted • SIED
575QX4493 • **Value $14**

(13) Child Care Giver
Acrylic • N/A
675QX3166 • **Value $14**

(14) Child's Fifth Christmas
Handcrafted • RHOD
675QX4876 • **Value $20**

(15) Child's Fourth
Christmas
Handcrafted • FRAN
675QX4873 • **Value $20**

(16) Child's Third Christmas
Handcrafted • FRAN
675QX4866 • **Value $23**

(17) Chiming In
Handcrafted/Brass • PIKE
975QX4366 • **Value $23**

(18) Christmas Croc
Handcrafted • PYDA
775QX4373 • **Value $24**

(19) Christmas Partridge
Dimensional Brass • SICK
775QX5246 • **Value $21**

(20) Claus Construction
(re-issued from 1989)
Handcrafted • SEAL
775QX4885 • **Value $37**

1990

GENERAL KEEPSAKE

	Price Paid	Value of My Collection
1.		
2.		
3.		
4.		
5.		
6.		
7.		
8.		
9.		
10.		
11.		
12.		
13.		
14.		
15.		
16.		
17.		
18.		
19.		
20.		
PENCIL TOTALS		

① Copy of Cheer
Handcrafted • SIED
775QX4486 • **Value $19**

② Country Angel
(canceled after limited production)
Handcrafted • N/A
675QX5046 • **Value $185**

③ Coyote Carols
Handcrafted • JLEE
875QX4993 • **Value $30**

④ Cozy Goose
Handcrafted • PIKE
575QX4966 • **Value $15**

⑤ Dad
Handcrafted • JLEE
675QX4533 • **Value $19**

⑥ Dad-to-Be
Handcrafted • SIED
575QX4913 • **Value $22**

⑦ Daughter
Handcrafted • SIED
575QX4496 • **Value $26**

⑧ Dickens Caroler Bell – Mr. Ashbourne
Porcelain • CHAD
2175QX5056 • **Value $50**

⑨ Donder's Diner
Handcrafted • DLEE
1375QX4823 • **Value $21**

⑩ Feliz Navidad
Handcrafted • N/A
675QX5173 • **Value $30**

⑪ Fifty Years Together
Faceted Glass • PATT
975QX4906 • **Value $20**

⑫ First Christmas Together
Acrylic • VOTR
675QX3146 • **Value $27**

⑬ First Christmas Together
Glass • VOTR
475QX2136 • **Value $28**

⑭ First Christmas Together
Handcrafted • PYDA
975QX4883 • **Value $30**

⑮ First Christmas Together – Photoholder
Fabric • VOTR
775QX4886 • **Value $20**

⑯ Five Years Together
Glass • VOTR
475QX2103 • **Value $20**

⑰ Forty Years Together
Faceted Glass • PATT
975QX4903 • **Value $21**

⑱ Friendship Kitten
Handcrafted • RHOD
675QX4143 • **Value $25**

⑲ From Our Home to Yours
Glass • N/A
475QX2166 • **Value $19**

⑳ GARFIELD®
Glass • N/A
475QX2303 • **Value $24**

GENERAL KEEPSAKE

	Price Paid	Value of My Collection
1.		
2.		
3.		
4.		
5.		
6.		
7.		
8.		
9.		
10.		
11.		
12.		
13.		
14.		
15.		
16.		
17.		
18.		
19.		
20.		

PENCIL TOTALS

1
Gentle Dreamers
Handcrafted • FRAN
875QX4756 • **Value $31**

2
Gingerbread Elf
Handcrafted • N/A
575QX5033 • **Value $20**

3
Godchild
Acrylic • FRAN
675QX3176 • **Value $18**

4
Golf's My Bag
Handcrafted • JLEE
775QX4963 • **Value $29**

5
Goose Cart
Handcrafted • N/A
775QX5236 • **Value $16**

6
Granddaughter
Glass • LYLE
475QX2286 • **Value $25**

7
Granddaughter's
First Christmas
Acrylic • FRAN
675QX3106 • **Value $21**

8
Grandmother
Glass • VOTR
475QX2236 • **Value $19**

9
Grandparents
Glass • N/A
475QX2253 • **Value $18**

10
Grandson
Glass • VOTR
475QX2293 • **Value $24**

11
Grandson's
First Christmas
Acrylic • FRAN
675QX3063 • **Value $22**

12
Hang in There
Handcrafted • SEAL
675QX4713 • **Value $23**

13
Happy Voices
Wood • VOTR
675QX4645 • **Value $15**

14
Happy Woodcutter
Handcrafted • JLEE
975QX4763 • **Value $25**

15
Holiday Cardinals
Dimensional Brass • LYLE
775QX5243 • **Value $22**

16
Home for the Owlidays
Handcrafted • N/A
675QX5183 • **Value $16**

17
Hot Dogger
Handcrafted • CROW
775QX4976 • **Value $18**

18
Jesus Loves Me
Acrylic • PATT
675QX3156 • **Value $14**

19
Jolly Dolphin
Handcrafted • RGRS
675QX4683 • **Value $35**

20
Joy is in the Air
Handcrafted • CROW
775QX5503 • **Value $26**

1990

GENERAL KEEPSAKE

	Price Paid	Value of My Collection
1.		
2.		
3.		
4.		
5.		
6.		
7.		
8.		
9.		
10.		
11.		
12.		
13.		
14.		
15.		
16.		
17.		
18.		
19.		
20.		

PENCIL TOTALS

Value Guide — Hallmark Keepsake Ornaments

(1) King Klaus *Handcrafted* • SEAL 775QX4106 • **Value $22**	**(2)** Kitty's Best Pal *Handcrafted* • FRAN 675QX4716 • **Value $26**	**(3)** Little Drummer Boy *Handcrafted* • UNRU 775QX5233 • **Value $24**	**(4)** Long Winter's Nap *Handcrafted* • RGRS 675QX4703 • **Value $25**
(5) Loveable Dears *Handcrafted* • UNRU 875QX5476 • **Value $20**	**(6)** Meow Mart *Handcrafted* • PIKE 775QX4446 • **Value $31**	**(7)** Mom and Dad *Handcrafted* • CHAD 875QX4593 • **Value $27**	**(8)** Mom-to-Be *Handcrafted* • SIED 575QX4916 • **Value $32**

General Keepsake

	Price Paid	Value of My Collection
1.		
2.		
3.		
4.		
5.		
6.		
7.		
8.		
9.		
10.		
11.		
12.		
13.		
14.		
15.		
16.		
17.		
18.		
19.		
20.		

PENCIL TOTALS

(9) Mooy Christmas *Handcrafted* • N/A 675QX4933 • **Value $32**	**(10)** Mother *Ceramic/Bisque* • VOTR 875QX4536 • **Value $27**	**(11)** Mouseboat *Handcrafted* • SEAL 775QX4753 • **Value $18**
(12) New Home *Handcrafted* • PYDA 675QX4343 • **Value $26**	**(13)** Norman Rockwell Art *Glass* • LYLE 475QX2296 • **Value $25**	**(14)** Nutshell Chat *Handcrafted* • N/A 675QX5193 • **Value $27**
(15) Nutshell Holiday (re-issued from 1989) *Handcrafted* • RGRS 575QX4652 • **Value $26**	**(16)** Peaceful Kingdom *Glass* • N/A 475QX2106 • **Value $23**	**(17)** PEANUTS® *Glass* • N/A 475QX2233 • **Value $31**
(18) Pepperoni Mouse *Handcrafted* • SIED 675QX4973 • **Value $23**	**(19)** Perfect Catch *Handcrafted* • SIED 775QX4693 • **Value $21**	**(20)** Polar Jogger *Handcrafted* • SIED 575QX4666 • **Value $19**

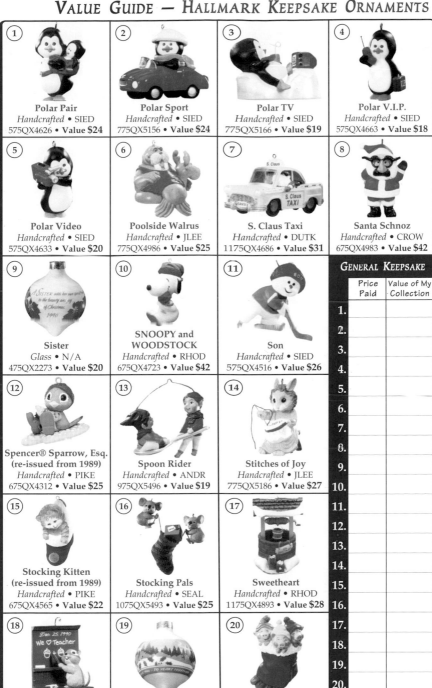

1 Polar Pair
Handcrafted • SIED
575QX4626 • **Value $24**

2 Polar Sport
Handcrafted • SIED
775QX5156 • **Value $24**

3 Polar TV
Handcrafted • SIED
775QX5166 • **Value $19**

4 Polar V.I.P.
Handcrafted • SIED
575QX4663 • **Value $18**

5 Polar Video
Handcrafted • SIED
575QX4633 • **Value $20**

6 Poolside Walrus
Handcrafted • JLEE
775QX4986 • **Value $25**

7 S. Claus Taxi
Handcrafted • DUTK
1175QX4686 • **Value $31**

8 Santa Schnoz
Handcrafted • CROW
675QX4983 • **Value $42**

9 Sister
Glass • N/A
475QX2273 • **Value $20**

10 SNOOPY and WOODSTOCK
Handcrafted • RHOD
675QX4723 • **Value $42**

11 Son
Handcrafted • SIED
575QX4516 • **Value $26**

12 Spencer® Sparrow, Esq.
(re-issued from 1989)
Handcrafted • PIKE
675QX4312 • **Value $25**

13 Spoon Rider
Handcrafted • ANDR
975QX5496 • **Value $19**

14 Stitches of Joy
Handcrafted • JLEE
775QX5186 • **Value $27**

15 Stocking Kitten
(re-issued from 1989)
Handcrafted • PIKE
675QX4565 • **Value $22**

16 Stocking Pals
Handcrafted • SEAL
1075QX5493 • **Value $25**

17 Sweetheart
Handcrafted • RHOD
1175QX4893 • **Value $28**

18 Teacher
Handcrafted • SEAL
775QX4483 • **Value $16**

19 Ten Years Together
Glass • LYLE
475QX2153 • **Value $23**

20 Three Little Piggies
Handcrafted • CROW
775QX4996 • **Value $30**

1990

GENERAL KEEPSAKE

	Price Paid	Value of My Collection
1.		
2.		
3.		
4.		
5.		
6.		
7.		
8.		
9.		
10.		
11.		
12.		
13.		
14.		
15.		
16.		
17.		
18.		
19.		
20.		
PENCIL TOTALS		

① Time for Love
Glass • LYLE
475QX2133 • **Value $24**

② Twenty-Five Years Together
Faceted Glass • PATT
975QX4896 • **Value $20**

③ Two Peas in a Pod
Handcrafted • ANDR
475QX4926 • **Value $37**

④ Welcome, Santa
Handcrafted • CROW
1175QX4773 • **Value $29**

⑤ Baby's First Christmas
Handcrafted • PALM
2800QLX7246 • **Value $68**

⑥ Beary Short Nap
Handcrafted • SIED
1000QLX7326 • **Value $31**

⑦ Blessings of Love
Panorama Ball • N/A
1400QLX7363 • **Value $53**

⑧ Children's Express
Handcrafted • SICK
2800QLX7243 • **Value $80**

⑨ Christmas Memories
Handcrafted • UNRU
2500QLX7276 • **Value $55**

⑩ Deer Crossing
Handcrafted • SIED
1800QLX7213 • **Value $48**

⑪ Elf of the Year
Handcrafted • ANDR
1000QLX7356 • **Value $24**

⑫ Elfin Whittler
Handcrafted • CROW
2000QLX7265 • **Value $50**

⑬ First Christmas Together
Handcrafted • DLEE
1800QLX7255 • **Value $46**

⑭ Holiday Flash
Handcrafted • CHAD
1800QLX7333 • **Value $34**

⑮ Hop 'N Pop Popper
Handcrafted • SIED
2000QLX7353 • **Value $100**

⑯ Letter to Santa
Handcrafted • RGRS
1400QLX7226 • **Value $39**

⑰ Mrs. Santa's Kitchen
Handcrafted • RHOD
2500QLX7263 • **Value $82**

⑱ Partridges in a Pear
Dimensional Brass • LYLE
1400QLX7212 • **Value $33**

⑲ Santa's Ho-Ho-Hoedown
Handcrafted • CROW
2500QLX7256 • **Value $90**

⑳ Song and Dance
Handcrafted • RGRS
2000QLX7253 • **Value $93**

GENERAL KEEPSAKE

	Price Paid	Value of My Collection
1.		
2.		
3.		
4.		

GENERAL MAGIC

5.		
6.		
7.		
8.		
9.		
10.		
11.		
12.		
13.		
14.		
15.		
16.		
17.		
18.		
19.		
20.		

PENCIL TOTALS

1 Starlight Angel
Handcrafted • RGRS
1400QLX7306 • **Value $37**

2 Starship Christmas
Handcrafted • SIED
1800QLX7336 • **Value $52**

3 Acorn Squirrel
(re-issued from 1989)
Handcrafted • PIKE
450QXM5682 • **Value $11**

4 Acorn Wreath
Handcrafted • CROW
600QXM5686 • **Value $12**

5 Air Santa
Handcrafted • N/A
450QXM5656 • **Value $14**

6 Baby's First Christmas
Handcrafted • FRAN
850QXM5703 • **Value $17**

7 Basket Buddy
Handcrafted/Wicker • RGRS
600QXM5696 • **Value $13**

8 Bear Hug
Handcrafted • PALM
600QXM5633 • **Value $14**

9 Brass Bouquet
Brass • LYLE
600QXM5776 • **Value $7**

10 Brass Horn
Brass • N/A
300QXM5793 • **Value $7**

11 Brass Peace
Brass • N/A
300QXM5796 • **Value $7**

12 Brass Santa
Brass • PATT
300QXM5786 • **Value $10**

13 Brass Year
Brass • N/A
300QXM5833 • **Value $8**

14 Busy Carver
Handcrafted • CROW
450QXM5673 • **Value $10**

15 Christmas Dove
Handcrafted • SIED
450QXM5636 • **Value $16**

16 Cloisonné Poinsettia
Cloisonné • VOTR
1050QXM5533 • **Value $22**

17 Country Heart
Handcrafted • RGRS
450QXM5693 • **Value $10**

18 Cozy Skater
(re-issued from 1989)
Handcrafted • LYLE
450QXM5735 • **Value $13**

19 First Christmas
Together
Porcelain • ANDR
600QXM5536 • **Value $14**

20 Going Sledding
Handcrafted • JLEE
450QXM5683 • **Value $16**

GENERAL MAGIC	Price Paid	Value of My Collection
1.		
2.		

GENERAL MINIATURE		
3.		
4.		
5.		
6.		
7.		
8.		
9.		
10.		
11.		
12.		
13.		
14.		
15.		
16.		
17.		
18.		
19.		
20.		
PENCIL TOTALS		

1990

1
Grandchild's First Christmas
Handcrafted • SIED
600QXM5723 • **Value $12**

2
Happy Bluebird
(re-issued from 1989)
Handcrafted • RGRS
450QXM5662 • **Value $16**

3
Holiday Cardinal
Acrylic • FRAN
300QXM5526 • **Value $11**

4
Lion and Lamb
Wood • SICK
450QXM5676 • **Value $11**

5
Little Soldier
(re-issued from 1989)
Handcrafted • SICK
450QXM5675 • **Value $11**

6
Loving Hearts
Acrylic • N/A
300QXM5523 • **Value $10**

7
Madonna and Child
Handcrafted • RGRS
600QXM5643 • **Value $13**

8
Mother
Cameo • LYLE
450QXM5716 • **Value $18**

9
Nativity
Handcrafted • UNRU
450QXM5706 • **Value $21**

10
Old-World Santa
(re-issued from 1989)
Handcrafted • SIED
300QXM5695 • **Value $10**

11
Panda's Surprise
Handcrafted • FRAN
450QXM5616 • **Value $14**

12
Perfect Fit
Handcrafted • CHAD
450QXM5516 • **Value $14**

13
Puppy Love
Handcrafted • PALM
600QXM5666 • **Value $15**

14
Roly-Poly Pig
(re-issued from 1989)
Handcrafted • PIKE
300QXM5712 • **Value $19**

15
Ruby Reindeer
Glass • PATT
600QXM5816 • **Value $13**

16
Santa's Journey
Handcrafted • SICK
850QXM5826 • **Value $24**

17
Santa's Streetcar
Handcrafted • DLEE
850QXM5766 • **Value $20**

18
Snow Angel
Handcrafted • JLEE
600QXM5773 • **Value $15**

19
Special Friends
Handcrafted • PIKE
600QXM5726 • **Value $14**

20
Stamp Collector
Handcrafted • CROW
450QXM5623 • **Value $11**

General Miniature

	Price Paid	Value of My Collection
1.		
2.		
3.		
4.		
5.		
6.		
7.		
8.		
9.		
10.		
11.		
12.		
13.		
14.		
15.		
16.		
17.		
18.		
19.		
20.		
PENCIL TOTALS		

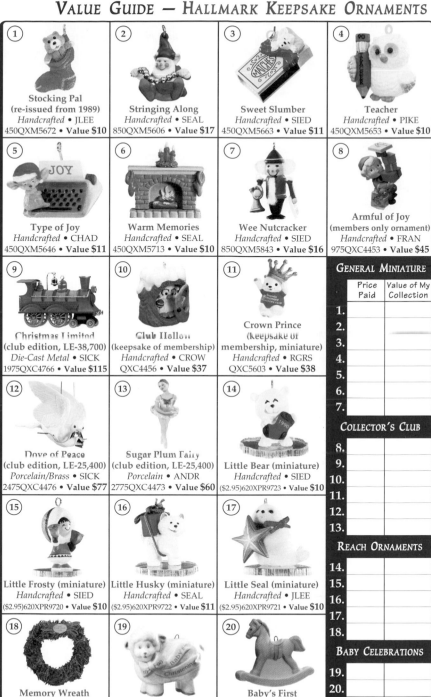

1 Stocking Pal
(re-issued from 1989)
Handcrafted • JLEE
450QXM5672 • **Value $10**

2 Stringing Along
Handcrafted • SEAL
850QXM5606 • **Value $17**

3 Sweet Slumber
Handcrafted • SIED
450QXM5663 • **Value $11**

4 Teacher
Handcrafted • PIKE
450QXM5653 • **Value $10**

5 Type of Joy
Handcrafted • CHAD
450QXM5646 • **Value $11**

6 Warm Memories
Handcrafted • SEAL
450QXM5713 • **Value $10**

7 Wee Nutcracker
Handcrafted • SIED
850QXM5843 • **Value $16**

8 Armful of Joy
(members only ornament)
Handcrafted • FRAN
975QXC4453 • **Value $45**

9 Christmas Limited
(club edition, LE-38,700)
Die-Cast Metal • SICK
1975QXC4766 • **Value $115**

10 Club Hollow
(keepsake of membership)
Handcrafted • CROW
QXC4456 • **Value $37**

11 Crown Prince
(keepsake of
membership, miniature)
Handcrafted • RGRS
QXC5603 • **Value $38**

12 Dove of Peace
(club edition, LE-25,400)
Porcelain/Brass • SICK
2475QXC4476 • **Value $77**

13 Sugar Plum Fairy
(club edition, LE-25,400)
Porcelain • ANDR
2775QXC4473 • **Value $60**

14 Little Bear (miniature)
Handcrafted • SIED
($2.95)620XPR9723 • **Value $10**

15 Little Frosty (miniature)
Handcrafted • SIED
($2.95)620XPR9720 • **Value $10**

16 Little Husky (miniature)
Handcrafted • SEAL
($2.95)620XPR9722 • **Value $11**

17 Little Seal (miniature)
Handcrafted • JLEE
($2.95)620XPR9721 • **Value $10**

18 Memory Wreath
(miniature)
Handcrafted • DLEE
($2.95)620XPR9724 • **Value $11**

19 Baby's Christening 1990
Porcelain • JLEE
1000BBY1326 • **Value $32**

20 Baby's First
Christmas 1990
Handcrafted • JLEE
1000BBY1454 • **Value $30**

GENERAL MINIATURE		
	Price Paid	Value of My Collection
1.		
2.		
3.		
4.		
5.		
6.		
7.		
COLLECTOR'S CLUB		
8.		
9.		
10.		
11.		
12.		
13.		
REACH ORNAMENTS		
14.		
15.		
16.		
17.		
18.		
BABY CELEBRATIONS		
19.		
20.		
PENCIL TOTALS		

1990

(1)

Baby's First Christmas 1990
Porcelain • RGRS
1000BBY1554 • **Value $30**

1989

In 1989 Hallmark debuted a popular collection of dated teddy bear ornaments celebrating a child's first five Christmases. In the 1989 collection, there were 123 Keepsake ornaments, 19 Magic ornaments and 41 Miniature ornaments. See the collectibles series section for more 1989 ornaments.

(2)

Baby Partridge
Handcrafted • FRAN
675QX4525 • **Value $15**

(3)

Baby's First Christmas
Acrylic • FRAN
675QX3815 • **Value $22**

(4)

Baby's First Christmas
Handcrafted • CHAD
725QX4492 • **Value $89**

(5)

Baby's First Christmas – Baby Boy
Satin • VOTR
475QX2725 • **Value $24**

BABY CELEBRATIONS

	Price Paid	Value of My Collection
1.		

GENERAL KEEPSAKE

2.		
3.		
4.		
5.		
6.		
7.		
8.		
9.		
10.		
11.		
12.		
13.		
14.		
15.		
16.		
17.		

(6)

Baby's First Christmas – Baby Girl
Satin • VOTR
475QX2722 • **Value $24**

(7)

Baby's First Christmas Photoholder
Handcrafted • VOTR
625QX4682 • **Value $50**

(8)

Baby's Second Christmas
Handcrafted • FRAN
675QX4495 • **Value $32**

(9)

Balancing Elf
Handcrafted • CHAD
675QX4895 • **Value $23**

(10)

Bear-i-Tone
Handcrafted • SIED
475QX4542 • **Value $20**

(11)

Brother
Handcrafted • LYLE
725QX4452 • **Value $20**

(12)

Cactus Cowboy
Handcrafted • DUTK
675QX4112 • **Value $48**

(13)

Camera Claus
Handcrafted • SIED
575QX5465 • **Value $22**

(14)

Carousel Zebra
Handcrafted • SICK
925QX4515 • **Value $22**

(15)

Cherry Jubilee
Handcrafted • SICK
500QX4532 • **Value $29**

(16)

Child's Fifth Christmas
Handcrafted • RHOD
675QX5435 • **Value $20**

(17)

Child's Fourth Christmas
Handcrafted • FRAN
675QX5432 • **Value $20**

PENCIL TOTALS

1
Child's Third Christmas
Handcrafted • FRAN
675QX4695 • **Value $21**

2
Claus Construction
(re-issued in 1990)
Handcrafted • SEAL
775QX4885 • **Value $37**

3
Cool Swing
Handcrafted • CROW
625QX4875 • **Value $34**

4
Country Cat
Handcrafted • PYDA
625QX4672 • **Value $19**

5
Cranberry Bunny
Handcrafted • RGRS
575QX4262 • **Value $19**

6
Dad
Handcrafted • N/A
725QX4412 • **Value $15**

7
Daughter
Handcrafted • SICK
625QX4432 • **Value $22**

8
Deer Disguise
Handcrafted • SIED
575QX4265 • **Value $23**

9
Feliz Navidad
Handcrafted • PYDA
675QX4392 • **Value $30**

10
Festive Angel
Dimensional Brass • N/A
675QX4635 • **Value $26**

11
Festive Year
Acrylic • VOTR
775QX3842 • **Value $24**

12
Fifty Years Together
Photoholder
Porcelain • RGRS
875QX4862 • **Value $20**

13
The First Christmas
Cameo • N/A
775QX5475 • **Value $18**

14
First Christmas
Together
Acrylic • RHOD
675QX3832 • **Value $24**

15
First Christmas
Together
Glass • N/A
475QX2732 • **Value $24**

16
First Christmas
Together
Handcrafted • RGRS
975QX4852 • **Value $25**

17
Five Years Together
Glass • N/A
475QX2735 • **Value $22**

18
Forty Years Together
Photoholder
Porcelain • RGRS
875QX5452 • **Value $18**

19
Friendship Time
Handcrafted • N/A
975QX4132 • **Value $33**

20
From Our
Home to Yours
Acrylic • N/A
625QX3845 • **Value $16**

GENERAL KEEPSAKE

	Price Paid	Value of My Collection
1.		
2.		
3.		
4.		
5.		
6.		
7.		
8.		
9.		
10.		
11.		
12.		
13.		
14.		
15.		
16.		
17.		
18.		
19.		
20.		
		PENCIL TOTALS

1989

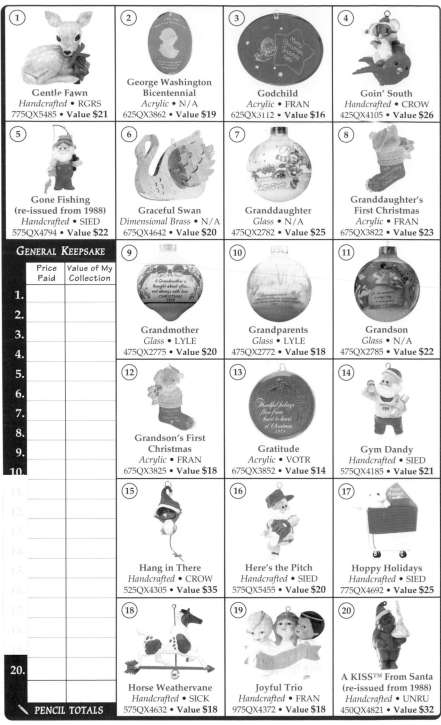

(1) Gentle Fawn
Handcrafted • RGRS
775QX5485 • **Value $21**

(2) George Washington Bicentennial
Acrylic • N/A
625QX3862 • **Value $19**

(3) Godchild
Acrylic • FRAN
625QX3112 • **Value $16**

(4) Goin' South
Handcrafted • CROW
425QX4105 • **Value $26**

(5) Gone Fishing
(re-issued from 1988)
Handcrafted • SIED
575QX4794 • **Value $22**

(6) Graceful Swan
Dimensional Brass • N/A
675QX4642 • **Value $20**

(7) Granddaughter
Glass • N/A
475QX2782 • **Value $25**

(8) Granddaughter's First Christmas
Acrylic • FRAN
675QX3822 • **Value $23**

GENERAL KEEPSAKE		
	Price Paid	Value of My Collection
1.		
2.		
3.		
4.		
5.		
6.		
7.		
8.		
9.		
10.		
11.		
12.		
13.		
14.		
15.		
16.		
17.		
18.		
19.		
20.		
PENCIL TOTALS		

(9) Grandmother
Glass • LYLE
475QX2775 • **Value $20**

(10) Grandparents
Glass • LYLE
475QX2772 • **Value $18**

(11) Grandson
Glass • N/A
475QX2785 • **Value $22**

(12) Grandson's First Christmas
Acrylic • FRAN
675QX3825 • **Value $18**

(13) Gratitude
Acrylic • VOTR
675QX3852 • **Value $14**

(14) Gym Dandy
Handcrafted • SIED
575QX4185 • **Value $21**

(15) Hang in There
Handcrafted • CROW
525QX4305 • **Value $35**

(16) Here's the Pitch
Handcrafted • SIED
575QX5455 • **Value $20**

(17) Hoppy Holidays
Handcrafted • SIED
775QX4692 • **Value $25**

(18) Horse Weathervane
Handcrafted • SICK
575QX4632 • **Value $18**

(19) Joyful Trio
Handcrafted • FRAN
975QX4372 • **Value $18**

(20) A KISS™ From Santa
(re-issued from 1988)
Handcrafted • UNRU
450QX4821 • **Value $32**

VALUE GUIDE — HALLMARK KEEPSAKE ORNAMENTS

(1) **Kristy Claus** *Handcrafted* • SIED 575QX4245 • **Value $15**	**(2)** **Language of Love** *Acrylic* • N/A 625QX3835 • **Value $25**	**(3)** **Let's Play** *Handcrafted* • CROW 725QX4882 • **Value $29**	**(4)** **Mail Call** *Handcrafted* • SEAL 875QX4522 • **Value $20**
(5) **Merry-Go-Round Unicorn** *Porcelain* • RGRS 1075QX4472 • **Value $24**	**(6)** **Mom and Dad** *Handcrafted* • PIKE 975QX4425 • **Value $24**	**(7)** **Mother** *Porcelain* • N/A 975QX4405 • **Value $32**	**(8)** **New Home** *Glass* • VOTR 475QX2755 • **Value $23**
(9) **Norman Rockwell** *Glass* • LYLE 475QX2762 • **Value $22**	**(10)** **North Pole Jogger** *Handcrafted* • SIED 575QX5462 • **Value $22**	**(11)** **Nostalgic Lamb** *Handcrafted* • PYDA 675QX4665 • **Value $16**	
(12) **Nutshell Dreams** *Handcrafted* • CHAD 575QX4655 • **Value $23**	**(13)** **Nutshell Holiday (re-issued in 1990)** *Handcrafted* • RGRS 575QX4652 • **Value $26**	**(14)** **Nutshell Workshop** *Handcrafted* • CHAD 575QX4872 • **Value $23**	
(15) **Old-World Gnome** *Handcrafted* • N/A 775QX4345 • **Value $27**	**(16)** **On the Links** *Handcrafted* • SIED 575QX4192 • **Value $24**	**(17)** **OREO® Chocolate Sandwich Cookies (re-issued from 1988)** *Handcrafted* • UNRU 400QX4814 • **Value $22**	
(18) **The Ornament Express (set/3)** *Handcrafted* • SICK 2200QX5805 • **Value $46**	**(19)** **Owliday Greetings** *Handcrafted* • PIKE 400QX4365 • **Value $21**	**(20)** **Paddington™ Bear** *Handcrafted* • FRAN 575QX4292 • **Value $25**	

GENERAL KEEPSAKE

	Price Paid	Value of My Collection
1.		
2.		
3.		
4.		
5.		
6.		
7.		
8.		
9.		
10.		
11.		
12.		
13.		
14.		
15.		
16.		
17.		
18.		
19.		
20.		
	PENCIL TOTALS	

1989

(1) Party Line
(re-issued from 1988)
Handcrafted • PIKE
875QX4761 • **Value $33**

(2) PEANUTS® – A Charlie
Brown Christmas
Glass • N/A
475QX2765 • **Value $42**

(3) Peek-a-Boo Kitties
(re-issued from 1988)
Handcrafted • CROW
750QX4871 • **Value $24**

(4) Peppermint Clown
Porcelain • DUTK
2475QX4505 • **Value $48**

(5) Playful Angel
Handcrafted • DLEE
675QX4535 • **Value $26**

(6) Polar Bowler
(re-issued from 1988)
Handcrafted • SIED
575QX4784 • **Value $20**

(7) Rodney Reindeer
Handcrafted • SIED
675QX4072 • **Value $16**

(8) Rooster Weathervane
Handcrafted • SICK
575QX4675 • **Value $19**

General Keepsake		
	Price Paid	Value of My Collection
1.		
2.		
3.		
4.		
5.		
6.		
7.		
8.		
9.		
10.		
11.		
12.		
13.		
14.		
15.		
16.		
17.		
18.		
19.		
20.		
PENCIL TOTALS		

(9) Sea Santa
Handcrafted • SIED
575QX4152 • **Value $31**

(10) Sister
Glass • N/A
475QX2792 • **Value $20**

(11) SNOOPY and
WOODSTOCK
Handcrafted • RHOD
675QX4332 • **Value $42**

(12) Snowplow Santa
Handcrafted • SIED
575QX4205 • **Value $23**

(13) Son
Handcrafted • SICK
625QX4445 • **Value $22**

(14) Sparkling Snowflake
Brass • LYLE
775QX5472 • **Value $23**

(15) Special Delivery
Handcrafted • RGRS
525QX4325 • **Value $24**

(16) Spencer® Sparrow, Esq.
(re-issued in 1990)
Handcrafted • PIKE
675QX4312 • **Value $25**

(17) Stocking Kitten
(re-issued in 1990)
Handcrafted • PIKE
675QX4565 • **Value $22**

(18) Sweet Memories
Photoholder
Handcrafted • N/A
675QX4385 • **Value $23**

(19) Sweetheart
Handcrafted • SICK
975QX4865 • **Value $34**

(20) Teacher
Handcrafted • SIED
575QX4125 • **Value $23**

1
Teeny Taster
(re-issued from 1988)
Handcrafted • SEAL
475QX4181 • **Value $30**

2
Ten Years Together
Glass • LYLE
475QX2742 • **Value $28**

3
TV Break
Handcrafted • DLEE
625QX4092 • **Value $20**

4
Twenty-Five Years Together Photoholder
Porcelain • RGRS
875QX4855 • **Value $17**

5
Wiggly Snowman
Handcrafted • RHOD
675QX4892 • **Value $25**

6
World of Love
Glass • N/A
475QX2745 • **Value $34**

7
Angel Melody
Acrylic • VOTR
950QLX7202 • **Value $24**

8
The Animals Speak
Panorama Ball • FRAN
1350QLX7232 • **Value $120**

9
Baby's First Christmas
Handcrafted • SEAL
3000QLX7272 • **Value $68**

10
Backstage Bear
Handcrafted • SIED
1350QLX7215 • **Value $36**

11
Busy Beaver
Handcrafted • DLEE
1750QLX7245 • **Value $50**

12
First Christmas Together
Handcrafted • DLEE
1750QLX7342 • **Value $45**

13
Holiday Bell
Lead Crystal • N/A
1750QLX7222 • **Value $33**

14
Joyous Carolers
Handcrafted • UNRU
3000QLX7295 • **Value $69**

15
Kringle's Toy Shop
(re-issued from 1988)
Handcrafted • SEAL
2450QLX7017 • **Value $50**

16
Loving Spoonful
Handcrafted • SIED
1950QLX7262 • **Value $37**

17
Metro Express
Handcrafted • SICK
2800QLX7275 • **Value $82**

18
Moonlit Nap
(re-issued from 1988)
Handcrafted • CHAD
875QLX7134 • **Value $29**

19
Rudolph the Red-Nosed Reindeer®
Handcrafted • CHAD
1950QLX7252 • **Value $70**

20
Spirit of St. Nick
Handcrafted • SEAL
2450QLX7285 • **Value $76**

1989

GENERAL KEEPSAKE	Price Paid	Value of My Collection
1.		
2.		
3.		
4.		
5.		
6.		
GENERAL MAGIC		
7.		
8.		
9.		
10.		
11.		
12.		
13.		
14.		
15.		
16.		
17.		
18.		
19.		
20.		
PENCIL TOTALS		

(1) Tiny Tinker
Handcrafted • CROW
1950QLX7174 • **Value $58**

(2) Unicorn Fantasy
Handcrafted • RHOD
950QLX7235 • **Value $22**

(3) Acorn Squirrel
(re-issued in 1990)
Handcrafted • PIKE
450QXM5682 • **Value $11**

(4) Baby's First Christmas
Handcrafted • PIKE
600QXM5732 • **Value $16**

(5) Brass Partridge
Brass • LYLE
300QXM5725 • **Value $12**

(6) Brass Snowflake
Dimensional Brass • LYLE
450QXM5702 • **Value $14**

(7) Bunny Hug
Acrylic • VOTR
300QXM5775 • **Value $11**

(8) Country Wreath
(re-issued from 1988)
Handcrafted • RGRS
450QXM5731 • **Value $13**

(9) Cozy Skater
(re-issued in 1990)
Handcrafted • LYLE
450QXM5735 • **Value $13**

(10) First Christmas Together
Ceramic • VOTR
850QXM5642 • **Value $11**

(11) Folk Art Bunny
Handcrafted • PATT
450QXM5692 • **Value $10**

(12) Happy Bluebird
(re-issued in 1990)
Handcrafted • RGRS
450QXM5662 • **Value $16**

(13) Holiday Deer
Acrylic • VOTR
300QXM5772 • **Value $11**

(14) Holy Family
(re-issued from 1988)
Handcrafted • UNRU
850QXM5611 • **Value $15**

(15) Kitty Cart
Wood • PATT
300QXM5722 • **Value $9**

(16) Little Soldier
(re-issued in 1990)
Handcrafted • SICK
450QXM5675 • **Value $11**

(17) Little Star Bringer
Handcrafted • LYLE
600QXM5622 • **Value $20**

(18) Load of Cheer
Handcrafted • RHOD
600QXM5745 • **Value $20**

(19) Lovebirds
Handcrafted/Brass • PIKE
600QXM5635 • **Value $15**

(20) Merry Seal
Porcelain • FRAN
600QXM5755 • **Value $15**

GENERAL MAGIC

	Price Paid	Value of My Collection
1.		
2.		

GENERAL MINIATURE

3.		
4.		
5.		
6.		
7.		
8.		
9.		
10.		
11.		
12.		
13.		
14.		
15.		
16.		
17.		
18.		
19.		
20.		

PENCIL TOTALS

1.
Mother
Cameo • N/A
600QXM5645 • **Value $14**

2.
Old-World Santa
(re-issued in 1990)
Handcrafted • SIED
300QXM5695 • **Value $10**

3.
Pinecone Basket
Handcrafted • RHOD
450QXM5734 • **Value $10**

4.
Puppy Cart
Wood • SICK
300QXM5715 • **Value $10**

5.
Rejoice
Acrylic • VOTR
300QXM5782 • **Value $10**

6.
Roly-Poly Pig
(re-issued in 1990)
Handcrafted • PIKE
300QXM5712 • **Value $19**

7.
Roly-Poly Ram
Handcrafted • N/A
300QXM5705 • **Value $14**

8.
Santa's Magic Ride
Handcrafted • RGRS
850QXM5632 • **Value $19**

9.
Santa's Roadster
Handcrafted • CROW
600QXM5665 • **Value $20**

10.
Scrimshaw Reindeer
Handcrafted • VOTR
450QXM5685 • **Value $9**

11.
Sharing a Ride
Handcrafted • DUTK
850QXM5765 • **Value $16**

12.
Slow Motion
Handcrafted • SIED
600QXM5752 • **Value $16**

13.
Special Friend
Handcrafted/Willow • N/A
450QXM5652 • **Value $13**

14.
Starlit Mouse
Handcrafted • RHOD
450QXM5655 • **Value $16**

15.
Stocking Pal
(re-issued in 1990)
Handcrafted • JLEE
450QXM5672 • **Value $10**

16.
Strollin' Snowman
Porcelain • SIED
450QXM5742 • **Value $18**

17.
Three Little Kitties
(re-issued from 1988)
Handcrafted/Willow • PIKE
600QXM5694 • **Value $20**

18.
Christmas is Peaceful
(club edition, LE-49,900)
Bone China • SEAL
1850QXC4512 • **Value $44**

19.
Collect a Dream
(club edition)
Handcrafted • PIKE
900QXC4285 • **Value $61**

20.
Noelle
(club edition, LE-49,900)
Porcelain • UNRU
1975QXC4483 • **Value $56**

1989

GENERAL MINIATURE

	Price Paid	Value of My Collection
1.		
2.		
3.		
4.		
5.		
6.		
7.		
8.		
9.		
10.		
11.		
12.		
13.		
14.		
15.		
16.		
17.		

COLLECTOR'S CLUB

18.		
19.		
20.		

PENCIL TOTALS

1. Sitting Purrty
(keepsake of
membership, miniature)
Handcrafted • DUTK
QXC5812 • **Value $35**

2. Visit From Santa
(keepsake of membership)
Handcrafted • CROW
QXC5802 • **Value $53**

3. Carousel Display Stand
Handcrafted/Brass • N/A
($1.00)629XPR9723 • **Value $10**

4. Ginger
Handcrafted/Brass • JLEE
($3.95)629XPR9721 • **Value $20**

5. Holly
Handcrafted/Brass • JLEE
($3.95)629XPR9722 • **Value $20**

6. Snow
Handcrafted/Brass • JLEE
($3.95)629XPR9719 • **Value $38**

7. Star
Handcrafted/Brass • JLEE
($3.95)629XPR9720 • **Value $20**

8. Baby's Christening
Keepsake
Acrylic • N/A
700BBY1325 • **Value $33**

COLLECTOR'S CLUB

	Price Paid	Value of My Collection
1.		
2.		

REACH ORNAMENTS

3.		
4.		
5.		
6.		
7.		

BABY CELEBRATIONS

8.		
9.		
10.		
11.		

GENERAL KEEPSAKE

12.		
13.		
14.		
15.		
16.		
17.		

PENCIL TOTALS

9. Baby's First Birthday
Acrylic • N/A
550BBY1729 • **Value $33**

10. Baby's First Christmas
– Baby Boy
(same as #475QX2725)
Satin • VOTR
475BBY1453 • **Value $15**

11. Baby's First Christmas
– Baby Girl
(same as #475QX2722)
Satin • VOTR
475BBY1553 • **Value $15**

1988

1988 was the year Hallmark introduced Miniature ornaments to the collection. In its debut year, the Miniature line featured 27 ornaments, while the Keepsake line had 118 and Magic had 20. See the collectible series section for more 1988 ornaments.

12. Americana Drum
Tin • SICK
775QX4881 • **Value $29**

13. Arctic Tenor
Handcrafted • SIED
400QX4721 • **Value $19**

14. Baby Redbird
Handcrafted • CHAD
500QX4101 • **Value $20**

15. Baby's First Christmas
Acrylic • PIKE
600QX3721 • **Value $22**

16. Baby's First Christmas
Handcrafted • CROW
975QX4701 • **Value $40**

17. Baby's First Christmas
– Baby Boy
Satin • N/A
475QX2721 • **Value $25**

1
Baby's First Christmas
– Baby Girl
Satin • N/A
475QX2724 • **Value $25**

2
Baby's First Christmas
Photoholder
Fabric • N/A
750QX4704 • **Value $28**

3
Baby's Second
Christmas
Handcrafted • PIKE
600QX4711 • **Value $34**

4
Babysitter
Glass • SICK
475QX2791 • **Value $10**

5
Child's Third Christmas
Handcrafted • CHAD
600QX4714 • **Value $29**

6
Christmas Cardinal
Handcrafted • RGRS
475QX4941 • **Value $19**

7
Christmas Cuckoo
Handcrafted • CROW
800QX4801 • **Value $38**

8
Christmas Memories
Photoholder
Acrylic • PATT
650QX3724 • **Value $22**

9
Cool Juggler
Handcrafted • CROW
650QX4874 • **Value $21**

10
Cymbals of Christmas
Handcrafted/Acrylic • DLEE
550QX4111 • **Value $29**

11
Dad
Handcrafted • SIED
700QX4141 • **Value $24**

12
Daughter
Handcrafted • PATT
575QX4151 • **Value $58**

13
Feliz Navidad
Handcrafted • UNRU
675QX4161 • **Value $33**

14
Fifty Years Together
Acrylic • N/A
675QX3741 • **Value $19**

15
Filled With Fudge
Handcrafted • SEAL
475QX4191 • **Value $32**

16
First Christmas
Together
Acrylic • VOTR
675QX3731 • **Value $25**

17
First Christmas
Together
Glass • N/A
475QX2741 • **Value $27**

18
First Christmas
Together
Handcrafted • PIKE
900QX4894 • **Value $27**

19
Five Years Together
Glass • MCGE
475QX2744 • **Value $21**

20
From Our
Home to Yours
Glass • PATT
475QX2794 • **Value $18**

	GENERAL KEEPSAKE	
	Price Paid	Value of My Collection
1.		
2.		
3.		
4.		
5.		
6.		
7.		
8.		
9.		
10.		
11.		
12.		
13.		
14.		
15.		
16.		
17.		
18.		
19.		
20.		
PENCIL TOTALS		

1988

1988 Collection

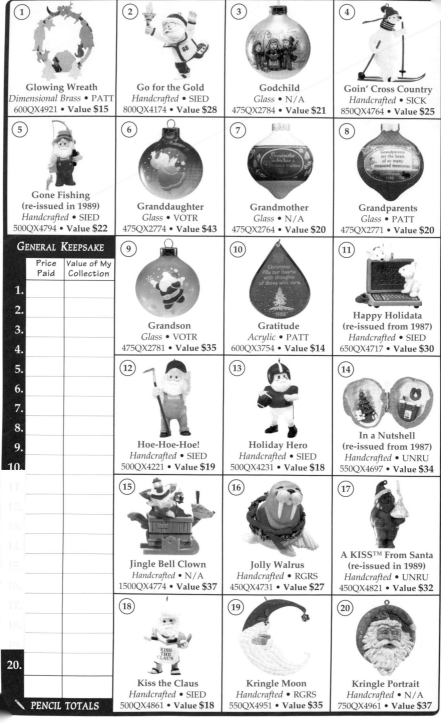

(1) Glowing Wreath
Dimensional Brass • PATT
600QX4921 • **Value $15**

(2) Go for the Gold
Handcrafted • SIED
800QX4174 • **Value $28**

(3) Godchild
Glass • N/A
475QX2784 • **Value $21**

(4) Goin' Cross Country
Handcrafted • SICK
850QX4764 • **Value $25**

(5) Gone Fishing
(re-issued in 1989)
Handcrafted • SIED
500QX4794 • **Value $22**

(6) Granddaughter
Glass • VOTR
475QX2774 • **Value $43**

(7) Grandmother
Glass • N/A
475QX2764 • **Value $20**

(8) Grandparents
Glass • PATT
475QX2771 • **Value $20**

General Keepsake

	Price Paid	Value of My Collection
1.		
2.		
3.		
4.		
5.		
6.		
7.		
8.		
9.		
10.		
11.		
12.		
13.		
14.		
15.		
16.		
17.		
18.		
19.		
20.		

PENCIL TOTALS

(9) Grandson
Glass • VOTR
475QX2781 • **Value $35**

(10) Gratitude
Acrylic • PATT
600QX3754 • **Value $14**

(11) Happy Holidata
(re-issued from 1987)
Handcrafted • SIED
650QX4717 • **Value $30**

(12) Hoe-Hoe-Hoe!
Handcrafted • SIED
500QX4221 • **Value $19**

(13) Holiday Hero
Handcrafted • SIED
500QX4231 • **Value $18**

(14) In a Nutshell
(re-issued from 1987)
Handcrafted • UNRU
550QX4697 • **Value $34**

(15) Jingle Bell Clown
Handcrafted • N/A
1500QX4774 • **Value $37**

(16) Jolly Walrus
Handcrafted • RGRS
450QX4731 • **Value $27**

(17) A KISS™ From Santa
(re-issued in 1989)
Handcrafted • UNRU
450QX4821 • **Value $32**

(18) Kiss the Claus
Handcrafted • SIED
500QX4861 • **Value $18**

(19) Kringle Moon
Handcrafted • RGRS
550QX4951 • **Value $35**

(20) Kringle Portrait
Handcrafted • N/A
750QX4961 • **Value $37**

1988 Collection

1 Kringle Tree
Handcrafted • N/A
650QX4954 • **Value $38**

2 Little Jack Horner
Handcrafted • SIED
800QX4081 • **Value $27**

3 Love Fills the Heart
Acrylic • VOTR
600QX3744 • **Value $25**

4 Love Grows
Glass • VOTR
475QX2754 • **Value $32**

5 Love Santa
Handcrafted • SIED
500QX4864 • **Value $19**

6 Loving Bear
Handcrafted • RGRS
475QX4934 • **Value $18**

7 Merry-Mint Unicorn
Porcelain • RGRS
850QX4234 • **Value $22**

8 Midnight Snack
Handcrafted • SIED
600QX4104 • **Value $21**

9 Mistletoad
(re-issued from 1987)
Handcrafted • CROW
700QX4687 • **Value $29**

10 Mother
Acrylic • N/A
650QX3751 • **Value $20**

11 Mother and Dad
Porcelain • LYLE
800QX4144 • **Value $19**

12 New Home
Acrylic • VOTR
600QX3761 • **Value $21**

13 Nick the Kick
Handcrafted • SIED
500QX4224 • **Value $25**

14 Night Before Christmas
(re-issued from 1987)
Handcrafted • CROW
650QX4517 • **Value $35**

15 Noah's Ark
Pressed Tin • SICK
850QX4904 • **Value $42**

16 Norman Rockwell: Christmas Scenes
Glass • LYLE
475QX2731 • **Value $26**

17 Old-Fashioned Church
Wood • SICK
400QX4981 • **Value $25**

18 Old-Fashioned Schoolhouse
Wood • SICK
400QX4971 • **Value $25**

19 OREO® Chocolate Sandwich Cookies
(re-issued in 1989)
Handcrafted • UNRU
400QX4814 • **Value $22**

20 "Owliday" Wish
(re-issued from 1987)
Handcrafted • PIKE
650QX4559 • **Value $23**

GENERAL KEEPSAKE

	Price Paid	Value of My Collection
1.		
2.		
3.		
4.		
5.		
6.		
7.		
8.		
9.		
10.		
11.		
12.		
13.		
14.		
15.		
16.		
17.		
18.		
19.		
20.		
PENCIL TOTALS		

1988

1
Par for Santa
Handcrafted • SIED
500QX4791 • **Value $20**

2
Party Line
(re-issued in 1989)
Handcrafted • PIKE
875QX4761 • **Value $33**

3
PEANUTS®
Glass • N/A
475QX2801 • **Value $50**

5
Polar Bowler
(re-issued in 1989)
Handcrafted • SIED
500QX4784 • **Value $20**

6
Purrfect Snuggle
Handcrafted • RGRS
625QX4744 • **Value $32**

7
Reindoggy
(re-issued from 1987)
Handcrafted • SIED
575QX4527 • **Value $35**

Sa
Pres
850QX4

GENERAL KEEPSAKE

	Price Paid	Value of My Collection
1.		
2.		
3.		
4.		
5.		
6.		
7.		
8.		
9.		
10.		
11.		
12.		
13.		
14.		
15.		
16.		
17.		
18.		
19.		
20.		

PENCIL TOTALS

9
St. Louie Nick
(re-issued from 1987)
Handcrafted • DUTK
775QX4539 • **Value $33**

10
Santa Flamingo
Handcrafted • PYDA
475QX4834 • **Value $36**

11
Shiny Slei
Dimensional Brass
575QX4924 • **Valu**

12
Sister
Porcelain • VOTR
800QX4994 • **Value $32**

13
Slipper Spaniel
Handcrafted • CROW
425QX4724 • **Value $20**

14
SNOOPY® and WOODSTOCK
Handcrafted • UNRU
600QX4741 • **Value $49**

15
Soft Landing
Handcrafted • CHAD
700QX4751 • **Value $25**

16
Son
Handcrafted • PATT
575QX4154 • **Value $40**

17
Sparkling Tree
Dimensional Brass • PATT
600QX4931 • **Value $20**

18
Spirit of Christmas
Glass • LYLE
475QX2761 • **Value $25**

19
Squeaky Clean
Handcrafted • PIKE
675QX4754 • **Value $24**

20
Starry Angel
Handcrafted • RGRS
475QX4944 • **Value $21**

(1) **Sweet Star** *Handcrafted* • SEAL 500QX4184 • **Value $32**	**(2)**  **Sweetheart** *Handcrafted* • UNRU 975QX4901 • **Value $23**	**(3)** **Teacher** *Handcrafted* • PIKE 625QX4171 • **Value $22**	**(4)** **Teeny Taster** (re-issued in 1989) *Handcrafted* • SEAL 475QX4181 • **Value $30**

(4) (spoon)

(5)  **Ten Years Together** *Glass* • N/A 475QX2751 • **Value $22**	**(6)** **The Town Crier** *Handcrafted* • SEAL 550QX4734 • **Value $22**	**(7)** **Travels with Santa** *Handcrafted* • DLEE 1000QX4771 • **Value $38**	**(8)** **Treetop Dreams** (re-issued from 1987) *Handcrafted* • SEAL 675QX4597 • **Value $30**

(8)

GENERAL KEEPSAKE

			Price Paid	Value of My Collection
(9) **Twenty-Five Years Together** *Acrylic* • PATT 675QX3734 • **Value $19**	**(10)** **Uncle Sam Nutcracker** *Handcrafted* • DLEE 700QX4884 • **Value $37**	**(11)**  **Very Strawbeary** *Handcrafted* • DUTK 475QX4091 • **Value $22**	1.	
			2.	
			3.	
			4.	

(12) **Winter Fun** *Handcrafted* • CHAD 850QX4781 • **Value $27**	**(13)** **The Wonderful Santacycle** *Handcrafted* • SEAL 2250QX4114 • **Value $47**	**(14)** **Year to Remember** *Ceramic* • N/A 700QX4164 • **Value $25**	5. 6. 7. 8. 9. 10.

(15) **Baby's First Christmas** *Handcrafted* • SEAL 2400QLX7184 • **Value $62**	**(16)** 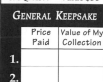 **Bearly Reaching** *Handcrafted* • SICK 950QLX7151 • **Value $39**	**(17)**  **Christmas Is Magic** *Handcrafted* • CROW 1200QLX7171 • **Value $57**	11. 12. 13. 14.

GENERAL MAGIC

(18) **Christmas Morning** (re-issued from 1987) *Handcrafted* • CROW 2450QLX7013 • **Value $48**	**(19)** **Circling the Globe** *Handcrafted* • CROW 1050QLX7124 • **Value $45**	**(20)** **Country Express** *Handcrafted* • SICK 2450QLX7211 • **Value $73**	15. 16. 17. 18. 19. 20.

PENCIL TOTALS

1988

1

Festive Feeder
Handcrafted • SICK
1150QLX7204 • **Value $52**

2

First Christmas Together
Handcrafted • SICK
1200QLX7027 • **Value $40**

3

Heavenly Glow
Brass • PYDA
1175QLX7114 • **Value $29**

4

Kitty Capers
Handcrafted • PIKE
1300QLX7164 • **Value $44**

5

Last-Minute Hug
Handcrafted • UNRU
2200QLX7181 • **Value $48**

6

Moonlit Nap
(re-issued in 1989)
Handcrafted • CHAD
875QLX7134 • **Value $29**

7

Parade of the Toys
Handcrafted • SICK
2450QLX7194 • **Value $50**

8

Radiant Tree
Brass • LYLE
1175QLX7121 • **Value $27**

GENERAL MAGIC

	Price Paid	Value of My Collection
1.		
2.		
3.		
4.		
5.		
6.		
7.		
8.		
9.		
10.		
11.		

GENERAL MINIATURE

12.		
13.		
14.		
15.		
16.		
17.		
18.		
19.		
20.		

9

Skater's Waltz
Handcrafted • UNRU
2450QLX7201 • **Value $61**

10

Song of Christmas
Acrylic • N/A
850QLX7111 • **Value $30**

11

Tree of Friendship
Acrylic • N/A
850QLX7104 • **Value $26**

12

Baby's First Christmas
Handcrafted • DLEE
600QXM5744 • **Value $14**

13

Brass Angel
Brass • LYLE
150QXM5671 • **Value $20**

14

Brass Star
Brass • LYLE
150QXM5664 • **Value $20**

15

Brass Tree
Brass • LYLE
150QXM5674 • **Value $20**

16

Candy Cane Elf
Handcrafted • SIED
300QXM5701 • **Value $20**

17

Country Wreath
(re-issued in 1989)
Handcrafted • RGRS
400QXM5731 • **Value $13**

18

First Christmas Together
Wood/Straw • MCGE
400QXM5741 • **Value $12**

19

Folk Art Lamb
Wood • PATT
275QXM5681 • **Value $23**

20

Folk Art Reindeer
Wood • PATT
300QXM5684 • **Value $19**

PENCIL TOTALS

(1) Friends Share Joy
Acrylic • PATT
200QXM5764 • **Value $13**

(2) Gentle Angel
Acrylic • VOTR
200QXM5771 • **Value $20**

(3) Happy Santa
Glass • PATT
450QXM5614 • **Value $22**

(4) Holy Family
(re-issued in 1989)
Handcrafted • UNRU
850QXM5611 • **Value $15**

(5) Jolly St. Nick
Handcrafted • UNRU
800QXM5721 • **Value $38**

(6) Joyous Heart
Wood • MCGE
350QXM5691 • **Value $30**

(7) Little Drummer Boy
Handcrafted • SIED
450QXM5784 • **Value $29**

(8) Love Is Forever
Acrylic • PATT
200QXM5774 • **Value $15**

(9) Mother
Handcrafted • PIKE
300QXM5724 • **Value $13**

(10) Skater's Waltz
Handcrafted • UNRU
700QXM5601 • **Value $23**

(11) Sneaker Mouse
Handcrafted • N/A
400QXM5711 • **Value $21**

(12) Snuggly Skater
Handcrafted • SIED
450QXM5714 • **Value $28**

(13) Sweet Dreams
Handcrafted • N/A
700QXM560-4 • **Value $23**

(14) Three Little Kitties
(re-issued in 1989)
Handcrafted/Willow • PIKE
600QXM5694 • **Value $20**

(15) Angelic Minstrel
(club edition, LE-49,900)
Porcelain • DLEE
2950QX4084 • **Value $65**

(16) Christmas is Sharing
(club edition, LE-49,900)
Bone China • SEAL
1750QX4071 • **Value $52**

(17) Hold on Tight
(early renewal piece,
miniature)
Handcrafted • SIED
QXC5704 • **Value $76**

(18) Our Clubhouse
(keepsake of membership)
Handcrafted • SIED
QXC5804 • **Value $44**

(19) Seal of Friendship
(gift membership bonus,
Merry Miniature)
Handcrafted • VOTR
QXC5104 • **Value $65**

(20) Sleighful of Dreams
(club edition)
Handcrafted • SICK
800QXC5801 • **Value $73**

GENERAL MINIATURE		
	Price Paid	Value of My Collection
1.		
2.		
3.		
4.		
5.		
6.		
7.		
8.		
9.		
10.		
11.		
12.		
13.		
14.		
COLLECTOR'S CLUB		
15.		
16.		
17.		
18.		
19.		
20.		
PENCIL TOTALS		

1988

(1)

Kringle's Toy Shop
(re-issued in 1989, magic)
Handcrafted • SEAL
2450QLX7017 • **Value $50**

1987

Among the most sought-after ornaments from 1987 is "Bright Christmas Dreams," which is coveted by collectors of the "CRAYOLA® Crayon" collectible series, although it is not officially a part of that series. Overall, there were 122 Keepsake ornaments and 18 Magic ornaments. See the collectible series section for more 1987 ornaments.

(2)

Baby Locket
Textured Metal • N/A
1500QX4617 • **Value $31**

(3)

Baby's First Christmas
Acrylic • N/A
600QX3729 • **Value $18**

(4)

Baby's First Christmas
Handcrafted • DLEE
975QX4113 • **Value $30**

(5)

**Baby's First Christmas
– Baby Boy**
Satin • PATT
475QX2749 • **Value $31**

OPEN HOUSE ORNAMENTS

	Price Paid	Value of My Collection
1.		
GENERAL KEEPSAKE		
2.		
3.		
4.		
5.		
6.		
7.		
8.		
9.		
10.		
11.		
12.		
13.		
14.		
15.		
16.		
17.		

PENCIL TOTALS

(6)

**Baby's First Christmas
– Baby Girl**
Satin • PATT
475QX2747 • **Value $28**

(7)

**Baby's First Christmas
Photoholder**
Fabric • N/A
750QX4619 • **Value $29**

(8)

**Baby's Second
Christmas**
Handcrafted • DLEE
575QX4607 • **Value $32**

(9)

Babysitter
Glass • PIKE
475QX2797 • **Value $19**

(10)

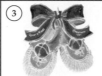

Beary Special
Handcrafted • SIED
475QX4557 • **Value $28**

(11)

**Bright
Christmas Dreams**
Handcrafted • SIED
725QX4737 • **Value $92**

(12)

Child's Third Christmas
Handcrafted • CROW
575QX4599 • **Value $28**

(13)

Chocolate Chipmunk
Handcrafted • SEAL
600QX4567 • **Value $58**

(14)

Christmas Cuddle
Handcrafted • N/A
575QX4537 • **Value $36**

(15)

Christmas Fun Puzzle
Handcrafted • DLEE
800QX4679 • **Value $30**

(16)

Christmas is Gentle
(LE-24,700)
Bone China • SEAL
1750QX4449 • **Value $90**

(17)

Christmas Keys
Handcrafted • UNRU
575QX4739 • **Value $34**

VALUE GUIDE — HALLMARK KEEPSAKE ORNAMENTS

(1) **Christmas Time Mime**
(LE-24,700)
Porcelain • UNRU
2750QX4429 • **Value $61**

(2) **The Constitution**
Acrylic • PATT
650QX3777 • **Value $28**

(3) **Country Wreath**
Wood/Straw • PYDA
575QX4709 • **Value $28**

(4) **Currier & Ives:**
American Farm Scene
Glass • LYLE
475QX2829 • **Value $30**

(5) **Dad**
Handcrafted • SIED
600QX4629 • **Value $40**

(6) **Daughter**
Handcrafted • SICK
575QX4637 • **Value $29**

(7) **December Showers**
Handcrafted • DLEE
550QX4487 • **Value $35**

(8) **Doc Holiday**
Handcrafted • SEAL
800QX4677 • **Value $45**

(9) **Dr. Seuss: The**
Grinch's Christmas
Glass • N/A
475QX2783 • **Value $96**

(10) **Favorite Santa**
Porcelain • DUTK
2250QX4457 • **Value $43**

(11) **Fifty Years Together**
Porcelain • SEAL
800QX4437 • **Value $25**

(12) **First Christmas**
Together
Acrylic • N/A
650QX3719 • **Value $19**

(13) **First Christmas**
Together
Glass • LYLE
475QX2729 • **Value $28**

(14) **First Christmas**
Together
Handcrafted • N/A
800QX4459 • **Value $38**

(15) **First Christmas**
Together
Handcrafted • DLEE
950QX4467 • **Value $28**

(16) **First Christmas**
Together
Textured Brass • N/A
1500QX4469 • **Value $30**

(17) **Folk Art Santa**
Handcrafted • SICK
525QX4749 • **Value $34**

(18) **From Our**
Home to Yours
Glass • PYDA
475QX2799 • **Value $46**

(19) **Fudge Forever**
Handcrafted • DUTK
500QX4497 • **Value $38**

(20) **Godchild**
Glass • PYDA
475QX2767 • **Value $22**

GENERAL KEEPSAKE

	Price Paid	Value of My Collection
1.		
2.		
3.		
4.		
5.		
6.		
7.		
8.		
9.		
10.		
11.		
12.		
13.		
14.		
15.		
16.		
17.		
18.		
19.		
20.		
PENCIL TOTALS		

Value Guide — Hallmark Keepsake Ornaments

(1)
Goldfinch
Porcelain • SICK
700QX4649 • **Value $78**

(2)
Grandchild's First Christmas
Handcrafted • SEAL
900QX4609 • **Value $25**

(3)
Granddaughter
Bezeled Satin • VOTR
600QX3747 • **Value $22**

(4)
Grandmother
Glass • N/A
475QX2779 • **Value $15**

(5)
Grandparents
Glass • PIKE
475QX2777 • **Value $19**

(6)
Grandson
Glass • VOTR
475QX2769 • **Value $29**

(7)
Happy Holidata (re-issued in 1988)
Handcrafted • SIED
650QX4717 • **Value $30**

(8)
Happy Santa
Handcrafted • CROW
475QX4569 • **Value $32**

(9)
Heart in Blossom
Acrylic • VOTR
600QX3727 • **Value $23**

(10)
Heavenly Harmony
Handcrafted • CROW
1500QX4659 • **Value $34**

(11)
Holiday Greetings
Bezeled Foil • N/A
600QX3757 • **Value $13**

(12)
Holiday Hourglass
Handcrafted • UNRU
800QX4707 • **Value $26**

(13)
Hot Dogger
Handcrafted • UNRU
650QX4719 • **Value $28**

(14)
Husband
Cameo • VOTR
700QX3739 • **Value $10**

(15)
I Remember Santa
Glass • LYLE
475QX278-9 • **Value $35**

(16)
Icy Treat
Handcrafted • SIED
450QX4509 • **Value $30**

(17)
In a Nutshell (re-issued in 1988)
Handcrafted • UNRU
550QX4697 • **Value $34**

(18)
Jack Frosting
Handcrafted • SEAL
700QX4499 • **Value $54**

(19)
Jammie Pies™
Glass • N/A
475QX2839 • **Value $19**

(20)
Jogging Through the Snow
Handcrafted • DUTK
725QX4577 • **Value $39**

General Keepsake		
	Price Paid	Value of My Collection
1.		
2.		
3.		
4.		
5.		
6.		
7.		
8.		
9.		
10.		
11.		
12.		
13.		
14.		
15.		
16.		
17.		
18.		
19.		
20.		
Pencil Totals		

1

Jolly Follies
Handcrafted • CROW
850QX4669 • **Value $36**

2

Jolly Hiker
(re-issued from 1986)
Handcrafted • SIED
500QX4832 • **Value $29**

3

Joy Ride
Handcrafted • SEAL
1150QX4407 • **Value $78**

4

Joyous Angels
Handcrafted • SEAL
775QX4657 • **Value $25**

5

Let It Snow
Handcrafted • N/A
650QX4589 • **Value $23**

6

L'il Jingler
(re-issued from 1986)
Handcrafted • SEAL
675QX4193 • **Value $42**

7

Little Whittler
Handcrafted • DUTK
600QX4699 • **Value $32**

8

Love Is Everywhere
Glass • LYLE
475QX2787 • **Value $25**

1987

9

Merry Koala
(re-issued from 1986)
Handcrafted • SICK
500QX4153 • **Value $23**

10

Mistletoad
(re-issued in 1988)
Handcrafted • CROW
700QX4687 • **Value $29**

11

Mother
Acrylic • PIKE
650QX3737 • **Value $15**

12

Mother and Dad
Porcelain • PIKE
700QX4627 • **Value $25**

13

Mouse in the Moon
(re-issued from 1986)
Handcrafted • SEAL
550QX4166 • **Value $26**

14

Nature's Decorations
Glass • VOTR
475QX2739 • **Value $35**

15

New Home
Acrylic • PATT
600QX3767 • **Value $26**

16

Niece
Glass • N/A
475QX2759 • **Value $16**

17

Night Before Christmas
(re-issued in 1988)
Handcrafted • CROW
650QX4517 • **Value $35**

18

Norman Rockwell:
Christmas Scenes
Glass • LYLE
475QX2827 • **Value $32**

19

Nostalgic Rocker
Wood • SICK
650QX4689 • **Value $30**

20

"Owliday" Wish
(re-issued in 1988)
Handcrafted • PIKE
650QX4559 • **Value $23**

General Keepsake

	Price Paid	Value of My Collection
1.		
2.		
3.		
4.		
5.		
6.		
7.		
8.		
9.		
10.		
11.		
12.		
13.		
14.		
15.		
16.		
17.		
18.		
19.		
20.		
PENCIL TOTALS		

Value Guide — Hallmark Keepsake Ornaments

(1) Paddington™ Bear
Handcrafted • PIKE
550QX4727 • **Value $34**

(2) PEANUTS®
Glass • N/A
475QX2819 • **Value $40**

(3) Pretty Kitty
Handcrafted/Glass • CROW
1100QX4489 • **Value $30**

(4) Promise of Peace
Acrylic • PIKE
650QX3749 • **Value $22**

(5) Raccoon Biker
Handcrafted • SIED
700QX4587 • **Value $29**

(6) Reindoggy (re-issued in 1988)
Handcrafted • SIED
575QX4527 • **Value $35**

(7) St. Louie Nick (re-issued in 1988)
Handcrafted • DUTK
775QX4539 • **Value $33**

(8) Santa at the Bat
Handcrafted • SIED
775QX4579 • **Value $28**

(9) Seasoned Greetings
Handcrafted • SEAL
625QX4549 • **Value $28**

(10) Sister
Wood • SICK
600QX4747 • **Value $14**

(11) Sleepy Santa
Handcrafted • CROW
625QX4507 • **Value $39**

(12) SNOOPY and WOODSTOCK
Handcrafted • SIED
725QX4729 • **Value $52**

(13) Son
Handcrafted • SICK
575QX4639 • **Value $46**

(14) Special Memories Photoholder
Fabric • N/A
675QX4647 • **Value $25**

(15) Spots 'n Stripes
Handcrafted • N/A
550QX4529 • **Value $26**

(16) Sweetheart
Handcrafted • SICK
1100QX4479 • **Value $30**

(17) Teacher
Handcrafted • SIED
575QX4667 • **Value $21**

(18) Ten Years Together
Porcelain • VOTR
700QX4447 • **Value $23**

(19) Three Men in a Tub
Handcrafted • DLEE
800QX4547 • **Value $30**

(20) Time for Friends
Glass • VOTR
475QX2807 • **Value $23**

GENERAL KEEPSAKE	Price Paid	Value of My Collection
1.		
2.		
3.		
4.		
5.		
6.		
7.		
8.		
9.		
10.		
11.		
12.		
13.		
14.		
15.		
16.		
17.		
18.		
19.		
20.		
PENCIL TOTALS		

(1)

Treetop Dreams
(re-issued in 1988)
Handcrafted • SEAL
675QX4597 • **Value $30**

(2)

Treetop Trio
(re-issued from 1986)
Handcrafted • DLEE
1100QX4256 • **Value $31**

(3)

Twenty-Five
Years Together
Porcelain • N/A
750QX4439 • **Value $27**

(4)

Walnut Shell Rider
(re-issued from 1986)
Handcrafted • SEAL
600QX4196 • **Value $28**

(5)

Warmth of Friendship
Acrylic • N/A
600QX3759 • **Value $11**

(6)

Wee Chimney Sweep
Handcrafted • SEAL
625QX4519 • **Value $28**

(7)

Word of Love
Porcelain • N/A
800QX4477 • **Value $24**

(8)
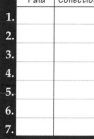
Angelic Messengers
Panorama Ball • UNRU
1875QLX7113 • **Value $61**

(9)

Baby's First Christmas
Handcrafted • N/A
1350QLX7049 • **Value $37**

(10)

Bright Noel
Acrylic • VOTR
700QLX7059 • **Value $32**

(11)

Christmas Morning
(re-issued in 1988)
Handcrafted • CROW
2450QLX7013 • **Value $48**

(12)

First Christmas
Together
Handcrafted • N/A
1150QLX7087 • **Value $48**

(13)
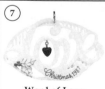
Good Cheer Blimp
Handcrafted • SICK
1600QLX7046 • **Value $60**

(14)

Keep on Glowin'!
(re-issued from 1986)
Handcrafted • CROW
1000QLX7076 • **Value $46**

(15)

Keeping Cozy
Handcrafted • CROW
1175QLX7047 • **Value $36**

(16)

Lacy Brass Snowflake
Brass • N/A
1150QLX7097 • **Value $27**

(17)

Loving Holiday
Handcrafted • SEAL
2200QLX7016 • **Value $53**

(18)

Memories Are Forever
Photoholder
Handcrafted • SEAL
850QLX7067 • **Value $34**

(19)

Meowy Christmas!
Handcrafted • PIKE
1000QLX7089 • **Value $62**

(20)

Season for Friendship
Acrylic • N/A
850QLX7069 • **Value $20**

	Price Paid	Value of My Collection
GENERAL KEEPSAKE		
1.		
2.		
3.		
4.		
5.		
6.		
7.		
GENERAL MAGIC		
8.		
9.		
10.		
11.		
12.		
13.		
14.		
15.		
16.		
17.		
18.		
19.		
20.		
PENCIL TOTALS		

1987

(1)

Train Station
Handcrafted • DLEE
1275QLX7039 • **Value $48**

(2)

Village Express
(re-issued from 1986)
Handcrafted • SICK
2450QLX7072 • **Value $120**

(3)

Carousel Reindeer
(club edition)
Handcrafted • SICK
800QXC5817 • **Value $63**

(4)

Wreath of Memories
(keepsake of membership)
Handcrafted • UNRU
QXC5809 • **Value $53**

(5)

North Pole Power & Light
Handcrafted • CROW
($2.95)627XPR9333 • **Value $27**

1986

One of the biggest stories among Hallmark collectors in 1986 was the hard-to-find porcelain "Magical Unicorn" ornament which was limited to 24,700 pieces. The 1986 collection featured 120 Keepsake ornaments and 16 Magic ornaments. See the collectible series section for more 1986 ornaments.

	Price Paid	Value of My Collection
General Magic		
1.		
2.		
Collector's Club		
3.		
4.		
Open House Ornaments		
5.		
General Keepsake		
6.		
7.		
8.		
9.		
10.		
11.		
12.		
13.		
14.		
15.		
16.		
17.		

PENCIL TOTALS

(6)

Acorn Inn
Handcrafted • UNRU
850QX4243 • **Value $30**

(7)

Baby Locket
Textured Brass • MCGE
1600QX4123 • **Value $28**

(8)

Baby's First Christmas
Acrylic • PALM
600QX3803 • **Value $26**

(9)

Baby's First Christmas
Handcrafted • SICK
900QX4126 • **Value $40**

(10)

Baby's First Christmas
Satin • PATT
550QX2713 • **Value $24**

(11)

Baby's First Christmas Photoholder
Fabric • PATT
800QX3792 • **Value $24**

(12)

Baby's Second Christmas
Handcrafted • SIED
650QX4133 • **Value $29**

(13)

Baby-Sitter
Glass • N/A
475QX2756 • **Value $11**

(14)

Beary Smooth Ride
(re-issued from 1985)
Handcrafted • SICK
650QX4805 • **Value $25**

(15)

Bluebird
Porcelain • SICK
725QX4283 • **Value $58**

(16)

Chatty Penguin
Plush • CROW
575QX4176 • **Value $26**

(17)

Child's Third Christmas
Fabric • VOTR
650QX4136 • **Value $26**

1
Christmas Beauty
Lacquer • PATT
600QX3223 • **Value $10**

2
Christmas Guitar
Handcrafted • UNRU
700QX5126 • **Value $25**

3
Cookies for Santa
Handcrafted • MCGE
450QX4146 • **Value $30**

4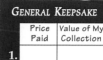
Country Sleigh
Handcrafted • SICK
1000QX5113 • **Value $28**

5
Daughter
Handcrafted • SEAL
575QX4306 • **Value $47**

6
Do Not Disturb Bear
(re-issued from 1985)
Handcrafted • SEAL
775QX4812 • **Value $32**

7
Father
Wood • VOTR
650QX4313 • **Value $14**

8
Favorite Tin Drum
Tin • SICK
850QX5143 • **Value $32**

9
Festive Treble Clef
Handcrafted • SIED
875QX5133 • **Value $26**

10
Fifty Years Together
Porcelain • PIKE
1000QX4006 • **Value $19**

11
First Christmas Together
Acrylic • MCGE
700QX3793 • **Value $22**

12
First Christmas Together
Glass • N/A
475QX2703 • **Value $25**

13
First Christmas Together
Handcrafted • SICK
1200QX4096 • **Value $28**

14
First Christmas Together
Textured Brass • N/A
1600QX4003 • **Value $21**

15
Friends Are Fun
Glass • CROW
475QX2723 • **Value $42**

16
Friendship Greeting
Fabric • N/A
800QX4273 • **Value $15**

17
Friendship's Gift
Acrylic • N/A
600QX3816 • **Value $15**

18
From Our Home to Yours
Acrylic • N/A
600QX3833 • **Value $15**

19
Glowing Christmas Tree
Acrylic • PATT
700QX4286 • **Value $16**

20
Godchild
Satin • N/A
475QX2716 • **Value $17**

General Keepsake

	Price Paid	Value of My Collection
1.		
2.		
3.		
4.		
5.		
6.		
7.		
8.		
9.		
10.		
11.		
12.		
13.		
14.		
15.		
16.		
17.		
18.		
19.		
20.		
PENCIL TOTALS		

Value Guide – Hallmark Keepsake Ornaments

1. Grandchild's First Christmas — *Handcrafted • N/A* — 1000QX4116 • **Value $16**

2. Granddaughter — *Glass • LYLE* — 475QX2736 • **Value $28**

3. Grandmother — *Satin • PATT* — 475QX2743 • **Value $16**

4. Grandparents — *Porcelain • PATT* — 750QX4323 • **Value $22**

5. Grandson — *Glass • VOTR* — 475QX2733 • **Value $35**

6. Gratitude — *Satin/Wood • PIKE* — 600QX4326 • **Value $11**

7. Happy Christmas to Owl — *Handcrafted • UNRU* — 600QX4183 • **Value $25**

8. Heathcliff — *Handcrafted • SEAL* — 750QX4363 • **Value $33**

9. Heavenly Dreamer — *Handcrafted • DLEE* — 575QX4173 • **Value $34**

10. Heirloom Snowflake — *Fabric • PATT* — 675QX5153 • **Value $21**

11. Holiday Horn — *Porcelain • UNRU* — 800QX5146 • **Value $34**

12. Holiday Jingle Bell — *Handcrafted • N/A* — 1600QX4046 • **Value $55**

13. Husband — *Cameo • PIKE* — 800QX3836 • **Value $14**

14. Jolly Hiker (re-issued in 1987) — *Handcrafted • SIED* — 500QX4832 • **Value $29**

15. Jolly St. Nick — *Porcelain • UNRU* — 2250QX4296 • **Value $75**

16. Joy of Friends — *Bezeled Satin • PATT* — 675QX3823 • **Value $18**

17. Joyful Carolers — *Handcrafted • SICK* — 975QX5136 • **Value $38**

18. Katybeth — *Porcelain • N/A* — 700QX4353 • **Value $25**

19. Kitty Mischief (re-issued from 1985) — *Handcrafted • DUTK* — 500QX4745 • **Value $24**

20. Li'l Jingler (re-issued in 1987) — *Handcrafted • SEAL* — 675QX4193 • **Value $42**

General Keepsake

	Price Paid	Value of My Collection
1.		
2.		
3.		
4.		
5.		
6.		
7.		
8.		
9.		
10.		
11.		
12.		
13.		
14.		
15.		
16.		
17.		
18.		
19.		
20.		
PENCIL TOTALS		

1
Little Drummers
Handcrafted • CROW
1250QX5116 • **Value $33**

2
Loving Memories
Handcrafted • SEAL
900QX4093 • **Value $34**

3
The Magi
Glass • PIKE
475QX2726 • **Value $23**

4
Magical Unicorn
(LE-24,700)
Porcelain • UNRU
2750QX4293 • **Value $100**

5
Marionette Angel
(canceled after
limited production)
Handcrafted • N/A
850QX4023 • **Value $425**

6
Mary Emmerling:
American Country
Collection
Glass • N/A
795QX2752 • **Value $26**

7
Memories to Cherish
Ceramic • VOTR
750QX4276 • **Value $28**

8
Merry Koala
(re-issued in 1987)
Handcrafted • SICK
500QX4153 • **Value $23**

9
Merry Mouse
(re-issued from 1985)
Handcrafted • DUTK
450QX4032 • **Value $31**

10
Mother
Acrylic • N/A
700QX3826 • **Value $20**

11
Mother and Dad
Porcelain • PYDA
750QX4316 • **Value $21**

12
Mouse in the Moon
(re-issued in 1987)
Handcrafted • SEAL
550QX4166 • **Value $26**

13
Nephew
Bezeled Lacquer • N/A
625QX3813 • **Value $14**

14
New Home
Glass • CROW
475QX2746 • **Value $50**

15
Niece
Fabric/Wood • N/A
600QX4266 • **Value $10**

16
Norman Rockwell
Glass • PIKE
475QX2763 • **Value $30**

17
Nutcracker Santa
Handcrafted • UNRU
1000QX5123 • **Value $53**

18
Open Me First
Handcrafted • N/A
725QX4226 • **Value $33**

19
Paddington™ Bear
Handcrafted • SIED
600QX4356 • **Value $40**

20
PEANUTS®
Glass • N/A
475QX2766 • **Value $42**

1986

General Keepsake

	Price Paid	Value of My Collection
1.		
2.		
3.		
4.		
5.		
6.		
7.		
8.		
9.		
10.		
11.		
12.		
13.		
14.		
15.		
16.		
17.		
18.		
19.		
20.		
PENCIL TOTALS		

VALUE GUIDE — HALLMARK KEEPSAKE ORNAMENTS

(1) Playful Possum	(2) Popcorn Mouse	(3) Puppy's Best Friend	(4) Rah Rah Rabbit
Handcrafted/Glass • CROW	Handcrafted • SICK	Handcrafted • UNRU	Handcrafted • CROW
1100QX4253 • **Value $33**	675QX4213 • **Value $53**	650QX4203 • **Value $29**	700QX4216 • **Value $38**

(5) Remembering Christmas	(6) Santa's Hot Tub	(7) Season of the Heart	(8) Shirt Tales™ Parade
Porcelain • N/A	Handcrafted • SEAL	Glass • PATT	Glass • N/A
875QX5106 • **Value $30**	1200QX4263 • **Value $60**	475QX2706 • **Value $17**	475QX2773 • **Value $18**

GENERAL KEEPSAKE

	Price Paid	Value of My Collection
1.		
2.		
3.		
4.		
5.		
6.		
7.		
8.		
9.		
10.		
11.		
12.		
13.		
14.		
15.		
16.		
17.		
18.		
19.		
20.		

PENCIL TOTALS

(9) Sister	(10) Skateboard Raccoon (re-issued from 1985)	(11) Ski Tripper
Bezeled Satin • VOTR	Handcrafted • DUTK	Handcrafted • SIED
675QX3806 • **Value $15**	650QX4732 • **Value $36**	675QX4206 • **Value $22**

(12) SNOOPY® and WOODSTOCK	(13) Snow Buddies	(14) Snow-Pitching Snowman (re-issued from 1985)
Handcrafted • SIED	Handcrafted • DUTK	Handcrafted • DLEE
800QX4346 • **Value $60**	800QX4236 • **Value $38**	450QX4702 • **Value $24**

(15) Soccer Beaver (re-issued from 1985)	(16) Son	(17) Special Delivery
Handcrafted • DUTK	Handcrafted • SEAL	Handcrafted • SIED
650QX4775 • **Value $26**	575QX4303 • **Value $35**	500QX4156 • **Value $30**

(18) Star Brighteners	(19) The Statue of Liberty	(20) Sweetheart
Acrylic • VOTR	Acrylic • PYDA	Handcrafted • SEAL
600QX3226 • **Value $19**	600QX3843 • **Value $25**	1100QX4086 • **Value $68**

1 **Teacher**
Glass • N/A
475QX2753 • **Value $12**

2 **Ten Years Together**
Porcelain • N/A
750QX4013 • **Value $19**

3 **Timeless Love**
Acrylic • VOTR
600QX3796 • **Value $35**

4 **Tipping the Scales**
Handcrafted • DUTK
675QX4186 • **Value $29**

5 **Touchdown Santa**
Handcrafted • DUTK
800QX4233 • **Value $42**

6 **Treetop Trio**
(re-issued in 1987)
Handcrafted • DLEE
1100QX4256 • **Value $31**

7 **Twenty-Five Years Together**
Porcelain • VOTR
800QX4103 • **Value $23**

8 **Walnut Shell Rider**
(re-issued in 1987)
Handcrafted • SEAL
600QX4196 • **Value $26**

9 **Welcome, Christmas**
Handcrafted • CROW
825QX5103 • **Value $33**

10 **Wynken, Blynken and Nod**
Handcrafted • DLEE
975QX4246 • **Value $45**

11 **Baby's First Christmas**
Panorama Ball • CROW
1950QLX7103 • **Value $48**

12 **Christmas Sleigh Ride**
Handcrafted • SEAL
2450QLX7012 • **Value $145**

13 **First Christmas Together**
Handcrafted • SEAL
1400QLX7073 • **Value $43**

14 **General Store**
Handcrafted • DLEE
1575QLX7053 • **Value $60**

15 **Gentle Blessings**
Panorama Ball • SICK
1500QLX7083 • **Value $185**

16 **Keep on Glowin'!**
(re-issued in 1987)
Handcrafted • CROW
1000QLX7076 • **Value $46**

17 **Merry Christmas Bell**
Acrylic • VOTR
850QLX7093 • **Value $24**

18 **Mr. and Mrs. Santa**
(re-issued from 1985)
Handcrafted • N/A
1450QLX7052 • **Value $85**

19 **Santa's On His Way**
Panorama Ball • UNRU
1500QLX7115 • **Value $73**

20 **Santa's Snack**
Handcrafted • CROW
1000QLX7066 • **Value $60**

1986

General Keepsake

	Price Paid	Value of My Collection
1.		
2.		
3.		
4.		
5.		
6.		
7.		
8.		
9.		
10.		

General Magic

11.		
12.		
13.		
14.		
15.		
16.		
17.		
18.		
19.		
20.		

PENCIL TOTALS

(1) **Sharing Friendship** *Acrylic* • VOTR 850QLX7063 • **Value $21**	(2)  **Sugarplum Cottage** **(re-issued from 1984)** *Handcrafted* • N/A 1100QLX7011 • **Value $45**	(3) **Village Express** **(re-issued in 1987)** *Handcrafted* • SICK 2450QLX7072 • **Value $120**	(4) **On the Right Track** *Porcelain* • DUTK 1500QSP4201 • **Value $48**
(5) **Coca-Cola® Santa** *Glass* • N/A 475QXO2796 • **Value $22**	(6) **Old-Fashioned Santa** *Handcrafted* • SICK 1275QXO4403 • **Value $60**	(7)  **Santa and His Reindeer** *Handcrafted* • N/A 975QXO4406 • **Value $40**	(8) **Santa's Panda Pal** *Handcrafted* • N/A 500QXO4413 • **Value $28**

1985

Some of the most popular pieces in 1985 were based on favorite themes such as Santa Claus, SNOOPY® and Norman Rockwell's art. For 1985, there were 114 Keepsake ornament designs and 14 Magic ornaments. See the collectible series section for more 1985 ornaments.

(9)  **Baby Locket** *Textured Brass* • MCGE 1600QX4012 • **Value $23**	(10) **Baby's First Christmas** *Acrylic* • N/A 575QX3702 • **Value $21**	(11) **Baby's First Christmas** *Embroidered Fabric* • N/A 700QX4782 • **Value $17**
(12)  **Baby's First Christmas** *Fabric* • N/A 1600QX4995 • **Value $44**	(13) **Baby's First Christmas** *Handcrafted* • DLEE 1500QX4992 • **Value $57**	(14) **Baby's First Christmas** *Satin* • VOTR 500QX2602 • **Value $26**
(15)  **Baby's Second Christmas** *Handcrafted* • N/A 600QX4785 • **Value $39**	(16) **Babysitter** *Glass* • PYDA 475QX2642 • **Value $13**	(17) **Baker Elf** *Handcrafted* • SEAL 575QX4912 • **Value $32**

GENERAL MAGIC

	Price Paid	Value of My Collection
1.		
2.		
3.		

GOLD CROWN ORNAMENTS

4.		

OPEN HOUSE ORNAMENTS

5.		
6.		
7.		
8.		

GENERAL KEEPSAKE

9.		
10.		

PENCIL TOTALS

1985

(1) **Beary Smooth Ride** (re-issued in 1986) *Handcrafted* • SICK 650QX4805 • **Value $25**	(2) **Betsey Clark** *Porcelain* • N/A 850QX5085 • **Value $33**	(3) **Bottlecap Fun Bunnies** *Handcrafted* • SIED 775QX4815 • **Value $36**	(4) **Candle Cameo** *Bezeled Cameo* • PIKE 675QX3742 • **Value $15**
(5) **Candy Apple Mouse** *Handcrafted* • SICK 650QX4705 • **Value $63**	(6) **Charming Angel** *Fabric* • PYDA 975QX5125 • **Value $25**	(7) **Children in the Shoe** *Handcrafted* • SEAL 950QX4905 • **Value $52**	(8) 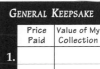 **Child's Third Christmas** *Handcrafted* • SEAL 600QX4755 • **Value $32**
(9) **Christmas Treats** *Bezeled Glass* • N/A 550QX5075 • **Value $18**	(10)  **Country Goose** *Wood* • PYDA 775QX5185 • **Value $16**	(11)  **Dapper Penguin** *Handcrafted* • SEAL 500QX4772 • **Value $33**	
(12) **Daughter** *Wood* • N/A 550QX5032 • **Value $22**	(13) **A DISNEY Christmas** *Glass* • N/A 475QX2712 • **Value $33**	(14) **Do Not Disturb Bear** (re-issued in 1986) *Handcrafted* • SEAL 775QX4812 • **Value $32**	
(15) **Doggy in a Stocking** *Handcrafted* • N/A 550QX4742 • **Value $41**	(16) 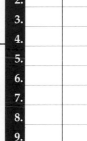 **Engineering Mouse** *Handcrafted* • SIED 550QX4735 • **Value $27**	(17)  **Father** *Wood* • VOTR 650QX3762 • **Value $12**	
(18)  **First Christmas Together** *Acrylic* • N/A 675QX3705 • **Value $20**	(19) **First Christmas Together** *Brass* • SEAL 1675QX4005 • **Value $27**	(20) **First Christmas Together** *Fabric/Wood* • N/A 800QX5072 • **Value $15**	

GENERAL KEEPSAKE

	Price Paid	Value of My Collection
1.		
2.		
3.		
4.		
5.		
6.		
7.		
8.		
9.		
10.		
11.		
12.		
13.		
14.		
15.		
16.		
17.		
18.		
19.		
20.		
PENCIL TOTALS		

1

First Christmas Together
Glass • N/A
475QX2612 • **Value $22**

2

First Christmas Together
Porcelain • SICK
1300QX4935 • **Value $27**

3

FRAGGLE ROCK™ Holiday
Glass • N/A
475QX2655 • **Value $32**

4

Friendship
Bezeled Satin • PYDA
675QX3785 • **Value $20**

5

Friendship
Embroidered Satin • PATT
775QX5062 • **Value $16**

6

From Our House to Yours
Needlepoint Fabric • PATT
775QX5202 • **Value $14**

7

Godchild
Bezeled Satin • MCGE
675QX3802 • **Value $14**

8

Good Friends
Glass • N/A
475QX2652 • **Value $32**

General Keepsake

	Price Paid	Value of My Collection
1.		
2.		
3.		
4.		
5.		
6.		
7.		
8.		
9.		
10.		
11.		
12.		
13.		
14.		
15.		
16.		
17.		
18.		
19.		
20.		

PENCIL TOTALS

9

Grandchild's First Christmas
Handcrafted • N/A
1100QX4955 • **Value $24**

10

Grandchild's First Christmas
Satin • VOTR
500QX2605 • **Value $15**

11

Granddaughter
Glass • N/A
475QX2635 • **Value $28**

12

Grandmother
Glass • PATT
475QX2625 • **Value $20**

13

Grandparents
Bezeled Lacquer • PIKE
700QX3805 • **Value $15**

14

Grandson
Glass • VOTR
475QX2622 • **Value $32**

15

Heart Full of Love
Bezeled Satin • N/A
675QX3782 • **Value $23**

16

Heavenly Trumpeter (LE-24,700)
Porcelain • DLEE
2750QX4052 • **Value $105**

17

Holiday Heart
Porcelain • N/A
800QX4982 • **Value $32**

18

Hugga Bunch™
Glass • N/A
500QX2715 • **Value $29**

19

Ice Skating Owl
Handcrafted • SIED
500QX4765 • **Value $26**

20

Keepsake Basket
Fabric • PIKE
1500QX5145 • **Value $21**

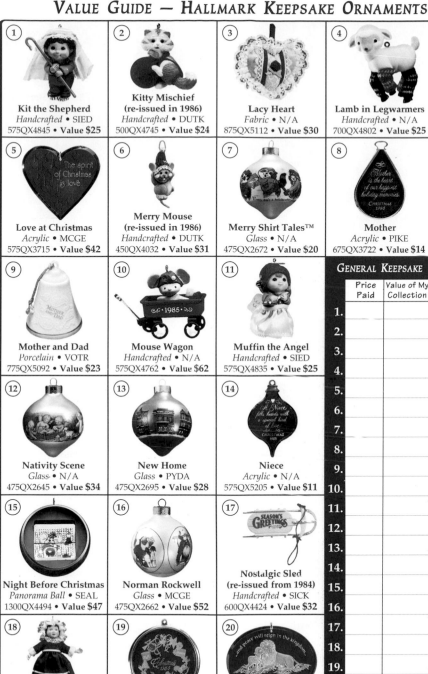

1 Kit the Shepherd
Handcrafted • SIED
575QX4845 • **Value $25**

2 Kitty Mischief
(re-issued in 1986)
Handcrafted • DUTK
500QX4745 • **Value $24**

3 Lacy Heart
Fabric • N/A
875QX5112 • **Value $30**

4 Lamb in Legwarmers
Handcrafted • N/A
700QX4802 • **Value $25**

5 Love at Christmas
Acrylic • MCGE
575QX3715 • **Value $42**

6 Merry Mouse
(re-issued in 1986)
Handcrafted • DUTK
450QX4032 • **Value $31**

7 Merry Shirt Tales™
Glass • N/A
475QX2672 • **Value $20**

8 Mother
Acrylic • PIKE
675QX3722 • **Value $14**

9 Mother and Dad
Porcelain • VOTR
775QX5092 • **Value $23**

10 Mouse Wagon
Handcrafted • N/A
575QX4762 • **Value $62**

11 Muffin the Angel
Handcrafted • SIED
575QX4835 • **Value $25**

12 Nativity Scene
Glass • N/A
475QX2645 • **Value $34**

13 New Home
Glass • PYDA
475QX2695 • **Value $28**

14 Niece
Acrylic • N/A
575QX5205 • **Value $11**

15 Night Before Christmas
Panorama Ball • SEAL
1300QX4494 • **Value $47**

16 Norman Rockwell
Glass • MCGE
475QX2662 • **Value $52**

17 Nostalgic Sled
(re-issued from 1984)
Handcrafted • SICK
600QX4424 • **Value $32**

18 Old-Fashioned Doll
Fabric/Porcelain • N/A
1450QX5195 • **Value $43**

19 Old-Fashioned Wreath
Brass/Acrylic • N/A
750QX3735 • **Value $26**

20 Peaceful Kingdom
Acrylic • PIKE
575QX3732 • **Value $30**

1985

GENERAL KEEPSAKE

	Price Paid	Value of My Collection
1.		
2.		
3.		
4.		
5.		
6.		
7.		
8.		
9.		
10.		
11.		
12.		
13.		
14.		
15.		
16.		
17.		
18.		
19.		
20.		
PENCIL TOTALS		

Value Guide — Hallmark Keepsake Ornaments

(1)
PEANUTS®
Glass • N/A
475QX2665 • **Value $38**

(2)
Porcelain Bird
Porcelain • SICK
650QX4795 • **Value $32**

(3)
Rainbow Brite™ and Friends
Glass • N/A
475QX2682 • **Value $26**

(4)
Rocking Horse Memories
Fabric/Wood • VOTR
1000QX5182 • **Value $16**

(5)
Roller Skating Rabbit (re-issued from 1984)
Handcrafted • SEAL
500QX4571 • **Value $34**

(6)
Santa Pipe
Handcrafted • DUTK
950QX4942 • **Value $26**

(7)
Santa's Ski Trip
Handcrafted • SEAL
1200QX4962 • **Value $62**

(8)
Sewn Photoholder
Embroidered Fabric • PIKE
700QX3795 • **Value $34**

GENERAL KEEPSAKE

	Price Paid	Value of My Collection
1.		
2.		
3.		
4.		
5.		
6.		
7.		
8.		
9.		
10.		
11.		
12.		
13.		
14.		
15.		
16.		
17.		
18.		
19.		
20.		

PENCIL TOTALS

(9)
Sheep at Christmas
Handcrafted • SICK
825QX5175 • **Value $28**

(10)
Sister
Porcelain • PATT
725QX5065 • **Value $24**

(11)
Skateboard Raccoon (re-issued in 1986)
Handcrafted • DUTK
650QX4732 • **Value $36**

(12)
SNOOPY® and WOODSTOCK
Handcrafted • SIED
750QX4915 • **Value $88**

(13)
Snowflake
Fabric • PATT
650QX5105 • **Value $25**

(14)
Snow-Pitching Snowman (re-issued in 1986)
Handcrafted • DLEE
450QX4702 • **Value $24**

(15)
Snowy Seal (re-issued from 1984)
Handcrafted • SEAL
400QX4501 • **Value $24**

(16)
Soccer Beaver (re-issued in 1986)
Handcrafted • DUTK
650QX4775 • **Value $26**

(17)
Son
Handcrafted • SIED
550QX5025 • **Value $53**

(18)
Special Friends
Arylic • PALM
575QX3725 • **Value $11**

(19)
The Spirit of Santa Claus
Handcrafted • DLEE
2250QX4985 • **Value $105**

(20)
Stardust Angel
Handcrafted • DLEE
575QX4752 • **Value $38**

1

Sun and Fun Santa
Handcrafted • SIED
775QX4922 • **Value $40**

2

Swinging Angel Bell
Handcrafted/Glass • SIED
1100QX4925 • **Value $35**

3

Teacher
Handcrafted • N/A
600QX5052 • **Value $20**

4

**Three Kittens
in a Mitten**
(re-issued from 1984)
Handcrafted • DLEE
800QX4311 • **Value $50**

5

Trumpet Panda
Handcrafted • SEAL
450QX4712 • **Value $25**

6

**Twenty-Five
Years Together**
Porcelain • N/A
800QX5005 • **Value $19**

7

Victorian Lady
Porcelain/Fabric • N/A
950QX5132 • **Value $25**

8

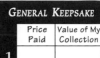

Whirligig Santa
Wood • N/A
1250QX5192 • **Value $30**

9

With Appreciation
Acrylic • N/A
675QX375? • **Value $11**

10

All Are Precious
(re-issued from 1984)
Acrylic • N/A
800QLX7044 • **Value $26**

11

Baby's First Christmas
Handcrafted • SEAL
1650QLX7005 • **Value $46**

12

Christmas Eve Visit
Etched Brass • N/A
1200QLX7105 • **Value $32**

13

Katybeth
Acrylic • N/A
1075QLX7102 • **Value $44**

14

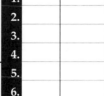

Little Red Schoolhouse
Handcrafted • DLEE
1575QLX7112 • **Value $98**

15

Love Wreath
Acrylic • VOTR
850QLX7025 • **Value $30**

16

Mr. and Mrs. Santa
(re-issued in 1986)
Handcrafted • N/A
1450QLX7052 • **Value $85**

17

Nativity
(re-issued from 1984)
Panorama Ball • SEAL
1200QLX7001 • **Value $32**

18

Santa's Workshop
(re-issued from 1984)
Panorama Ball • N/A
1300QLX7004 • **Value $63**

19

Season of Beauty
Classic Shape • LYLE
800QLX7122 • **Value $30**

20

Sugarplum Cottage
(re-issued from 1984)
Handcrafted • N/A
1100QLX7011 • **Value $45**

1985

General Keepsake

	Price Paid	Value of My Collection
1.		
2.		
3.		
4.		
5.		
6.		
7.		
8.		
9.		

General Magi

10.		
11.		
12.		
13.		
14.		
15.		
16.		
17.		
18.		
19.		
20.		

Pencil Total

①

Swiss Cheese Lane
Handcrafted • N/A
1300QLX7065 • **Value $48**

②

Village Church
(re-issued from 1984)
Handcrafted • DLEE
1500QLX7021 • **Value $51**

③

Santa Claus
Lacquer • N/A
675QX3005 • **Value $12**

④

Santa's Village
Lacquer • N/A
675QX3002• **Value $12**

1984

1984 was a landmark year for Hallmark ornaments with the debut of lighted Magic ornaments (then called "Lighted Ornaments"). In later years, these ornaments would also incorporate motion and sound. There were 10 Magic ornaments issued in 1984, as well as 110 Keepsake designs. See the collectible series section for more 1984 ornaments.

⑤

Alpine Elf
Handcrafted • SEAL
600QX4521 • **Value $38**

GENERAL MAGIC	Price Paid	Value of My Collection
1.		
2.		
SANTA CLAUS – THE MOVIE		
3.		
4.		
GENERAL KEEPSAKE		
5.		
6.		
7.		
8.		
9.		
10.		

⑥

Amanda
Fabric/Porcelain • N/A
900QX4321 • **Value $32**

⑦

Baby's First Christmas
Acrylic • N/A
600QX3401 • **Value $41**

⑧

Baby's First Christmas
Classic Shape • DLEE
1600QX9041 • **Value $50**

⑨

Baby's First Christmas
Handcrafted • N/A
1400QX4381 • **Value $50**

⑩

Baby's First
Christmas – Boy
Satin • N/A
450QX2404 • **Value $32**

⑪

Baby's First
Christmas – Girl
Satin • N/A
450QX2401 • **Value $31**

⑫

Baby's First Christmas
– Photoholder
Fabric • N/A
700QX3001 • **Value $20**

⑬

Baby's Second
Christmas
Satin • N/A
450QX2411 • **Value $43**

⑭

Baby-sitter
Glass • N/A
450QX2531 • **Value $15**

⑮

Bell Ringer Squirrel
Handcrafted/Glass • SEAL
1000QX4431 • **Value $42**

⑯

Betsey Clark Angel
Porcelain • N/A
900QX4624 • **Value $34**

⑰

Chickadee
Porcelain • SICK
600QX4514 • **Value $42**

PENCIL TOTALS

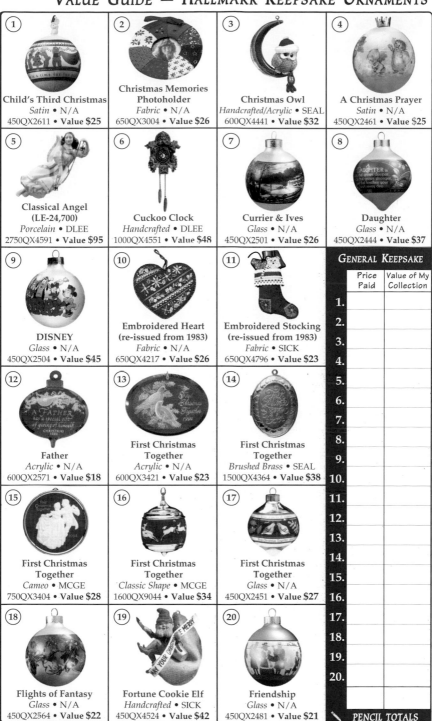

1. Child's Third Christmas
Satin • N/A
450QX2611 • **Value $25**

2. Christmas Memories Photoholder
Fabric • N/A
650QX3004 • **Value $26**

3. Christmas Owl
Handcrafted/Acrylic • SEAL
600QX4441 • **Value $32**

4. A Christmas Prayer
Satin • N/A
450QX2461 • **Value $25**

5. Classical Angel (LE-24,700)
Porcelain • DLEE
2750QX4591 • **Value $95**

6. Cuckoo Clock
Handcrafted • DLEE
1000QX4551 • **Value $48**

7. Currier & Ives
Glass • N/A
450QX2501 • **Value $26**

8. Daughter
Glass • N/A
450QX2444 • **Value $37**

9. DISNEY
Glass • N/A
450QX2504 • **Value $45**

10. Embroidered Heart (re-issued from 1983)
Fabric • N/A
650QX4217 • **Value $26**

11. Embroidered Stocking (re-issued from 1983)
Fabric • SICK
650QX4796 • **Value $23**

12. Father
Acrylic • N/A
600QX2571 • **Value $18**

13. First Christmas Together
Acrylic • N/A
600QX3421 • **Value $23**

14. First Christmas Together
Brushed Brass • SEAL
1500QX4364 • **Value $38**

15. First Christmas Together
Cameo • MCGE
750QX3404 • **Value $28**

16. First Christmas Together
Classic Shape • MCGE
1600QX9044 • **Value $34**

17. First Christmas Together
Glass • N/A
450QX2451 • **Value $27**

18. Flights of Fantasy
Glass • N/A
450QX2564 • **Value $22**

19. Fortune Cookie Elf
Handcrafted • SICK
450QX4524 • **Value $42**

20. Friendship
Glass • N/A
450QX2481 • **Value $21**

GENERAL KEEPSAKE		
	Price Paid	Value of My Collection
1.		
2.		
3.		
4.		
5.		
6.		
7.		
8.		
9.		
10.		
11.		
12.		
13.		
14.		
15.		
16.		
17.		
18.		
19.		
20.		
PENCIL TOTALS		

1984

VALUE GUIDE – HALLMARK KEEPSAKE ORNAMENTS

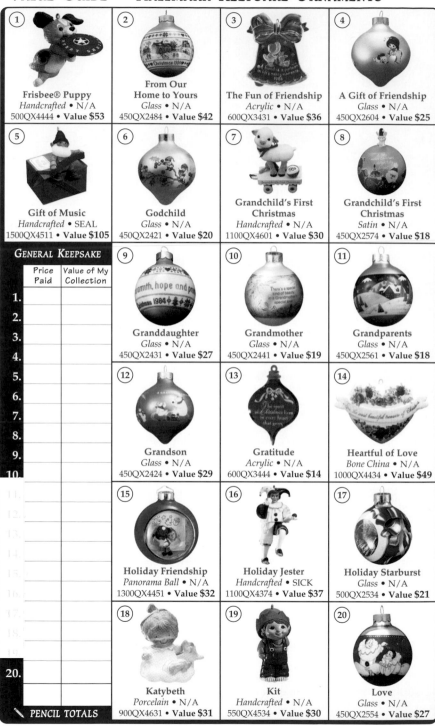

(1) Frisbee® Puppy
Handcrafted • N/A
500QX4444 • **Value $53**

(2) From Our Home to Yours
Glass • N/A
450QX2484 • **Value $42**

(3) The Fun of Friendship
Acrylic • N/A
600QX3431 • **Value $36**

(4) A Gift of Friendship
Glass • N/A
450QX2604 • **Value $25**

(5) Gift of Music
Handcrafted • SEAL
1500QX4511 • **Value $105**

(6) Godchild
Glass • N/A
450QX2421 • **Value $20**

(7) Grandchild's First Christmas
Handcrafted • N/A
1100QX4601 • **Value $30**

(8) Grandchild's First Christmas
Satin • N/A
450QX2574 • **Value $18**

(9) Granddaughter
Glass • N/A
450QX2431 • **Value $27**

(10) Grandmother
Glass • N/A
450QX2441 • **Value $19**

(11) Grandparents
Glass • N/A
450QX2561 • **Value $18**

(12) Grandson
Glass • N/A
450QX2424 • **Value $29**

(13) Gratitude
Acrylic • N/A
600QX3444 • **Value $14**

(14) Heartful of Love
Bone China • N/A
1000QX4434 • **Value $49**

(15) Holiday Friendship
Panorama Ball • N/A
1300QX4451 • **Value $32**

(16) Holiday Jester
Handcrafted • SICK
1100QX4374 • **Value $37**

(17) Holiday Starburst
Glass • N/A
500QX2534 • **Value $21**

(18) Katybeth
Porcelain • N/A
900QX4631 • **Value $31**

(19) Kit
Handcrafted • N/A
550QX4534 • **Value $30**

(20) Love
Glass • N/A
450QX2554 • **Value $27**

1
Love . . . the Spirit
of Christmas
Glass • N/A
450QX2474 • **Value $44**

2
Madonna and Child
Acrylic • PALM
600QX3441 • **Value $52**

3
Marathon Santa
Handcrafted • SEAL
800QX4564 • **Value $42**

4
The Miracle of Love
Acrylic • N/A
600QX3424 • **Value $34**

5
Mother
Acrylic • N/A
600QX3434 • **Value $18**

6
Mother and Dad
Bone China • N/A
650QX2581 • **Value $27**

7
Mountain
Climbing Santa
(re-issued from 1983)
Handcrafted • SEAL
650QX4077 • **Value $40**

8
Muffin
Handcrafted • DLEE
550QX4421 • **Value $32**

1984

9
The MUPPETS™
Glass • N/A
450QX2514 • **Value $37**

10
Musical Angel
Handcrafted • DLEE
550QX4344 • **Value $73**

11
Napping Mouse
Handcrafted • N/A
550QX4351 • **Value $52**

12
Needlepoint Wreath
Fabric • PIKE
650QX4594 • **Value $15**

13
New Home
Glass • N/A
450QX2454 • **Value $70**

14
Norman Rockwell
Glass • MCGE
450QX2511 • **Value $33**

15
Nostalgic Sled
(re-issued in 1985)
Handcrafted • SICK
600QX4424 • **Value $32**

16
Old Fashioned
Rocking Horse
Acrylic/Brass • N/A
750QX3464 • **Value $21**

17
Peace on Earth
Cameo • N/A
750QX3414 • **Value $32**

18
PEANUTS®
Satin • N/A
450QX2521 • **Value $37**

19
Peppermint 1984
Handcrafted • DLEE
450QX4561 • **Value $53**

20
Polar Bear Drummer
Handcrafted • SEAL
450QX4301 • **Value $30**

GENERAL KEEPSAKE		
	Price Paid	Value of My Collection
1.		
2.		
3.		
4.		
5.		
6.		
7.		
8.		
9.		
10.		
11.		
12.		
13.		
14.		
15.		
16.		
17.		
18.		
19.		
20.		
PENCIL TOTALS		

VALUE GUIDE — HALLMARK KEEPSAKE ORNAMENTS

(1) **Raccoon's Christmas** *Handcrafted* • SEAL 900QX4474 • **Value $56**	**(2)** **Reindeer Racetrack** *Glass* • N/A 450QX2544 • **Value $26**	**(3)** **Roller Skating Rabbit (re-issued in 1985)** *Handcrafted* • SEAL 500QX4571 • **Value $34**	**(4)** **Santa** *Fabric* • N/A 750QX4584 • **Value $20**
(5) **Santa Mouse** *Handcrafted* • SIED 450QX4334 • **Value $53**	**(6)** **Santa Star** *Handcrafted* • N/A 550QX4504 • **Value $38**	**(7)** **Santa Sulky Driver** *Etched Brass* • N/A 900QX4361 • **Value $35**	**(8)** **A Savior is Born** *Glass* • N/A 450QX2541 • **Value $34**

GENERAL KEEPSAKE

	Price Paid	Value of My Collection
1.		
2.		
3.		
4.		
5.		
6.		
7.		
8.		
9.		
10.		
11.		
12.		
13.		
14.		
15.		
16.		
17.		
18.		
19.		
20.		

PENCIL TOTALS

(9) **Shirt Tales™** *Satin* • N/A 450QX2524 • **Value $21**	**(10)** **Sister** *Bone China* • N/A 650QX2594 • **Value $32**	**(11)** **SNOOPY® and WOODSTOCK** *Handcrafted* • SEAL 750QX4391 • **Value $105**
(12) **Snowmobile Santa** *Handcrafted* • N/A 650QX4314 • **Value $38**	**(13)** **Snowshoe Penguin** *Handcrafted* • SICK 650QX4531 • **Value $52**	**(14)** **Snowy Seal (re-issued in 1985)** *Handcrafted* • SEAL 400QX4501 • **Value $24**
(15) **Son** *Glass* • N/A 450QX2434 • **Value $33**	**(16)** **Teacher** *Glass* • N/A 450QX2491 • **Value $15**	**(17)** **Ten Years Together** *Bone China* • N/A 650QX2584 • **Value $24**
(18) **Three Kittens in a Mitten (re-issued in 1985)** *Handcrafted* • DLEE 800QX4311 • **Value $50**	**(19)** **Twelve Days of Christmas** *Handcrafted* • SEAL 1500QX4159 • **Value $125**	**(20)** **Twenty-Five Years Together** *Bone China* • N/A 650QX2591 • **Value $23**

1. Uncle Sam
Pressed Tin • SICK
600QX4491 • **Value $49**

2. White Christmas
Classic Shape • N/A
1600QX9051 • **Value $98**

3. All Are Precious
(re-issued in 1985)
Acrylic • N/A
800QLX7044 • **Value $26**

4. Brass Carousel
Etched Brass • N/A
900QLX7071 • **Value $100**

5. Christmas in the Forest
Classic Shape • N/A
800QLX7034 • **Value $21**

6. City Lights
Handcrafted • SIED
1000QLX7014 • **Value $55**

7. Nativity
(re-issued in 1985)
Panorama Ball • SEAL
1200QLX7001 • **Value $32**

8. Santa's Arrival
Panorama Ball • DLEE
1300QLX7024 • **Value $67**

9. Santa's Workshop
(re-issued in 1985)
Panorama Ball • N/A
1300QLX7004 • **Value $63**

10. Stained Glass
Classic Shape • N/A
800QLX7031 • **Value $20**

11. Sugarplum Cottage
(re-issued in
1985 and 1986)
Handcrafted • N/A
1100QLX7011 • **Value $45**

12. Village Church
(re-issued in 1985)
Handcrafted • DLEE
1500QLX7021 • **Value $51**

1983

1983 marked the 10th anniversary of Keepsake ornaments. Among the popular pieces from 1983 were a pair of angel ornaments, "Baroque Angels" and "Rainbow Angel," as well as three ornaments featuring Muppets™ characters. The 1983 line featured 111 Keepsake ornaments. See the collectible series section for more 1983 ornaments.

13. 25th Christmas Together
Glass • N/A
450QX2247 • **Value $22**

14. 1983
Glass • N/A
450QX2209 • **Value $32**

15. Angel Messenger
Handcrafted • SEAL
650QX4087 • **Value $97**

1983

GENERAL KEEPSAKE		
	Price Paid	Value of My Collection
1.		
2.		
GENERAL MAGI		
3.		
4.		
5.		
6.		
7.		
8.		
9.		
10.		
11.		
12.		
GENERAL KEEPSAKE		
13.		
14.		
15.		
PENCIL TOTALS		

VALUE GUIDE — HALLMARK KEEPSAKE ORNAMENTS

(1) **Angels**
Glass • N/A
500QX2197 • **Value $26**

(2) **The Annunciation**
Glass • N/A
450QX2167 • **Value $31**

(3) **Baby's First Christmas**
Acrylic • N/A
700QX3029 • **Value $25**

(4) **Baby's First Christmas**
Cameo • SICK
750QX3019 • **Value $18**

(5) **Baby's First Christmas**
Handcrafted • DLEE
1400QX4027 • **Value $40**

(6) **Baby's First Christmas – Boy**
Satin • N/A
450QX2009 • **Value $27**

(7) **Baby's First Christmas – Girl**
Satin • N/A
450QX2007 • **Value $29**

(8) **Baby's Second Christmas**
Satin • N/A
450QX2267 • **Value $36**

GENERAL KEEPSAKE

	Price Paid	Value of My Collection
1.		
2.		
3.		
4.		
5.		
6.		
7.		
8.		
9.		
10.		
11.		
12.		
13.		
14.		
15.		
16.		
17.		
18.		
19.		
20.		

PENCIL TOTALS

(9) **Baroque Angels**
Handcrafted • DLEE
1300QX4229 • **Value $138**

(10) **Bell Wreath**
Brass • SICK
650QX4209 • **Value $34**

(11) **Betsey Clark**
Handcrafted • SEAL
650QX4047 • **Value $33**

(12) **Betsey Clark**
Porcelain • N/A
900QX4401 • **Value $36**

(13) **Brass Santa**
Brass • SEAL
900QX4239 • **Value $24**

(14) **Caroling Owl**
Handcrafted • SEAL
450QX4117 • **Value $42**

(15) **Child's Third Christmas**
Satin Piqué • N/A
450QX2269 • **Value $26**

(16) **Christmas Joy**
Satin • N/A
450QX2169 • **Value $32**

(17) **Christmas Kitten (re-issued from 1982)**
Handcrafted • N/A
400QX4543 • **Value $37**

(18) **Christmas Koala**
Handcrafted • SEAL
400QX4199 • **Value $33**

(19) **Christmas Stocking**
Acrylic • N/A
600QX3039 • **Value $41**

(20) **Christmas Wonderland**
Glass • N/A
450QX2219 • **Value $125**

VALUE GUIDE – HALLMARK KEEPSAKE ORNAMENTS

① Currier & Ives
Glass • N/A
450QX2159 • **Value $25**

② Cycling Santa
(re-issued from 1982)
Handcrafted • N/A
2000QX4355 • **Value $160**

③ Daughter
Glass • N/A
450QX2037 • **Value $44**

④ DISNEY
Glass • N/A
450QX2129 • **Value $55**

⑤ Embroidered Heart
(re-issued in 1984)
Fabric • N/A
650QX4217 • **Value $26**

⑥ Embroidered Stocking
(re-issued in 1984)
Fabric • SICK
650QX4796 • **Value $23**

⑦ Enameled Christmas
Wreath
Enameled • N/A
900QX3119 • **Value $16**

⑧ First Christmas
Together
Acrylic • N/A
600QX3069 • **Value $24**

⑨ First Christmas
Together
Cameo • N/A
750QX3017 • **Value $24**

⑩ First Christmas
Together
Classic Shape • N/A
600QX3107 • **Value $43**

⑪ First Christmas
Together
Glass • SICK
450QX2089 • **Value $30**

⑫ First Christmas
Together – Brass Locket
Brass • SEAL
1500QX4329 • **Value $39**

⑬ Friendship
Acrylic • N/A
600QX3059 • **Value $20**

⑭ Friendship
Glass • N/A
450QX2077 • **Value $20**

⑮ Godchild
Glass • N/A
450QX2017 • **Value $17**

⑯ Grandchild's First
Christmas
Classic Shape • N/A
600QX3129 • **Value $24**

⑰ Grandchild's First
Christmas
Handcrafted • N/A
1400QX4309 • **Value $40**

⑱ Granddaughter
Glass • N/A
450QX2027 • **Value $30**

⑲ Grandmother
Glass • N/A
450QX2057 • **Value $20**

⑳ Grandparents
Ceramic • N/A
650QX4299 • **Value $22**

1983

GENERAL KEEPSAKE		
	Price Paid	Value of My Collection
1.		
2.		
3.		
4.		
5.		
6.		
7.		
8.		
9.		
10.		
11.		
12.		
13.		
14.		
15.		
16.		
17.		
18.		
19.		
20.		
PENCIL TOTALS		

(1) Grandson
Satin • N/A
450QX2019 • **Value $30**

(2) Heart
Acrylic • SICK
400QX3079 • **Value $50**

(3) Here Comes Santa
Glass • N/A
450QX2177 • **Value $47**

(4) Hitchhiking Santa
Handcrafted • SEAL
800QX4247 • **Value $42**

(5) Holiday Puppy
Handcrafted • N/A
350QX4127 • **Value $29**

(6) Jack Frost
Handcrafted • N/A
900QX4079 • **Value $60**

(7) Jolly Santa
Handcrafted • N/A
350QX4259 • **Value $37**

(8) KERMIT the FROG™
(re-issued from 1982)
Handcrafted • DLEE
1100QX4956 • **Value $105**

General Keepsake

	Price Paid	Value of My Collection
1.		
2.		
3.		
4.		
5.		
6.		
7.		
8.		
9.		
10.		
11.		
12.		
13.		
14.		
15.		
16.		
17.		
18.		
19.		
20.		

PENCIL TOTALS

(9) Love
Acrylic • N/A
600QX3057 • **Value $18**

(10) Love
Classic Shape • N/A
600QX3109 • **Value $40**

(11) Love
Glass • N/A
450QX2079 • **Value $60**

(12) Love
Porcelain • SICK
1300QX4227 • **Value $42**

(13) Love Is a Song
Glass • N/A
450QX2239 • **Value $30**

(14) Madonna and Child
Porcelain • N/A
1200QX4287 • **Value $48**

(15) Mailbox Kitten
Handcrafted • N/A
650QX4157 • **Value $63**

(16) Mary Hamilton
Glass • N/A
450QX2137 • **Value $43**

(17) Memories to Treasure
Acrylic • N/A
700QX3037 • **Value $30**

(18) MISS PIGGY™
Handcrafted • N/A
1300QX4057 • **Value $240**

(19) Mom and Dad
Ceramic • PIKE
650QX4297 • **Value $25**

(20) Mother
Acrylic • N/A
600QX3067 • **Value $20**

1983

1. Mother and Child
Cameo • N/A
750QX3027 • **Value $42**

2. Mountain Climbing Santa
(re-issued in 1984)
Handcrafted • SEAL
650QX4077 • **Value $40**

3. Mouse in Bell
Handcrafted/Glass • N/A
1000QX4197 • **Value $68**

4. Mouse on Cheese
Handcrafted • SICK
650QX4137 • **Value $50**

5. The MUPPETS™
Satin • N/A
450QX2147 • **Value $52**

6. New Home
Satin • N/A
450QX2107 • **Value $34**

7. Norman Rockwell
Glass • N/A
450QX2157 • **Value $55**

8. An Old Fashioned Christmas
Glass • N/A
450QX2179 • **Value $35**

9. Old-Fashioned Santa
Handcrafted • SICK
1100QX4099 • **Value $68**

10. Oriental Butterflies
Glass • N/A
450QX2187 • **Value $31**

11. PEANUTS®
Satin • N/A
450QX2127 • **Value $40**

12. Peppermint Penguin
Handcrafted • N/A
650QX4089 • **Value $47**

13. Porcelain Doll, Diana
Porcelain/Fabric • DLEE
900QX4237 • **Value $32**

14. Rainbow Angel
Handcrafted • DLEE
550QX4167 • **Value $115**

15. Santa
Acrylic • N/A
400QX3087 • **Value $34**

16. Santa's Many Faces
Classic Shape • N/A
600QX3117 • **Value $32**

17. Santa's on His Way
Handcrafted • N/A
1000QX4269 • **Value $37**

18. Santa's Workshop
(re-issued from 1982)
Handcrafted • DLEE
1000QX4503 • **Value $88**

19. Scrimshaw Reindeer
Handcrafted • SEAL
800QX4249 • **Value $35**

20. Season's Greetings
Glass • N/A
450QX2199 • **Value $23**

General Keepsake

	Price Paid	Value of My Collection
1.		
2.		
3.		
4.		
5.		
6.		
7.		
8.		
9.		
10.		
11.		
12.		
13.		
14.		
15.		
16.		
17.		
18.		
19.		
20.		
PENCIL TOTALS		

Value Guide – Hallmark Keepsake Ornaments

1. SHIRT TALES™
Glass • N/A
450QX2149 • **Value $26**

2. Sister
Glass • N/A
450QX2069 • **Value $24**

3. Skating Rabbit
Handcrafted • N/A
800QX4097 • **Value $53**

4. Ski Lift Santa
Handcrafted/Brass • N/A
800QX4187 • **Value $74**

5. Skiing Fox
Handcrafted • DLEE
800QX4207 • **Value $41**

6. Sneaker Mouse
Handcrafted • SEAL
450QX4009 • **Value $43**

7. Son
Satin • N/A
450QX2029 • **Value $42**

8. Star of Peace
Acrylic • SEAL
600QX3047 • **Value $20**

9. Teacher
Acrylic • N/A
600QX3049 • **Value $14**

10. Teacher
Glass • N/A
450QX2249 • **Value $17**

11. Tenth Christmas Together
Ceramic • N/A
650QX4307 • **Value $25**

12. Time for Sharing
Acrylic • N/A
600QX3077 • **Value $40**

13. Tin Rocking Horse
Pressed Tin • SICK
650QX4149 • **Value $52**

14. Unicorn
Porcelain • N/A
1000QX4267 • **Value $66**

15. The Wise Men
Glass • N/A
450QX2207 • **Value $63**

16. Baby's First Christmas
Classic Shape • N/A
1600QMB9039 • **Value $95**

17. Friendship
Classic Shape • N/A
1600QMB9047 • **Value $120**

18. Nativity
Classic Shape • N/A
1600QMB9049 • **Value $125**

19. Twelve Days of Christmas
Handcrafted • SEAL
1500QMB4159 • **Value $100**

General Keepsake

	Price Paid	Value of My Collection
1.		
2.		
3.		
4.		
5.		
6.		
7.		
8.		
9.		
10.		
11.		
12.		
13.		
14.		
15.		

Musical Ornaments

16.		
17.		
18.		
19.		

PENCIL TOTALS

1982

The 1982 collection was highlighted by the always-popular creations of Hallmark artist, Donna Lee. Among her sought-after 1982 designs were "Baroque Angel," "Pinecone Home" and "Raccoon Surprises." Overall, there were 104 Keepsake ornaments issued in 1982. See the collectible series section for more 1982 ornaments.

①

25th Christmas Together
Glass • N/A
450QX2116 • **Value $19**

②

50th Christmas Together
Glass • N/A
450QX2123 • **Value $20**

③

Angel
Acrylic • N/A
550QX3096 • **Value $36**

④

Angel Chimes
Chrome-Plated Brass • N/A
550QX5026 • **Value $30**

⑤

Arctic Penguin
Acrylic • N/A
400QX3003 • **Value $21**

⑥

Baby's First Christmas
Acrylic • SEAL
550QX3023 • **Value $41**

⑦

Baby's First Christmas
Handcrafted • SEAL
1300QX4553 • **Value $50**

⑧
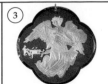
Baby's First Christmas – Boy
Satin • N/A
450QX2163 • **Value $28**

⑨

Baby's First Christmas – Girl
Satin • N/A
450QX2073 • **Value $29**

⑩

Baby's First Christmas – Photoholder
Acrylic • N/A
650QX3126 • **Value $27**

⑪

Baroque Angel
Handcrafted/Brass • DLEE
1500QX4566 • **Value $170**

⑫

Bell Chimes
Chrome-Plated Brass • SICK
550QX4943 • **Value $30**

⑬

Betsey Clark
Cameo • N/A
850QX3056 • **Value $26**

⑭

Brass Bell
Brass • DLEE
1200QX4606 • **Value $27**

⑮

Christmas Angel
Glass • N/A
450QX2206 • **Value $26**

⑯

Christmas Fantasy
(re-issued from 1981)
Handcrafted/Brass • N/A
1300QX1554 • **Value $90**

⑰

Christmas Kitten
(re-issued in 1983)
Handcrafted • N/A
400QX4543 • **Value $37**

GENERAL KEEPSAKE

	Price Paid	Value of My Collection
1.		
2.		
3.		
4.		
5.		
6.		
7.		
8.		
9.		
10.		
11.		
12.		
13.		
14.		
15.		
16.		
17.		
PENCIL TOTALS		

(1)

Christmas Magic
Acrylic • N/A
550QX3113 • **Value $30**

(2)

Christmas Memories
– Photoholder
Acrylic • SICK
650QX3116 • **Value $24**

(3)

Christmas Owl
(re-issued from 1980)
Handcrafted • N/A
400QX1314 • **Value $48**

(4)

Christmas Sleigh
Acrylic • N/A
550QX3093 • **Value $77**

(5)

Cloisonné Angel
Cloisonné • N/A
1200QX1454 • **Value $95**

(6)

Cookie Mouse
Handcrafted • SICK
450QX4546 • **Value $60**

(7)

Cowboy Snowman
Handcrafted • N/A
800QX4806 • **Value $55**

(8)

Currier & Ives
Glass • N/A
450QX2013 • **Value $26**

GENERAL KEEPSAKE

	Price Paid	Value of My Collection
1.		
2.		
3.		
4.		
5.		
6.		
7.		
8.		
9.		
10.		
11.		
12.		
13.		
14.		
15.		
16.		
17.		
18.		
19.		
20.		

PENCIL TOTALS

(9)

Cycling Santa
(re-issued in 1983)
Handcrafted • N/A
2000QX4355 • **Value $160**

(10)

Daughter
Satin • N/A
450QX2046 • **Value $36**

(11)

DISNEY
Satin • N/A
450QX2173 • **Value $39**

(12)

THE DIVINE
MISS PIGGY™
(re-issued from 1981)
Handcrafted • FRAN
1200QX4255 • **Value $98**

(13)

Dove Love
Acrylic • SICK
450QX4623 • **Value $57**

(14)

Elfin Artist
Handcrafted • SICK
900QX4573 • **Value $51**

(15)

Embroidered Tree
Fabric • N/A
650QX4946 • **Value $39**

(16)

Father
Satin • SICK
450QX2056 • **Value $20**

(17)

First Christmas
Together
Acrylic • SEAL
550QX3026 • **Value $21**

(18)

First Christmas
Together
Cameo • N/A
850QX3066 • **Value $46**

(19)

First Christmas
Together
Glass • N/A
450QX2113 • **Value $41**

(20)

First Christmas
Together – Locket
Brass • SEAL
1500QX4563 • **Value $30**

1 Friendship
Acrylic • N/A
550QX3046 • **Value $25**

2 Friendship
Satin • N/A
450QX2086 • **Value $22**

3 Godchild
Glass • N/A
450QX2226 • **Value $23**

4 Granddaughter
Glass • N/A
450QX2243 • **Value $28**

5 Grandfather
Satin • N/A
450QX2076 • **Value $20**

6 Grandmother
Satin • N/A
450QX2003 • **Value $18**

7 Grandparents
Glass • N/A
450QX2146 • **Value $17**

8 Grandson
Satin • N/A
450QX2246 • **Value $31**

9 Ice Sculptor
(re-issued from 1981)
Handcrafted • DLEE
800QX4322 • **Value $105**

10 Jingling Teddy
Brass • SEAL
400QX4776 • **Value $41**

11 Joan Walsh Anglund
Satin • N/A
450QX2193 • **Value $20**

12 Jogging Santa
Handcrafted • N/A
800QX4576 • **Value $50**

13 Jolly Christmas Tree
Handcrafted • N/A
650QX4653 • **Value $85**

14 KERMIT the FROG™
(re-issued in 1983)
Handcrafted • DLEE
1100QX4956 • **Value $105**

15 Love
Acrylic • N/A
550QX3043 • **Value $30**

16 Love
Satin • N/A
450QX2096 • **Value $20**

17 Mary Hamilton
Satin • N/A
450QX2176 • **Value $26**

18 Merry Christmas
Glass • N/A
450QX2256 • **Value $22**

19 Merry Moose
Handcrafted • N/A
550QX4155 • **Value $57**

20 MISS PIGGY™ and KERMIT™
Satin • N/A
450QX2183 • **Value $42**

1982

GENERAL KEEPSAKE

	Price Paid	Value of My Collection
1.		
2.		
3.		
4.		
5.		
6.		
7.		
8.		
9.		
10.		
11.		
12.		
13.		
14.		
15.		
16.		
17.		
18.		
19.		
20.		

PENCIL TOTALS

Value Guide — Hallmark Keepsake Ornaments

(1) Moments of Love
Satin • N/A
450QX2093 • **Value $18**

(2) Mother
Glass • N/A
450QX2053 • **Value $20**

(3) Mother and Dad
Glass • N/A
450QX2223 • **Value $18**

(4) MUPPETS™ Party
Satin • N/A
450QX2186 • **Value $42**

(5) Musical Angel
Handcrafted • DLEE
550QX4596 • **Value $130**

(6) Nativity
Acrylic • N/A
450QX3083 • **Value $51**

(7) New Home
Satin • N/A
450QX2126 • **Value $23**

(8) Norman Rockwell
Satin • N/A
450QX2023 • **Value $30**

General Keepsake

	Price Paid	Value of My Collection
1.		
2.		
3.		
4.		
5.		
6.		
7.		
8.		
9.		
10.		
11.		
12.		
13.		
14.		
15.		
16.		
17.		
18.		
19.		
20.		

PENCIL TOTALS

(9) Old Fashioned Christmas
Glass • N/A
450QX2276 • **Value $60**

(10) Old World Angels
Glass • N/A
450QX2263 • **Value $25**

(11) Patterns of Christmas
Glass • N/A
450QX2266 • **Value $22**

(12) PEANUTS®
Satin • N/A
450QX2006 • **Value $41**

(13) Peeking Elf
Handcrafted • N/A
650QX4195 • **Value $38**

(14) Perky Penguin (re-issued from 1981)
Handcrafted • N/A
400QX4095 • **Value $62**

(15) Pinecone Home
Handcrafted • DLEE
800QX4613 • **Value $175**

(16) Raccoon Surprises
Handcrafted • DLEE
900QX4793 • **Value $150**

(17) Santa
Glass • BLAC
450QX2216 • **Value $21**

(18) Santa and Reindeer
Handcrafted/Brass • SICK
900QX4676 • **Value $50**

(19) Santa Bell
Porcelain • N/A
1500QX1487 • **Value $60**

(20) Santa's Flight
Acrylic • N/A
450QX3086 • **Value $50**

1 Santa's Sleigh
Brass • SEAL
900QX4786 • **Value $33**

2 Santa's Workshop
(re-issued in 1983)
Handcrafted • DLEE
1000QX4503 • **Value $88**

3 Season for Caring
Satin • N/A
450QX2213 • **Value $23**

4 Sister
Glass • N/A
450QX2083 • **Value $28**

5 Snowy Seal
Acrylic • N/A
400QX3006 • **Value $21**

6 Son
Satin • N/A
450QX2043 • **Value $30**

7 The Spirit of Christmas
Handcrafted • SICK
1000QX4526 • **Value $135**

8 Stained Glass
Glass • N/A
450QX2283 • **Value $23**

9 Teacher
Acrylic • SICK
650QX3123 • **Value $18**

10 Teacher
Glass • N/A
450QX2143 • **Value $14**

11 Teacher – Apple
Acrylic • SEAL
550QX3016 • **Value $14**

12 Three Kings
Cameo • BLAC
850QX3073 • **Value $27**

13 Tin Soldier
Pressed Tin • SICK
650QX4836 • **Value $51**

14 Tree Chimes
Stamped Brass • SEAL
550QX4846 • **Value $50**

15 Twelve Days
of Christmas
Glass • N/A
450QX2036 • **Value $24**

16 Dimensional Ornament
Dimensional Brass • N/A
($3.50) No stock # • **Value $42**

17 Baby's First Christmas
Classic Shape • N/A
1600QMB9007 • **Value $85**

18 First Christmas
Together
Classic Shape • N/A
1600QMB9019 • **Value $80**

19 Love
Classic Shape • N/A
1600QMB9009 • **Value $85**

1982

General Keepsake		
	Price Paid	Value of My Collection
1.		
2.		
3.		
4.		
5.		
6.		
7.		
8.		
9.		
10.		
11.		
12.		
13.		
14.		
15.		
Early Promotional Ornaments		
16.		
Musical Ornaments		
17.		
18.		
19.		
Pencil Totals		

1981

Santa Claus was well-represented in Hallmark's collection for 1981 with several coveted designs, including the handcrafted ornaments "Sailing Santa" and "Space Santa," as well as the ball ornament "Traditional (Black Santa)." The 1981 line featured 99 Keepsake ornaments. See the collectible series section for more 1981 ornaments.

1

25th Christmas Together
Acrylic • N/A
550QX5042 • **Value $23**

2

25th Christmas Together
Glass • N/A
450QX7075 • **Value $22**

3

50th Christmas
Glass • N/A
450QX7082 • **Value $19**

4

Angel
Acrylic • N/A
400QX5095 • **Value $65**

5

Angel
Acrylic • N/A
450QX5075 • **Value $27**

GENERAL KEEPSAKE

	Price Paid	Value of My Collection
1.		
2.		
3.		
4.		
5.		
6.		
7.		
8.		
9.		
10.		
11.		
12.		
13.		
14.		
15.		
16.		
17.		

PENCIL TOTALS

6

Angel
(re-issued from 1980)
Yarn • N/A
300QX1621 • **Value $10**

7

Baby's First Christmas
Acrylic • N/A
550QX5162 • **Value $32**

8

Baby's First Christmas
Cameo • N/A
850QX5135 • **Value $20**

9

Baby's First Christmas
Handcrafted • N/A
1300QX4402 • **Value $51**

10

Baby's First Christmas – Black
Satin • N/A
450QX6022 • **Value $26**

11

Baby's First Christmas – Boy
Satin • N/A
450QX6015 • **Value $24**

12

Baby's First Christmas – Girl
Satin • N/A
450QX6002 • **Value $24**

13

Betsey Clark
Cameo • N/A
850QX5122 • **Value $30**

14

Betsey Clark
Handcrafted • FRAN
900QX4235 • **Value $80**

15

Calico Kitty
Fabric • N/A
300QX4035 • **Value $20**

16

Candyville Express
Handcrafted • N/A
750QX4182 • **Value $100**

17

Cardinal Cutie
Fabric • N/A
300QX4002 • **Value $22**

1
Checking It Twice
(re-issued from 1980)
Handcrafted • BLAC
2250QX1584 • **Value $205**

2
Christmas 1981 –
Schneeberg
Satin • N/A
450QX8095 • **Value $25**

3
Christmas Dreams
Handcrafted • DLEE
1200QX4375 • **Value $220**

4
Christmas Fantasy
(re-issued in 1982)
Handcrafted • N/A
1300QX1554 • **Value $90**

5
Christmas in the Forest
Glass • N/A
450QX8135 • **Value $160**

6
Christmas Magic
Satin • N/A
450QX8102 • **Value $26**

7
Christmas Star
Acrylic • N/A
550QX5015 • **Value $28**

8
Christmas Teddy
Plush • N/A
550QX4042 • **Value $25**

9
Clothespin
Drummer Boy
Handcrafted • N/A
450QX4082 • **Value $44**

10
Daughter
Satin • N/A
450QX6075 • **Value $40**

11
DISNEY
Satin • N/A
450QX8055 • **Value $32**

12
THE DIVINE MISS
PIGGY™
(re-issued in 1982)
Handcrafted • FRAN
1200QX4255 • **Value $98**

13
Dough Angel
(re-issued from 1978)
Handcrafted • DLEE
550QX1396 • **Value $100**

14
Drummer Boy
Wood • N/A
250QX1481 • **Value $47**

15
Father
Satin • N/A
450QX6095 • **Value $19**

16
First Christmas Together
Acrylic • N/A
550QX5055 • **Value $24**

17
First Christmas Together
Glass • N/A
450QX7062 • **Value $28**

18
The Friendly Fiddler
Handcrafted • DLEE
800QX4342 • **Value $80**

19
Friendship
Acrylic • N/A
550QX5035 • **Value $31**

20
Friendship
Satin • N/A
450QX7042 • **Value $30**

1981

	GENERAL KEEPSAKE	
	Price Paid	Value of My Collection
1.		
2.		
3.		
4.		
5.		
6.		
7.		
8.		
9.		
10.		
11.		
12.		
13.		
14.		
15.		
16.		
17.		
18.		
19.		
20.		
PENCIL TOTALS		

VALUE GUIDE — HALLMARK KEEPSAKE ORNAMENTS

1 The Gift of Love *Glass* • N/A 450QX7055 • **Value $26**	**2** Gingham Dog *Fabric* • N/A 300QX4022 • **Value $21**	**3** Godchild *Satin* • N/A 450QX6035 • **Value $20**	**4** Granddaughter *Satin* • N/A 450QX6055 • **Value $28**
5 Grandfather *Glass* • N/A 450QX7015 • **Value $20**	**6** Grandmother *Satin* • N/A 450QX7022 • **Value $22**	**7** Grandparents *Glass* • N/A 450QX7035 • **Value $20**	**8** Grandson *Satin* • N/A 450QX6042 • **Value $28**

GENERAL KEEPSAKE

	Price Paid	Value of My Collection
1.		
2.		
3.		
4.		
5.		
6.		
7.		
8.		
9.		
10.		
11.		
12.		
13.		
14.		
15.		
16.		
17.		
18.		
19.		
20.		

PENCIL TOTALS

9 A Heavenly Nap
(re-issued from 1980)
Handcrafted • DLEE
650QX1394 • **Value $58**

10 Home
Satin • N/A
450QX7095 • **Value $21**

11 Ice Fairy
Handcrafted • DLEE
650QX4315 • **Value $105**

12 The Ice Sculptor
(re-issued in 1982)
Handcrafted • DLEE
800QX4322 • **Value $105**

13 Joan Walsh Anglund
Satin • N/A
450QX8042 • **Value $31**

14 Jolly Snowman
Handcrafted • N/A
350QX4075 • **Value $62**

15 KERMIT the FROG™
Handcrafted • FRAN
900QX4242 • **Value $100**

16 Let Us Adore Him
Glass • N/A
450QX8115 • **Value $68**

17 Love
Acrylic • N/A
550QX5022 • **Value $50**

18 Love and Joy
(Porcelain Chimes)
Porcelain • N/A
900QX4252 • **Value $98**

19 Marty Links™
Satin • N/A
450QX8082 • **Value $21**

20 Mary Hamilton
Glass • N/A
450QX8062 • **Value $20**

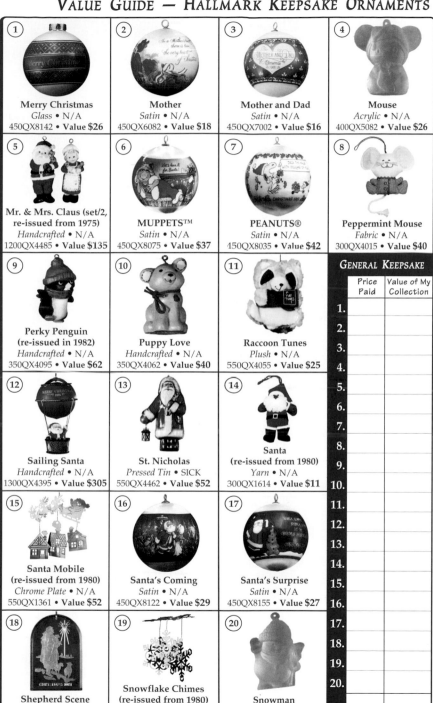

1.
Merry Christmas
Glass • N/A
450QX8142 • **Value $26**

2.
Mother
Satin • N/A
450QX6082 • **Value $18**

3.
Mother and Dad
Satin • N/A
450QX7002 • **Value $16**

4.
Mouse
Acrylic • N/A
400QX5082 • **Value $26**

5.
Mr. & Mrs. Claus (set/2, re-issued from 1975)
Handcrafted • N/A
1200QX4485 • **Value $135**

6.
MUPPETS™
Satin • N/A
450QX8075 • **Value $37**

7.
PEANUTS®
Satin • N/A
450QX8035 • **Value $42**

8.
Peppermint Mouse
Fabric • N/A
300QX4015 • **Value $40**

9.
Perky Penguin (re-issued in 1982)
Handcrafted • N/A
350QX4095 • **Value $62**

10.
Puppy Love
Handcrafted • N/A
350QX4062 • **Value $40**

11.
Raccoon Tunes
Plush • N/A
550QX4055 • **Value $25**

12.
Sailing Santa
Handcrafted • N/A
1300QX4395 • **Value $305**

13.
St. Nicholas
Pressed Tin • SICK
550QX4462 • **Value $52**

14.
Santa (re-issued from 1980)
Yarn • N/A
300QX1614 • **Value $11**

15.
Santa Mobile (re-issued from 1980)
Chrome Plate • N/A
550QX1361 • **Value $52**

16.
Santa's Coming
Satin • N/A
450QX8122 • **Value $29**

17.
Santa's Surprise
Satin • N/A
450QX8155 • **Value $27**

18.
Shepherd Scene
Acrylic • N/A
550QX5002 • **Value $30**

19.
Snowflake Chimes (re-issued from 1980)
Chrome Plate • SICK
550QX1654 • **Value $37**

20.
Snowman
Acrylic • N/A
400QX5102 • **Value $27**

GENERAL KEEPSAKE		
	Price Paid	Value of My Collection
1.		
2.		
3.		
4.		
5.		
6.		
7.		
8.		
9.		
10.		
11.		
12.		
13.		
14.		
15.		
16.		
17.		
18.		
19.		
20.		
PENCIL TOTALS		

1981

Value Guide – Hallmark Keepsake Ornaments

1
Snowman
(re-issued from 1980)
Yarn • N/A
300QX1634 • **Value $10**

2
Snowman Chimes
Chrome Plate • N/A
550QX4455 • **Value $31**

3
Soldier
(re-issued from 1980)
Yarn • N/A
300QX1641 • **Value $10**

4
Son
Satin • N/A
450QX6062 • **Value $31**

5
Space Santa
Handcrafted • N/A
650QX4302 • **Value $130**

6
Star Swing
Handcrafted/Brass • SICK
550QX4215 • **Value $36**

7
The Stocking Mouse
Handcrafted • N/A
450QX4122 • **Value $110**

8
Teacher
Satin • N/A
450QX8002 • **Value $14**

9
Topsy-Turvy Tunes
Handcrafted • DLEE
750QX4295 • **Value $82**

10
Traditional (Black Santa)
Satin • N/A
450QX8015 • **Value $100**

11
Tree Photoholder
Acrylic • N/A
550QX5155 • **Value $30**

12
Unicorn
Cameo • N/A
850QX5165 • **Value $28**

13
A Well-Stocked Stocking
Handcrafted • N/A
900QX1547 • **Value $80**

GENERAL KEEPSAKE

	Price Paid	Value of My Collection
1.		
2.		
3.		
4.		
5.		
6.		
7.		
8.		
9.		
10.		
11.		
12.		
13.		

GENERAL KEEPSAKE

14.		
15.		
16.		

PENCIL TOTALS

1980

Teddy bear lovers have always been able to find great Hallmark bear ornaments and in 1980 Hallmark offered up two special treats in "Caroling Bear" and "Christmas Teddy." In the collection for 1980 there were a total of 85 Keepsake ornaments. See the collectible series section for more 1980 ornaments.

14
25th Christmas Together
Glass • N/A
400QX2061 • **Value $23**

15
Angel
(re-issued in 1981)
Yarn • N/A
300QX1621 • **Value $10**

16
Angel Music
(re-issued from 1979)
Fabric • N/A
200QX3439 • **Value $21**

1
The Animals' Christmas
Handcrafted • DLEE
800QX1501 • **Value $55**

2
Baby's First Christmas
Handcrafted • SICK
12QX1561 • **Value $50**

3
Baby's First Christmas
Satin • N/A
400QX2001 • **Value $30**

4
Beauty of Friendship
Acrylic • N/A
400QX3034 • **Value $70**

5
Betsey Clark
Cameo • N/A
650QX3074 • **Value $62**

6
Betsey Clark's Christmas
Handcrafted • N/A
750X1494 • **Value $38**

7
Black Baby's First Christmas
Satin • N/A
400QX2294 • **Value $30**

8
Caroling Bear
Handcrafted • DLEE
750QX1401 • **Value $150**

1980

9
Checking It Twice (re-issued in 1981)
Handcrafted • BLAC
2000QX1584 • **Value $205**

10
Christmas at Home
Glass • N/A
400QX2101 • **Value $39**

11
Christmas Cardinals
Glass • N/A
400QX2241 • **Value $32**

12
Christmas Choir
Glass • N/A
400QX2281 • **Value $90**

13
Christmas is for Children (re-issued from 1979)
Handcrafted • N/A
550QX1359 • **Value $97**

14
Christmas Love
Glass • N/A
400QX2074 • **Value $50**

15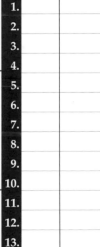
Christmas Owl (re-issued in 1982)
Handcrafted • N/A
400QX1314 • **Value $48**

16
Christmas Teddy
Handcrafted • N/A
250QX1354 • **Value $135**

17
Christmas Time
Satin • N/A
400QX2261 • **Value $30**

18
A Christmas Treat (re-issued from 1979)
Handcrafted • N/A
550QX1347 • **Value $88**

19
A Christmas Vigil
Handcrafted • DLEE
900QX1441 • **Value $110**

20
Clothespin Soldier
Handcrafted • N/A
350QX1341 • **Value $42**

21

22

GENERAL KEEPSAKE

	Price Paid	Value of My Collection
1.		
2.		
3.		
4.		
5.		
6.		
7.		
8.		
9.		
10.		
11.		
12.		
13.		
14.		
15.		
16.		
17.		
18.		
19.		
20.		
PENCIL TOTALS		

VALUE GUIDE — HALLMARK KEEPSAKE ORNAMENTS

1
Dad
Glass • N/A
400QX2141 • **Value $18**

2
Daughter
Glass • N/A
400QX2121 • **Value $41**

3
DISNEY
Satin • N/A
400QX2181 • **Value $33**

4
Dove
Acrylic • N/A
400QX3081 • **Value $40**

5
Drummer Boy
Acrylic • N/A
400QX3094 • **Value $27**

6
Drummer Boy
Handcrafted • DLEE
550QX1474 • **Value $95**

7
Elfin Antics
Handcrafted • N/A
900QX1421 • **Value $230**

8
First
Christmas Together
Acrylic • N/A
400QX3054 • **Value $50**

9
First
Christmas Together
Glass • N/A
400QX2054 • **Value $42**

10
Friendship
Glass • N/A
400QX2081 • **Value $20**

11
Granddaughter
Satin • N/A
400QX2021 • **Value $36**

12
Grandfather
Glass • N/A
400QX2314 • **Value $20**

13
Grandmother
Glass • N/A
400QX2041 • **Value $20**

14
Grandparents
Glass • N/A
400QX2134 • **Value $41**

15
Grandson
Satin • N/A
400QX2014 • **Value $35**

16
Happy Christmas
Satin • N/A
400QX2221 • **Value $30**

17
Heavenly Minstrel
Handcrafted • DLEE
1500QX1567 • **Value $355**

18
A Heavenly Nap
(re-issued in 1981)
Handcrafted • DLEE
650QX1394 • **Value $58**

19
Heavenly Sounds
Handcrafted • N/A
750QX1521 • **Value $98**

20
Joan Walsh Anglund
Satin • N/A
400QX2174 • **Value $26**

	Price Paid	Value of My Collection
GENERAL KEEPSAKE		
1.		
2.		
3.		
4.		
5.		
6.		
7.		
8.		
9.		
10.		
11.		
12.		
13.		
14.		
15.		
16.		
17.		
18.		
19.		
20.		
PENCIL TOTALS		

1 Jolly Santa
Glass • N/A
400QX2274 • **Value $32**

2 Joy
Acrylic • N/A
400QX3501 • **Value $24**

3 Love
Acrylic • N/A
400QX3021 • **Value $64**

4 Marty Links™
Satin • N/A
400QX2214 • **Value $23**

5 Mary Hamilton
Glass • N/A
400QX2194 • **Value $23**

6 Merry Redbird
Handcrafted • N/A
350QX1601 • **Value $67**

7 Merry Santa
(re-issued from 1979)
Fabric • N/A
200QX3427 • **Value $20**

8 Mother
Acrylic • N/A
400QX3041 • **Value $35**

1980

9 Mother
Satin • N/A
400QX2034 • **Value $24**

10 Mother and Dad
Glass • N/A
400QX2301 • **Value $23**

11 MUPPETS™
Satin • N/A
400QX2201 • **Value $41**

12 Nativity
Glass • N/A
400QX2254 • **Value $90**

13 PEANUTS®
Satin • N/A
400QX2161 • **Value $42**

14 Reindeer Chimes
(re-issued from 1978)
Chrome Plate • SICK
550QX3203 • **Value $45**

15 Rocking Horse
(re-issued from 1979)
Fabric • N/A
200QX3407 • **Value $23**

16 Santa
Acrylic • N/A
400QX3101 • **Value $24**

17 Santa
(re-issued in 1981)
Yarn • N/A
300QX1614 • **Value $11**

18 Santa 1980
Handcrafted • N/A
550QX1461 • **Value $97**

19 Santa Mobile
(re-issued in 1981)
Chrome Plate • N/A
550QX1361 • **Value $52**

20 Santa's Flight
Pressed Tin • SICK
550QX1381 • **Value $115**

GENERAL KEEPSAKE

	Price Paid	Value of My Collection
1.		
2.		
3.		
4.		
5.		
6.		
7.		
8.		
9.		
10.		
11.		
12.		
13.		
14.		
15.		
16.		
17.		
18.		
19.		
20.		
PENCIL TOTALS		

① Santa's Workshop
Satin • N/A
400QX2234 • **Value $31**

② Skating Snowman
(re-issued from 1979)
Handcrafted • DLEE
550QX1399 • **Value $82**

③ Snowflake Chimes
(re-issued in 1981)
Chrome Plate • SICK
550QX1654 • **Value $37**

④ The Snowflake Swing
Handcrafted • N/A
400QX1334 • **Value $45**

⑤ Snowman
(re-issued in 1981)
Yarn • N/A
300QX1634 • **Value $10**

⑥ Soldier
(re-issued in 1981)
Yarn • N/A
300QX1641 • **Value $10**

⑦ Son
Glass • N/A
400QX2114 • **Value $35**

⑧ A Spot of Christmas Cheer
Handcrafted • DLEE
800QX1534 • **Value $153**

⑨ Stuffed Full Stocking
(re-issued from 1979)
Fabric • N/A
200QX3419 • **Value $25**

⑩ Swingin' on a Star
Handcrafted • N/A
400QX1301 • **Value $86**

⑪ Teacher
Satin • N/A
400QX2094 • **Value $20**

⑫ Three Wise Men
Acrylic • N/A
400QX3001 • **Value $31**

⑬ Wreath
Acrylic • N/A
400QX3014 • **Value $83**

	Price Paid	Value of My Collection
GENERAL KEEPSAKE		
1.		
2.		
3.		
4.		
5.		
6.		
7.		
8.		
9.		
10.		
11.		
12.		
13.		
GENERAL KEEPSAKE		
14.		
15.		
16.		
PENCIL TOTALS		

1979

Among the most popular Hallmark ornaments in the early years were the ball ornaments commemorating "Baby's First Christmas." In 1979, Hallmark released its first handcrafted ornament with this theme. Overall, there were 65 Keepsake ornaments in 1979. See the collectible series section for more 1979 ornaments.

⑭ Angel Delight
Handcrafted • N/A
300QX1307 • **Value $95**

⑮ Angel Music
(re-issued in 1980)
Fabric • N/A
200QX3439 • **Value $21**

⑯ Baby's First Christmas
Handcrafted • N/A
800QX1547 • **Value $120**

VALUE GUIDE — HALLMARK KEEPSAKE ORNAMENTS

① Baby's First Christmas
Satin • N/A
350QX2087 • **Value $30**

② Behold the Star
Satin • N/A
350QX2559 • **Value $40**

③ Black Angel
Glass • BLAC
350QX2079 • **Value $26**

④ Christmas Angel
Acrylic • N/A
350QX3007 • **Value $145**

⑤ Christmas Cheer
Acrylic • N/A
350QX3039 • **Value $88**

⑥ Christmas Chickadees
Glass • N/A
350QX2047 • **Value $34**

⑦ Christmas Collage
Glass • N/A
350QX2579 • **Value $40**

⑧ Christmas Eve Surprise
Handcrafted • N/A
650QX1579 • **Value $67**

⑨ Christmas Heart
Handcrafted • SICK
650QX1407 • **Value $110**

⑩ Christmas is for Children
(re-issued in 1980)
Handcrafted • N/A
500QX1359 • **Value $97**

⑪ Christmas Traditions
Glass • SICK
350QX2539 • **Value $36**

⑫ A Christmas Treat
(re-issued in 1980)
Handcrafted • N/A
500QX1347 • **Value $88**

⑬ Christmas Tree
Acrylic • N/A
350QX3027 • **Value $73**

⑭ The Downhill Run
Handcrafted • DLEE
650QX1459 • **Value $172**

⑮ The Drummer Boy
Handcrafted • N/A
800QX1439 • **Value $125**

⑯ Friendship
Glass • N/A
350QX2039 • **Value $24**

⑰ Granddaughter
Satin • N/A
350QX2119 • **Value $37**

⑱ Grandmother
Glass • N/A
350QX2527 • **Value $22**

⑲ Grandson
Satin • N/A
350QX2107 • **Value $34**

⑳ Green Boy
(re-issued from 1978)
Yarn • N/A
200QX1231 • **Value $26**

	GENERAL KEEPSAKE	
	Price Paid	Value of My Collection
1.		
2.		
3.		
4.		
5.		
6.		
7.		
8.		
9.		
10.		
11.		
12.		
13.		
14.		
15.		
16.		
17.		
18.		
19.		
20.		
PENCIL TOTALS		

1979

VALUE GUIDE — HALLMARK KEEPSAKE ORNAMENTS

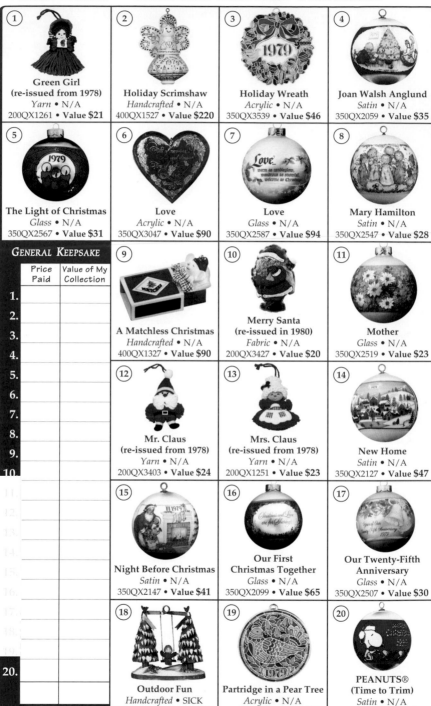

1
Green Girl
(re-issued from 1978)
Yarn • N/A
200QX1261 • **Value $21**

2
Holiday Scrimshaw
Handcrafted • N/A
400QX1527 • **Value $220**

3
Holiday Wreath
Acrylic • N/A
350QX3539 • **Value $46**

4
Joan Walsh Anglund
Satin • N/A
350QX2059 • **Value $35**

5
The Light of Christmas
Glass • N/A
350QX2567 • **Value $31**

6
Love
Acrylic • N/A
350QX3047 • **Value $90**

7
Love
Glass • N/A
350QX2587 • **Value $94**

8
Mary Hamilton
Satin • N/A
350QX2547 • **Value $28**

GENERAL KEEPSAKE

	Price Paid	Value of My Collection
1.		
2.		
3.		
4.		
5.		
6.		
7.		
8.		
9.		
10.		
11.		
12.		
13.		
14.		
15.		
16.		
17.		
18.		
19.		
20.		

PENCIL TOTALS

9
A Matchless Christmas
Handcrafted • N/A
400QX1327 • **Value $90**

10
Merry Santa
(re-issued in 1980)
Fabric • N/A
200QX3427 • **Value $20**

11
Mother
Glass • N/A
350QX2519 • **Value $23**

12
Mr. Claus
(re-issued from 1978)
Yarn • N/A
200QX3403 • **Value $24**

13
Mrs. Claus
(re-issued from 1978)
Yarn • N/A
200QX1251 • **Value $23**

14
New Home
Satin • N/A
350QX2127 • **Value $47**

15
Night Before Christmas
Satin • N/A
350QX2147 • **Value $41**

16
Our First
Christmas Together
Glass • N/A
350QX2099 • **Value $65**

17
Our Twenty-Fifth
Anniversary
Glass • N/A
350QX2507 • **Value $30**

18
Outdoor Fun
Handcrafted • SICK
800QX1507 • **Value $133**

19
Partridge in a Pear Tree
Acrylic • N/A
350QX3519 • **Value $46**

20
PEANUTS®
(Time to Trim)
Satin • N/A
350QX2027 • **Value $44**

①
Raccoon
(re-issued from 1978)
Handcrafted • DLEE
650QX1423 • **Value $96**

②
Ready for Christmas
Handcrafted • DLEE
650QX1339 • **Value $155**

③
Reindeer Chimes
(re-issued from 1978)
Chrome Plate • SICK
450QX3203 • **Value $45**

④
Rocking Horse
(re-issued in 1980)
Fabric • N/A
200QX3407 • **Value $23**

⑤
Santa
(re-issued from 1978)
Handcrafted • N/A
300QX1356 • **Value $68**

⑥
Santa's Here
Handcrafted • SICK
500QX1387 • **Value $75**

⑦
The Skating Snowman
(re-issued in 1980)
Handcrafted • DLEE
500QX1399 • **Value $82**

⑧
Snowflake
Acrylic • N/A
350QX3019 • **Value $41**

⑨
Spencer® Sparrow, Esq.
Satin • N/A
350QX2007 • **Value $42**

⑩
Star Chimes
Chrome Plate • SICK
450QX1379 • **Value $73**

⑪
Star Over Bethlehem
Acrylic • SICK
350QX3527 • **Value $74**

⑫
Stuffed Full Stocking
(re-issued in 1980)
Fabric • N/A
200QX3419 • **Value $25**

⑬
Teacher
Satin • N/A
350QX2139 • **Value $15**

⑭
Winnie-the-Pooh
Satin • N/A
350QX2067 • **Value $52**

⑮
Words of Christmas
Acrylic • N/A
350QX3507 • **Value $80**

GENERAL KEEPSAKE

	Price Paid	Value of My Collection
1.		
2.		
3.		
4.		
5.		
6.		
7.		
8.		
9.		
10.		
11.		
12.		
13.		
14.		
15.		
	PENCIL TOTALS	

1978

In the 6th year of Hallmark ornaments several unique handcrafted ornaments proved to be the most popular, including "Angels," "Animal Home," "Calico Mouse," "Red Cardinal" and "Schneeberg Bell." The 1978 collection featured 54 Keepsake ornaments. See the collectible series section for more 1978 ornaments.

(1)
25th Christmas Together
Glass • N/A
350QX2696 • **Value $34**

(2)

Angel
Acrylic • N/A
350QX3543 • **Value $49**

(3)

Angel
(re-issued in 1981)
Handcrafted • DLEE
450QX1396 • **Value $100**

(4)

Angels
Handcrafted • N/A
800QX1503 • **Value $355**

(5)

Animal Home
Handcrafted • DLEE
600QX1496 • **Value $180**

General Keepsake

	Price Paid	Value of My Collection
1.		
2.		
3.		
4.		
5.		
6.		
7.		
8.		
9.		
10.		
11.		
12.		
13.		
14.		
15.		
16.		
17.		

(6)

Baby's First Christmas
Satin • N/A
350QX2003 • **Value $88**

(7)

Calico Mouse
Handcrafted • N/A
450QX1376 • **Value $175**

(8)

Candle
Acrylic • N/A
350QX3576 • **Value $88**

(9)

DISNEY
Satin • N/A
350QX2076 • **Value $130**

(10)

Dove
Acrylic •PALM
350QX3103 • **Value $130**

(11)

Dove
Handcrafted • SICK
450QX1903 • **Value $87**

(12)

Drummer Boy
Glass • N/A
350QX2523 • **Value $45**

(13)

Drummer Boy
Handcrafted • N/A
250QX1363 • **Value $70**

(14)

First Christmas Together
Satin • N/A
350QX2183 • **Value $49**

(15)

For Your New Home
Satin • N/A
350QX2176 • **Value $26**

(16)
Granddaughter
Satin • N/A
350QX2163 • **Value $50**

(17)
Grandmother
Satin • N/A
350QX2676 • **Value $45**

PENCIL TOTALS

1
Grandson
Satin • N/A
350QX2156 • **Value $47**

2
Green Boy
(re-issued in 1979)
Yarn • N/A
200QX1231 • **Value $26**

3
Green Girl
(re-issued in 1979)
Yarn • N/A
200QX1261 • **Value $21**

4
**Hallmark's Antique
Card Collection Design**
Satin • N/A
350QX2203 • **Value $44**

5
**Holly and
Poinsettia Ball**
Handcrafted • SICK
600QX1476 • **Value $84**

6
Joan Walsh Anglund
Satin • N/A
350QX2216 • **Value $69**

7
Joy
Glass • N/A
350QX2543 • **Value $48**

8
Joy
Handcrafted • N/A
450QX1383 • **Value $86**

9
Locomotive
Acrylic • N/A
350QX3563 • **Value $56**

10
Love
Glass • N/A
350QX2683 • **Value $57**

11
Merry Christmas
Acrylic • PALM
350QX3556 • **Value $51**

12
Merry Christmas (Santa)
Satin • N/A
350QX2023 • **Value $57**

13
Mother
Glass • N/A
350QX2663 • **Value $53**

14
**Mr. Claus
(re-issued in 1979)**
Yarn • N/A
200QX3403 • **Value $24**

15
**Mrs. Claus
(re-issued in 1979)**
Yarn • N/A
200QX1251 • **Value $23**

16
Nativity
Acrylic • PALM
350QX3096 • **Value $100**

17
Nativity
Glass • N/A
350QX2536 • **Value $75**

18
Panorama Ball
Handcrafted • N/A
600QX1456 • **Value $138**

19
PEANUTS®
Satin • N/A
250QX2036 • **Value $63**

1978

General Keepsake

	Price Paid	Value of My Collection
1.		
2.		
3.		
4.		
5.		
6.		
7.		
8.		
9.		
10.		
11.		
12.		
13.		
14.		
15.		
16.		
17.		
18.		
19.		

PENCIL TOTALS

①
PEANUTS®
Satin • N/A
250QX2043 • **Value $67**

②
PEANUTS®
Satin • N/A
350QX2056 • **Value $70**

③
PEANUTS®
Satin • N/A
350QX2063 • **Value $63**

④
Praying Angel
Handcrafted • DLEE
250QX1343 • **Value $93**

⑤
The Quail
Glass • N/A
350QX2516 • **Value $44**

⑥
Red Cardinal
Handcrafted • UNRU
450QX1443 • **Value $175**

⑦
Reindeer Chimes
(re-issued in 1979 and 1980)
Chrome Plate • SICK
450QX3203 • **Value $45**

⑧
Rocking Horse
Handcrafted • N/A
600QX1483 • **Value $92**

GENERAL KEEPSAKE

	Price Paid	Value of My Collection
1.		
2.		
3.		
4.		
5.		
6.		
7.		
8.		
9.		
10.		
11.		
12.		
13.		
14.		
15.		

⑨
Santa
Acrylic • PALM
350QX3076 • **Value $77**

⑩
Santa
(re-issued in 1979)
Handcrafted • N/A
250QX1356 • **Value $68**

⑪
Schneeberg Bell
Handcrafted • N/A
800QX1523 • **Value $184**

⑫
Skating Raccoon
(re-issued in 1979)
Handcrafted • DLEE
600QX1423 • **Value $96**

⑬
Snowflake
Acrylic • PALM
350QX3083 • **Value $66**

⑭
Spencer® Sparrow, Esq.
Satin • N/A
350QX2196 • **Value $50**

⑮
Yesterday's Toys
Glass • N/A
350QX2503 • **Value $30**

✎ PENCIL TOTALS

1977

The 1977 collection was highlighted by a group of handcrafted ornaments designed to have an antique wooden appearance. Called the "Nostalgia Collection," these ornaments were "Angel," "Antique Car," "Nativity," and "Toys." In 1977, there were 53 Keepsake ornaments. See the collectible series section for more 1977 ornaments.

(1)

Angel
Cloth • N/A
175QX2202 • **Value $51**

(2)

Angel
Handcrafted • DLEE
500QX1822 • **Value $130**

(3)

Angel
Handcrafted • N/A
600QX1722 • **Value $120**

(4)

Antique Car
Handcrafted • SICK
500QX1802 • **Value $63**

(5)

Baby's First Christmas
Satin • N/A
350QX1315 • **Value $82**

(6)

Bell
Acrylic • SICK
350QX2002 • **Value $52**

(7)

Bell
Glass • N/A
350QX1542 • **Value $40**

(8)

Bellringer
Handcrafted • N/A
600QX1922 • **Value $58**

(9)

Candle
Acrylic • N/A
350QX2035 • **Value $62**

(10)

Charmers
Glass • N/A
350QX1535 • **Value $63**

(11)

Christmas Mouse
Satin • N/A
350QX1342 • **Value $60**

(12)

Currier & Ives
Satin • N/A
350QX1302 • **Value $56**

(13)

Della Robia Wreath
Handcrafted • DLEE
450QX1935 • **Value $120**

(14)

Desert
Glass • N/A
250QX1595 • **Value $43**

(15)

DISNEY
Satin • N/A
350QX1335 • **Value $68**

(16)

DISNEY (set/2)
Satin • N/A
400QX1375 • **Value $45**

(17)

Drummer Boy
Acrylic • N/A
350QX3122 • **Value $67**

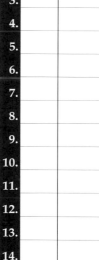

GENERAL KEEPSAKE

	Price Paid	Value of My Collection
1.		
2.		
3.		
4.		
5.		
6.		
7.		
8.		
9.		
10.		
11.		
12.		
13.		
14.		
15.		
16.		
17.		
PENCIL TOTALS		

1977

VALUE GUIDE — HALLMARK KEEPSAKE ORNAMENTS

(1) First Christmas Together
Satin • N/A
350QX1322 • **Value $70**

(2) For Your New Home
Glass • N/A
350QX2635 • **Value $36**

(3) Granddaughter
Satin • N/A
350QX2082 • **Value $37**

(4) Grandma Moses
Glass • N/A
350QX1502 • **Value $63**

(5) Grandmother
Glass • N/A
350QX2602 • **Value $48**

(6) Grandson
Satin • N/A
350QX2095 • **Value $33**

(7) House
Handcrafted • N/A
600QX1702 • **Value $129**

(8) Jack-in-the-Box
Handcrafted • N/A
600QX1715 • **Value $120**

(9) Joy
Acrylic • N/A
350QX2015 • **Value $54**

(10) Joy
Acrylic • N/A
350QX3102 • **Value $47**

(11) Love
Glass • N/A
350QX2622 • **Value $28**

(12) Mandolin
Glass • N/A
350QX1575 • **Value $38**

(13) Mother
Glass • N/A
350QX2615 • **Value $38**

(14) Mountains
Glass • N/A
250QX1582 • **Value $35**

(15) Nativity
Handcrafted • N/A
500QX1815 • **Value $140**

(16) Norman Rockwell
Glass • N/A
350QX1515 • **Value $77**

(17) Ornaments
Glass • N/A
350QX1555 • **Value $41**

(18) Peace on Earth
Acrylic • N/A
350QX3115 • **Value $58**

(19) PEANUTS®
Glass • N/A
250QX1622 • **Value $75**

(20) PEANUTS® (set/2)
Glass • N/A
400QX1635 • **Value $89**

GENERAL KEEPSAKE

	Price Paid	Value of My Collection
1.		
2.		
3.		
4.		
5.		
6.		
7.		
8.		
9.		
10.		
11.		
12.		
13.		
14.		
15.		
16.		
17.		
18.		
19.		
20.		

PENCIL TOTALS

VALUE GUIDE — HALLMARK KEEPSAKE ORNAMENTS

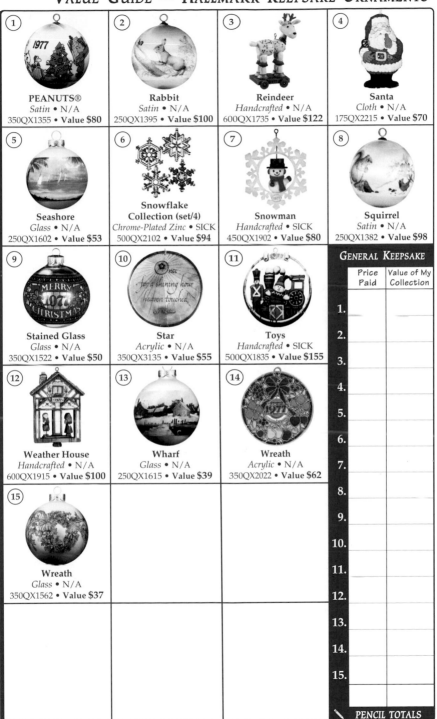

(1)
PEANUTS®
Satin • N/A
350QX1355 • **Value $80**

(2)
Rabbit
Satin • N/A
250QX1395 • **Value $100**

(3)
Reindeer
Handcrafted • N/A
600QX1735 • **Value $122**

(4)
Santa
Cloth • N/A
175QX2215 • **Value $70**

(5)
Seashore
Glass • N/A
250QX1602 • **Value $53**

(6)
Snowflake
Collection (set/4)
Chrome-Plated Zinc • SICK
500QX2102 • **Value $94**

(7)
Snowman
Handcrafted • SICK
450QX1902 • **Value $80**

(8)
Squirrel
Satin • N/A
250QX1382 • **Value $98**

(9)
Stained Glass
Glass • N/A
350QX1522 • **Value $50**

(10)
Star
Acrylic • N/A
350QX3135 • **Value $55**

(11)
Toys
Handcrafted • SICK
500QX1835 • **Value $155**

(12)
Weather House
Handcrafted • N/A
600QX1915 • **Value $100**

(13)
Wharf
Glass • N/A
250QX1615 • **Value $39**

(14)
Wreath
Acrylic • N/A
350QX2022 • **Value $62**

(15)
Wreath
Glass • N/A
350QX1562 • **Value $37**

1977

GENERAL KEEPSAKE

	Price Paid	Value of My Collection
1.		
2.		
3.		
4.		
5.		
6.		
7.		
8.		
9.		
10.		
11.		
12.		
13.		
14.		
15.		
PENCIL TOTALS		

1976

The 1976 collection of ornaments featured popular themes such as Santa Claus, locomotives, partridges and drummer boys, all in a variety of different handcrafted styles. For the Bicentennial year, Hallmark issued a total of 39 Keepsake ornaments. See the collectible series section for more 1976 ornaments.

(1) Angel
Handcrafted • N/A
300QX1761 • **Value $196**

(2) Angel
Handcrafted • SICK
450QX1711 • **Value $175**

(3) Baby's First Christmas
Satin • N/A
250QX2111 • **Value $150**

(4) Betsey Clark
Satin • N/A
250QX2101 • **Value $68**

(5) Betsey Clark (set/3)
Satin • N/A
450QX2181 • **Value $55**

GENERAL KEEPSAKE

	Price Paid	Value of My Collection
1.		
2.		
3.		
4.		
5.		
6.		
7.		
8.		
9.		
10.		
11.		
12.		
13.		
14.		
15.		
16.		
17.		

PENCIL TOTALS

(6) Bicentennial '76 Commemorative
Satin • N/A
250QX2031 • **Value $61**

(7) Bicentennial Charmers
Glass • N/A
300QX1981 • **Value $95**

(8) Cardinals
Glass • N/A
225QX2051 • **Value $80**

(9) Caroler
(re-issued from 1975)
Yarn • N/A
175QX1261 • **Value $21**

(10) Charmers (set/2)
Satin • N/A
350QX2151 • **Value $80**

(11) Chickadees
Glass • N/A
225QX2041 • **Value $64**

(12) Colonial Children (set/2)
Glass • N/A
400QX2081 • **Value $82**

(13) Currier & Ives
Glass • N/A
300QX1971 • **Value $50**

(14) Currier & Ives
Satin • N/A
250QX2091 • **Value $48**

(15) Drummer Boy
(re-issued from 1975)
Handcrafted • SICK
400QX1301 • **Value $178**

(16) Drummer Boy
Handcrafted • N/A
500QX1841 • **Value $152**

(17) Drummer Boy
(re-issued from 1975)
Yarn • N/A
175QX1231 • **Value $26**

1
Happy the
Snowman (set/2)
Satin • N/A
350QX2161 • **Value $50**

2
Locomotive
(re-issued from 1975)
Handcrafted • SICK
400QX2221 • **Value $210**

3
Marty Links™ (set/2)
Glass • N/A
400QX2071 • **Value $63**

4
Mrs. Santa
(re-issued from 1975)
Yarn • N/A
175QX1251 • **Value $24**

5
Norman Rockwell
Glass • N/A
300QX1961 • **Value $72**

6
Partridge
Handcrafted • SICK
450QX1741 • **Value $193**

7
Partridge
Handcrafted • N/A
500QX1831 • **Value $116**

8
Peace on Earth
(re-issued from 1975)
Handcrafted • SICK
400QX2231 • **Value $165**

9
Raggedy Andy™
(re-issued from 1975)
Yarn • N/A
175QX1221 • **Value $45**

10
Raggedy Ann™
Satin • N/A
250X2121 • **Value $63**

11
Raggedy Ann™
(re-issued from 1975)
Yarn • N/A
175QX1211 • **Value $44**

12
Reindeer
Handcrafted • N/A
300QX1781 • **Value $113**

13
Rocking Horse
(re-issued from 1975)
Handcrafted • SICK
400QX1281 • **Value $172**

14
Rudolph and Santa
Satin • N/A
250QX2131 • **Value $90**

15
Santa
Handcrafted • N/A
300QX1771 • **Value $222**

16
Santa
Handcrafted • SICK
450QX1721 • **Value $128**

17
Santa
Handcrafted • N/A
500QX1821 • **Value $166**

18
Santa
(re-issued from 1975)
Yarn • N/A
175QX1241 • **Value $24**

19
Shepherd
Handcrafted • N/A
300QX1751 • **Value $120**

20
Soldier
Handcrafted • SICK
450QX1731 • **Value $98**

1976

General Keepsake

	Price Paid	Value of My Collection
1.		
2.		
3.		
4.		
5.		
6.		
7.		
8.		
9.		
10.		
11.		
12.		
13.		
14.		
15.		
16.		
17.		
18.		
19.		
20.		
PENCIL TOTALS		

Train
Handcrafted • N/A
500QX1811 • **Value $160**

1975

A whole new era of Christmas ornaments began when Hallmark debuted 12 handcrafted ornaments in 1975. These early handcrafted designs are highly sought-after by collectors. Overall, there were 32 Keepsake ornaments issued in 1975, double the total of the previous year. See the collectible series section for more 1975 ornaments.

Betsey Clark
Handcrafted • DLEE
250QX1571 • **Value $240**

Betsey Clark
Satin • N/A
250QX1631 • **Value $41**

Betsey Clark (set/2)
Satin • N/A
350QX1671 • **Value $46**

Betsey Clark (set/4)
Satin • N/A
450QX1681 • **Value $52**

GENERAL KEEPSAKE

	Price Paid	Value of My Collection
1.		

GENERAL KEEPSAKE

2.		
3.		
4.		
5.		
6.		
7.		
8.		
9.		
10.		
11.		
12.		
13.		
14.		
15.		
16.		
17.		

Buttons & Bo (set/4)
Glass • N/A
500QX1391 • **Value $50**

Charmers
Glass • N/A
300QX1351 • **Value $47**

Currier & Ives (set/2)
Glass • N/A
400QX1371 • **Value $38**

Currier & Ives
Satin • N/A
250QX1641 • **Value $40**

Drummer Boy
Handcrafted • DLEE
250QX1611 • **Value $232**

Drummer Boy
(re-issued in 1976)
Handcrafted • SICK
350QX1301 • **Value $178**

Drummer Boy
(re-issued in 1976)
Yarn • N/A
175QX1231 • **Value $26**

Joy
Handcrafted • SICK
350QX1321 • **Value $233**

Little Girl
(re-issued in 1976)
Yarn • N/A
175QX1261 • **Value $21**

Little Miracles (set/4)
Glass • N/A
500QX1401 • **Value $40**

Locomotive
(re-issued in 1976)
Handcrafted • SICK
350QX1271 • **Value $210**

Marty Links™
Glass • N/A
300QX1361 • **Value $57**

PENCIL TOTALS

Value Guide — Hallmark Keepsake Ornaments

(1) **Mrs. Santa** **(re-issued in 1981)** *Handcrafted* • DLEE 250QX1561 • **Value $225**	**(2)** **Mrs. Santa** **(re-issued in 1976)** *Yarn* • N/A 175QX1251 • **Value $24**
(3) **Norman Rockwell** *Glass* • N/A 300QX1341 • **Value $66**	**(4)** **Norman Rockwell** *Satin* • N/A 250QX1661 • **Value $58**
(5) **Peace On Earth** **(re-issued in 1976)** *Handcrafted* • SICK 350QX1311 • **Value $165**	**(6)** **Raggedy Andy™** *Handcrafted* • DLEE 250QX1601 • **Value $365**
(7) **Raggedy Andy™** **(re-issued in 1976)** *Yarn* • N/A 175QX1221 • **Value $45**	**(8)** **Raggedy Ann™** *Handcrafted* • DLEE 250QX1591 • **Value $315**
(9) **Raggedy Ann™** *Satin* • N/A 250QX1651 • **Value $50**	**(10)** **Raggedy Ann™** **(re-issued in 1976)** *Yarn* • N/A 175QX1211 • **Value $44**
(11) **Raggedy Ann™ and Raggedy Andy™ (set/2)** *Glass* • N/A 400QX1381 • **Value $68**	
(12) **Rocking Horse** **(re-issued in 1976)** *Handcrafted* • SICK 350QX1281 • **Value $172**	**(13)** **Santa** **(re-issued in 1981)** *Handcrafted* • DLEE 250QX1551 • **Value $220**
(14) **Santa** **(re-issued in 1976)** *Yarn* • N/A 175QX1241 • **Value $24**	
(15) **Santa & Sleigh** *Handcrafted* • SICK 350QX1291 • **Value $250**	

General Keepsake

	Price Paid	Value of My Collection
1.		
2.		
3.		
4.		
5.		
6.		
7.		
8.		
9.		
10.		
11.		
12.		
13.		
14.		
15.		
PENCIL TOTALS		

1975

1975 Collection 239

1974

In the second year of Keepsake ornaments, the collection featured popular Christmas scenes from Norman Rockwell, Betsey Clark and Currier & Ives. Of the 16 Keepsake designs or sets offered in 1974, 10 were ball ornaments and 6 were made from yarn. See the collectible series section for more 1974 ornaments.

①
Angel
Glass • N/A
250QX1101 • **Value $76**

②
Angel
Yarn • N/A
150QX1031 • **Value $32**

③
Buttons & Bo (set/2)
Glass • N/A
350QX1131 • **Value $52**

④
Charmers
Glass • N/A
250QX1091 • **Value $49**

⑤
Currier & Ives (set/2)
Glass • N/A
350QX1121 • **Value $56**

⑥
Elf
Yarn • N/A
150QX1011 • **Value $26**

⑦
Little Miracles (set/4)
Glass • N/A
450QX1151 • **Value $58**

⑧
Mrs. Santa
Yarn • N/A
150QX1001 • **Value $24**

⑨
Norman Rockwell
Glass • N/A
250QX1061 • **Value $98**

⑩
Norman Rockwell
Glass • N/A
250QX1111 • **Value $86**

⑪
Raggedy Ann™ and Raggedy Andy™ (set/4)
Glass • N/A
450QX1141 • **Value $88**

⑫
Santa
Yarn • N/A
150QX1051 • **Value $27**

⑬
Snowgoose
Glass • N/A
250QX1071 • **Value $76**

⑭
Snowman
Yarn • N/A
150QX1041 • **Value $25**

⑮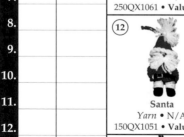
Soldier
Yarn • N/A
150QX1021 • **Value $25**

GENERAL KEEPSAKE	Price Paid	Value of My Collection
1.		
2.		
3.		
4.		
5.		
6.		
7.		
8.		
9.		
10.		
11.		
12.		
13.		
14.		
15.		
PENCIL TOTALS		

1973

The very first year of Hallmark Keepsake Ornaments was 1973. This year's debut offering consisted of 6 ball ornaments and 12 yarn ornaments, making a total of 18 Keepsake designs. The first Keepsake series, "Betsey Clark," began this year. See the collectible series section for more 1973 ornaments.

(1)

Angel
Yarn • N/A
125XHD785 • **Value $28**

---

(2)

Betsey Clark
Glass • N/A
250XHD1002 • **Value $105**

(3)

Blue Girl
Yarn • N/A
125XHD852 • **Value $25**

(4)

Boy Caroler
Yarn • N/A
125XHD832 • **Value $25**

(5)

Choir Boy
Yarn • N/A
125XHD805 • **Value $26**

(6)

Christmas Is Love
Glass • N/A
250XHD1062 • **Value $82**

(7)

Elf
Yarn • N/A
125XHD792 • **Value $26**

(8)

Elves
Glass • N/A
250XHD1035 • **Value $88**

(9)

Green Girl
Yarn • N/A
125XHD845 • **Value $26**

(10)

Little Girl
Yarn • N/A
125XHD825 • **Value $26**

(11)

Manger Scene
Glass • N/A
250XHD1022 • **Value $100**

(12)

Mr. Santa
Yarn • N/A
125XHD745 • **Value $27**

(13)

Mrs. Santa
Yarn • N/A
125XHD752 • **Value $25**

(14)

Mr. Snowman
Yarn • N/A
125XHD765 • **Value $25**

(15)

Mrs. Snowman
Yarn • N/A
125XHD772 • **Value $25**

(16)

Santa with Elves
Glass • N/A
250XHD1015 • **Value $87**

(17)

Soldier
Yarn • N/A
100XHD812 • **Value $24**

GENERAL KEEPSAKE

	Price Paid	Value of My Collection
1.		
2.		
3.		
4.		
5.		
6.		
7.		
8.		
9.		
10.		
11.		
12.		
13.		
14.		
15.		
16.		
17.		
PENCIL TOTALS		

1973

Spring Ornaments

Hallmark created a new way to collect ornaments in 1991 with the introduction of Spring Ornaments. Springtime themes and playful animals abound in this collection, while familiar faces like BARBIE™ and Winnie the Pooh are featured prominently. There have been a total of 148 Spring Ornaments, including 43 that belong to collectible series.

Collectible Series

(1) Apple Blossom Lane
(1st, 1995)
Handcrafted • FRAN
895QEO8207 • **Value $24**

(2) Apple Blossom Lane
(2nd, 1996)
Handcrafted • FRAN
895QEO8084 • **Value $17**

(3) Apple Blossom Lane
(3rd & final, 1997)
Handcrafted • FRAN
895QEO8662 • **Value $18**

(4) Peter Rabbit™
(1st, 1996)
Handcrafted • VOTR
895QEO8071 • **Value $78**

APPLE BLOSSOM LANE

	Price Paid	Value of My Collection
1.		
2.		
3.		

BEATRIX POTTER™

4.		
5.		
6.		

CHILDREN'S COLLECTOR BARBIE™ ORNAMENT

7.		
8.		

COLLECTOR'S PLATE

9.		
10.		
11.		
12.		

COTTONTAIL EXPRESS

13.		
14.		
15.		

PENCIL TOTALS

(5) Jemima Puddle-duck™
(2nd, 1997)
Handcrafted • VOTR
895QEO8645 • **Value $23**

 NEW!

(6) Benjamin Bunny™
Beatrix Potter™
(3rd, 1998)
Handcrafted • VOTR
895QEO8383 • **Value $8.95**

(7) Based on the BARBIE® as Rapunzel Doll (1st, 1997)
Handcrafted • RGRS
1495QEO8635 • **Value $32**

 NEW!

(8) Based on the BARBIE® as Little Bo Peep Doll
(2nd, 1998)
Handcrafted • RGRS
1495QEO8373 • **Value $14.95**

(9) "Gathering Sunny Memories" (1st, 1994)
Porcelain • VOTR
775QEO8233 • **Value $32**

(10) "Catching the Breeze"
(2nd, 1995)
Porcelain • VOTR
795QEO8219 • **Value $21**

(11) "Keeping a Secret"
(3rd, 1996)
Porcelain • VOTR
795QEO8221 • **Value $17**

(12) "Sunny Sunday Best"
(4th & final, 1997)
Porcelain • VOTR
795QEO8675 • **Value $16**

(13) Locomotive (1st, 1996)
Handcrafted • CROW
895QEO8074 • **Value $42**

(14) Colorful Coal Car
(2nd, 1997)
Handcrafted • CROW
895QEO8652 • **Value $18**

 NEW!

(15) Passenger Car (3rd, 1998)
Handcrafted • CROW
995QEO8376 • **Value $9.95**

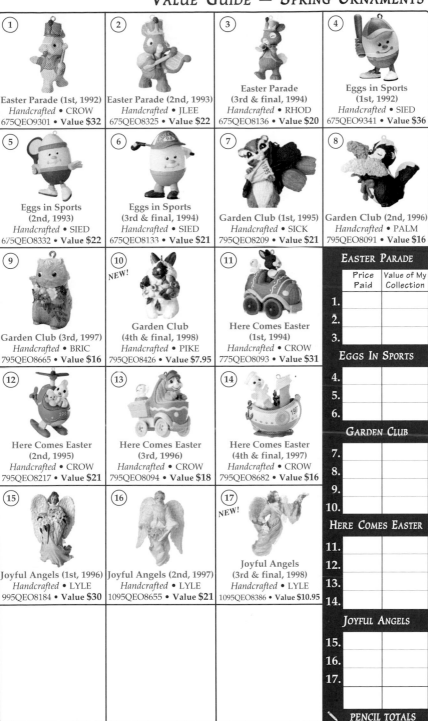

1 — Easter Parade (1st, 1992)
Handcrafted • CROW
675QEO9301 • **Value $32**

2 — Easter Parade (2nd, 1993)
Handcrafted • JLEE
675QEO8325 • **Value $22**

3 — Easter Parade (3rd & final, 1994)
Handcrafted • RHOD
675QEO8136 • **Value $20**

4 — Eggs in Sports (1st, 1992)
Handcrafted • SIED
675QEO9341 • **Value $36**

5 — Eggs in Sports (2nd, 1993)
Handcrafted • SIED
675QEO8332 • **Value $22**

6 — Eggs in Sports (3rd & final, 1994)
Handcrafted • SIED
675QEO8133 • **Value $21**

7 — Garden Club (1st, 1995)
Handcrafted • SICK
795QEO8209 • **Value $21**

8 — Garden Club (2nd, 1996)
Handcrafted • PALM
795QEO8091 • **Value $16**

9 — Garden Club (3rd, 1997)
Handcrafted • BRIC
795QEO8665 • **Value $16**

10 NEW! — Garden Club (4th & final, 1998)
Handcrafted • PIKE
795QEO8426 • **Value $7.95**

11 — Here Comes Easter (1st, 1994)
Handcrafted • CROW
775QEO8093 • **Value $31**

12 — Here Comes Easter (2nd, 1995)
Handcrafted • CROW
795QEO8217 • **Value $21**

13 — Here Comes Easter (3rd, 1996)
Handcrafted • CROW
795QEO8094 • **Value $18**

14 — Here Comes Easter (4th & final, 1997)
Handcrafted • CROW
795QEO8682 • **Value $16**

15 — Joyful Angels (1st, 1996)
Handcrafted • LYLE
995QEO8184 • **Value $30**

16 — Joyful Angels (2nd, 1997)
Handcrafted • LYLE
1095QEO8655 • **Value $21**

17 NEW! — Joyful Angels (3rd & final, 1998)
Handcrafted • LYLE
1095QEO8386 • **Value $10.95**

EASTER PARADE	Price Paid	Value of My Collection
1.		
2.		
3.		
EGGS IN SPORTS		
4.		
5.		
6.		
GARDEN CLUB		
7.		
8.		
9.		
10.		
HERE COMES EASTER		
11.		
12.		
13.		
14.		
JOYFUL ANGELS		
15.		
16.		
17.		
PENCIL TOTALS		

SPRING ORNAMENTS

VALUE GUIDE − SPRING ORNAMENTS

(1) 1935 Steelcraft Streamline Velocipede by Murray® (1st, 1997)
Die-Cast Metal • RHOD
1295QEO8632 • **Value $25**

(2) NEW! 1939 Mobo Horse (2nd, 1998)
Die-Cast Metal • N/A
1295QEO8393 • **Value $12.95**

(3) Springtime BARBIE™ (1st, 1995)
Handcrafted • ANDR
1295QEO8069 • **Value $38**

(4) Springtime BARBIE™ (2nd, 1996)
Handcrafted • ANDR
1295QEO8081 • **Value $30**

(5) Springtime BARBIE™ (3rd & final, 1997)
Handcrafted • ANDR
1295QEO8642 • **Value $23**

(6) Springtime Bonnets (1st, 1993)
Handcrafted • DLEE
775QEO8322 • **Value $31**

(7) Springtime Bonnets (2nd, 1994)
Handcrafted • BISH
775QEO8096 • **Value $28**

(8) Springtime Bonnets (3rd, 1995)
Handcrafted • UNRU
795QEO8227 • **Value $21**

(9) Springtime Bonnets (4th, 1996)
Handcrafted • PIKE
795QEO8134 • **Value $27**

(10) Springtime Bonnets (5th & final, 1997)
Handcrafted • PIKE
795QEO8672 • **Value $16**

(11) NEW! 1931 Ford Model A Roadster (1st, 1998)
Die-Cast Metal • PALM
1495QEO8416 • **Value $14.95**

1998

(12) Bashful Gift (set/2)
Handcrafted • AUBE
1195QEO8446 • **Value $11.95**

(13) Bouquet of Memories
Handcrafted • TAGU
795QEO8456 • **Value $7.95**

(14) Forever Friends The Andrew Brownsword Collection
Handcrafted • PIKE
995QEO8423 • **Value $9.95**

(15) The Garden of Piglet and Pooh (set/2)
Handcrafted • N/A
1295QEO8403 • **Value $12.95**

(16) Going Up? Charlie Brown – PEANUTS®
Handcrafted • PIKE
995QEO8433 • **Value $9.95**

(17) Happy Diploma Day!
Handcrafted • HADD
795QEO8476 • **Value $7.95**

(18) Midge™ – 35th Anniversary
Handcrafted • ANDR
1495QEO8413 • **Value $14.95**

(19) Practice Swing – Donald Duck
Handcrafted • N/A
1095QEO8396 • **Value $10.95**

SIDEWALK CRUISERS

	Price Paid	Value of My Collection
1.		
2.		

SPRINGTIME BARBIE™

3.		
4.		
5.		

SPRINGTIME BONNETS

6.		
7.		
8.		
9.		
10.		

VINTAGE ROADSTER

11.		

1998 COLLECTION

12.		
13.		
14.		
15.		
16.		
17.		
18.		
19.		

PENCIL TOTALS

(1) Precious Baby
Handcrafted • TAGU
995QEO8463 • **Value $9.95**

(2) Special Friends
Handcrafted • VOTR
1295QEO8523 • **Value $12.95**

(3) STAR WARS™
Pressed Tin • N/A
1295QEO8406 • **Value $12.95**

(4) Sweet Birthday
Handcrafted • KLIN
795QEO8473 • **Value $7.95**

(5) Tigger in the Garden (Spring Preview)
Handcrafted • N/A
995QEO8436 • **Value $9.95**

(6) Victorian Cross
Pewter • UNRU
895QEO8453 • **Value $8.95**

(7) Wedding Memories
Porcelain • VOTR
995QEO8466 • **Value $9.95**

(8) What's Your Name?
Handcrafted • KLIN
795QEO8443 • **Value $7.95**

(9) Fair Valentine™ BARBIE® Doll (3rd in *Be My Valentine Collector Series™*)
Vinyl • N/A
5000QHV8743 • **Value $50**

1997

(10) Bumper Crop, Tender Touches (set/3)
Handcrafted • SEAL
1495QEO8735 • **Value $25**

(11) Digging In
Handcrafted • SEAL
795QEO8712 • **Value $16**

(12) Eggs-pert Artist, CRAYOLA® Crayon
Handcrafted • TAGU
895QEO8695 • **Value $16**

(13) Garden Bunnies, Nature's Sketchbook
Handcrafted • UNRU
1495QEO8702 • **Value $26**

(14) Gentle Guardian
Handcrafted • LARS
695QEO8732 • **Value $13**

(15) A Purr-fect Princess
Handcrafted • PIKE
795QEO8715 • **Value $16**

(16) Swing-Time
Handcrafted • TAGU
795QEO8705 • **Value $15**

(17) Victorian Cross
Pewter • N/A
895QEO8725 • **Value $18**

(18) Sentimental Valentine™ BARBIE® Doll (2nd in *Be My Valentine Collector Series™*)
Vinyl • N/A
5000QHV8742 • **Value N/E**

	Price Paid	Value of My Collection
1998 COLLECTION		
1.		
2.		
3.		
4.		
5.		
6.		
7.		
8.		
9.		
1997 COLLECTION		
10.		
11.		
12.		
13.		
14.		
15.		
16.		
17.		
18.		
PENCIL TOTALS		

SPRING ORNAMENTS

1996

(1)
Daffy Duck,
LOONEY TUNES
Handcrafted • RGRS
895QEO8154 • **Value $18**

(2)
Easter Morning
Handcrafted • UNRU
795QEO8164 • **Value $15**

(3)
Eggstra Special Surprise,
Tender Touches
Handcrafted • SEAL
895QEO8161 • **Value $20**

(4)
Hippity-Hop Delivery,
CRAYOLA® Crayon
Handcrafted • CROW
795QEO8144 • **Value $18**

(5)
Look What I Found!
Handcrafted • FRAN
795QEO8181 • **Value $15**

(6)
Parade Pals, PEANUTS®
Handcrafted • RHOD
795QEO8151 • **Value $17**

(7)
Pork 'n Beans
Handcrafted • CHAD
795QEO8174 • **Value $15**

(8)
Strawberry Patch
Handcrafted • SEAL
695QEO8171 • **Value $17**

(9)
Strike up the Band! (set/3)
Handcrafted • UNRU
1495QEO8141 • **Value $27**

(10)
Sweet Valentine™
BARBIE® Doll
(1st in *Be My Valentine
Collector Series*™)
Vinyl • N/A
4500QHV8131 • **Value N/E**

1995

(11)
April Shower
Handcrafted • SIED
695QEO8253 • **Value $15**

(12)
Baby's First Easter
Handcrafted • PALM
795QEO8237 • **Value $18**

(13)
Bugs Bunny,
LOONEY TUNES™
Handcrafted • CHAD
895QEO8279 • **Value $21**

(14)
Daughter
Handcrafted • RGRS
595QEO8239 • **Value $14**

(15)
Easter Eggspress
Handcrafted • SIED
495QEO8269 • **Value $15**

(16)
Elegant Lily
Brass • VOTR
695QEO8267 • **Value $15**

(17)
Flowerpot Friends (set/3)
Handcrafted • ANDR
1495QEO8229 • **Value $26**

(18)
Ham 'n Eggs
Handcrafted • CHAD
795QEO8277 • **Value $15**

1996 Collection

	Price Paid	Value of My Collection
1.		
2.		
3.		
4.		
5.		
6.		
7.		
8.		
9.		
10.		

1995 Collection

11.		
12.		
13.		
14.		
15.		
16.		
17.		
18.		

PENCIL TOTALS

1
High Hopes,
Tender Touches
Handcrafted • SEAL
895QEO8259 • **Value $20**

2
PEANUTS®
Handcrafted • RHOD
795QEO8257 • **Value $25**

3
Picture Perfect,
Handcrafted • CROW
795QEO8249 • **Value $21**

4
Son
Handcrafted • RGRS
595QEO8247 • **Value $17**

1994

5
Baby's First Easter
Handcrafted • FRAN
675QEO8153 • **Value $20**

6
Colorful Spring
Handcrafted • CROW
775QEO8166 • **Value $30**

7
Daughter
Handcrafted • ANDR
575QEO8156 • **Value $15**

8
Divine Duet
Handcrafted • VOTR
675QEO8183 • **Value $17**

9
Easter Art Show
Handcrafted • VOTR
775QEO8193 • **Value $18**

10
Joyful Lamb
Handcrafted • UNRU
575QEO8206 • **Value $15**

11
PEANUTS®
Handcrafted • UNRU
775QEO8176 • **Value $48**

12
Peeping Out
Handcrafted • UNRU
675QEO8203 • **Value $15**

13
Riding a Breeze
Handcrafted • PALM
575QEO8213 • **Value $16**

14
Son
Handcrafted • ANDR
575QEO8163 • **Value $16**

15
Sunny Bunny
Garden (set/3)
Handcrafted • SEAL
1500QEO8146 • **Value $32**

16
Sweet as Sugar
Handcrafted • RGRS
875QEO8086 • **Value $20**

17
Sweet Easter Wishes,
Tender Touches
Handcrafted • SEAL
875QEO8196 • **Value $26**

18
Treetop Cottage
Handcrafted • SICK
975QEO8186 • **Value $20**

19
Yummy Recipe
Handcrafted • RGRS
775QEO8143 • **Value $21**

	Price Paid	Value of My Collection
1995 COLLECTION		
1.		
2.		
3.		
4.		
1994 COLLECTION		
5.		
6.		
7.		
8.		
9.		
10.		
11.		
12.		
13.		
14.		
15.		
16.		
17.		
18.		
19.		
PENCIL TOTALS		

SPRING ORNAMENTS

1993

1
Baby's First Easter
Handcrafted • PALM
675QEO8345 • **Value $16**

2
Backyard Bunny
Handcrafted • SICK
675QEO8405 • **Value $17**

3
Barrow of Giggles
Handcrafted • ANDR
875QEO8402 • **Value $21**

4
Beautiful Memories
Handcrafted • UNRU
675QEO8362 • **Value $13**

5
Best-dressed Turtle
Handcrafted • JLEE
575QEO8392 • **Value $16**

6
Chicks-on-a-Twirl
Handcrafted • LYLE
775QEO8375 • **Value $18**

7
Daughter
Handcrafted • ANDR
575QEO8342 • **Value $17**

1993 Collection

	Price Paid	Value of My Collection
1.		
2.		
3.		
4.		
5.		
6.		
7.		
8.		
9.		
10.		
11.		
12.		
13.		
14.		
15.		
16.		

8
Grandchild
Handcrafted • SIED
675QEO8352 • **Value $20**

9
Li'l Peeper
Handcrafted • JLEE
775QEO8312 • **Value $22**

10
Lop-eared Bunny
Handcrafted • SICK
575QEO8315 • **Value $21**

11
Lovely Lamb
Porcelain • VOTR
975QEO8372 • **Value $23**

12
Maypole Stroll (set/3)
Handcrafted/Wood •
CHAD/FRAN
2800QEO8395 • **Value $53**

13
Nutty Eggs
Handcrafted • JLEE
675QEO8382 • **Value $15**

14
Radiant Window
Handcrafted • UNRU
775QEO8365 • **Value $19**

15
Son
Handcrafted • ANDR
575QEO8335 • **Value $16**

16
Time for Easter
Handcrafted • CHAD
875QEO8385 • **Value $22**

1992 Collection

17.		
18.		

1992

17
Baby's First Easter
Handcrafted • FRAN
675QEO9271 • **Value $24**

18
Belle Bunny
Porcelain • VOTR
975QEO9354 • **Value $20**

PENCIL TOTALS

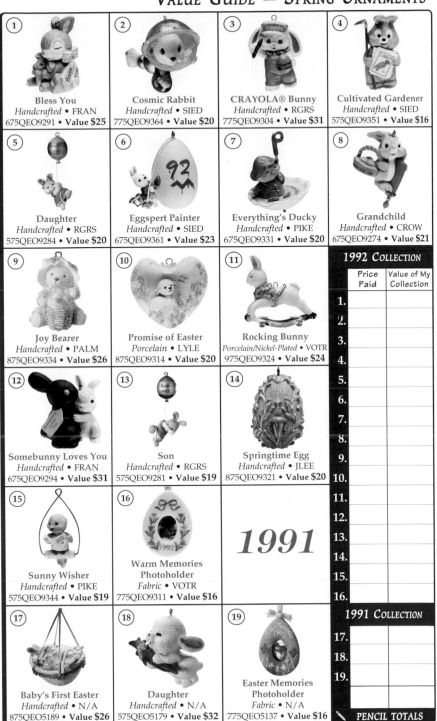

1 Bless You
Handcrafted • FRAN
675QEO9291 • **Value $25**

2 Cosmic Rabbit
Handcrafted • SIED
775QEO9364 • **Value $20**

3 CRAYOLA® Bunny
Handcrafted • RGRS
775QEO9304 • **Value $31**

4 Cultivated Gardener
Handcrafted • SIED
575QEO9351 • **Value $16**

5 Daughter
Handcrafted • RGRS
575QEO9284 • **Value $20**

6 Eggspert Painter
Handcrafted • SIED
675QEO9361 • **Value $23**

7 Everything's Ducky
Handcrafted • PIKE
675QEO9331 • **Value $20**

8 Grandchild
Handcrafted • CROW
675QEO9274 • **Value $21**

9 Joy Bearer
Handcrafted • PALM
875QEO9334 • **Value $26**

10 Promise of Easter
Porcelain • LYLE
875QEO9314 • **Value $20**

11 Rocking Bunny
Porcelain/Nickel-Plated • VOTR
975QEO9324 • **Value $24**

12 Somebunny Loves You
Handcrafted • FRAN
675QEO9294 • **Value $31**

13 Son
Handcrafted • RGRS
575QEO9281 • **Value $19**

14 Springtime Egg
Handcrafted • JLEE
875QEO9321 • **Value $20**

15 Sunny Wisher
Handcrafted • PIKE
575QEO9344 • **Value $19**

16 Warm Memories
Photoholder
Fabric • VOTR
775QEO9311 • **Value $16**

1991

17 Baby's First Easter
Handcrafted • N/A
875QEO5189 • **Value $26**

18 Daughter
Handcrafted • N/A
575QEO5179 • **Value $32**

19 Easter Memories
Photoholder
Fabric • N/A
775QEO5137 • **Value $16**

1992 Collection

	Price Paid	Value of My Collection
1.		
2.		
3.		
4.		
5.		
6.		
7.		
8.		
9.		
10.		
11.		
12.		
13.		
14.		
15.		
16.		

1991 Collection

17.		
18.		
19.		
	PENCIL TOTALS	

①	② 	③	④
Full of Love *Handcrafted* • N/A 775QEO5149 • **Value $46**	**Gentle Lamb** *Handcrafted* • N/A 675QEO5159 • **Value $21**	**Grandchild** *Handcrafted* • N/A 675QEO5177 • **Value $20**	**Li'l Dipper** *Handcrafted* • N/A 675QEO5147 • **Value $24**
⑤	⑥	⑦	⑧
Lily Egg *Porcelain* • UNRU 975QEO5139 • **Value $23**	**Son** *Handcrafted* • N/A 575QEO5187 • **Value $26**	**Spirit of Easter** *Handcrafted* • N/A 775QEO5169 • **Value $35**	**Springtime Stroll** *Handcrafted* • N/A 675QEO5167 • **Value $24**

1991 COLLECTION

	Price Paid	Value of My Collection
1.		
2.		
3.		
4.		
5.		
6.		
7.		
8.		

1998 COLLECTION

9.		
10.		

Merry Miniatures

As the name implies, Merry Miniatures figurines have been a delight for collectors since their debut in 1974. Popular features of the collection include collectible series, holiday themes and groupings of recurring characters. Some popular Merry Miniatures have been issued for more than one year. There have been over 500 Merry Miniatures figurines released.

1998

⑨	⑩ 	
Bride and Groom–1996 Madame Alexander® (Premiere) *Handcrafted* • FRAN 1295QFM8486 • **Value $12.95**	**Donald's Passenger Car** *Handcrafted* • N/A 595QRP8513 • **Value $5.95**	
⑪ 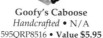	⑫	⑬
Goofy's Caboose *Handcrafted* • N/A 595QRP8516 • **Value $5.95**	**HERSHEY'S™** (Premiere, set/2, 2nd, *HERSHEY'S*™) *Handcrafted* • BRIC 1095QFM8493 • **Value $10.95**	**Mickey's Locomotive** *Handcrafted* • N/A 595QRP8496 • **Value $5.95**
⑭	⑮	⑯
Minnie's Luggage Car *Handcrafted* • N/A 595QRP8506 • **Value $5.95**	**Pluto's Coal Car** *Handcrafted* • N/A 595QRP8503 • **Value $5.95**	**Rapunzel** (Spring Preview, set/2) *Handcrafted* • TAGU 1295QSM8483 • **Value $12.95**

PENCIL TOTALS

1997

(1)
Apple Harvest – Mary's Bears (set/3)
Handcrafted • HAMI
1295QFM8585 • **Value $22**

(2)
Bashful Visitors (set/3)
Handcrafted • AUBE
1295QFM8582 • **Value $22**

(3)
Cupid Cameron
Handcrafted • N/A
495QSM8552 • **Value $13**

(4)
Easter Parade (set/2)
Handcrafted • TAGU
795QSM8562 • **Value $16**

(5)
Getting Ready for Spring (set/3)
Handcrafted • TAGU
1295QSM8575 • **Value $21**

(6)
Happy Birthday Clowns (3rd & final, *Happy Birthday Clowns*)
Handcrafted • N/A
495QSM8565 • **Value $15**

(7)
HERSHEY'S™ (set/2, 1st, *HERSHEY'S™*)
Handcrafted • BRIC
1295QFM8625 • **Value $23**

(8)
Holiday Harmony (set/3)
Handcrafted • TAGU
1295QFM8612 • **Value $21**

(9)
Making a Wish (set/2)
Handcrafted • TAGU
795QFM8592 • **Value $14**

(10)
The Nativity (set/2)
Handcrafted • N/A
795QFM8615 • **Value $15**

(11)
Noah's Friends (set/2)
Handcrafted • ESCH
795QSM8572 • **Value $20**

(12)
Peter Pan (set/5)
Handcrafted • TAGU
1995QSM8605 • **Value $36**

(13)
Santa Cameron
Handcrafted • N/A
495QFM8622 • **Value $15**

(14)
Six Dwarfs (set/3)
Handcrafted • ESCH
1295QFM8685 • **Value $20**

(15)
Snow White and Dancing Dwarf (set/2)
Handcrafted • ESCH
795QFM8535 • **Value $16**

(16)
Snowbear Season (Premiere, set/3)
Handcrafted • ESCH
1295QFM8602 • **Value $21**

(17)
Sule and Sara – PendaKids™ (set/2)
Handcrafted • JOHN
795QSM8545 • **Value $12**

(18)
Tea Time – Mary's Bears (set/3)
Handcrafted • HAMI
1295QSM8542 • **Value $22**

(19)
Three Wee Kings (set/3)
Handcrafted • N/A
1295QFM8692 • **Value $20**

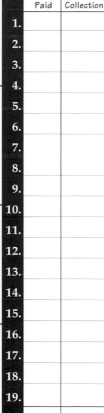

1997 COLLECTION		
	Price Paid	Value of My Collection
1.		
2.		
3.		
4.		
5.		
6.		
7.		
8.		
9.		
10.		
11.		
12.		
13.		
14.		
15.		
16.		
17.		
18.		
19.		
PENCIL TOTALS		

MERRY MINIATURES

1996

(1) Alice in Wonderland (set/5)
Handcrafted • N/A
1995QSM8014 • **Value $35**

(2) Bashful Mistletoe (Premiere, set/3)
Handcrafted • N/A
1295QFM8319 • **Value $23**

(3) Blue-Ribbon Bunny
Handcrafted • N/A
495QSM8064 • **Value $12**

(4) Busy Bakers (set/2)
Handcrafted • N/A
795QFM8121 • **Value $14**

(5) Cowboy Cameron (set/3)
Handcrafted • N/A
1295QFM8041 • **Value $27**

(6) Easter Egg Hunt
Handcrafted • N/A
495QSM8024 • **Value $15**

(7) Giving Thanks (set/3)
Handcrafted • N/A
1295QFM8134 • **Value $24**

1996 COLLECTION

	Price Paid	Value of My Collection
1.		
2.		
3.		
4.		
5.		
6.		
7.		
8.		
9.		
10.		
11.		
12.		
13.		
14.		
15.		
16.		
17.		

(8) Happy Birthday Clowns (set/2, 2nd, *Happy Birthday Clowns*)
Handcrafted • N/A
795QSM8114 • **Value $15**

(9) Happy Haunting (set/2)
Handcrafted • N/A
1295QFM8124 • **Value $25**

(10) Lucky Cameron (set/2)
Handcrafted • N/A
795QSM8021 • **Value $16**

(11) Mr. and Mrs. Claus Bears (set/2)
Handcrafted • N/A
795QFM8044 • **Value $17**

(12) Noah and Friends (set/5)
Handcrafted • N/A
1995QSM8111 • **Value $32**

(13) PEANUTS® Pumpkin Patch (set/5)
Handcrafted • N/A
1995QFM8131 • **Value $35**

(14) Penda Kids (set/2)
Handcrafted • N/A
795QSM8011 • **Value $15**

(15) Santa's Helpers (set/3)
Handcrafted • N/A
1295QFM8051 • **Value $23**

(16) The Sewing Club (set/3)
Handcrafted • N/A
1295QFM8061 • **Value $23**

1995 COLLECTION

18.		

PENCIL TOTALS

(17) Sweetheart Cruise (set/3)
Handcrafted • N/A
1295QSM8004 • **Value $22**

1995

(18) Bashful Boy
Handcrafted • N/A
300QSM8107 • **Value $16**

Value Guide – Merry Miniatures

1 Bashful Girl *Handcrafted* • N/A 300QSM8109 • **Value $16**	**2** Beauregard *Handcrafted* • N/A 300QSM8047 • **Value N/E**	**3** Birthday Bear (1st, *Happy Birthday Clowns*) *Handcrafted* • N/A 375QSM8057 • **Value $15**	**4** Bride & Groom *Handcrafted* • N/A 375QSM8067 • **Value $15**
5 Cameron *Handcrafted* • N/A 375QSM8009 • **Value $20**	**6** Cameron/Bunny *Handcrafted* • N/A 375QSM8029 • **Value $20**	**7** Cameron in Pumpkin Costume *Handcrafted* • N/A 375QFM8147 • **Value $17**	**8** Cameron on Sled *Handcrafted* • N/A 375QFM8199 • **Value $14**
9 Cameron Pilgrim *Handcrafted* • N/A 375QFM8169 • **Value $17**	**10** Cameron w/Camera *Handcrafted* • N/A 375QSM8077 • **Value $18**	**11** Caroling Bear *Handcrafted* • N/A 325QFM8307 • **Value $13**	
12 Caroling Bunny *Handcrafted* • N/A 325QFM8309 • **Value $13**	**13** Caroling Mouse *Handcrafted* • N/A 300QFM8317 • **Value $12**	**14** Chipmunk with Corn *Handcrafted* • N/A 375QFM8179 • **Value $12**	
15 Christmas Tree *Handcrafted* • N/A 675QFM8197 • **Value $18**	**16** Cinderella *Handcrafted* • N/A 400QSM8117 • **Value $40**	**17** Cottage *Handcrafted* • N/A 675QSM8027 • **Value $21**	
18 Cute Witch *Handcrafted* • N/A 300QFM8157 • **Value $11**	**19** Fairy Godmother *Handcrafted* • N/A 400QSM8089 • **Value $22**	**20** Feast Table *Handcrafted* • N/A 475QFM8167 • **Value $13**	

1995 Collection

	Price Paid	Value of My Collection
1.		
2.		
3.		
4.		
5.		
6.		
7.		
8.		
9.		
10.		
11.		
12.		
13.		
14.		
15.		
16.		
17.		
18.		
19.		
20.		
PENCIL TOTALS		

MERRY MINIATURES

VALUE GUIDE — MERRY MINIATURES

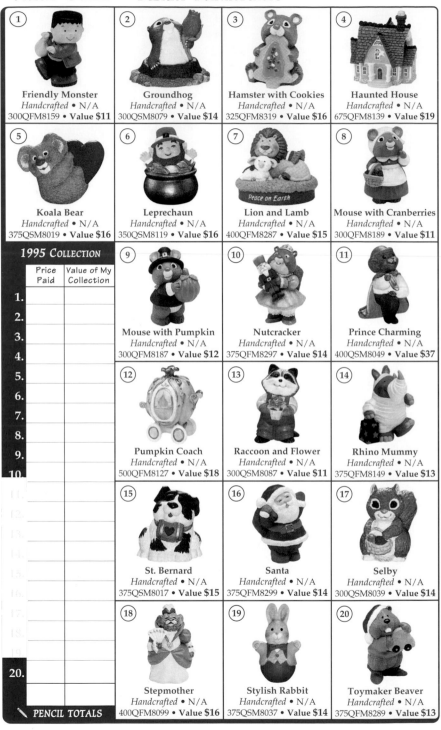

1 Friendly Monster
Handcrafted • N/A
300QFM8159 • **Value $11**

2 Groundhog
Handcrafted • N/A
300QSM8079 • **Value $14**

3 Hamster with Cookies
Handcrafted • N/A
325QFM8319 • **Value $16**

4 Haunted House
Handcrafted • N/A
675QFM8139 • **Value $19**

5 Koala Bear
Handcrafted • N/A
375QSM8019 • **Value $16**

6 Leprechaun
Handcrafted • N/A
350QSM8119 • **Value $16**

Peace on Earth
7 Lion and Lamb
Handcrafted • N/A
400QFM8287 • **Value $15**

8 Mouse with Cranberries
Handcrafted • N/A
300QFM8189 • **Value $11**

1995 COLLECTION

	Price Paid	Value of My Collection
1.		
2.		
3.		
4.		
5.		
6.		
7.		
8.		
9.		
10.		
11.		
12.		
13.		
14.		
15.		
16.		
17.		
18.		
19.		
20.		

PENCIL TOTALS

9 Mouse with Pumpkin
Handcrafted • N/A
300QFM8187 • **Value $12**

10 Nutcracker
Handcrafted • N/A
375QFM8297 • **Value $14**

11 Prince Charming
Handcrafted • N/A
400QSM8049 • **Value $37**

12 Pumpkin Coach
Handcrafted • N/A
500QFM8127 • **Value $18**

13 Raccoon and Flower
Handcrafted • N/A
300QSM8087 • **Value $11**

14 Rhino Mummy
Handcrafted • N/A
375QFM8149 • **Value $13**

15 St. Bernard
Handcrafted • N/A
375QSM8017 • **Value $15**

16 Santa
Handcrafted • N/A
375QFM8299 • **Value $14**

17 Selby
Handcrafted • N/A
300QSM8039 • **Value $14**

18 Stepmother
Handcrafted • N/A
400QFM8099 • **Value $16**

19 Stylish Rabbit
Handcrafted • N/A
375QSM8037 • **Value $14**

20 Toymaker Beaver
Handcrafted • N/A
375QFM8289 • **Value $13**

(1) Tree
Handcrafted • N/A
675QSM8007 • **Value $20**

(2) Turkey
Handcrafted • N/A
375QFM8177 • **Value $13**

1994

(3) Basket of Apples
Handcrafted • N/A
275QFM8356 • **Value $13**

(4) Bear Letter Carrier
Handcrafted • N/A
375QSM8006 • **Value $13**

(5) Bear on Skates
Handcrafted • N/A
375QFM8293 • **Value $14**

(6) Bear with Flag
Handcrafted • N/A
375QSM8043 • **Value $22**

(7) Beaver
Handcrafted • N/A
375QFM8336 • **Value $14**

(8) Beaver
Handcrafted • N/A
375QSM8013 • **Value $12**

(9) Birds in Nest
Handcrafted • N/A
375QSM8116 • **Value $14**

(10) Black Kitten
Handcrafted • N/A
325QFM8273 • **Value $12**

(11) Bunny Alien
Handcrafted • N/A
375QFM8266 • **Value $15**

(12) Chick in Wagon
Handcrafted • N/A
375QSM8123 • **Value $20**

(13) Chipmunk with Kite
Handcrafted • N/A
300QSM8003 • **Value $16**

(14) Corn Stalk
Handcrafted • N/A
675QFM8363 • **Value $19**

(15) Dock
Handcrafted • N/A
675QSM8076 • **Value $23**

(16) Document
Handcrafted • N/A
275QSM8053 • **Value $15**

(17) Eagle with Hat
Handcrafted • N/A
375QSM8036 • **Value $15**

(18) Fence with Lantern
Handcrafted • N/A
675QFM8283 • **Value $18**

(19) Flag
Handcrafted • N/A
675QSM8056 • **Value $23**

1995 COLLECTION

	Price Paid	Value of My Collection
1.		
2.		

1994 COLLECTION

3.		
4.		
5.		
6.		
7.		
8.		
9.		
10.		
11.		
12.		
13.		
14.		
15.		
16.		
17.		
18.		
19.		
PENCIL TOTALS		

MERRY MINIATURES

(1) Fox on Skates *Handcrafted* • N/A 375QFM8303 • **Value $14**	**(2)** Indian Bunny *Handcrafted* • N/A 275QFM8353 • **Value $11**	**(3)** Indian Chickadee *Handcrafted* • N/A 325QFM8346 • **Value $14**	**(4)** Lamb *Handcrafted* • N/A 325QSM8132• **Value $12**
(5) Mailbox *Handcrafted* • N/A 675QSM8023 • **Value $15**	**(6)** Mouse with Flower *Handcrafted* • N/A 275QSM8243 • **Value $13**	**(7)** Mrs. Claus *Handcrafted* • N/A 375QFM8286 • **Value $17**	**(8)** North Pole Sign *Handcrafted* • N/A 675QFM8333 • **Value $19**

1994 COLLECTION

	Price Paid	Value of My Collection
1.		
2.		
3.		
4.		
5.		
6.		
7.		
8.		
9.		
10.		
11.		
12.		
13.		
14.		
15.		
16.		
17.		
18.		
19.		
20.		

PENCIL TOTALS

(9) Owl in Stump *Handcrafted* • N/A 275QSM8243 • **Value $13**	**(10)** Pail of Seashells *Handcrafted* • N/A 275QSM8052 • **Value $14**	**(11)** Penguin *Handcrafted* • N/A 275QFM8313 • **Value $18**
(12) Pilgrim Bunny *Handcrafted* • N/A 375QFM8343 • **Value $13**	**(13)** Polar Bears *Handcrafted* • N/A 325QFM8323 • **Value $16**	**(14)** Pumpkin with Hat *Handcrafted* • N/A 275QFM8276 • **Value $12**
(15) Rabbit *Handcrafted* • N/A 275QSM8066 • **Value $13**	**(16)** Rabbit *Handcrafted* • N/A 325QSM8016 • **Value $12**	**(17)** Rabbit with Can *Handcrafted* • N/A 325QSM8083 • **Value $13**
(18) Rabbit with Croquet *Handcrafted* • N/A 375QSM8113 • **Value $10**	**(19)** Raccoon *Handcrafted* • N/A 375QSM8063 • **Value $20**	**(20)** Sled Dog *Handcrafted* • N/A 325QFM8306 • **Value $16**

①
Snowman
Handcrafted • N/A
275QFM8316 • **Value $11**

②
Squirrel as Clown
Handcrafted • N/A
375QFM8263 • **Value $14**

③
Tree
Handcrafted • N/A
275QFM8326 • **Value $11**

④
Wishing Well
Handcrafted • N/A
675QSM8033 • **Value $22**

1993

⑤

⑥

⑦

Animated Cauldron
Handcrafted • N/A
250QFM8425 • **Value $14**

Arctic Fox
Handcrafted • N/A
350QFM8242 • **Value $16**

Arctic Scene Backdrop
Paper • N/A
175QFM8205 • **Value $7**

⑧
Baby Walrus
Handcrafted • N/A
300QFM8232 • **Value $11**

⑨
Baby Whale
Handcrafted • N/A
350QFM8222 • **Value $11**

⑩
Beach Scene Backdrop
Paper • N/A
175QSM8042 • **Value $8**

⑪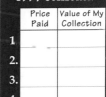
Bear dressed as Bat
Handcrafted • N/A
300QFM8285 • **Value $10**

⑫
Bear with Surfboard
Handcrafted • N/A
350QSM8015 • **Value $15**

⑬
Betsey Ross Lamb
Handcrafted • N/A
350QSM8482 • **Value $17**

⑭
Bobcat Pilgrim
Handcrafted • N/A
350QFM8172 • **Value $15**

⑮
Box of Candy
Handcrafted • N/A
250QSM8095 • **Value $21**

⑯
Bunny Painting Egg
Handcrafted • N/A
350QSM8115 • **Value $10**

⑰
Bunny with Basket
Handcrafted • N/A
250QSM8142 • **Value $13**

⑱
Bunny with Egg
Handcrafted • N/A
300QSM8125 • **Value $12**

⑲
Bunny with Scarf
Handcrafted • N/A
250QFM8235 • **Value $16**

1994 COLLECTION

	Price Paid	Value of My Collection
1		
2.		
3.		
4.		

1993 COLLECTION

5.		
6.		
7.		
8.		
9.		
10.		
11.		
12.		
13.		
14.		
15.		
16.		
17.		
18.		
19.		
PENCIL TOTALS		

MERRY MINIATURES

VALUE GUIDE — MERRY MINIATURES

(1) Bunny with Seashell
Handcrafted • N/A
350QSM8005 • **Value $20**

(2) Cat & Mouse (3rd & final, *Hugs and Kisses***)**
Handcrafted • N/A
350QSM8102 • **Value $16**

(3) Chipmunk
Handcrafted • N/A
350QSM8002 • **Value $16**

(4) Display Stand
Handcrafted • N/A
675QFM8055 • **Value $10**

(5) Dog with Balloon
Handcrafted • N/A
250QSM8092 • **Value $10**

(6) Dragon Dog
Handcrafted • N/A
300QFM8295 • **Value $10**

(7) Duck with Egg
Handcrafted • N/A
300QSM8135 • **Value $11**

(8) Easter Basket
Handcrafted • N/A
250QSM8145 • **Value $15**

1993 COLLECTION

	Price Paid	Value of My Collection
1.		
2.		
3.		
4.		
5.		
6.		
7.		
8.		
9.		
10.		
11.		
12.		
13.		
14.		
15.		
16.		
17.		
18.		
19.		
20.		
PENCIL TOTALS		

(9) Easter Garden Backdrop
Paper • N/A
175QSM8152 • **Value $7**

(10) Eskimo Child
Handcrafted • N/A
300QFM8215 • **Value $21**

(11) Fox with Heart
Handcrafted • N/A
350QSM8065 • **Value $11**

(12) Ghost on Tombstone
Handcrafted • N/A
250QFM8282 • **Value $9**

(13) Goat Uncle Sam
Handcrafted • N/A
300QSM8472 • **Value $15**

(14) Haunted Halloween Backdrop
Paper • N/A
175QFM8275 • **Value $7**

(15) Heartland Forest Backdrop
Paper • N/A
175QSM8082 • **Value $7**

(16) Hedgehog
Handcrafted • N/A
300QSM8026 • **Value $15**

(17) Hedgehog Patriot
Handcrafted • N/A
350QSM8492 • **Value $13**

(18) Hippo
Handcrafted • N/A
300QSM8032 • **Value $14**

(19) Husky Puppy
Handcrafted • N/A
350QFM8245 • **Value $13**

(20) Igloo
Handcrafted • N/A
300QFM8252 • **Value $18**

Value Guide — Merry Miniatures

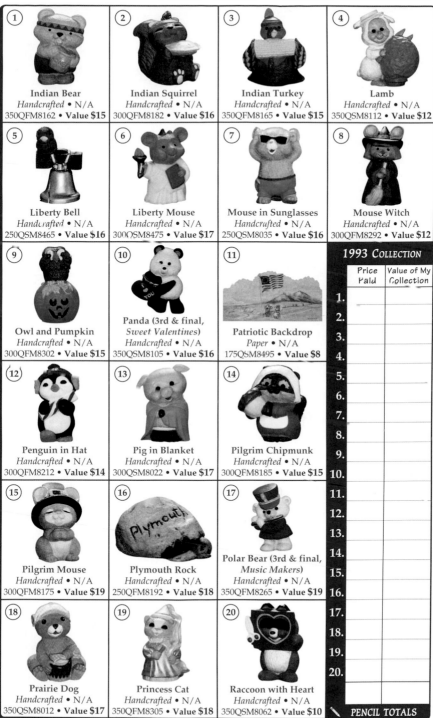

1 Indian Bear
Handcrafted • N/A
350QFM8162 • **Value $15**

2 Indian Squirrel
Handcrafted • N/A
300QFM8182 • **Value $16**

3 Indian Turkey
Handcrafted • N/A
350QFM8165 • **Value $15**

4 Lamb
Handcrafted • N/A
350QSM8112 • **Value $12**

5 Liberty Bell
Handcrafted • N/A
250QSM8465 • **Value $16**

6 Liberty Mouse
Handcrafted • N/A
300QSM8475 • **Value $17**

7 Mouse in Sunglasses
Handcrafted • N/A
250QSM8035 • **Value $16**

8 Mouse Witch
Handcrafted • N/A
300QFM8292 • **Value $12**

9 Owl and Pumpkin
Handcrafted • N/A
300QFM8302 • **Value $15**

10 Panda (3rd & final, *Sweet Valentines*)
Handcrafted • N/A
350QSM8105 • **Value $16**

11 Patriotic Backdrop
Paper • N/A
175QSM8495 • **Value $8**

12 Penguin in Hat
Handcrafted • N/A
300QFM8212 • **Value $14**

13 Pig in Blanket
Handcrafted • N/A
300QSM8022 • **Value $17**

14 Pilgrim Chipmunk
Handcrafted • N/A
300QFM8185 • **Value $15**

15 Pilgrim Mouse
Handcrafted • N/A
300QFM8175 • **Value $19**

16 Plymouth Rock
Handcrafted • N/A
250QFM8192 • **Value $18**

17 Polar Bear (3rd & final, *Music Makers*)
Handcrafted • N/A
350QFM8265 • **Value $19**

18 Prairie Dog
Handcrafted • N/A
350QSM8012 • **Value $17**

19 Princess Cat
Handcrafted • N/A
350QFM8305 • **Value $18**

20 Raccoon with Heart
Handcrafted • N/A
350QSM8062 • **Value $10**

1993 Collection

	Price Paid	Value of My Collection
1.		
2.		
3.		
4.		
5.		
6.		
7.		
8.		
9.		
10.		
11.		
12.		
13.		
14.		
15.		
16.		
17.		
18.		
19.		
20.		
PENCIL TOTALS		

MERRY MINIATURES

VALUE GUIDE — MERRY MINIATURES

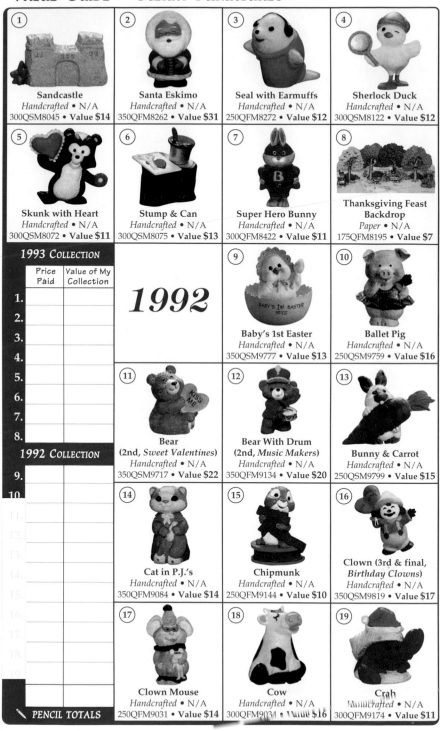

① Sandcastle
Handcrafted • N/A
300QSM8045 • **Value $14**

② Santa Eskimo
Handcrafted • N/A
350QFM8262 • **Value $31**

③ Seal with Earmuffs
Handcrafted • N/A
250QFM8272 • **Value $12**

④ Sherlock Duck
Handcrafted • N/A
300QSM8122 • **Value $12**

⑤ Skunk with Heart
Handcrafted • N/A
300QSM8072 • **Value $11**

⑥ Stump & Can
Handcrafted • N/A
300QSM8075 • **Value $13**

⑦ Super Hero Bunny
Handcrafted • N/A
300QFM8422 • **Value $11**

⑧ Thanksgiving Feast Backdrop
Paper • N/A
175QFM8195 • **Value $7**

1993 COLLECTION

	Price Paid	Value of My Collection
1.		
2.		
3.		
4.		
5.		
6.		
7.		
8.		

1992 COLLECTION

9.		
10.		
11.		
12.		
13.		
14.		
15.		
16.		
17.		
18.		
19.		

1992

⑨ Baby's 1st Easter
Handcrafted • N/A
350QSM9777 • **Value $13**

⑩ Ballet Pig
Handcrafted • N/A
250QSM9759 • **Value $16**

⑪ Bear
(2nd, *Sweet Valentines*)
Handcrafted • N/A
350QSM9717 • **Value $22**

⑫ Bear With Drum
(2nd, *Music Makers*)
Handcrafted • N/A
350QFM9134 • **Value $20**

⑬ Bunny & Carrot
Handcrafted • N/A
250QSM9799 • **Value $15**

⑭ Cat in P.J.'s
Handcrafted • N/A
350QFM9084 • **Value $14**

⑮ Chipmunk
Handcrafted • N/A
250QFM9144 • **Value $10**

⑯ Clown (3rd & final, *Birthday Clowns*)
Handcrafted • N/A
350QSM9819 • **Value $17**

⑰ Clown Mouse
Handcrafted • N/A
250QFM9031 • **Value $14**

⑱ Cow
Handcrafted • N/A
300QFM9031 • **Value $16**

⑲ Crab
Handcrafted • N/A
300QFM9174 • **Value $11**

✎ PENCIL TOTALS

Value Guide — Merry Miniatures

1
Dog
Handcrafted • N/A
300QSM9847 • **Value $18**

2
Dog in P.J.'s
Handcrafted • N/A
350QFM9081 • **Value $13**

3
Ghost with Corn Candy
Handcrafted • N/A
300QFM9014 • **Value $15**

4
Giraffe as Tree
Handcrafted • N/A
300QFM9141 • **Value $15**

5
Goldfish
Handcrafted • N/A
300QFM9181 • **Value $12**

6
Goose in Bonnet
Handcrafted • N/A
300QSM9789 • **Value $13**

7
Grad Dog
Handcrafted • N/A
250QSM9817 • **Value $13**

8
Haunted House
Handcrafted • N/A
350QFM9024 • **Value $14**

9
Hedgehog
Handcrafted • N/A
250QSM9859 • **Value $13**

10
Horse
Handcrafted • N/A
300QFM9051 • **Value $20**

11
Indian Bunnies
Handcrafted • N/A
350QFM9004 • **Value $15**

12
Kitten for Dad
Handcrafted • N/A
350QSM9839 • **Value $15**

13
Kitten for Mom
Handcrafted • N/A
350QSM9837 • **Value $15**

14
Kitten in Bib
Handcrafted • N/A
350QSM9829 • **Value $13**

15
Lamb
Handcrafted • N/A
250QFM9044 • **Value $17**

16
Lamb
Handcrafted • N/A
350QSM9787 • **Value $15**

17
Lion
Handcrafted • N/A
350QSM9719 • **Value $14**

18
Mouse
Handcrafted • N/A
300QSM9769 • **Value $12**

19
Mouse in Car
Handcrafted • N/A
300QFM9114 • **Value $13**

20
Nina Ship
Handcrafted • N/A
350QFM9154 • **Value $12**

1992 Collection

	Price Paid	Value of My Collection
1.		
2.		
3.		
4.		
5.		
6.		
7.		
8.		
9.		
10.		
11.		
12.		
13.		
14.		
15.		
16.		
17.		
18.		
19.		
20.		
PENCIL TOTALS		

MERRY MINIATURES

1. Octopus
Handcrafted • N/A
300QFM9171 • **Value $13**

2. Party Dog
Handcrafted • N/A
300QFM9191 • **Value $13**

3. Penguin in Tux
Handcrafted • N/A
300QSM9757 • **Value $16**

4. Penguin Skating
Handcrafted • N/A
350QFM9091 • **Value $15**

5. Pig
Handcrafted • N/A
250QFM9041 • **Value $20**

6. Pilgrim Beaver
Handcrafted • N/A
300QFM9011 • **Value $13**

7. Pinta Ship
Handcrafted • N/A
350QFM9161 • **Value $12**

8. Praying Chipmunk
Handcrafted • N/A
300QSM9797 • **Value $15**

9. Pumpkin
Handcrafted • N/A
300QFM9021 • **Value $13**

10. Puppy
Handcrafted • N/A
250QSM9767 • **Value $17**

11. Rabbit & Squirrel
(2nd, *Hugs and Kisses*)
Handcrafted • N/A
350QSM9827 • **Value $21**

12. Rabbit Holding
Heart Carrot
Handcrafted • N/A
350QFM9201 • **Value $15**

13. Rabbit On Sled
Handcrafted • N/A
300QFM9151 • **Value $12**

14. Santa Bee
Handcrafted • N/A
300QFM9061 • **Value $12**

15. Santa Bell (3rd & final,
Jingle Bell Santa)
Handcrafted • N/A
350QFM9131 • **Value $20**

16. Santa Maria Ship
Handcrafted • N/A
350QFM9164 • **Value $12**

17. Seal
Handcrafted • N/A
300QSM9849 • **Value $13**

18. Skunk with Butterfly
Handcrafted • N/A
350QFM9184 • **Value $13**

19. Snow Bunny
Handcrafted • N/A
400QFM9071 • **Value $12**

20. Squirrel Pal (3rd &
final, *Gentle Pals*)
Handcrafted • N/A
350QFM9094 • **Value $21**

1992 Collection

	Price Paid	Value of My Collection
1.		
2.		
3.		
4.		
5.		
6.		
7.		
8.		
9.		
10.		
11.		
12.		
13.		
14.		
15.		
16.		
17.		
18.		
19.		
20.		
PENCIL TOTALS		

1 Squirrels in Nutshell
Handcrafted • N/A
350QFM9064 • **Value $14**

2 Sweatshirt Bunny
Handcrafted • N/A
350QSM9779 • **Value $17**

3 Sweet Angel
Handcrafted • N/A
300QFM9124 • **Value $16**

4 Teacher Cat
Handcrafted • N/A
350QFM9074 • **Value $10**

5 Teddy Bear
Handcrafted • N/A
250QFM9194 • **Value $15**

6 Thankful Turkey (3rd & final, *Thankful Turkey*)
Handcrafted • N/A
350QFM9001 • **Value $23**

7 Turtle & Mouse
Handcrafted • N/A
300QSM9857 • **Value $26**

8 Walrus & Bird
Handcrafted • N/A
350QFM9054 • **Value $16**

9 Waving Reindeer
Handcrafted • N/A
300QFM9121 • **Value $15**

1991

10 1st Christmas Together
Handcrafted • N/A
350QFM1799 • **Value $13**

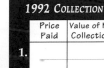

11 Aerobic Bunny
Handcrafted • N/A
250QFM1817 • **Value $20**

12 Artist Mouse
Handcrafted • N/A
250QSM1519 • **Value $16**

13 Baby Bunny
Handcrafted • N/A
350QSM1619 • **Value $13**

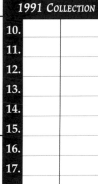

14 Baby's 1st Christmas
Handcrafted • N/A
300QFM1797 • **Value $11**

15 Baby's 1st Easter
Handcrafted • N/A
300QSM1557 • **Value $15**

16 Backpack Chipmunk
Handcrafted • N/A
250QFM1809 • **Value $17**

17 Baseball Bear
Handcrafted • N/A
300QFM1827 • **Value $23**

18 Bear
Handcrafted • N/A
250QFM1669 • **Value $25**

19 Bear
(also avail. in Carousel Set, #2000QSM1667)
Handcrafted • N/A
300QSM1637 • **Value $13**

1992 COLLECTION	
	Price Paid	Value of My Collection
1.		
2.		
3.		
4.		
5.		
6.		
7.		
8.		
9.		
1991 COLLECTION		
10.		
11.		
12.		
13.		
14.		
15.		
16.		
17.		
18.		
19.		
PENCIL TOTALS		

MERRY MINIATURES

1 — Bear
(1st, *Sweet Valentines*)
Handcrafted • N/A
350QSM1509 • **Value $24**

2 — Bears Hugging
(1st, *Hugs and Kisses*)
Handcrafted • N/A
350QSM1609 • **Value $25**

3 — Birthday Clown
(2nd, *Birthday Clowns*)
Handcrafted • N/A
350QSM1617 • **Value $21**

4 — Bunny
Handcrafted • N/A
300QFM1719 • **Value $12**

5 — Bunny
Handcrafted • N/A
300QSM1537 • **Value $16**

6 — Bunny Praying
Handcrafted • N/A
250QSM1597 • **Value $17**

7 — Camel
(also avail. in Carousel
Set, #2000QSM1667)
Handcrafted • N/A
300QSM1629 • **Value $13**

8 — Carousel Display
(also avail. in Carousel
Set, #2000QSM1667)
Handcrafted • N/A
500QSM1627 • **Value $17**

1991 Collection

	Price Paid	Value of My Collection
1.		
2.		
3.		
4.		
5.		
6.		
7.		
8.		
9.		
10.		
11.		
12.		
13.		
14.		
15.		
16.		
17.		
18.		
19.		
20.		

PENCIL TOTALS

9 — Cat Witch
Handcrafted • N/A
300QFM1677 • **Value $16**

10 — Cookie Elf
Handcrafted • N/A
300QFM1769 • **Value $12**

11 — Cookie Reindeer
Handcrafted • N/A
300QFM1777 • **Value $12**

12 — Cookie Santa
Handcrafted • N/A
300QFM1767 • **Value $12**

13 — Daughter Bunny
Handcrafted • N/A
250QSM1587 • **Value $15**

14 — Dog in Cap & Gown
Handcrafted • N/A
250QSM1607 • **Value $15**

15 — Duck
Handcrafted • N/A
300QSM1549 • **Value $21**

16 — Elephant
(also avail. in Carousel
Set, #2000QSM1667)
Handcrafted • N/A
300QSM1647 • **Value $14**

17 — Football Beaver
Handcrafted • N/A
350QFM1829 • **Value $24**

18 — Fox
Handcrafted • N/A
350QFM1689 • **Value $13**

19 — Frog
Handcrafted • N/A
300QFM1729 • **Value $13**

20 — Gentle Pals Kitten
(2nd, *Gentle Pals*)
Handcrafted • N/A
350QFM1709 • **Value $19**

1
Horse
(also avail. in Carousel
Set, #2000QSM1667)
Handcrafted • N/A
300QSM1649 • **Value $25**

2
I Love Dad
Handcrafted • N/A
250QSM1657 • **Value $14**

3
I Love Mom
Handcrafted • N/A
250QSM1659 • **Value $14**

4
Indian Maiden
Handcrafted • N/A
250QFM1687 • **Value $12**

5
Irish Frog
Handcrafted • N/A
350QSM1539 • **Value $16**

6
Jingle Bell Santa
(2nd, *Jingle Bell Santa*)
Handcrafted • N/A
350QFM1717 • **Value $24**

7
Kitten
Handcrafted • N/A
300QFM1737 • **Value $13**

8
Lamb & Duck
Handcrafted • N/A
350QSM1569 • **Value $16**

9
Lion
(also avail. in Carousel
Set, #2000QSM1667)
Handcrafted • N/A
300QSM1639 • **Value $20**

10
Mother Bunny
Handcrafted • N/A
300QSM1577 • **Value $16**

11
Mouse
Handcrafted • N/A
250QFM1789 • **Value $15**

12
Mummy
Handcrafted • N/A
250QFM1679 • **Value $15**

13
Music Makers Bear
(1st, *Music Makers*)
Handcrafted • N/A
300QFM1779 • **Value $23**

14
Pig
Handcrafted • N/A
300QFM1739 • **Value $15**

15
Puppy
Handcrafted • N/A
300QFM1727 • **Value $15**

16
Puppy
Handcrafted • N/A
300QFM1787 • **Value $14**

17
Puppy
Handcrafted • N/A
300QSM1529 • **Value $26**

18
Raccoon Thief
Handcrafted • N/A
350QSM1517 • **Value $13**

19
Skating Raccoon
Handcrafted • N/A
350QFM1837 • **Value $23**

20
Snow Bunny
Handcrafted • N/A
250QFM1749 • **Value $13**

1991 COLLECTION

	Price Paid	Value of My Collection
1.		
2.		
3.		
4.		
5.		
6.		
7.		
8.		
9.		
10.		
11.		
12.		
13.		
14.		
15.		
16.		
17.		
18.		
19.		
20.		
PENCIL TOTALS		

MERRY MINIATURES

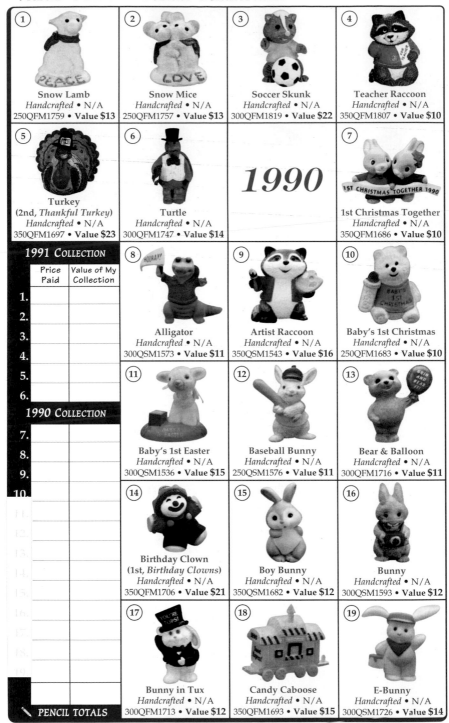

(1) **Snow Lamb** Handcrafted • N/A 250QFM1759 • **Value $13**	**(2)** **Snow Mice** Handcrafted • N/A 250QFM1757 • **Value $13**	**(3)** **Soccer Skunk** Handcrafted • N/A 300QFM1819 • **Value $22**	**(4)** **Teacher Raccoon** Handcrafted • N/A 350QFM1807 • **Value $10**
(5) **Turkey** (2nd, *Thankful Turkey*) Handcrafted • N/A 350QFM1697 • **Value $23**	**(6)** **Turtle** Handcrafted • N/A 300QFM1747 • **Value $14**	*1990*	**(7)** **1st Christmas Together** Handcrafted • N/A 350QFM1686 • **Value $10**

1991 COLLECTION

	Price Paid	Value of My Collection
1.		
2.		
3.		
4.		
5.		
6.		

1990 COLLECTION

7.		
8.		
9.		
10.		

(8) **Alligator** Handcrafted • N/A 300QSM1573 • **Value $11**	**(9)** **Artist Raccoon** Handcrafted • N/A 350QSM1543 • **Value $16**	**(10)** **Baby's 1st Christmas** Handcrafted • N/A 250QFM1683 • **Value $10**
(11) **Baby's 1st Easter** Handcrafted • N/A 300QSM1536 • **Value $15**	**(12)** **Baseball Bunny** Handcrafted • N/A 250QSM1576 • **Value $11**	**(13)** **Bear & Balloon** Handcrafted • N/A 300QFM1716 • **Value $11**
(14) **Birthday Clown** (1st, *Birthday Clowns*) Handcrafted • N/A 350QFM1706 • **Value $21**	**(15)** **Boy Bunny** Handcrafted • N/A 350QSM1682 • **Value $12**	**(16)** **Bunny** Handcrafted • N/A 300QSM1593 • **Value $12**
(17) **Bunny in Tux** Handcrafted • N/A 300QFM1713 • **Value $12**	**(18)** **Candy Caboose** Handcrafted • N/A 350QFM1693 • **Value $15**	**(19)** **E-Bunny** Handcrafted • N/A 300QSM1726 • **Value $14**

PENCIL TOTALS

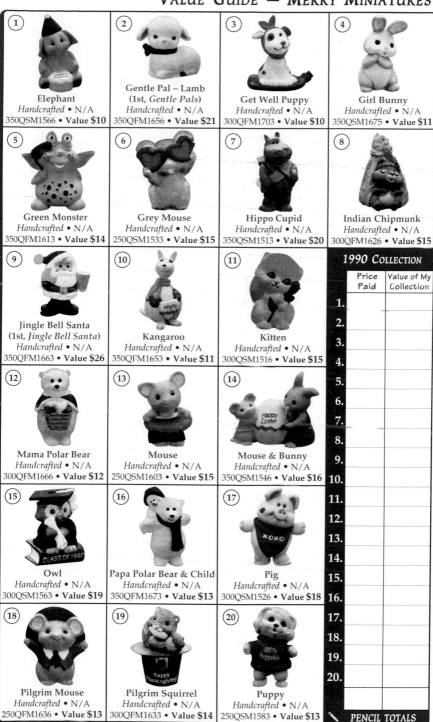

1 Elephant
Handcrafted • N/A
350QSM1566 • **Value $10**

2 Gentle Pal – Lamb
(1st, *Gentle Pals*)
Handcrafted • N/A
350QFM1656 • **Value $21**

3 Get Well Puppy
Handcrafted • N/A
300QFM1703 • **Value $10**

4 Girl Bunny
Handcrafted • N/A
350QSM1675 • **Value $11**

5 Green Monster
Handcrafted • N/A
350QFM1613 • **Value $14**

6 Grey Mouse
Handcrafted • N/A
250QSM1533 • **Value $15**

7 Hippo Cupid
Handcrafted • N/A
350QSM1513 • **Value $20**

8 Indian Chipmunk
Handcrafted • N/A
300QFM1626 • **Value $15**

9 Jingle Bell Santa
(1st, *Jingle Bell Santa*)
Handcrafted • N/A
350QFM1663 • **Value $26**

10 Kangaroo
Handcrafted • N/A
350QFM1653 • **Value $11**

11 Kitten
Handcrafted • N/A
300QSM1516 • **Value $15**

12 Mama Polar Bear
Handcrafted • N/A
300QFM1666 • **Value $12**

13 Mouse
Handcrafted • N/A
250QSM1603 • **Value $15**

14 Mouse & Bunny
Handcrafted • N/A
350QSM1546 • **Value $16**

15 Owl
Handcrafted • N/A
300QSM1563 • **Value $19**

16 Papa Polar Bear & Child
Handcrafted • N/A
350QFM1673 • **Value $13**

17 Pig
Handcrafted • N/A
300QSM1526 • **Value $18**

18 Pilgrim Mouse
Handcrafted • N/A
250QFM1636 • **Value $13**

19 Pilgrim Squirrel
Handcrafted • N/A
300QFM1633 • **Value $14**

20 Puppy
Handcrafted • N/A
250QSM1583 • **Value $13**

1990 Collection

	Price Paid	Value of My Collection
1.		
2.		
3.		
4.		
5.		
6.		
7.		
8.		
9.		
10.		
11.		
12.		
13.		
14.		
15.		
16.		
17.		
18.		
19.		
20.		
PENCIL TOTALS		

Merry Miniatures

① Raccoon
Handcrafted • N/A
350QSM1586 • **Value $14**

② Scarecrow
Handcrafted • N/A
350QFM1616 • **Value $14**

③ Snowman
Handcrafted • N/A
250QFM1646 • **Value $14**

④ Squirrel
Handcrafted • N/A
250QSM1553 • **Value $20**

⑤ Squirrel Caroler
Handcrafted • N/A
300QFM1696 • **Value $20**

⑥ Squirrel Hobo
Handcrafted • N/A
300QFM1606 • **Value $14**

⑦ Stitched Teddy
Handcrafted • N/A
350QSM1506 • **Value $28**

⑧ Teacher Mouse
Handcrafted • N/A
300QFM1676 • **Value $10**

⑨ Thankful Turkey
(1st, *Thankful Turkey*)
Handcrafted • N/A
350QFM1623 • **Value $24**

⑩ Walrus
Handcrafted • N/A
250QFM1643 • **Value $14**

1989

⑪ Baby Boy
Handcrafted • N/A
300QFM1585 • **Value $20**

⑫ Baby Girl
Handcrafted • N/A
300QFM1592 • **Value $20**

⑬ Baby's 1st Christmas
Handcrafted • N/A
300QFM1615 • **Value $15**

⑭ Bear
Handcrafted • N/A
250QSM1525 • **Value $21**

⑮ Bear Baker
Handcrafted • N/A
350QSM1522 • **Value $20**

⑯ Blue King
(also avail. in Nativity Set, #3550QFM1685)
Handcrafted • N/A
300QFM1632 • **Value $25**

⑰ Bunny
Handcrafted • N/A
250QSM1512 • **Value $19**

⑱ Bunny
Handcrafted • N/A
300QFM1565 • **Value $13**

⑲ Bunny
Handcrafted • N/A
350QSM1552 • **Value $16**

1990 COLLECTION

	Price Paid	Value of My Collection
1.		
2.		
3.		
4.		
5.		
6.		
7.		
8.		
9.		
10.		

1989 COLLECTION

11.		
12.		
13.		
14.		
15.		
16.		
17.		
18.		

PENCIL TOTALS

1
Bunny & Skateboard
Handcrafted • N/A
350EBO3092 • **Value $29**

2
Bunny Caroler
Handcrafted • N/A
300QFM1662 • **Value $22**

3
Dog & Kitten
Handcrafted • N/A
350QSM1515 • **Value $33**

4
Elf
Handcrafted • N/A
300QFM1622 • **Value $16**

5
Grey Mouse
Handcrafted • N/A
250QSM1502 • **Value $23**

6
Joy Elf
Handcrafted • N/A
300QFM1605 • **Value $14**

7
Kitten
Handcrafted • N/A
250QSM1505 • **Value $26**

8
Lamb
Handcrafted • N/A
350QSM1545 • **Value $22**

9
Momma Bear
Handcrafted • N/A
350QFM1582 • **Value $18**

10
Mouse
Handcrafted • N/A
250QFM1572 • **Value $21**

11
Mouse Caroler
Handcrafted • N/A
250QFM1655 • **Value $22**

12
Mr. Claus
Handcrafted • N/A
350QFM1595 • **Value $15**

13
Mrs. Claus
Handcrafted • N/A
350QFM1602 • **Value $15**

14
Owl
Handcrafted • N/A
250QSM1555 • **Value $18**

15
Pink King
(also avail. in Nativity
Set, #3550QFM1685)
Handcrafted • N/A
300QFM1642 • **Value $13**

16
Raccoon
Handcrafted • N/A
250QFM1575 • **Value $15**

17
Raccoon Caroler
Handcrafted • N/A
350QFM1652 • **Value $20**

18
Teacher Elf
Handcrafted • N/A
300QFM1612 • **Value $14**

19
Train Car
Handcrafted • N/A
350QFM1562 • **Value $16**

20
Yellow King
(also avail. in Nativity
Set, #3550QFM1685)
Handcrafted • N/A
300QFM1635 • **Value $12**

1989 COLLECTION

	Price Paid	Value of My Collection
1.		
2.		
3.		
4.		
5.		
6.		
7.		
8.		
9.		
10.		
11.		
12.		
13.		
14.		
15.		
16.		
17.		
18.		
19.		
20.		
PENCIL TOTALS		

MERRY MINIATURES

1988

(1) Dog
Handcrafted • N/A
200GHA3524 • Value **$14**

(2) Donkey
(also avail. in Nativity
Set, #3550QFM1685)
Handcrafted • N/A
225QFM1581 • Value **$10**

(3) Indian Bear
Handcrafted • N/A
325QFM1511 • Value **$18**

(4) Jesus
(also avail. in Nativity
Set, #3550QFM1685)
Handcrafted • N/A
250QFM1564 • Value **$21**

(5) Joseph
(also avail. in Nativity
Set, #3550QFM1685)
Handcrafted • N/A
250QFM1561 • Value **$12**

(6) Kitten in Slipper
Handcrafted • N/A
250QFM1544 • Value **$20**

(7) Koala & Hearts
Handcrafted • N/A
200VHA3531 • Value **$11**

(8) Koala & Lollipop
Handcrafted • N/A
200VHA3651 • Value **$23**

(9) Koala & Ruffled Heart
Handcrafted • N/A
200VHA3631 • Value **$67**

**(10) Koala with
Bow & Arrow**
Handcrafted • N/A
200VHA3624 • Value **$14**

(11) Lamb
(also avail. in Nativity
Set, #3550QFM1685)
Handcrafted • N/A
225QFM1574 • Value **$27**

(12) Mary
(also avail. in Nativity
Set, #3550QFM1685)
Handcrafted • N/A
250QFM1554 • Value **$13**

(13) Mouse Angel
Handcrafted • N/A
250QFM1551 • Value **$29**

(14) Mouse in Cornucopia
Handcrafted • N/A
225QFM1514 • Value **$15**

(15) Mouse/Pumpkin
Handcrafted • N/A
225QFM1501 • Value **$50**

(16) Owl
Handcrafted • N/A
225QFM1504 • Value **$18**

(17) Penguin
Handcrafted • N/A
375QFM1541 • Value **$23**

(18) Santa
Handcrafted • N/A
375QFM1521 • Value **$42**

(19) Shepherd
(also avail. in Nativity
Set, #3550QFM1685)
Handcrafted • N/A
250QFM1571 • Value **$11**

1988 COLLECTION

	Price Paid	Value of My Collection
1.		
2.		
3.		
4.		
5.		
6.		
7.		
8.		
9.		
10.		
11.		
12.		
13.		
14.		
15.		
16.		
17.		
18.		
19.		

PENCIL TOTALS

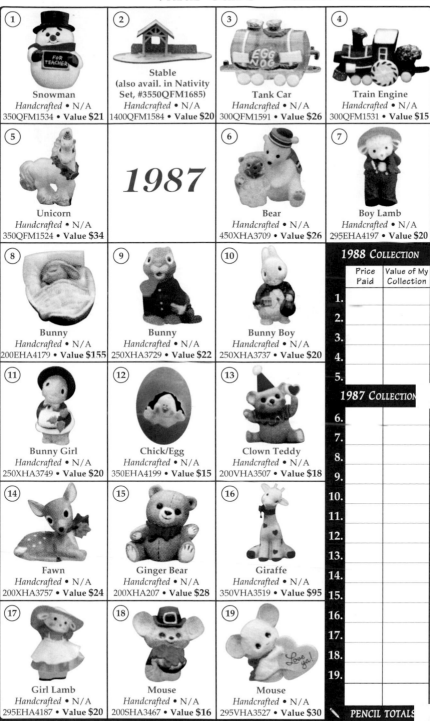

1 Snowman
Handcrafted • N/A
350QFM1534 • **Value $21**

2 Stable
(also avail. in Nativity
Set, #3550QFM1685)
Handcrafted • N/A
1400QFM1584 • **Value $20**

3 Tank Car
Handcrafted • N/A
300QFM1591 • **Value $26**

4 Train Engine
Handcrafted • N/A
300QFM1531 • **Value $15**

5 Unicorn
Handcrafted • N/A
350QFM1524 • **Value $34**

1987

6 Bear
Handcrafted • N/A
450XHA3709 • **Value $26**

7 Boy Lamb
Handcrafted • N/A
295EHA4197 • **Value $20**

8 Bunny
Handcrafted • N/A
200EHA4179 • **Value $155**

9 Bunny
Handcrafted • N/A
250XHA3729 • **Value $22**

10 Bunny Boy
Handcrafted • N/A
250XHA3737 • **Value $20**

11 Bunny Girl
Handcrafted • N/A
250XHA3749 • **Value $20**

12 Chick/Egg
Handcrafted • N/A
350EHA4199 • **Value $15**

13 Clown Teddy
Handcrafted • N/A
200VHA3507 • **Value $18**

14 Fawn
Handcrafted • N/A
200XHA3757 • **Value $24**

15 Ginger Bear
Handcrafted • N/A
200XHA207 • **Value $28**

16 Giraffe
Handcrafted • N/A
350VHA3519 • **Value $95**

17 Girl Lamb
Handcrafted • N/A
295EHA4187 • **Value $20**

18 Mouse
Handcrafted • N/A
200SHA3467 • **Value $16**

19 Mouse
Handcrafted • N/A
295VHA3527 • **Value $30**

1988 Collection	Price Paid	Value of My Collection
1.		
2.		
3.		
4.		
5.		
1987 Collection		
6.		
7.		
8.		
9.		
10.		
11.		
12.		
13.		
14.		
15.		
16.		
17.		
18.		
19.		
PENCIL TOTALS		

MERRY MINIATURES

VALUE GUIDE — MERRY MINIATURES

(1)
Puppy
Handcrafted • N/A
200XHA3769 • **Value $21**

(2)
Raccoon Witch
Handcrafted • N/A
200HHA3487 • **Value $21**

(3)
Santa
Handcrafted • N/A
350XHA3717 • **Value $43**

(4)
Sebastian
Handcrafted • N/A
200EHA4167 • **Value $55**

(5)
Turkey
Handcrafted • N/A
375THA49 • **Value $18**

1986

(6)
Boy Bunny
Handcrafted • N/A
295EPF4133 • **Value $20**

(7)
Bunny
Handcrafted • N/A
350EHA3476 • **Value $20**

1987 COLLECTION

	Price Paid	Value of My Collection
1.		
2.		
3.		
4.		
5.		

1986 COLLECTION

6.		
7.		
8.		
9.		
10.		
11.		
12.		
13.		
14.		
15.		
16.		
17.		
18.		
19.		

PENCIL TOTALS

(8)
Bunny Girl
Handcrafted • N/A
295EPF4106 • **Value $20**

(9)
Cat
Handcrafted • N/A
200HHA3486 • **Value $23**

(10)
Duck
Handcrafted • N/A
295EHA3463 • **Value $15**

(11)
Duck Sailor
Handcrafted • N/A
295EPF4113 • **Value $16**

(12)
Girl Bunny
Handcrafted • N/A
200EHA3503 • **Value $33**

(13)
Goose
Handcrafted • N/A
200EHA3516 • **Value $17**

(14)
Katybeth
Handcrafted • N/A
200XHA3666 • **Value $46**

(15)
Mouse
Handcrafted • N/A
200XHA3533 • **Value $72**

(16)
Mr. Mouse
Handcrafted • N/A
200XHA3573 • **Value $30**

(17)
Mr. Squirrel
Handcrafted • N/A
200THA3403 • **Value $20**

(18)
Mrs. Mouse
Handcrafted • N/A
200XHA3653 • **Value $30**

(19)
Mrs. Squirrel
Handcrafted • N/A
200THA3416 • **Value $20**

1
Owl
Handcrafted • N/A
200GHA3456 • **Value $16**

2
Pandas
Handcrafted • N/A
350VHA3523 • **Value $25**

3
Penguin
Handcrafted • N/A
295XHA4413 • **Value $26**

4
Rhonda
Handcrafted • N/A
350XHA3553 • **Value $42**

5
Rodney
Handcrafted • N/A
350XHA3546 • **Value $26**

6
Santa
Handcrafted • N/A
350XHA3673 • **Value $44**

7
Sebastian
Handcrafted • N/A
200VHA3516 • **Value $80**

8
Sebastian
Handcrafted • N/A
200XHA3566 • **Value $96**

9
Sheep & Bell
Handcrafted • N/A
295EPF4126 • **Value $15**

10
Unicorn
Handcrafted • N/A
200VHA3503 • **Value $16**

11
Witch
Handcrafted • N/A
300HHS3473 • **Value $100**

1985

12
Basket
Handcrafted • N/A
200EHA3495 • **Value $45**

13
Bears
Handcrafted • N/A
450XHA3392 • **Value $31**

14
Bunny
Handcrafted • N/A
200EHA3482 • **Value $38**

15
Cat
Handcrafted • N/A
200XHA3482 • **Value $45**

16
Ceramic Bunny
Handcrafted • N/A
(N/A)EPR3701 • **Value $14**

17
Goose
Handcrafted • N/A
250XHA3522 • **Value $18**

18
Horse
Handcrafted • N/A
350XHA3412 • **Value $11**

19
Kitten
Handcrafted • N/A
200VHA3495 • **Value $30**

1986 COLLECTION	Price Paid	Value of My Collection
1.		
2.		
3.		
4.		
5.		
6.		
7.		
8.		
9.		
10.		
11.		
1985 COLLECTION		
12.		
13.		
14.		
15.		
16.		
17.		
18.		
19.		
PENCIL TOTALS		

MERRY MINIATURES

Value Guide — Merry Miniatures

(1) Lamb
Handcrafted • N/A
350EHA3442 • **Value $20**

(2) Mouse
Handcrafted • N/A
350EHA3455 • **Value $25**

(3) Mouse
Handcrafted • N/A
350XHA3405 • **Value $24**

(4) Mr. Santa
Handcrafted • N/A
200XHA3495 • **Value $25**

(5) Mrs. Santa
Handcrafted • N/A
200XHA3502 • **Value $30**

(6) Rocking Horse
Handcrafted • N/A
200XHA3515 • **Value $33**

(7) Shamrock
Handcrafted • N/A
200SHA3452 • **Value $19**

(8) Skunk
Handcrafted • N/A
200VHA3482 • **Value $23**

1985 Collection

	Price Paid	Value of My Collection
1.		
2.		
3.		
4.		
5.		
6.		
7.		
8.		
9.		

1984 Collection

10.		
11.		
12.		
13.		
14.		
15.		
16.		
17.		
18.		
19.		

(9) Turkey
Handcrafted • N/A
295THA3395 • **Value $22**

1984

(10) Brown Bunny
Handcrafted • N/A
350EHA3401 • **Value $16**

(11) Chick
Handcrafted • N/A
200EHA3461 • **Value $34**

(12) Dog
Handcrafted • N/A
200VHA3451 • **Value $68**

(13) Duck
Handcrafted • N/A
200EHA3474 • **Value $35**

(14) Duck
Handcrafted • N/A
350EHA3434 • **Value $24**

(15) Hedgehog
Handcrafted • N/A
200THA3444 • **Value $20**

(16) Jack-O-Lantern
Handcrafted • N/A
200HHA3454 • **Value $26**

(17) Kitten
Handcrafted • N/A
200HHA3441 • **Value $25**

(18) Koala
Handcrafted • N/A
295XHA3401 • **Value $30**

(19) Mouse
Handcrafted • N/A
200THA3451 • **Value $47**

PENCIL TOTALS

(1) Panda
Handcrafted • N/A
200VHA3471 • **Value $28**

(2) Penguin
Handcrafted • N/A
200VHA3464 • **Value $32**

(3) Puppy
Handcrafted • N/A
200XHA3494 • **Value $58**

(4) Redbird
Handcrafted • N/A
200XHA3501 • **Value $50**

(5) Rodney
Handcrafted • N/A
295XHA3391 • **Value $40**

(6) Soldier
Handcrafted • N/A
200XHA3481 • **Value $41**

1983

(7) Angel
Handcrafted • N/A
200XHA3467 • **Value $55**

(8) Animals
Handcrafted • N/A
750XHA3487 • **Value $42**

(9) Betsey Clark
Handcrafted • N/A
350EHA2429 • **Value $33**

(10) Bunny
Handcrafted • N/A
250EHA3457 • **Value $17**

(11) Cherub
Handcrafted • N/A
350VHA3497 • **Value $28**

(12) Chick
Handcrafted • N/A
250EHA3469 • **Value $240**

(13) Cupid
Handcrafted • N/A
550VHA4099 • **Value $440**

(14) Deer
Handcrafted • N/A
350XHA3419 • **Value $55**

(15) Duck
Handcrafted • N/A
250EHA3477 • **Value $240**

(16) Flocked Bunny
Handcrafted • N/A
350EHA3417 • **Value $17**

(17) Kitten
Handcrafted • N/A
200XHA3447 • **Value $46**

(18) Kitten
Handcrafted • N/A
350VHA3489 • **Value $128**

(19) Mouse
Handcrafted • N/A
200XHA3459 • **Value $47**

1984 COLLECTION

	Price Paid	Value of My Collection
1.		
2.		
3.		
4.		
5.		
6.		

1983 COLLECTION

7.		
8.		
9.		
10.		
11.		
12.		
13.		
14.		
15.		
16.		
17.		
18.		
19.		
PENCIL TOTALS		

MERRY MINIATURES

(1) Mouse
Handcrafted • N/A
350SHA3407 • **Value $21**

(2) Penguin
Handcrafted • N/A
295XHA3439 • **Value $80**

(3) Polar Bear
Handcrafted • N/A
350XHA3407 • **Value $260**

(4) Santa
Handcrafted • N/A
295XHA3427 • **Value $45**

(5) Shirt Tales
Handcrafted • N/A
295HHA3437 • **Value $42**

(6) Snowman
Handcrafted • N/A
300XHA3479 • **Value $43**

(7) Turkey
Handcrafted • N/A
295THA207 • **Value $45**

1982

1983 COLLECTION

	Price Paid	Value of My Collection
1.		
2.		
3.		
4.		
5.		
6.		
7.		

1982 COLLECTION

8.		
9.		
10.		
11.		
12.		
13.		
14.		
15.		
16.		
17.		
18.		

(8) Ceramic Bunny
Handcrafted • N/A
300EPF3702 • **Value $50**

(9) Duck
Handcrafted • N/A
300EHA3403 • **Value $33**

(10) Kermit
Handcrafted • N/A
395VHA3403 • **Value $30**

(11) Kitten
Handcrafted • N/A
395HHA3466 • **Value $56**

(12) Miss Piggy
Handcrafted • N/A
395VHA3416 • **Value $30**

(13) Mouse
Handcrafted • N/A
450XHA5023 • **Value $66**

(14) Pilgrim Mouse
Handcrafted • N/A
295THA3433 • **Value $228**

(15) Rocking Horse
Handcrafted • N/A
450XHA5003 • **Value $100**

(16) Santa (rigid)
Handcrafted • N/A
450XHA5016 • **Value $192**

(17) Tree
Handcrafted • N/A
450XHA5006 • **Value $160**

(18) Witch
Handcrafted • N/A
395HHA3456 • **Value $400**

PENCIL TOTALS

1981

(1) Cupid
Handcrafted • N/A
300VPF3465 • **Value $61**

(2) Ghost
Handcrafted • N/A
300HHA3402 • **Value $330**

(3) Lamb
Handcrafted • N/A
300EPF402 • **Value $30**

(4) Leprechaun
Handcrafted • N/A
300SHA3415 • **Value $56**

(5) Penguin
Handcrafted • N/A
300XHA3412 • **Value $110**

(6) Raccoon Pilgrim
Handcrafted • N/A
300THA3402 • **Value $51**

(7) Redbird
Handcrafted • N/A
300XHA3405 • **Value $40**

(8) Squirrel Indian
Handcrafted • N/A
300THA3415 • **Value $53**

(9) Turkey
Handcrafted • N/A
300THA22 • **Value $55**

1980

(10) Angel
Handcrafted • N/A
300XPF3471 • **Value $42**

(11) Kitten
Handcrafted • N/A
300XPF3421 • **Value $41**

(12) Pipe
Handcrafted • N/A
75SPF1017 • **Value $65**

(13) Reindeer
Handcrafted • N/A
300XPF3464 • **Value $106**

(14) Santa
Handcrafted • N/A
300XPF39 • **Value $35**

(15) Sleigh
Handcrafted • N/A
300XPF3451 • **Value $50**

(16) Turkey
Handcrafted • N/A
200TPF3441 • **Value $88**

(17) Turtle
Handcrafted • N/A
200VPF3451 • **Value $57**

1981 COLLECTION

	Price Paid	Value of My Collection
1.		
2.		
3.		
4.		
5.		
6.		
7.		
8.		
9.		

1980 COLLECTION

10.		
11.		
12.		
13.		
14.		
15.		
16.		
17.		
PENCIL TOTALS		

MERRY MINIATURES

1979

(1) **Bunny**
Handcrafted • N/A
200EPF377 • **Value $93**

(2) **Duck**
Handcrafted • N/A
200EPF397 • **Value $62**

(3) **Love**
Handcrafted • N/A
150VPF1007 • **Value $125**

(4) **Mouse**
Handcrafted • N/A
150XPF1017 • **Value $127**

1978

(5) **Joy Elf**
Handcrafted • N/A
150XPF1003 • **Value $110**

(6) **Kitten**
Handcrafted • N/A
150HPF1013 • **Value $29**

(7) **Mrs. Snowman**
Handcrafted • N/A
150XPF23 • **Value $100**

(8) **Pilgrim Boy**
Handcrafted • N/A
150TPF1003 • **Value $30**

(9) **Pilgrim Girl**
Handcrafted • N/A
150TPF1016 • **Value $30**

(10) **Turkey**
Handcrafted • N/A
150TPF12 • **Value $93**

1977

(11) **Barnaby**
Handcrafted • N/A
125EPF12 • **Value $230**

(12) **Bernadette**
Handcrafted • N/A
125EPF25 • **Value $230**

(13) **Chick**
Handcrafted • N/A
125EPF32 • **Value $235**

(14) **Mouse**
Handcrafted • N/A
125XPF122 • **Value $125**

(15) **Pilgrims**
Handcrafted • N/A
150TPF502 • **Value $255**

(16) **Witch**
Handcrafted • N/A
125HPF32 • **Value $200**

1979 Collection

	Price Paid	Value of My Collection
1.		
2.		
3.		
4.		

1978 Collection

5.		
6.		
7.		
8.		
9.		
10.		

1977 Collection

11.		
12.		
13.		
14.		
15.		
16.		
PENCIL TOTALS		

VALUE GUIDE — MERRY MINIATURES

1976

① Betsey Clark
Handcrafted • N/A
125XPF151 • **Value $275**

② Drummer Boy
Handcrafted • N/A
125XPF144 • **Value $270**

③ Owl
Handcrafted • N/A
100HPF515 • **Value $350**

④ Pilgrims
Handcrafted • N/A
100TPF502 • **Value $225**

⑤ Pipe
Handcrafted • N/A
89SPF266 • **Value $152**

⑥ Santa
Handcrafted • N/A
125XPF131 • **Value $85**

⑦ Scarecrow
Handcrafted • N/A
100HPF522 • **Value $325**

⑧ Snowman
Handcrafted • N/A
125XPF44 • **Value $72**

⑨ Turkey
Handcrafted • N/A
100TPF512 • **Value $172**

1975

⑩ Bunny
Handcrafted • N/A
125EPF49 • **Value $705**

⑪ Devil
Handcrafted • N/A
125HPF29 • **Value $375**

⑫ Duck
Handcrafted • N/A
125EPF69 • **Value $710**

⑬ Girl
Handcrafted • N/A
125EPF57 • **Value $600**

⑭ Indian
Handcrafted • N/A
125TPF29 • **Value $53**

⑮ Santa
Handcrafted • N/A
125XPF49 • **Value $305**

1974

⑯ Angel
Handcrafted • N/A
125XPF506 • **Value $485**

⑰ Bunny
Handcrafted • N/A
59EPF186 • **Value $705**

1976 COLLECTION		
	Price Paid	Value of My Collection
1.		
2.		
3.		
4.		
5.		
6.		
7.		
8.		
9.		
1975 COLLECTION		
10.		
11.		
12.		
13.		
14.		
15.		
1974 COLLECTION		
16.		
17.		
PENCIL TOTALS		

MERRY MINIATURES

Merry Miniatures **279**

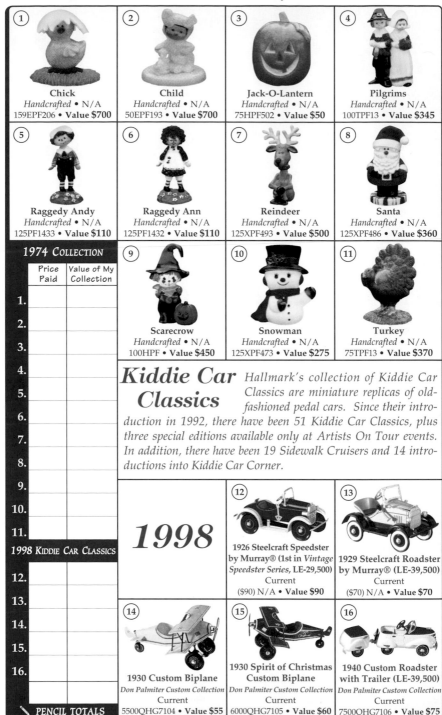

(1) Chick
Handcrafted • N/A
159EPF206 • **Value $700**

(2) Child
Handcrafted • N/A
50EPF193 • **Value $700**

(3) Jack-O-Lantern
Handcrafted • N/A
75HPF502 • **Value $50**

(4) Pilgrims
Handcrafted • N/A
100TPF13 • **Value $345**

(5) Raggedy Andy
Handcrafted • N/A
125PF1433 • **Value $110**

(6) Raggedy Ann
Handcrafted • N/A
125PF1432 • **Value $110**

(7) Reindeer
Handcrafted • N/A
125XPF493 • **Value $500**

(8) Santa
Handcrafted • N/A
125XPF486 • **Value $360**

1974 COLLECTION

	Price Paid	Value of My Collection
1.		
2.		
3.		
4.		
5.		
6.		
7.		
8.		
9.		
10.		
11.		
1998 KIDDIE CAR CLASSICS		
12.		
13.		
14.		
15.		
16.		
PENCIL TOTALS		

(9) Scarecrow
Handcrafted • N/A
100HPF • **Value $450**

(10) Snowman
Handcrafted • N/A
125XPF473 • **Value $275**

(11) Turkey
Handcrafted • N/A
75TPF13 • **Value $370**

Kiddie Car Classics

Hallmark's collection of Kiddie Car Classics are miniature replicas of old-fashioned pedal cars. Since their introduction in 1992, there have been 51 Kiddie Car Classics, plus three special editions available only at Artists On Tour events. In addition, there have been 19 Sidewalk Cruisers and 14 introductions into Kiddie Car Corner.

1998

(12) 1926 Steelcraft Speedster
by Murray® (1st in *Vintage Speedster* Series, LE-29,500)
Current
($90) N/A • **Value $90**

(13) 1929 Steelcraft Roadster
by Murray® (LE-39,500)
Current
($70) N/A • **Value $70**

(14) 1930 Custom Biplane
Don Palmiter Custom Collection
Current
5500QHG7104 • **Value $55**

(15) 1930 Spirit of Christmas Custom Biplane
Don Palmiter Custom Collection
Current
6000QHG7105 • **Value $60**

(16) 1940 Custom Roadster with Trailer (LE-39,500)
Don Palmiter Custom Collection
Current
7500QHG7106 • **Value $75**

(1)
1941 Steelcraft Chrysler by Murray®
Current
5500QHG9044 • **Value $55**

(2)
1941 Steelcraft Fire Truck by Murray®
Current
6000QHG9042 • **Value $60**

(3)
1950 Custom Convertible
Don Palmiter Custom Collection
Current
6000QHG7101 • **Value $60**

(4)
1958 Murray® Champion
Current
5500QHG9041 • **Value $55**

(5)
1960 Eight Ball Racer (3rd in *Winner's Circle Collector's Series*)
Current
5500QHG9039 • **Value $55**

(6)
1998 Nascar® 50th Anniversary Custom Champion
Don Palmiter Custom Collection
Current
6000QHG7110 • **Value $60**

(7)
Don's Street Rod
Don Palmiter Custom Collection
Current
5500QHG7102 • **Value $55**

(8)
1955 Custom Chevy®
Don Palmiter Custom Collection
Current
5000QHG7103 • **Value $50**

(9)
Car Lift and Tool Box (set/2)
Current
2500QHG3608 • **Value $25**

(10)
Corner Drive-In (LE-39,500)
Current
7000QHG3610 • **Value $70**

(11)
Famous Food Sign (2nd in *Bill's Boards Series*)
Current
3000QHG3614 • **Value $30**

(12)
KC's Motor Oil
Current
1500QHG3609 • **Value $15**

(13)
Menu Station with Food Trays (set/3)
Current
3000QHG3611 • **Value $30**

(14)
Newspaper Box & Trash Can Set (set/2)
Current
2000QHG3613 • **Value $20**

(15)
1932 Keystone Coast-to-Coast Bus (LE-29,500)
Current
4500QHG6320 • **Value $45**

(16)
1934 Mickey Mouse Velocipede
Current
4800QHG6316 • **Value $48**

(17)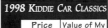
1937 De Luxe Velocipede
Current
4500QHG6319 • **Value $45**

(18)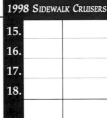
1960s Sealtest Milk Truck
Current
4000QHG6315 • **Value $40**

1998 KIDDIE CAR CLASSICS

	Price Paid	Value of My Collection
1.		
2.		
3.		
4.		
5.		
6.		
7.		

1998 KIDDIE CAR CORNER

8.		
9.		
10.		
11.		
12.		
13.		
14.		

1998 SIDEWALK CRUISERS

15.		
16.		
17.		
18.		
PENCIL TOTALS		

KIDDIE CAR CLASSICS

1997

(1) 	(2) 	(3) 
1937 GARTON® Ford (LE-24,500) Retired 1997 6500QHG9035 • **Value $120**	1938 GARTON® Lincoln Zephyr (LE-24,500) Retired 1997 6500QHG9038 • **Value $130**	1939 GARTON® Ford Station Wagon Current 5500QHG9034 • **Value $55**

(4)	(5)	(6)	(7)
1939 GARTON® Ford Station Wagon (Artists On Tour, brown) Retired 1997 (N/C) No stock # • **Value N/E**	1940 Gendron "Red Hot" Roadster (2nd in *Winner's Circle Collector's Series*) Current 5500QHG9037 • **Value $55**	1941 Steelcraft Oldsmobile by Murray® Current 5500QHG9036 • **Value $55**	1956 Murray® Golden Eagle (LE-29,500) Retired 1997 5000QHG9033 • **Value $90**

1997 KIDDIE CAR CLASSICS

	Price Paid	Value of My Collection
1.		
2.		
3.		
4.		

(8)	(9)	(10)
1941 Murray® Junior Service Truck Current 5500QHG9031 • **Value $55**	KC's Garage (LE-29,500) Retired 1997 7000QHG3601 • **Value $100**	Pedal Petroleum Gas Pump Current 2500QHG3602 • **Value $25**

5.	
6.	
7.	

1997 KIDDIE CAR CORNER

(11)	(12)	(13)
Pedal Power Premium Lighted Gas Pump Current 3000QHG3603 • **Value $30**	Sidewalk Sales Signs Current 1500QHG3605 • **Value $15**	Sidewalk Service Signs Current 1500QHG3604 • **Value $15**

8.	
9.	
10.	

(14) 	(15)	(16)
Welcome Sign (1st in *Bill's Boards Series*) Current 3000QHG3606 • **Value $30**	1937 Scamp Wagon (LE-29,500) Current 4800QHG6318 • **Value $48**	1939 American National Pedal Bike Current 3800QHG6314 • **Value $38**

1997 SIDEWALK CRUISERS

(17)	(18)
1939 GARTON® Batwing Scooter Retired 1997 3800QHG6317 • **Value N/E**	1960 Murray® Blaz-O-Jet Tricycle Current 4500QHG6313 • **Value $45**

PENCIL TOTALS

1996

(1)

1935 Steelcraft Airplane
by Murray® (LE-29,500)
Retired 1997
5000QHG9032 • **Value $125**

(2)

1935 Steelcraft by
Murray® (LE-24,500)
Retired 1996
6500QHG9029 • **Value $145**

(3)

1937 Steelcraft Airflow
by Murray® (Artists
On Tour, red)
(N/C) No stock # • **Value N/E**

(4)

1956 GARTON® Hot Rod
Racer (1st in *Winner's
Circle Collector's Series*)
Current
5500QHG9028 • **Value $55**

(5)

1961 Murray®
Super Deluxe
Tractor with Trailer
Current
5500QHG9027 • **Value $55**

(6)

1964-1/2 Ford Mustang
Current
5500QHG9030 • **Value $55**

(7)

1935 Sky King
Velocipede
Current
4500QHG6311 • **Value $45**

(8)

1935 American Airflow
Coaster (LE-29,500)
Current
4800QHG6310 • **Value $48**

(9)

1941 Keystone
Locomotive
Current
4500QHG6312 • **Value $45**

(10)

1950 GARTON®
Delivery Cycle
Current
3800QHG6309 • **Value $38**

(11)

Late 1940s Mobo Sulky
(LE-29,500)
Current
4800QHG6308 • **Value $48**

1995

(12)

1937 Steelcraft Airflow
by Murray® (LE-24,500)
Retired 1996
6500QHG9024 • **Value $125**

(13)

1937 Steelcraft Auburn
(LE-24,500)
Retired 1996
6500QHG9021 • **Value $165**

(14)

1937 Steelcraft Auburn
(Artists On Tour,
dark green)
Retired 1995
(N/C) No stock # • **Value N/E**

(15)

1948 Murray® Pontiac
Retiring by June 1998
5000QHG9026 • **Value $50**

(16)

1950 Murray® Torpedo
Retired 1996
5000QHG9020 • **Value $170**

(17)

1955 Murray® Royal
Deluxe (LE-29,500)
Current
5500QHG9025 • **Value $55**

(18)

1959 GARTON®
Deluxe Kidillac
Retired 1996
5500QHG9017 • **Value $122**

1996 KIDDIE CAR CLASSICS		
	Price Paid	Value of My Collection
1.		
2.		
3.		
4.		
5.		
6.		
1996 SIDEWALK CRUISERS		
7.		
8.		
9.		
10.		
11.		
1995 KIDDIE CAR CLASSICS		
12.		
13.		
14.		
15.		
16.		
17.		
18.		
PENCIL TOTALS		

KIDDIE CAR CLASSICS

VALUE GUIDE — KIDDIE CAR CLASSICS

(1)	**(2)**	**(3)**	**(4)**
1961 GARTON® Casey Jones Locomotive Retired 1996 5500QHG9019 • **Value $100**	**1962 Murray® Super Deluxe Fire Truck** Retired 1997 5500QHG9095 • **Value $55**	**1964 GARTON® Tin Lizzie** Retired 1997 5000QHG9023 • **Value $72**	**1935 Steelcraft Streamline Velocipede by Murray®** Current 4500QHG6306 • **Value $45**
(5)	**(6)**	**(7)**	**(8)**
1937 Steelcraft Streamline Scooter by Murray® Retired 1997 3500QHG6301 • **Value $43**	**1939 Mobo Horse** Current 4500QHG6304 • **Value $45**	**1940 GARTON® Aero Flite Wagon (LE-29,500)** Current 4800QHG6305 • **Value $48**	**1958 Murray® Police Cycle (LE-29,500)** Current 5500QHG6307 • **Value $55**

1995 KIDDIE CAR CLASSICS

	Price Paid	Value of My Collection
1.		
2.		
3.		

1995 SIDEWALK CRUISERS

4.		
5.		
6.		
7.		
8.		
9.		
10.		

1994 KIDDIE CAR CLASSICS

11.		
12.		
13.		
14.		
15.		
16.		
17.		
18.		
19.		

(9)	**(10)**
1963 GARTON® Speedster Current 3800QHG6303 • **Value $38**	**1966 GARTON® Super-Sonda** Retired 1997 4500QHG6302 • **Value $55**

1994

(11)	**(12)**	**(13)**
1939 Steelcraft Lincoln Zephyr by Murray® (LE-24,500) Retired 1996 5000QHG9015 • **Value $120**	**1941 Steelcraft Spitfire Airplane by Murray® (LE-19,500)** Retired 1996 5000QHG9009 • **Value $190**	**1955 Murray® Dump Truck (LE-19,500)** Retired 1996 4800QHG9011 • **Value $130**
(14)	**(15)**	**(16)**
1955 Murray® Fire Truck (LE-19,500, white) Retired 1996 5000QHG9010 • **Value $290**	**1955 Murray® Ranch Wagon (LE-19,500)** Retired 1996 4800QHG9007 • **Value $120**	**1955 Murray® Red Champion (LE-19,500)** Retired 1996 4500QHG9002 • **Value $124**
(17)	**(18)**	**(19)**
1956 GARTON® Dragnet® Police Car (LE-24,500) Retired 1997 5000QHG9016 • **Value $80**	**1956 GARTON® Kidillac** Retired 1994 5000QHX9094 • **Value $79**	**1956 GARTON® Mark V (LE-24,500)** Retired 1997 4500QHG9022 • **Value $72**

PENCIL TOTALS

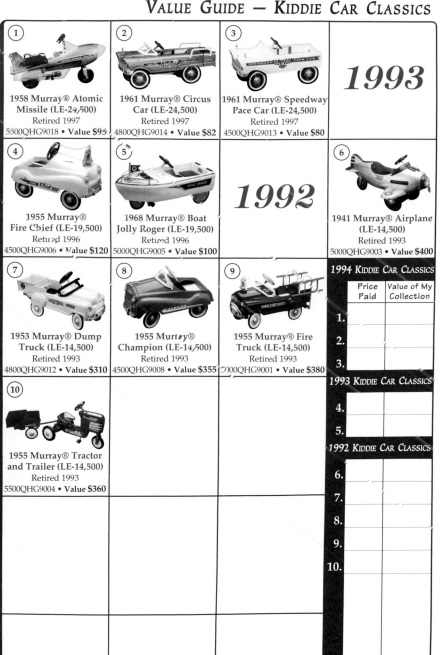

1
1958 Murray® Atomic
Missile (LE-24,500)
Retired 1997
5500QHG9018 • **Value $95**

2
1961 Murray® Circus
Car (LE-24,500)
Retired 1997
4800QHG9014 • **Value $82**

3
1961 Murray® Speedway
Pace Car (LE-24,500)
Retired 1997
4500QHG9013 • **Value $80**

1993

4
1955 Murray®
Fire Chief (LE-19,500)
Retired 1996
4500QHG9006 • **Value $120**

5
1968 Murray® Boat
Jolly Roger (LE-19,500)
Retired 1996
5000QHG9005 • **Value $100**

1992

6
1941 Murray® Airplane
(LE-14,500)
Retired 1993
5000QHG9003 • **Value $400**

7
1953 Murray® Dump
Truck (LE-14,500)
Retired 1993
4800QHG9012 • **Value $310**

8
1955 Murray®
Champion (LE-14,500)
Retired 1993
4500QHG9008 • **Value $355**

9
1955 Murray® Fire
Truck (LE-14,500)
Retired 1993
5000QHG9001 • **Value $380**

10
1955 Murray® Tractor
and Trailer (LE-14,500)
Retired 1993
5500QHG9004 • **Value $360**

	Price Paid	Value of My Collection
1994 KIDDIE CAR CLASSICS		
1.		
2.		
3.		
1993 KIDDIE CAR CLASSICS		
4.		
5.		
1992 KIDDIE CAR CLASSICS		
6.		
7.		
8.		
9.		
10.		

PENCIL TO

SSICS

Kiddie Car C

VALUE GUIDE — FUTURE RELEASES

Use these pages to record future Hallmark releases.

FUTURE RELEASES	Material	Artist	Stock #	Price Paid	Value of My Collection
			PENCIL TOTALS		
				PRICE PAID	MARKET VALUE

VALUE GUIDE — FUTURE RELEASES

Use these pages to record future Hallmark releases.

FUTURE RELEASES	Material	Artist	Stock #	Price Paid	Value of My Collection

✏ PENCIL TOTALS

PRICE PAID

TOTAL VALUE OF MY COLLECTION

*Record the value of your collection here by adding the pencil totals
from the bottom of each Value Guide page.*

HALLMARK KEEPSAKE ORNAMENTS	Price Paid	Market Value
Page 45		
Page 46		
Page 47		
Page 48		
Page 49		
Page 50		
Page 51		
Page 52		
Page 53		
Page 54		
Page 55		
Page 56		
Page 57		
Page 58		
Page 59		
Page 60		
Page 61		
Page 62		
Page 63		
Page 64		
Page 65		
Page 66		
Page 67		
Page 68		
Page 69		
TOTAL		

HALLMARK KEEPSAKE ORNAMENTS	Price Paid	Market Value
Page 70		
Page 71		
Page 72		
Page 73		
Page 74		
Page 75		
Page 76		
Page 77		
Page 78		
Page 79		
Page 80		
Page 81		
Page 82		
Page 83		
Page 84		
Page 85		
Page 86		
Page 87		
Page 88		
Page 89		
Page 90		
Page 91		
Page 92		
Page 93		
Page 94		
TOTAL		

PAGE SUBTOTALS		
	PRICE PAID	MARKET VALUE

Total Value Of My Collection

Record the value of your collection here by adding the pencil totals from the bottom of each Value Guide page.

Hallmark Keepsake Ornaments	Price Paid	Market Value
Page 95		
Page 96		
Page 97		
Page 98		
Page 99		
Page 100		
Page 101		
Page 102		
Page 103		
Page 104		
Page 105		
Page 106		
Page 107		
Page 108		
Page 109		
Page 110		
Page 111		
Page 112		
Page 113		
Page 114		
Page 115		
Page 116		
Page 117		
Page 118		
Page 119		
TOTAL		

Hallmark Keepsake Ornaments	Price Paid	Market Value
Page 120		
Page 121		
Page 122		
Page 123		
Page 124		
Page 125		
Page 126		
Page 127		
Page 128		
Page 129		
Page 130		
Page 131		
Page 132		
Page 133		
Page 134		
Page 135		
Page 136		
Page 137		
Page 138		
Page 139		
Page 140		
Page 141		
Page 142		
Page 143		
Page 144		
TOTAL		

Page Subtotals

Price Paid	Market Value

Total Value Of My Collection

Record the value of your collection here by adding the pencil totals from the bottom of each Value Guide page.

Hallmark Keepsake Ornaments	Price Paid	Market Value
Page 145		
Page 146		
Page 147		
Page 148		
Page 149		
Page 150		
Page 151		
Page 152		
Page 153		
Page 154		
Page 155		
Page 156		
Page 157		
Page 158		
Page 159		
Page 160		
Page 161		
Page 162		
Page 163		
Page 164		
Page 165		
Page 166		
Page 167		
Page 168		
Page 169		
TOTAL		

Hallmark Keepsake Ornaments	Price Paid	Market Value
Page 170		
Page 171		
Page 172		
Page 173		
Page 174		
Page 175		
Page 176		
Page 177		
Page 178		
Page 179		
Page 180		
Page 181		
Page 182		
Page 183		
Page 184		
Page 185		
Page 186		
Page 187		
Page 188		
Page 189		
Page 190		
Page 191		
Page 192		
Page 193		
Page 194		
TOTAL		

Page Subtotals		
	Price Paid	Market Value

TOTAL VALUE OF MY COLLECTION

Record the value of your collection here by adding the pencil totals from the bottom of each Value Guide page.

HALLMARK KEEPSAKE ORNAMENTS	Price Paid	Market Value
Page 195		
Page 196		
Page 197		
Page 198		
Page 199		
Page 200		
Page 201		
Page 202		
Page 203		
Page 204		
Page 205		
Page 206		
Page 207		
Page 208		
Page 209		
Page 210		
Page 211		
Page 212		
Page 213		
Page 214		
Page 215		
Page 216		
Page 217		
Page 218		
TOTAL		

HALLMARK KEEPSAKE ORNAMENTS	Price Paid	Market Value
Page 219		
Page 220		
Page 221		
Page 222		
Page 223		
Page 224		
Page 225		
Page 226		
Page 227		
Page 228		
Page 229		
Page 230		
Page 231		
Page 232		
Page 233		
Page 234		
Page 235		
Page 236		
Page 237		
Page 238		
Page 239		
Page 240		
Page 241		
TOTAL		

PAGE SUBTOTALS	PRICE PAID	MARKET VALUE

TOTAL VALUE OF MY COLLECTION

*Record the value of your collection here by adding the pencil totals
from the bottom of each Value Guide page.*

SPRING ORNAMENTS/MERRY MINIATURES	Price Paid	Market Value
Page 242		
Page 243		
Page 244		
Page 245		
Page 246		
Page 247		
Page 248		
Page 249		
Page 250		
Page 251		
Page 252		
Page 253		
Page 254		
Page 255		
Page 256		
Page 257		
Page 258		
Page 259		
Page 260		
Page 261		
Page 262		
Page 263		
Page 264		
Page 265		
TOTAL		

MERRY MINIATURES/KIDDIE CAR CLASSICS	Price Paid	Market Value
Page 266		
Page 267		
Page 268		
Page 269		
Page 270		
Page 271		
Page 272		
Page 273		
Page 274		
Page 275		
Page 276		
Page 277		
Page 278		
Page 279		
Page 280		
Page 281		
Page 282		
Page 283		
Page 284		
Page 285		
Page 286		
Page 287		
TOTAL		

GRAND TOTALS		
	PRICE PAID	MARKET VALUE

*H*ow much do you know about Hallmark Keepsake ornaments and collectibles? To find out your ornament "IQ," take our quiz and then check your answers on page 307!

1. What is the longest running Keepsake Ornament series in Hallmark history?

2. In what year was motion added to Hallmark's Magic Ornaments?

3. In what year did ornament expert Clara Johnson Scroggins publish the first-ever guide to Hallmark Keepsake Ornaments?

4. Hallmark artist Linda Sickman's "Welcome Sign" was the first addition to the *Bill's Boards Series* in Kiddie Car Corner. According to the sign, in which direction should one turn to get to KC's Garage?

5. What is the name of the Hallmark Keepsake Ornament Collector's Club newsletter?

6. Walt Disney characters have been featured on many Hallmark ornaments. Which Disney character was originally named "Dippy Dawg"?

7. The artwork of what famous American painter was first featured on a Hallmark glass ball ornament in 1974?

8. What type of "break" has Santa had in the 1993 Keepsake Ornament entitled "Christmas Break?"

9. What is the name of the Hallmark Cards, Inc. animated spokeswoman and in what year did she make her debut as a Keepsake ornament?

10. The first ornament in the "unannounced" series "Feliz Navidad" was issued in 1988. What type of animal was featured on this piece?

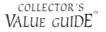

*N*o doubt about it, 1997 was a great year, with the release of many exciting Hallmark ornaments. Collectors had a plentiful supply of new series to choose from – 17 in all. Now that the 1997 line has come and gone, Collectors' Publishing has asked Hallmark retailers and collectors what the big stories were for 1997.

The one ornament everyone seemed to be talking about was "The Lone Ranger™." This wonderful tin lunch box ornament (which actually opens and closes) struck a chord with collectors everywhere. Fans of this ornament should definitely look for the "STAR WARS™" (from the Spring Ornaments) and "Superman™" lunch box ornaments available in 1998.

Another big hit from 1997 was the first edition in the *Lighthouse Greetings* series, perhaps spurred on by the rising popularity of lighthouse figurines. Among the other popular ornaments mentioned frequently were "Little Red Riding Hood – 1991," the second edition of the *Madame Alexander®* series, and the "Tonka® Mighty Front Loader," the second in an "unannounced" series depicting Tonka® vehicles. Old favorites like *Frosty Friends*, *Here Comes Santa* and *Kiddie Car Classics* remained popular and several nostalgic pieces like "Howdy Doody™" and "Mr. Potato Head®" attracted fans.

What will be the big hits of 1998? We'll just have to wait and see.

All The Right Moves

Ornaments celebrating the power of transportation also proved to be collector favorites in 1997. One store owner in North Carolina (where the Wright brothers' famous first flight took place) remarked that the first piece in the *Sky's The Limit* series, "Flight at Kitty Hawk," all but flew off the shelves. Kiddie Car Classics are always favorites, and the 1997 releases did not fail to cruise into the hearts of collectors. And then there were bicycles, showboats, Tonka® trucks . . . .

This section highlights the ten most valuable Hallmark ornaments as determined by their secondary market value. Not surprisingly, most of these are first editions in collectible series. Are you lucky enough to have any of these coveted treasures?

#1 SANTA'S MOTORCAR (1979)
1st in the Here Comes Santa series
#900QX1559
Original Price: $9
Market Value: $710

#2 TIN LOCOMOTIVE (1982)
1st in the Tin Locomotive series
#1300QX4603
Original Price: $13
Market Value: $695

#3 A COOL YULE (1980)
1st in the Frosty Friends series
#650QX1374
Original Price: $6.50
Market Value: $655

#4 ROCKING HORSE (1981)
1st in the Rocking Horse series
#900QX4222
Original Price: $9
Market Value: $580

#5 FROSTY FRIENDS (1981)
2nd in the Frosty Friends series
#800QX4335
Original Price: $8
Market Value: $495

#6 TRUEST JOYS OF CHRISTMAS (1977)
5th in the Betsey Clark series
#350QX2642
Original Price: $3.50
Market Value: $450

#7 THE BELLSWINGER (1979)
1st in The Bellringers series
#1000QX1479
Original Price: $10
Market Value: $425

#8 ROCKING HORSE (1982)
2nd in the Rocking Horse series
#1000QX5023
Original Price: $10
Market Value: $420

#9 ANTIQUE TOYS (1978)
1st in the Carrousel Series
#600QX1463
Original Price: $6
Market Value: $400

#10 CARDINALIS (1982)
1st in the Holiday Wildlife series
#700QX3133
Original Price: $7
Market Value: $395

HONORABLE MENTION

Other pieces with very limited distribution have also seen skyrocketing secondary market values, such as "Kansas City Santa" (1991, $900), "K.C. Angel" (1993, $500) and "Marionette Angel" (1986, $425).

*W*ith the staggering number of ornaments and wide variety of designs released by Hallmark each year, almost every home in America has had a Hallmark ornament in it at one time or another, whether the lucky owner knows it or not. When these would-be collectors discover what they have, they often begin the search for new ornaments to add to their collection. And regardless of their collecting experience, these ornament lovers need somewhere to turn to find these highly-coveted pieces.

What Is The Secondary Market And
What Makes Hallmark Unique?

For most collectible lines, secondary market demand is created when pieces are removed from production and are no longer available in retail stores. This results in an increase in their value, based on collector demand for these now hard-to-find pieces.

While the Hallmark secondary market is based on the same principle, it functions a bit differently due to the nature of the line. Production of the ornaments is limited to only one year and once that year is over, these ornaments (except in very rare cases) will never be produced again. And as they typically do not appear in retail stores until July and disappear in December, collectors only have about six months to purchase these limited pieces. It might be said, then, that every Hallmark ornament is a "limited edition" which, after its year of issue, can only be found on the secondary market.

If you're looking for the "one that got away," you do have somewhere to turn. Keep in mind, however, that while the range of prices on each piece will fluctuate over time, ornaments purchased through the secondary market are likely to be more expensive than those purchased through retail outlets. While most ornaments retail between $8 and $20, some may cost hundreds of dollars on the secondary market. This phenomenon is due to the limited availability of each ornament, as well as Hallmark's honored status as one of the oldest collectible lines, having started in 1973.

How Do I Shop The Secondary Market?

So where can you find the secondary market? There are various ways in which to buy and sell ornaments through this system. Your first step should be to contact your local retailer. Although most retailers aren't actively involved in the secondary market, they can often be a good source of information or advice for collectors. They also may be able to tell you about upcoming secondary market collector shows or put you in touch with other like-minded collectors.

You can also try a secondary market exchange service, with which collectors list the pieces they would like to buy or sell and the asking price. The exchange is considered the middleman in the transaction and is paid a fee for the service, usually between 10% and 20%. Such exchanges generally publish monthly newsletters and may require a subscription or membership fee. A few exchanges generate daily listings.

Most of these secondary market exchanges list other collectible items as well as Hallmark Ornaments, so these may not be the best

---

A Hit Series

Ornaments that are part of a collectible series often command the highest values on the secondary market. For example, the first editions of *Frosty Friends*, *Here Comes Santa*, and *Tin Locomotive* series today are valued at over $600. Other "theme" ornaments, such as BARBIE™ ornaments, have also proven popular (and more valuable) on the secondary market. Were you lucky enough to grab these ornaments while you had the chance?

---

choice if you're looking to do some serious ornament "shopping." Instead, there are a handful of secondary market dealers who specialize in Hallmark Ornaments and are noted ornament authorities. These dealers maintain price listings of their own and many collectors give these dealers more credibility when it comes to buying or selling ornaments. You'll find a list of some dealers and exchanges that specialize in Hallmark Ornaments on page 301.

Another option is to place an advertisement in a magazine or newsletter, many of which have "swap & sell" sections for just this purpose. A listing in the classifieds section of your local newspaper (usually under Antiques/Collectibles) is also a possibility. However, because newspapers reach a general readership and are not aimed at collectors specifically, this route may take a bit longer.

The newest and most exciting way to access the secondary market is by using the Internet. Here collectors can find a wealth of information on Hallmark Ornaments without leaving their homes! On the Internet, you can visit bulletin boards and other websites where collectors can share information and buy, sell and trade pieces. Many sites even publish online price listings, which can be updated immediately and be used for quick sales and trades, making it much easier to "shop around."

Web searches will lead you to retailers, collectors, publishers and dealers who can help you find what you're looking for. Start by conducting a search using words like "Hallmark," "ornaments" and "secondary market." You may also want to visit Hallmark's own webpage (www.hallmark.com) which is a great source for general information.

What Might Affect Values On The Secondary Market?

An important factor to keep in mind when buying and selling ornaments on the secondary market is their packaging. In the "real world," a box is just a box; but in the world of collectibles, boxes can have a significant effect on the secondary market value of an ornament. Many collectors consider an ornament without its original box to be "incomplete" and these will usually command a lower price on the secondary market.

When searching for ornaments, keep in mind the following abbreviations that are often used: "MIB" ("mint in box"), "NB" (no box), "DB" (damaged box) and "NT" (no original price tag). These conditions will usually reduce the value of an ornament by 10%, 20% or even 40%, especially for ornaments with no box at all.

Should I Consider My Collection An Investment?

While the high values of some Hallmark Ornaments can be attractive, it's important to remember that not every ornament appreciates by as much. Collectors who engage in collecting solely for monetary rewards may be disappointed. Collecting should be fun, and the pieces should bring joy and pleasure into your life. If you see your collection as a personal investment in happiness, you're guaranteed to enjoy Hallmark Ornaments for a lifetime!

Exchanges, Dealers & Newsletters

The Baggage Car
Meredith DeGood
3100 Justin Drive, Suite B
Des Moines, IA 50322
515-270-9080

Cherished Collectibles
Victoria Marling
2643 Campbellstown Road
Eaton, OH 45320
937-456-6781

Christmas in Vermont
Kathy Parrott
51 Jalber Road
Barre, VT 05641
802-479-2024

The Christmas Shop
Shirley Trexler
P.O. Box 5221
Cary, NC 27512
919-469-5264

Collectible Exchange, Inc.
6621 Columbiana Road
New Middletown, OH 44442
800-752-3208
330-542-9646

Mary Johnson
P.O. Box 1015
Marion, NC 28752-1015
828-652-2910

Ronnie Kesterson
300 Camelot Court
Knoxville, TN 37922
423-675-7511

New England Collectibles Exchange
Bob Dorman
201 Pine Avenue
Clarksburg, MA 01247
413-663-3643

The Ornament Trader Magazine
P. O. Box 469
Lavonia, GA 30553-0469
800-441-1551
770-650-2726

Morris Antiques
Allen and Pat Morris
2716 Flintlock Drive
Henderson, KY 42420
502-826-8378

Twelve Months of Christmas
Joan Ketterer
P.O. Box 97172
Pittsburgh, PA 15229
412-367-2352

*W*hen insuring your collection, there are three major points to consider:

1 **Know your coverage** — Collectibles are typically included in homeowner's or renter's insurance policies. Ask your agent if your policy covers fire, theft, floods, hurricanes, earthquakes and damage or breakage from routine handling. Also, ask if your policy covers claims at "current replacement value" – the amount it would cost to replace items if they were damaged, lost or stolen – which is extremely important since the secondary market value of some pieces may well exceed their original retail price.

2 **Document your collection** — In the event of a loss, you will need a record of the contents and value of your collection. Ask your insurance agent what information is acceptable. Keep receipts and an inventory of your collection in a different location, such as a safe deposit box. Include the pur-

> Many companies will accept a reputable secondary market price guide – such as the Collector's Value Guide™ – as a valid source for determining your collection's value.

chase date, price paid, size, issue year, edition limit/number, special markings and secondary market value for each piece. Photographs and video footage with close-up views of each piece are good back-ups.

3 **Weigh the risk** — To determine the coverage you need, calculate how much it would cost to replace your collection and compare it to the total amount your current policy would pay. To insure your collection for a specific dollar amount, ask your agent about adding a Personal Articles Floater or a Fine Arts Floater or "rider" to your policy, or insuring your collection under a totally separate policy. As with all insurance, you must weigh the risk of loss against the cost of additional coverage.

*A*mong ornament collectors, Clara Johnson Scroggins is a household name. Having collected ornaments for over 30 years, Clara now has "lots and lots and lots" of ornaments in her collection and is regarded as the foremost authority on Hallmark Ornaments.

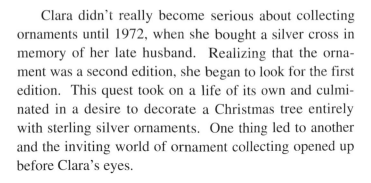

Clara spent many of her early childhood years in Little Village, Arkansas, where she was born and later moved to Illinois. Having grown up in a large family, she often encountered the "hand-me-down" phenomenon, in which everything she owned would eventually be passed down to her younger siblings. As a result, it wasn't until much later that she was able to cultivate her passion for collecting with such items as nativities, antique sterling napkin rings, rare books, dolls and original artwork.

Clara didn't really become serious about collecting ornaments until 1972, when she bought a silver cross in memory of her late husband. Realizing that the ornament was a second edition, she began to look for the first edition. This quest took on a life of its own and culminated in a desire to decorate a Christmas tree entirely with sterling silver ornaments. One thing led to another and the inviting world of ornament collecting opened up before Clara's eyes.

As she became more and more serious about collecting, Clara looked for a source of information on ornaments. Keeping track of what ornaments were available and finding accurate information on them was extremely difficult during the early stages of her collection, as many companies did not even keep track of the ornaments they themselves had produced. So, as education had always played a large part in her life (quizzical games were a passion among Clara and her brothers and sisters), Clara decided to submerge herself in the study of ornaments and published her first book on them in 1980. Clara recalls that the people at Hallmark were helpful, but "thought I was a little bit nuts." At the time, the entire Keepsake staff consisted of three artists, an office manager and a department manager (the department was then called "Trim-A-Home"), housed in three little rooms over the parking garage at corporate headquarters and they didn't really believe anyone was collecting Hallmark ornaments.

Clara has also become well-known for her display of Christmas trees. It is not unusual to find separate trees in her home decorated entirely with blown glass, porcelain or sterling silver ornaments, for example and of course, she always has a tree full of Hallmark ornaments. As the passing years have seen a decline in the celebration of the true Christmas spirit, Clara looks to tree decoration as a way of bringing a bit of it back. As part of this revival, Clara likes to share her passion with all who visit her home (whether it be family members or friends, neighbors or UPS delivery workers) by placing a basket full of ornaments beneath the tree and inviting each visitor to take part in the decorating experience.

It's a grand year for Hallmark Keepsake Ornaments as it celebrates its 25th Anniversary! In honor of this tremendous milestone, Collectors' Publishing asked nationally-recognized ornament expert Clara Johnson Scroggins to share some of her thoughts regarding the anniversary.

Collectors' Publishing: You began collecting ornaments in 1972, just one year before Hallmark introduced the first Keepsake Ornaments. How does it feel to be celebrating the 25th anniversary of the collection?

Clara Johnson Scroggins: Wonderful! It doesn't seem like 25 years!

CP: Why do you think people collect ornaments? What has made collecting them so popular?

CJS: People collect to bring back memories, to have a more beautiful tree. Collecting has been made easier because of the clubs (national and local) that have formed, and because people are more aware of what is out there due to the catalogs and flyers that are now available. Ornaments also are designed to appeal to the user. Many ornaments have been created in licensed programs to recall better, easier, more simple times: childhood, dating days, marriage, births, friendships, vacations, weddings and other life events.

CP: How do you feel about the fact that many of today's ornaments don't seem to be related to Christmas?

CJS: But they are, because they represent times, events and people in our lives. A train ornament can be for someone who loves trains. Ornaments can recall a happy vacation or commemorate a baby's first Christmas. The Christmas tree has changed according to our needs and times, just like everything else. We can put the things that mean the most to us on it. A spider ornament on a tree has as much right as a walnut from the 1800s. You can put what you want on the tree. It's your tree – do what you want to do!

CP: Ornaments with motion and sound were introduced in 1986 and 1989, respectively. In what ways do you think this impacted the collecting of ornaments?

CJS: Motion and sound impacted Christmas the way lights did. We once lit our trees with candles – we can now light our trees with our ornaments. We've just advanced to the degree where we can hear songs, leave messages, record messages, hear rockets go up, hear Christmas carols. Our trees give us action, light and voices now, which is simply another stage of growth. Who knows what the next big thing will be!

CP: What has surprised you in the 25 years of Hallmark Ornaments?

CJS: How Americans and the world have fallen in love with beautiful ornaments and are so thrilled to be collecting beautiful memories.

CP: What do you think the future holds for ornament collecting?

CJS: This is not a fad – it has staying power. I believe that as people are collecting finer ornaments, companies will create nicer, finer ornaments. I anticipate more heirloom pieces. I feel there will never be a time that people won't decorate.

*W*e asked Clara to list some of her favorite ornaments from the past 25 years. Although she insists that she loves all of them, she agreed to name several of the ornaments which she has enjoyed the most over the years. She is quick to point out, however, that they are in no particular order! (We have put them in chronological order for simplicity's sake.)

1973 Christmas 1973
(1st in *Betsey Clark* series)

1975 Joy

1976 Bicentennial Charmers

1979 Ice Hockey Holiday
(1st in SNOOPY® And *Friends* series)

1981 Christmas Fantasy

1985 Night Before Christmas

1986 Magical Unicorn (LE-24,700)

1987 Mistletoad

1988 Filled With Fudge

1990 Two Peas in a Pod

1995 Heaven's Gift (set/2)

1997 The Night Before Christmas

*I*t may seem hard to believe, but 1998 marks the 25th Anniversary of Hallmark Keepsake Ornaments! To celebrate, Hallmark has a grand celebration planned!

The events of the 25th Anniversary Celebration are scheduled to take place in Kansas City, Missouri in mid-August, and are exclusive to those whose membership in the Hallmark Keepsake Ornament Collector's Club was current during 1997. If you were lucky enough to get your name on the admittance list, here are some of the events you can look forward to:

- Meet the Keepsake Ornament artists
- Opportunities to purchase exclusive event pieces
- Keepsake Ornament exhibits
- Presentations, seminars and workshops
- Special tours of the Hallmark Visitors Center
- Special surprises including gifts, prizes and games
- A dinner party with live entertainment
- Special guests
- A farewell banquet with music provided by a 20-piece orchestra

Because this celebration will be such an immense undertaking, there will be no Artists On Tour events or other club events this year. Have a great time!

Visit The Hallmark Showroom

Anyone who isn't able to attend the 25th Anniversary Celebration should still make a trip to Kansas City and visit the Hallmark Visitors Center, located in the Crown Center complex. Exhibits include original artwork from contributing artists and an ornament display area.

*T*he Christmas season marks a time to celebrate traditions; from hanging the mistletoe to baking gingerbread cookies. But perhaps the most beloved tradition of all is decorating the family Christmas tree with special, one-of-a-kind collectible ornaments.

Collectors can add exquisitely-crafted, uniquely-designed ornaments to their collections – ornaments that are not available to the general public – when they join the Hallmark Keepsake Ornament Collector's Club.

For a $22.50 fee, members receive three free Membership Ornaments when they sign up and have the opportunity to purchase exclusive Club Edition ornaments that year. Members also receive the Club newsletter, the *Collector's Courier*, a copy of Hallmark's annual Dream Book, invitations to attend special Hallmark events and a personalized membership card.

Established in 1987 as a way for collectors to learn more about collecting ornaments and about the Keepsake Ornament artists who design them, the Club today has more than 300,000 members.

Collectors who join the Club in 1998 will receive three exclusive Membership Ornaments depicting different versions of Santa Claus inspired by Hallmark artwork from the 1960s, 1970s and 1980s:

★ "Kringle Bells," an elfin Santa Keepsake Miniature Ornament inspired by a 1965 holiday card.

★ "Making His Way," an old-fashioned St. Nicholas inspired by 1970s woodcut artwork, and which complements the Hallmark Keepsake Ornament "Folk Art Americana Collection."

★ "New Christmas Friend," featuring a jolly Santa and little puppy based on a 1982 holiday card.

Members who sign up in 1998 will also receive a special anniversary surprise that commemorates the 25th Anniversary of Hallmark Keepsake Ornaments.

In addition to these free benefits, 1998 Club members will have the opportunity to purchase three Club Edition ornaments that are not available in stores:

★ "Follow the Leader," set of two PEANUTS® ornaments featuring Lucy, Linus, Snoopy and Charlie Brown on ice skates.

★ "Based on the 1990 Happy Holidays® BARBIE® Doll," is the third BARBIE™ ornament in the Club-exclusive series. This complements the Keepsake Ornament Holiday BARBIE™ series that has depicted Mattel's annual doll since 1993.

★ "1935 Steelcraft by Murray®," a die-cast pedal car that complements the *Kiddie Car Classics* series.

Club members also have the opportunity to attend Hallmark conventions and Artists On Tour events, where they can participate in workshops, watch demonstrations, meet Hallmark artists and obtain exclusive special event ornaments. To sign up, contact your local retailer or the Club.

> Hallmark Keepsake Ornament
> Collector's Club
> P.O. Box 419824
> Kansas City, MO 64141-6824
> (800) 523-5839

*W*hile each Hallmark Ornament artist may have his or her own style, their artwork is produced in much the same way. Each ornament first begins as an idea. An artist may get their inspiration from almost any source: a childhood memory, an age-old story that has been handed down from generation to generation or a personal hobby or interest. Once the idea is envisioned, the artist will then put the image on paper. From that example, a three-dimensional model of the ornament is sculpted and painted. If this particular ornament has been chosen to be produced, molds will be fashioned in order to facilitate the production of large quantities of the ornament.

While the majority of Hallmark Ornaments are made of plastic, examples of other media that have been used in years past include acrylic, porcelain, glass, pewter, wood, brass and other metals. Sometimes a combination of materials are used.

Most of the ornaments are marked with the Hallmark copyright and year. Some older ones are not marked at all, however. Pieces in collectible series are marked with a small pine tree and a number. Again, as with the regular ornaments, some of the earlier pieces were not marked in this way.

Prices for Hallmark Keepsake Ornaments can vary, but generally range between $5 and $10 for the Miniature ornaments and between $10 and $16 for the general Keepsake ornaments. Magic ornaments usually range between $18 and $50.

Ornaments are packaged in individual boxes featuring a photograph of the piece on the front, the logo, year, stock number and the country in which it was produced.

Ornaments are protected by various packing materials, including plastic bags and trays, bubble wrap, Styrofoam and small sheets of foam rubber.

As you may already be aware, it is important to keep the original box in which the ornament comes. The market values of pieces without their original packaging or with damaged boxes can be greatly reduced. See the "Secondary Market Overview" on page 297 for more information. The boxes are also perfect for storing your ornaments when they are not on display.

The Selection Process

Have you ever wondered how Hallmark Ornaments are chosen? Once the decision to employ a particular theme is reached, artists then submit their own renditions of the piece. One version will be chosen and that artist will have the honor of designing and sculpting the ornament. This means that the artist who ultimately designs and sculpts the ornament is not always the one who came up with the idea in the first place!

*W*ith the Hallmark Keepsake Ornament collection containing over 3,000 pieces by itself and additional lines like Kiddie Car Classics and Spring Ornaments growing every year, collectors are finding that display opportunities are endless! Today, decorating with ornaments is a fun and exciting form of self-expression. So, whatever the holiday, season or mood, let your creative side loose and enjoy your collection. The following is a list of 12 fun and easy ideas to help get your "creative juices" flowing and to remind you that ornaments aren't just for trees anymore!

1 As your collection grows you may find that just one tree is not enough! How about multiple trees set up throughout your house as a way to help spread the Christmas spirit? Each tree can be used as a reflection of the room that houses it when it's decorated with a certain theme. For example, use ornaments involving food on a tree in the kitchen, and decorate a tree out on the porch with ornaments featuring nature scenes!

2 For the holidays, twist garlands, tulle and strands of beads through banisters or chandeliers and attach your favorite ornaments with decorative strips of cording or fabric.

3 Bring your collection to the kitchen! Miniature ornaments are a nice decorative accent to cakes and cupcakes. The Hallmark collection also makes a great addition to your kitchen when ornaments are hung on cup hooks and cabinets or displayed on a pedestal cake dish, interspersed with dried flowers or evergreens!

4 Create personalized Christmas stockings for friends and family. This easy project can be completed by using thread or ribbon to attach ornaments to "store-bought"

stockings, or make your own stocking that works as a complementary backdrop for your ornaments!

5 The perfect (needle-less) tree! Cover a flat piece of wood or corkboard with any color fabric. Next, go to work attaching ornaments (either with thread or gold hooks) to the fabric in the shape of a tree. Once complete, remove the protective glass from the frame of your choice and insert your creation for a fun and exciting 3-D wall hanging!

6 Dress up your windows year-round by attaching Miniature ornaments to the edges of your valances and curtains or to the cords of shades and blinds! Attach ornaments to suction cups and affix to windows throughout your house.

7 Display your ornaments on wreaths, using different themes for different occasions (heart ornaments on a heart-shaped wreath for Valentine's Day, for example.) Or try different styles to match the decor in your home (use selections from the *Folk Art Americana Collection* for a "country" style or ornaments from the *CRAYOLA® Crayon* series for a child's room). Keep in mind that wreaths do not always have to be made of dried flowers or grapevine!

8 Use ornaments as accents for a variety of objects already in your home. Coupled with ribbon or lace, ornaments can be used to dress up mirrors and frames or can add elegance to throw pillows in your living room or bedroom.

9 Wear your collection! Attach your favorite Miniature ornaments to your mittens, scarves or lapels, or cover an entire sweatshirt with them! Spice up a child's barrette by adding a row of musical bears from the Miniature series *March of the Teddy Bears.* Miniature ornaments also make great jewelry. They can be added to costume necklaces or turned into earrings for a fun, inexpensive alternative to run-of-the-mill fashion accessories.

10 For a beautiful alternative to the Christmas tree, select a medium-sized branch from a deciduous tree after the leaves have fallen off and spray paint it the color of your choice. After allowing it to dry, secure it to a base and use string or fabric to hang your favorite ornaments from it!

11 Use ornaments to create display vignettes. Try placing your collection of *Nostalgic Houses And Shops* on your mantle. Enhance the scene by using polyester quilt batting for snow and by adding miniature trees you can find at your local hobby shop! You can also use more than one series or collection at the same time. For example, add your *Classic American Cars* to your winter village scene. Settings can be as simple or as complex as you wish and can be placed anywhere throughout the house. Place displays on curio shelves, book shelves and in shadow boxes, or use wicker baskets to house your ornaments. For holiday parties, use one vignette as the centerpiece for your dining room table.

12 For more holiday festivities, use ornaments as place settings that can also double as party favors for your guests. (Be sure to match the ornaments to the recipients' hobbies or interests.) Ornaments tied with ribbon or cording can also be fastened around linen napkins to make napkin rings and can be used to add flair to a pair of simple candlesticks.

COLLECTOR'S CALENDAR

May

S	M	T	W	T	F	S
					1	2
3	4	5	6	7	8	9
10	11	12	13	14	15	16
17	18	19	20	21	22	23
24	25	26	27	28	29	30
31						

New Kiddie Car Classics arrive

Notes: _____

_____

_____

July

S	M	T	W	T	F	S
			1	2	3	4
5	6	7	8	9	10	11
12	13	14	15	16	17	(18)
(19)	20	21	22	23	24	25
26	27	28	29	30	31	

July 18-19: Keepsake Premiere
1998 Ornaments In Stores Now!

Notes: _____

_____

_____

August

S	M	T	W	T	F	S
						1
2	3	4	5	6	7	8
9	10	11	12	13	14	15
16	17	18	19	(20)	(21)	(22)
23	24	25	26	27	28	29
30	31					

Aug. 20-22: 25th Anniversary
Celebration, Kansas City, MO
In Stores Now: STAR TREK™

Notes: _____

_____

_____

September

S	M	T	W	T	F	S
		1	2	3	4	5
6	7	8	9	10	11	12
13	14	15	16	17	18	19
20	21	22	23	24	25	26
27	28	29	30			

New Kiddie Car Classics arrive
In Stores Now: Sports Collection

Notes: _____

_____

_____

Oct. 3-4: Keepsake Ornaments 25th
Anniversary In-Store Events
In Stores Now: Crown Reflections,
Disney, Spoonful of Stars

Notes: _____

_____

_____

October

S	M	T	W	T	F	S
				1	2	③
④	5	6	7	8	9	10
11	12	13	14	15	16	17
18	19	20	21	22	23	24
25	26	27	28	29	30	31

Nov. 14-15: Holiday Open House
In Stores Now: "The Grinch,"
"Flik," "Holiday BARBIE™,"
Mickey Express (Merry Miniatures),
Lionel®, School Days Lunch Boxes

Notes: _____

_____

_____

November

S	M	T	W	T	F	S
1	2	3	4	5	6	7
8	9	10	11	12	13	⑭
⑮	16	17	18	19	20	21
22	23	24	25	26	27	28
29	30					

Local Events: _____

_____

_____

_____

_____

_____

_____

_____

_____

_____

_____

_____

GLOSSARY

Artists On Tour—artist signing events held for Hallmark Keepsake Ornament Collector's Club members. Events are held across the country, and collectors can meet with artists, win prizes and purchase exclusive ornaments.

Club Edition—ornaments which are made available for purchase only to members of the Hallmark Keepsake Ornament Collector's Club.

collectibles—anything and everything that is "able to be collected." Figurines, dolls . . . or even *wooden decoys* can be considered a "collectible," but it is generally recognized that a true collectible should be something that increases in value over time.

collectible series—a succession of ornaments released as annual editions (one ornament per year) over several years.

collection—several ornaments with a common theme that are released in one year (unlike a collectible series, which is spread over several years).

Collector's Choice—title awarded each year by Hallmark Ornament historian Clara Johnson Scroggins. Ornaments chosen typically exemplify the spirit of Christmas or are "can't miss" ornaments.

commemoratives—ornaments that celebrate special people (mother or sister) or special events (anniversaries or baby's first Christmas).

damaged box (DB)—a secondary market term used when a collectible's original box is in poor condition, in most cases diminishing the value of the item.

Dream Book—catalog issued by Hallmark debuting that year's ornaments and collectibles. The Dream Book contains color photographs and other information about the ornaments.

editions (ed.)—new ornaments released each year that belong to a new or ongoing series. For example, "Mop Top Wendy" is the 3rd edition in the Madame Alexander® series.

exchanges—a secondary market service that lists pieces that collectors wish to buy or sell. The exchange works as a middleman and usually requires a commission.

Gold Crown Store—Hallmark stores that meet certain criteria. Selected products (either entire lines or specific ornaments) are often available exclusively through such stores.

handcrafted—the manufacturing process of many Hallmark Ornaments where pieces are hand-assembled and hand-painted.

Keepsake Ornaments—brand name for Hallmark's line of ornaments, including miniature, light and motion and full-sized ornaments. The term "Keepsake" is also used to distinguish the regular ornament line from the Magic and Miniature lines.

limited edition—a piece scheduled for a predetermined production quantity or time period. Most ornaments are limited to one year of availability but can have varied production runs depending upon the demand for the ornament.

Magic Ornaments—the Hallmark line of ornaments, first introduced in 1984, that incorporates features such as light, motion and sound.

Membership Ornaments—exclusive ornaments given as gifts to Hallmark Keepsake Ornament Collector's Club members.

mint in box (MIB)—a secondary market term used when a collectible's original box is in "as good as new" condition, in most cases adding value to the item.

no box (NB)—a secondary market term used when a collectible's original box is missing. For most collectibles, having the original box is a factor in its value on the secondary market.

Ornament Premiere—Hallmark store event featuring the debut of that year's new ornaments. Some special pieces are available only at this event.

personalized ornaments—ornaments offered through Gold Crown dealers between 1993 and 1995 that could be sent to Hallmark to be imprinted with personal messages.

primary market—the conventional collectibles purchasing process in which collectors buy at issue price through retail stores, direct mail or home shopping networks.

room hopping—the practice of going from one hotel room to another at a collectibles show to look at other attendees' collections or to see collectibles that guests are selling.

REACH Program—program that ran from 1989 to 1995 at selected retailers and featured promotional products available with a minimum Hallmark purchase.

secondary market—the source for buying and selling collectibles according to basic supply-and-demand principles. Pieces which are popular, retired or with low production quantities can appreciate in value far above the original retail issue price.

Showcase Ornaments—collection of ornaments that ran from 1993 to 1996 and featured traditional designs and materials, such as porcelain, die-cast metal and silver-plating.

trimmers—tree decorations which are not part of the Keepsake Ornament Collection, are not boxed and are generally lower in price.

"unannounced" series—ornaments released in consecutive years that are not part of official series, but can be connected by theme. For example, the Tonka® vehicles from 1996, 1997 and 1998 are considered an "unannounced" series.

ALPHABETICAL INDEX
– Key –

All Hallmark Keepsake Ornaments, Spring Ornaments, Merry Miniatures and Kiddie Car Classics are listed below in alphabetical order. The first number refers to the piece's location within the Value Guide section and the second to the box in which it is pictured on that page.

Alphabetical Index

ALPHABETICAL INDEX

ALPHABETICAL INDEX

ALPHABETICAL INDEX

ALPHABETICAL INDEX

ALPHABETICAL INDEX

Look for these other

COLLECTOR'S
VALUE GUIDE™

titles at fine gift and collectible stores everywhere.

The BOYDS COLLECTION LTD.

Cherished
Teddies®
by ENESCO®

HARBOUR
LIGHTS™

Dreamsicles™

HALLMARK
Keepsake Ornaments

SWAROVSKI
Silver Crystal

Department 56®
Villages

Department 56®
Snowbabies©

PRECIOUS
MOMENTS
by ENESCO

Charming
Tails

LOONEY TUNES™
SPOTLIGHT COLLECTION™

Beanie Babies®

HARMONY
KINGDOM

COLLECTORS'
PUBLISHING

598 Pomeroy Ave., Meriden, CT 06450
www.collectorspub.com